THE BOY IN THE MASK
THE HIDDEN WORLD OF
LAWRENCE OF ARABIA

To the Dear Memory of my Father and Mother,
always loving, always giving

DICK BENSON-GYLES

THE BOY IN THE MASK

THE HIDDEN WORLD OF

LAWRENCE OF ARABIA

Foreword by MALCOLM BROWN

THE LILLIPUT PRESS
DUBLIN

First published 2016 by
THE LILLIPUT PRESS
62–63 Sitric Road, Arbour Hill,
Dublin 7, Ireland
www.lilliputpress.ie

A CIP record for this title is available
from The British Library.

10 9 8 7 6 5 4 3 2 1

ISBN 978 1 84351 656 9

Set in 11 pt on 15.2 pt Garamond by Marsha Swan
Printed in Navarre, Spain, by GraphyCems

Contents

Illustrations

Illustrations

There was a sort of dual personality – there was – the boy – and there was also – I think he called it a mask. That's rather crude – but it is – the boy in the mask. We all liked him – but he began to be quite different.

Canon Edgar Hall (Omnibus. BBC 2, 18 April 1986)

My self-distrusting shyness held a mask, often a mask of indifference or flippancy, before my face, and puzzled me. My thoughts clawed at this apparent peace, wondering what was underneath, knowing that it was only a mask.

T.E. Lawrence (*Seven Pillars of Wisdom*, 2004, p. 679)

T.E. Lawrence – A Chronology

16 August 1888. Born North Wales, second of five 'Lawrence' brothers.

1896. Family settles in Oxford.

September 1896 – July 1907. Attends Oxford High School.

Summers 1906 and 1907. Studies castles in northern France.

October, 1907 – June 1910. Attends Jesus College, Oxford.

Summers 1908 and 1909. Studies castles in France and in Syria for degree thesis.

Winter 1909-1910, Writes *Crusader Castles*. Awarded First Class Honours in History.

Summer 1910. Studies medieval pottery in France.

Winter 1910 – 1911. Studies Arabic at Jebail, Syria.

March – July 1911. Excavating at Carchemish (Jerablus) with British Museum Expedition under D.G. Hogarth and R. Campbell Thompson.

Summer 1911. Walks through northern Syria.

Early 1912. Excavating in Egypt under Flinders Petrie.

Spring 1912 – spring 1914. Excavating at Carchemish under C.L Woolley.

Summer 1913. Home in Oxford.

January – February 1914, Survey of Sinai.

Summer 1914. Completes *Wilderness of Zin* (report on Sinai work) in Oxford and London, then in War Office, London.

December, 1914 – May 1916. In Egypt with Intelligence Department.

March – May 1916. Journey to Iraq.

October 1916 – October 1918. With Arab forces during Arab Revolt, Syria (rising in rank from Lieutenant to Colonel).

October – December 1918. In London and Oxford.

January – October 1919. In Paris for Peace Conference.

May 1919. By air to Egypt.

October 1919 – 1921. At All Souls College, Oxford, and in London.

1921 – 1922. Adviser to Colonial Office.

August-December 1921. Missions to Aden, Jeddah and Transjordan.

Second half 1922 – January 1923. Aircraftman Ross, Royal Air Force (RAF). Discharged on discovery of identity.

March, 1923 – August, 1925. Private Shaw, Royal Tank Corps, Bovington, Dorset. Acquires cottage, Clouds Hill, near Bovington. Transfers to RAF.

August 1926. Aircraftman Shaw RAF at Cranwell.

1926. *Seven Pillars of Wisdom* (SPoW) published.

January, 1927 – 1928. India, RAF, Karachi and North-West frontier.

Revolt in the Desert (abridgement of SPoW) published and withdrawn in British Empire.

Completes *The Mint* (account of time in RAF as Aircraftman Ross).

1930 – 1935, RAF Mountbatten, with work around Britain on marine air-sea rescue craft.

February 1935. RAF Bridlington, discharged. Returns to civilian life, Clouds Hill.

19 May 1935. Dies after motorcycling accident near Clouds Hill, Dorset, aged forty-six.

Foreword

MALCOLM BROWN

My initial response when asked to write a foreword to, or a review of, yet another book on one of Britain's most enduring heroes is usually 'No'. I've been involved in the T.E. Lawrence world for many years and am very suspicious of ninety plus per cent of any new authors coming out of the blue with the claim: 'Look, I've got the Holy Grail.'

But this book is different. It's an amazing story, powerful, moving and a genuinely fresh perspective on Lawrence's life. It is, in fact, an original, both in the material it's offering and its exceptional, indeed unique approach. It's a book that has been lived as much as written by its author, who was captivated through the David Lean film and has ever since turned Lawrence into an aid and a companion, almost a doppelgänger. So, rightly, he calls the book a personal quest and has had the energy, insight and ability to translate his extraordinary story into an absorbing written account. It is brilliantly lucid and compulsive for pages on end and the author, a practised journalist as well as a gifted writer, has imposed order and clarity on complex argument and analysis while retaining the romance and evocative lyricism of an enthralling narrative.

What's new in this book? This will undoubtedly be the question immediately asked. Well, for me, in the first part he has illuminated an area long dark about the Anglo-Irish background from which Lawrence emerged. We all knew his father was an Eton-educated aristocrat who left a socially prominent family of a wife and four daughters in Ireland to run off with their Anglo-Scottish governess and found a family of five illegitimate sons under an assumed name, the second of whom was to become the legendary Lawrence of Arabia; but Dick Benson-Gyles has put reality and detail into the story, so that we now know this was not just, as it were, any old Rochester running off with a Jane Eyre, but in social terms a cataclysmic fall from grace within a highly reputable and well connected social circle which left seriously hurt people all over the place and put a far bigger wound into Lawrence's psyche than we had ever thought. He has also placed the story powerfully in the context of Irish history and of that fading clan of Anglo-Irish whose decline almost parallels that of the British in India. This is *Jewel in the Crown* stuff Irish style.

Then, in the second half of the book, he takes us to where the story of Lawrence simply has to go – Arabia. The author went in pursuit of one of the great enigmas Lawrence left behind – who was the character 'S.A.' to whom he dedicated his most famous work, *Seven Pillars of Wisdom*? His conclusion, which is both surprising and persuasive, was reached after a quest which took him to, among other places, the deserts

| XIII |

and mountains of Syria. As a by-product, this part of the narrative contains some very good travel writing. Finally, the book has a substantial number of genuinely exclusive illustrations, which even I hadn't seen.

Anyone who reads this compelling story will be both moved and enlightened. After the plethora of biographies and studies published over the years it might be thought that there would be little of real consequence left to say about Lawrence. The author has proved such a belief emphatically wrong. Dick Benson-Gyles has achieved something rather remarkable.

THE BOY IN THE MASK
THE HIDDEN WORLD OF
LAWRENCE OF ARABIA

ONE

A Meeting

I FIRST MET T.E. Lawrence in the Odeon Cinema, Richmond.

David Lean's epic film, *Lawrence of Arabia*, had just moved out from the big screens of London's West End to the suburbs and provinces. I decided to go and see it, expecting a lot of sound, fury and colour as well as the usual cinematic distortions, in short, a sort of Cecil B. DeMille *Ten Commandments* with Bedouin, camels, sheikhs and British army officers. Nevertheless, I was looking forward to enjoying what I imagined would be the desert exploits of an unusual First World War soldier brought vividly to life on the screen. Yet I had too a strong sense of something subliminal at work, an undercurrent of attraction that seemed to be drawing me like a magnet to the film.

When I came out of the cinema four hours later my student doldrums had been blown away. I was stunned. It wasn't the film's heroic narrative, sweeping grandeur, romantic backdrop or luxuriant photography that had so moved me. It was something transcending this, a glimmering suggestion of the apocalyptic, which troubled and tantalized me. As I emerged into the bright twilight of that never-to-be-forgotten summer evening, everything but the film seemed suddenly absurdly inconsequential. I have never discovered what happened, only that some inner alchemy responded like reawakened consciousness to this celluloid T.E. Lawrence luminously alive in the dreamworld of the Odeon. As soon as the house lights had dimmed and Lawrence's motorbike appeared, gleaming in summer sunlight filtered through translucent green leaves in a quiet Dorset farmyard, the hair went up on the back of my neck. I sensed, despite the incongruity of the venue, that this was somehow a watershed for me. My body had gone, only my heart and soul were there. In such simple moments are lifelong involvements born. Since then down the years Lawrence has haunted me with a quiet, questioning persistence.

After the motorbike crash on a heathland road in Dorset in May 1935 and Lawrence's death comes the funeral scene at St Paul's Cathedral. The story then goes back to its beginnings in the Intelligence Department in Cairo in 1916. Lieutenant T.E. Lawrence, disguised as a rather taller Peter O'Toole, is in a basement office with an orderly, awaiting the arrival of his copy of the *Arab Bulletin*. He is soon summoned by Dryden – his political guide through the bewildering corridors of power in the rambling mansion of British Levantine policy – to see General Murray, Commander of the Egyptian Expeditionary Force (EEF). Murray reluctantly permits the unconventional subaltern a temporary secondment to Arabia. Lawrence lights a match, looks at it and says, almost to himself, 'It's going to be fun.' Then, in close-up profile, he blows it out. Instantaneously, in total silence, the giant screen turns an incandescent flame-red – the red of dawn in the desert. A huge, molten sun inches up over the austere, empty wastes and Maurice Jarre's sweeping score swells to a powerful crescendo. Arabia in all its vast, purged expanses is slowly revealed in exquisite gradations of colour. I was mesmerised. Like so many others I had experienced the Lawrence moment. It takes hold of you quietly and firmly and doesn't let go. Lawrence would probably have laughed at such a reaction, yet he knew that he and his life exuded a magnetism that invariably held an irresistible attraction for people. At the same time his personality contained paradoxes that he never fully reconciled, and, if he had an uncanny ability to understand others, he struggled to understand himself.

I have searched myself in vain to discover what happened to me that day in the cinema. It was David Lean's film that urged me to go in search of the real Lawrence, in the hope that I might stumble upon something essential about him and, in the process, about myself. I had hoped that finding the truth behind Lawrence's renunciation of the material and physical might somehow bring understanding and order to my own life. It hasn't. Nevertheless, I picked up the gauntlet thrown down by the film, and the challenge ever since has been unfailingly dynamic: a quest, a continual meeting with the unexpected, the astonishing, and, occasionally, the unpalatable.

In our family house my father had a cosy little study just off the hall and in it were two home-made wooden bookcases containing an eclectic but modest collection. Among the books was a two-volume economy edition of *Seven Pillars of Wisdom* by T.E. Lawrence. Its unusual title had caught my eye. I was young and hungry for spiritual food and the title held a strange fascination. Now, overwhelmed by the film, I went straight to the book. It promised something special, something mind-opening, even perhaps something mystical, and it more than exceeded the film in the indelible impression it made on me. I was on fire with the effects of reading this compelling work of extraordinary literary juxtapositions – the vivid chronicling of a medieval campaign in a modern theatre and an ancient land; the movingly lyrical evocation of a vast, primal landscape; the raw, unsparing recording of the brutalities of war; the unflinching self-analysis.

Lean's seductive treatment of the Arabian campaign had first attracted me to the legendary Lawrence, but after the book I developed an obsessive urge to uncover what I sensed was another Lawrence, a very private person concealed behind the pages of *Seven Pillars*. Despite years of intensive study, his nature and his life have stubbornly refused to yield up their secrets. Hence, of course, his continuing fascination. Lawrence was always trying to discover who he really was. He was the arch-introspective, the constant self-inquisitor, a man of both self-assurance and self-doubt. He was preoccupied with the hidden wellsprings that drove him, more interested in the 'why' than the 'how' or 'when' of things. Extrovert and introvert, actor and audience, which was the real Lawrence? Was there one at all? Yet I was certain that there was one promising route to discovery – a pathway that led all the way back to his childhood and beyond.

As for his legendary status, if he hadn't been in the right place at the right time – Arabia at the onset of the Great War – it is likely that there would have been no celebrated hero at all. He might have become well-known within academic circles, perhaps as an archaeologist or traveller, but without the Arab Revolt he would not have achieved the worldwide fame which is his today. And yet it is as though it was all pre-ordained. Nevertheless, a doubt stubbornly persisted. Did the events that effectively began in 1916 sweep him reluctantly into the spotlight, or did he purposely wait in the wings and on cue step out onto the boards and assume the lead role? A bit of each, I suspected. Neither the film, nor in fact the book, had really provided the answer, so I decided that before I looked anywhere else I would take a key, controversial area of his war service and subject it to as exhaustive and critical an examination as possible. That, surely, would provide a pretty good testing ground for the truth about him. If the Arabian Lawrence turned out to have been just a very good actor, or worse, a self-promoting charlatan, then there would be little point in researching further.

On the eve of the Great War the British Empire was hugely extended and cumbersome, and in the political context it was often a matter of the right hand not knowing what the left was doing. The strains imposed on the Empire's policymakers by having to conduct Imperial business through Byzantine channels of communication are well summarized by Sir Ronald Wingate, kinsman of Sir Reginald Wingate, who in the war years was firstly Governor-General of the Sudan and then High Commissioner of Egypt:

> England herself, though she had a general and right idea of what should be her policy towards Islam – as from the population standpoint the greatest Muslim power – was prevented both by the extent of her empire and by her administrative machinery from being particularly coherent on the subject. The Foreign Office was responsible for England's policy towards Turkey and the Middle East generally… This area of Foreign Office control included Egypt and the Sudan, where however the Foreign Office for years past had been accustomed to leave everything to the man on the spot … Then there was the India Office in London, which, through the Viceroy of India, was responsible for the Indian sphere of influence, which in those days included Aden, Oman, the Persian Gulf and Mesopotamia – Here again, the India Office had been content to leave everything to the men on the spot … Lastly there was the War Office in London – to which Kitchener came in August 1914 – which was directly concerned, from the intelligence standpoint, with the military potentialities of Turkey in the event of war … The result of all this was that, as regards Arabia and its problems, though the War Office, the Viceroy of India, and the British Agent in Egypt were all well informed and kept in touch with each other, the Foreign Office and the India Office in London had little to say and were not particularly interested. And so the British Government had no clear-cut policy in the Islamic Field, and often found itself, when the crisis of the war with Turkey came, in a cross-fire between advocates of one course or another.[1]

Into this bewildering network of Imperial rule in 1914, unsuspected and as yet unapplied, came the iron will and idealistic fire of T.E. Lawrence. Soon he would be adding his considerable intellect to that coterie of pragmatic luminaries in Cairo, which became the Arab Bureau. Under its shrewd Director, Colonel (later Brigadier-General) Sir Gilbert Clayton, Acting Director, Commander D.G. Hogarth, and his deputy, Captain Kinahan Cornwallis, and answering to the High Commissioner in Egypt and the Foreign Office, the Bureau rapidly developed into the hub of intelligence on Arab affairs. Hogarth, Lawrence's mentor, wrote of the members of this brilliant club created to serve British intelligence and policy in Arabia:

> Do you know
> The Arab Bureau?
> Clayton stability,
> Symes versatility,
> Cornwallis is practical,
> Dawnay syntactical,
> Mackintosh havers,
> And Fielding palavers,
> Mackindoe easy,
> And Wordie not breezy:
> Lawrence licentiate to dream and to dare
> And yours Very Faithfully, bon à tout faire.[2]

This gifted group of men believed in the Empire and took it almost for granted that Britain's birthright was to oversee the governance of much of the world; but they were not blinkered chauvinists. They were certainly privileged but they were also highly educated Oxbridge scholars, Arabists, linguists and travellers. They were dedicated to ensuring the Empire a dominant stake in the Levant in the event of the collapse of 'the sick man of Europe' – Turkey and its crumbling Empire. And some of these men – like Lawrence, who knew the area and its nomadic inhabitants well after four years of archaeology at Carchemish in northern Syria – had already been infected with an abiding fascination with the Near East, the cradle of civilization and the spiritual home of three of the world's great religions.

These servants and savants of empire were intoxicated with the region's long, rich history, its elemental deserts, the venerability of its cities, and the bewildering variety of its peoples. Nor were they immune to the powerful aura of romance and mystique that suffuses the Levant, its polyglot races spun by the centuries into a complex web of spiritual, political and nationalist allegiance, an ethnic and religious coat of many colours. There is even today an air of musty antiquity and shadowy intrigue about the cities of the Middle East. Memories of ancient dynastic struggle and religious revelation and persecution hover like ghosts in the dancing heat of the noisy, dusty streets of the old quarters of Damascus, Jerusalem, Baghdad and Cairo. It invests the region with a seductive power that British orientalists like Lawrence have always found hard to resist.

The story of his rise in the Great War from relative obscurity as a Lieutenant and an intelligence officer in the Arab Bureau in Cairo to Colonel Lawrence, legendary among the desert tribes as El Aurens, arriving triumphantly in Damascus in 1918 at the head of an irregular army of bedouin, has become almost a cliché. Put at its simplest, the legend has it that his unique vision and burning determination allowed him to appreciate what might be made of the initially disparate, and not particularly promising, materials at his disposal to build his 'seven-pillared worthy house', namely the Bedouin tribes and their potential as guerrilla fighters.

In the early stages Lawrence had little executive clout with policy-making superiors, many of whom were unconvinced of the military value of untrained native forces. However, his pre-war years living in Syria, a working knowledge of Arabic, powers of endurance well beyond the average, a natural gift for leadership, dissimulation and manipulation, and a driven urge to succeed, all suggested that he was tailor-made for the job of motivating and orchestrating bedouin irregulars. Few of his contemporaries saw this at first. In fact, he rubbed a lot of people up the wrong way with his outspoken opinions and unconventional behaviour and what they saw as his precocious belief in the rightness of his own views to the disparagement of those of others, even of those of much more senior officers. Lieutenant-Colonel Cyril Wilson, the British Representative in Jiddah on the Red Sea's Hejaz coast, wrote to Clayton in November 1916:

> Lawrence wants kicking and kicking hard at that then he would [illegible word]. At present I look upon him as a bumptious young ass who spoils his undoubted knowledge of Syrian Arabs etc. by making himself out to be the only authority on war, engineering, running HM's ships and everything else. He put every single person's back up I've met from the Admiral down to the most junior fellow on the RW team.[3]

Someone, however, who did appreciate Lawrence's remarkable potential was David Hogarth, and with his support Lawrence now carved out his place in history. The Arab Revolt of 1916–18 was always a piecemeal movement, and without General Sir Edmund Allenby (from June 1917 the General Officer Commanding-in-Chief of the EEF) there would most probably have been no revolt of any significance. It was initially a tribal insurgency launched in June 1916 by the Hejaz's Sherif Hussein bin Ali, the Emir of Mecca and Guardian of the Holy Places of Mecca and Medina. He had not taken the British into his confidence and so the Revolt took them, and the Turks, by surprise. Nevertheless, the British reacted positively, providing intelligence officers (among them Lawrence), advisers, money, arms, and later some artillery.

The British had been ambivalent about what military value an uprising of Arab irregulars would have. They tended to view the Bedouin through conventional military eyes as irredeemably tribal – volatile, untrustworthy nomads who could never be marshalled into a reliable, effective or regular fighting force. Lawrence was one of only a few who saw their real potential as guerilla fighters, and he later devoted considerable space in *Seven Pillars* to explaining how he had envisaged their productive deployment, presenting his ideas as almost a new philosophy of irregular warfare. Elusive tribal units, avoiding direct confrontation with the enemy, would be armed with explosives as well as guns and swords and be despatched on desert raids to harass and cut the north-south Hejaz railway. This would theoretically tie down Turkish forces and create the illusion of a significant armed threat lurking hidden in the deserts to the south and east.

Lawrence, however, came perilously close to missing his chance altogether. Sir Reginald Wingate, Sirdar of the Egyptian Army, had originally chosen Captain Stewart Newcombe, RE, in Military Intelligence in Cairo, to liaise with the Revolt's *de facto* leader, King Hussein's son, Prince Feisal. Newcombe had first met Lawrence during his pre-war archaeological days and was to become a good friend. In November 1916 Wingate telegrammed Clayton: 'I propose sending Newcombe to Yenbo but in view of possible delay of his arrival I think Lawrence would do the work excellently as a temporary arrangement.'⁴ So Lawrence made sure that his services as liaison officer with Feisal became virtually indispensable. He was to forge an enduring rapport with the impressive Prince, a tall, slender, quietly heroic figure, subtly insinuating his strategic vision into Feisal's mind, nudging the determined but sometimes vacillating Emir ever onward towards Damascus.

That accepted, how did Lawrence manage to become a major player in the Middle-East theatre? The received view is that it was a touch of genius by him— in the form of an unorthodox and secret plan in 1917 to take the northern Red Sea port of Aqaba by surprise attack from inland – that put him, and the Revolt, firmly centre stage. If executed successfully, it would be a giant strategic step, transforming the fledgling and uncoordinated Arab Revolt from a parochial one confined to the Hejaz into a much larger, organized movement with a new and permanent base in Syria. With Feisal's approval Lawrence and a carefully chosen party of Arabs would cross hundreds of miles of desert, re-emerge in south-east Syria, and, capturing the Turkish posts en route, march down to Aqaba. The Royal Navy would then supply the new base and a growing Arab army with munitions, provisions, money and British military advisers. Aqaba would then be the perfect springboard for an advance into Syria and the eventual capture of Damascus. In the event, it would also become the anchor of a right flank for the EEF under Allenby when British Imperial forces later advanced into Palestine.

If it was to succeed, the Aqaba plan – as apparently conceived by Lawrence with Feisal's full, and essential, backing – would require the vital support of Auda abu Tayi, the chief of the eastern Howeitat, whose tribal territories lay dotted about the Aqaba region. The plan in detail was to take a small party of sherifian-led bedouin from the Revolt's new base at Wejh on the upper Red Sea coast and set off north-east through the vast, empty and mercilessly hot hinterland, skirting the forbidding Nefud desert and riding up the snake-infested Wadi Sirhan. The forty-strong expedition would establish a propaganda presence and set about persuading the northern tribes to enrol under Feisal's banner. From there, after a feint or two to put the Turks off the scent, the force would turn south-west and capture the Turkish posts in the defiles and rugged terrain along the final fifty-mile ride down Wadi Ithm to Aqaba and the sea.

This great turning movement across hundreds of barren miles was an ambitious mission and a tremendous gamble, the more so because Lawrence claimed that he undertook it without either Cairo's authorization or knowledge. He told his biographer Basil Liddell Hart: 'The venture was a private one. I had no orders to do it, and took nothing British with me. Feisal provided money, camels, stores, and explosives. That explains why I had no help from the Navy.'[5] The gamble paid off, and it turned out to be Lawrence's first step to fame. With £1000 of sherifs' money in his saddlebags, given to him by Feisal in Wejh on 8 May, Lawrence set off the next day with the little party of camel-mounted bedouin under Sherif Nasir, Feisal's cousin, and accompanied by the Damascene Nesib el Bekri as political officer and a few others, on the long, dangerous trek northward.[6] Two months later this initially insignificant Arab force, now 2000 strong, rode through Wadi Ithm winning several fierce engagements. On 6 July they swept triumphantly down to Aqaba, herding six hundred prisoners in front of them.

The port itself was defended by only a token presence because the bulk of the garrison had earlier withdrawn to the surrounding hills after a Royal Navy vessel on a chance reconnaissance had loosed off a few rounds at the beach, ignorant of the force advancing in numbers on the port from inland. In Aqaba Lawrence and the Arabs found only three hundred panicking defenders, among them a bewildered German military well-borer called Liesegang, who hadn't the faintest idea what was going on and had never heard of an Arab Army!

Aqaba's thin sea-defences had, in fact, already been breached three months earlier by Royal Navy ships commanded by Captain 'Ginger' Boyle, subsequently Admiral of the Fleet, the Earl of Cork and Orrery. Boyle's exploratory action to clear mines from the port waters, and his brief landing, had resulted in the taking of eleven Turkish prisoners. Boyle later commented: 'The capture of prisoners was important and welcomed by Lawrence, who was anxious to get information as to the Turkish forces in the Aqaba district. He was already plotting his descent upon that place, which he carried out in such a gallant manner a few weeks later.'[7]

Nevertheless, there has always been controversy about who actually conceived the Aqaba scheme. Establishing whose initiative it was was important because it was the taking of Aqaba which launched the Revolt proper, elevated Lawrence to a pre-eminent role, gave him direct access to his chiefs in Cairo and Khartoum, and thereafter lent his tactical and strategic views considerable weight. It also opened the door to the creation of the Lawrence legend.

Some Arab scholars have claimed that the Aqaba plan had been an entirely Arab idea first suggested by Auda abu Tayi in consultation with Feisal and other senior sherifs when Auda and Feisal met for the first time at Wejh.[8] British officers in the field, though, were adamant that it was entirely Lawrence's brainchild. Lawrence himself wrote that Aqaba had been taken 'on my plan by my effort', and years later, discussing *Seven Pillars* in a letter to Charlotte Shaw, the playwright George Bernard Shaw's wife, he confirmed the imperative of capturing Aqaba from the land and that it was his idea: 'Yes, of course, the Aqaba ride was when first I was conscious of my aim in Arabia. It represents the changeover of the book from accident to intention.'[9][10] In 1934 he told her: 'Aqaba beach could have been taken by ship's gunfire, like the beach of Gallipoli. What I wanted was the 50 miles of mountain defiles behind the beach, which could (I still think) only have been taken by us from inland.'[11]

There is documentary evidence to support Lawrence's claim. By early 1917 the goals of the fragile but growing Revolt were still ill-defined, its progress driven more by hope than expectation. Newcombe outlined ideas for its advance in a note to Wingate of 24 May, both the date and the contents suggesting that Feisal had not taken Newcombe into his confidence about the secret ride to capture Aqaba, which, of course, was already under way: 'On May 31st Sherif Feisal hopes to leave Wejh to attack El Ula or Bedia while Sherif Abdullah destroys the railway from the South …'

In another comment he said:

From Uweinid Feisal with his escort moves to Jafar East of Ma'an, 150 miles. He might get there by July 7th. Auda Abu Tayi and Lawrence are to be told to collect there food for 1000 men for 10 days and food for mules: and a large number of camels, say 1000; until Feisal gets into that neighbourhood, these camels will not move South to Uweinid … [Newcombe continued, saying that Feisal would] then move to Kasr el Azrak about July 17th where food will also be prepared. Thence he will start his campaign. [He then added significantly that the capture of the northern port would be essential for success:] The importance of Aqaba is both political and tactical. Sherif Faisal considers it indispensable politically to encourage the Beni Sakhr, Huwitat, and Druzes. Once taken he thinks the Turks would not move towards it from Ma'an through a hostile country, any more than they did from El Ula after Wejh was taken, though water was ample. To take Aqaba, he will have 1500 Meccans at Wejh by June 24th. He would like to move these to Aqaba, though only partially trained, about July 15th. And would therefore want steamers about that date.[12]

Of key relevance here is the mention of the need for steamers. It further supports the view that Feisal was keeping his strategic cards close to his chest and, by placing emphasis on a capture by sea, was deflecting attention away from the overland expedition and maintaining its secrecy. Nevertheless, he probably did envisage a seaborne attack as a genuine fall-back option in the event of Nasir, Lawrence and Auda failing to achieve their objective. That Lawrence was the driving force behind the Aqaba plan is supported in an interview given by Newcombe to Frenchman Jean Beraud Villars for his 1955 Lawrence biography. He wrote that Newcombe had told him, 'in a personal conversation in 1954', that Lawrence had indeed been the originator of the plan.[13]

Villars wrote:

… all the witnesses are agreed on this point, and they prove that things did happen as they have just been related. Colonel Newcombe who had Lawrence under his command at the time has said so himself. During this period, he said, the leaders of the English mission were still groping in the dark, each one of them doing his best in his own sphere. Everyone had noticed the extraordinary ascendancy which T.E. had gained over Feisal, and they were pleased to see him decide the Sherifs' men on effective action; they allowed their comrade to operate on his own so long as he only used native units and did not draw on the still limited resources of the allied base. Colonel Newcombe has confirmed that the Aqaba exploit was entirely conceived by Lawrence who was its real leader and animating spirit, although for reasons of diplomacy that are understandable the official command was left in the hands of the Arab chieftains.[14]

That the Aqaba initiative was Lawrence's is further supported, if indirectly, by evidence of Feisal's increasing dependence on him for advice and guidance. A month before the Aqaba expedition and shortly before a major tribal council at Wejh Feisal wrote to Lawrence, who was engaged on railway demolition raids in Wadi Ais, anxiously appealing to him to return to Wejh as soon as possible. He said: 'I am waiting for your coming because I want to see you very much because I have many things to tell you.'[15] And in another anxious communication he entreated: 'You are much needed here more than the destruction of the line because I am in very great complication which I had never expected…'[16]

Feisal's increasing trust in Lawrence was to give him a vital credibility with the tribal sheikhs and by extension with the tribesmen themselves. This bond with Feisal, together with British funding and military support and his own extraordinary abilities, allowed Lawrence to pull the strings and in crucial measure to control the direction of the Revolt. He also knew that the desert Arabs believed in people not in institutions or in strategies dictated impersonally from on high, so, to identify himself more closely with them and to gain their confidence, he proved he could equal them in endurance and share their harsh life. He also dressed, with Feisal's approval, like a Sherif. To the tribesmen such rich apparel marked and significantly enhanced authority and status. In combination, all these elements allowed Lawrence to build an unrivalled reputation among them. He also avoided leading from the front. He would drop well-considered ideas into conversations with the ashraf (the tribal chiefs) as though they were just passing thoughts, knowing that the Arab leaders, while often not admitting as much, would appreciate their value and usually ultimately adopt them as their own. That suited Lawrence. He was not in the business of self-aggrandizement, in directly establishing his own ascendancy, but in implementing vital plans. Who took credit for their execution didn't matter, so long as they were executed successfully.

Lawrence's fellow British officers confirm this psychological approach. Hogarth said of him in an article written after the war in 1919: 'Pushing (not himself) he finds more congenial than leading and he loves to push the unsuspecting body: but if it does not get on as fast as he thinks it should, he pushes it into the gutter and steps to the front.'[17] Captain Boyle wrote that this policy of Lawrence's was evident well before the taking of Aqaba: 'Lawrence by this time had completely won over the Arab leaders. His influence with them was very great and most wisely used.'[18] Irishman Major (later Colonel) Pierce Joyce, a regular officer of the Connaught Rangers who was to become base commandant at Aqaba and was technically Lawrence's superior officer but in practical terms his coeval, said of him: 'At Arab conferences he spoke little, but he knew beforehand that his plan would be adopted, while the task of kindling enthusiasm amongst the tribesmen was better left to the Arab leaders'. He further commented: 'as at dozens of other conferences we attended together, Lawrence rarely spoke. He merely studied the men around him and when the arguments ended as they usually did in smoke, he then dictated his plan of action, which was usually adopted and everyone went away satisfied.'[19]

One of Lawrence's great virtues was patience, particularly with the volatile and unreliable tribesmen, who would only commit to action when it suited them, with money or loot often their prime motivation. Bedouin vision was localized; they could appreciate an immediate part of a strategy but seldom the whole, so Lawrence cajoled them along, biding his time for the judicious moment to act. During the long march to Aqaba he wrote in his message-pad, 'Mem. don't attempt too much'. Many of the British officers seconded to the Revolt lacked his reservoir of tact, their military training tending to demand unquestioning obedience. This didn't suit the maverick bedouin at all and they often showed as much, on one occasion taking pot-shots at Newcombe for pushing them too hard.[20] The only authority they accepted, and even then not always, was that of their sheikhs. Lawrence's shrewd, kid-glove approach to dealing with the bedouin is perfectly encapsulated in his now well-known 'Twenty-Seven Articles', a set of guidance notes for working with the tribes, which first appeared in the August 1917 issue of the secret *Arab Bulletin*, published in Cairo for restricted Intelligence circulation (still consulted to this day by American and British forces in Afghanistan).[21]

While Lawrence was disappearing from Wejh into the desert wilderness, Anglo-French policy on a post-war Middle East had been hardening into official expressions of territorial covetousness such as the 1916 Sykes-Picot Treaty, which was a blueprint for draconian geopolitical dispositions, including French control of Syria. Lawrence loved France, particularly French medieval history and literature, but he had developed an implacable hatred of French designs on his beloved Syria. The Treaty was, of course, top secret, but Lawrence, kept informed by Hogarth and others in the Arab Bureau, knew that the promised reward of freedom and autonomy for the Arabs in the event of the defeat of their Turkish overlords was, in the final analysis, a deception and a lie.

Out in the wilds on the hazardous northern trek and weakened by illness and the extreme conditions of heat and terrain, which taxed even his hardened body and mind to their limits, Lawrence began to have misgivings and to suffer serious pangs of conscience. On the seemingly never-ending desert ride he had time to mull over the complex politics of the war in Arabia in which he was becoming more and more embroiled. He started to doubt both the feasibility of the Aqaba adventure and Imperial policy. Two days into the march he was 'Tired and sorry'; the next day he was 'V. sick'; the day after that he wrote in his diary: 'The weight is bearing me down now. Auda last night, and pain and agony today.' A further two days on he seemed close to giving up, recording: 'If I could only get out.'[22]

Nevertheless, Lawrence persevered and got across the vast tracts of desert to the planned Syrian recruiting base of Nebk at the head of Wadi Sirhan. Weeks on the march had not changed his outlook. On 5 June he was still having serious doubts, writing in his diary: 'Can't stand another day here. Will ride N & chuck it.'[23] His urge to quit the Revolt just as it was starting to burgeon seems initially to have been triggered by no more elevated consideration than his disgust and impatience with the delay caused by the gluttonous tribal feasting going on day after day at the march's northern end, at Isawiyeh, Abu Tareifiyat and Nebk. Lawrence scribbled in his message-pad: 'I had been twenty eight years well fed & had no right to despise these fellows for loving their mutton'. But politics were clearly still uppermost in his mind because his next comment was: 'Nesib was of their race, and brothers and sisters may tell the truth where we cannot. But I wish to God I was quit of it' – a clear, if oblique, reference to the Sykes-Picot Treaty and the false position he felt it was putting him in.[24] However, in his *Seven Pillars'* accounts of the expedition to Nebk Lawrence makes no mention of wanting to give up.

It was now dawning on him that in order to achieve his strategic aims he would have to don a mantle of deceit and lie to his Arab comrades-in-arms, denying the existence of the secret Imperial agenda, which underlay Britain's qualified support for Arab independence. His response to this moral dilemma was extraordinary. He would throw himself on the mercy of fate and go off by camel on another long, northward ride, half hoping not to survive. On the impulse of the moment he drafted a note to his superiors in Cairo (which he then crossed out) expressing his extreme disquiet with the way the Arabs were being treated: 'Clayton. I've decided to go off alone to Damascus hoping to get killed on the way. For all sakes try and clear this show up before it goes further. We are telling them to fight for no motive, and I can't stand it.'[25] This momentary, and probably unsent, cry from the heart was written in a very small hand for, as his friend the poet Robert Graves astutely noticed many years later, whenever Lawrence was depressed his handwriting shrank in proportion to the degree of his despondency.[26] Yet he always had an eye to the main chance and, ever the pragmatist and looking to the long term, he would also have known that priceless intelligence could be garnered on a secret northern reconnaissance, which, if he survived, would be invaluable to the Revolt, if and when it advanced into Syria in strength.

Astonishingly, having already covered six hundred miles of largely uncharted desert, he was now setting off again, initially with just two bedouin companions, then alone, to cross several hundred miles more of wilderness. He left Nebk on this impulsive and extremely risky spying venture on 5 June. His solitary ride into the unknown took him up the eastern desert as far as Tudmor and Ras Baalbek, sounding out tribal leaders and blowing up a bridge or two for propaganda purposes, and back down to the outskirts of Damascus, where he had a secret meeting with Ali Rida Pasha al-Rikabi, who had been General Officer Commanding the city but who was also covertly President of the Syrian branch of the Arab Secret Society. When Lawrence got back to Nebk on or about 18 June, the enrolment of men for the campaign proper was well under way. The road to Aqaba and into the pages of history beckoned.

Lawrence's solo ride was an extraordinary feat that would have been beyond the physical and mental capabilities of most men. Wingate, Clayton, Newcombe, Hogarth and others were fulsome in their praise of his major role in the capture of Aqaba, but it was his northern reconnaissance with its vital prize of invaluable intelligence, which attracted the most lavish praise and for which he was recommended for the Victoria Cross. Wingate wrote to the politician Mark Sykes on 16 July 1917:

> Lawrence's exploit in the Syrian Hinterland was really splendid and I hope you will have an opportunity of putting in a word that will help him to get the V.C, which, in my opinion, he has so thoroughly earned. Clayton and G.H.Q. are now digesting the information he has collected with a view to working out a scheme of co-operation from Sinai, Baghdad and the Hedjaz...[27]

On the same day Wingate also wrote to Wilson, in even more glowing terms, about Lawrence's northern ride: 'I have very strongly recommended Lawrence for the Victoria Cross for his magnificent achievement – in my opinion one of the finest done during the whole war...'[28] In the end, in Hogarth's words: 'His V.C. was not given because of the proviso in the Charter of the Order that there must be British officer witnesses of the deed.'[29]

Critics of Lawrence later fastened onto this lack of corroboration to cast doubt on the whole journey. However, a scrutiny of Lawrence's notes and pocket diaries in the British Library makes it abundantly clear that his secret ride *did* take place. These writings are what Lawrence called 'observations on the road, scribbled at random in the saddle'. The pencilled diary entries are inevitably brief and dotted with erasures, faint, almost illegible words, isolated letters, and coded characters, all consistent with the constant dangers and difficulties of such a venture into remote enemy territory: 'Riding since yesterday morning without stop'; 'More miles Burga last night'; 'S. Biar watered'; 'My camel is done B'; 'R. Baalb'; 'Wanted to see M. but (He)–X.'[30]

The significance of the surprise capture of Aqaba was that it was achieved by an independent Arab force without any outside support. This gave the Arab irregulars a new credibility. It also altered the balance of power in the eastern theatre. An hitherto unstable and largely untested alliance of bedouin tribes was now set to play a crucial part in the subsequent British advance northward. The Arab Revolt had come of age and at a stroke Lawrence had become the indispensable link between the Arab insurgents and the British Forces. He now had the attentive ear not only of Feisal but also of his chiefs in Cairo. He was promoted Major and thenceforward to a role of increasing importance.

The securing of Aqaba brought him not just to the attention of the top brass in Egypt but also to the rarefied heights of the War Cabinet in Britain. Wingate wrote to Lawrence: 'The Chief of the Imperial General Staff has requested me to convey his congratulations on your recent exploit and I do so with the liveliest satisfaction.'[31] In fact, the news of Lawrence's extraordinary success reached the very highest in the land – the King himself. In late July 1917 Lawrence's immediate chief, Brigadier-General Clayton, wrote to the King's Private Secretary, Colonel Clive Wigram, describing in some detail both Lawrence's secret northern ride and the taking of Aqaba, commenting: 'His recent trip in enemy country ranks among the really gallant deeds of the war.'[32]

These fulsome plaudits are a major confirmation of some of Lawrence's achievements, but in the years after his death came the inevitable backlash. More recently, hostile critics pronounced the charismatic brilliance and meteoric rise of the twenty-eight-year-old from junior officer to colonel commanding thousands of Arab tribesmen as largely a triumph of promotion and self-promotion. They added that the legend had been given a crucial fillip by the impact on the British public of a post-war picture show about the Middle East campaign, put on in London theatres by a money-making American journalist. There is some truth in this but the central claims of these critics are being proved wrong. A more balanced perspective, provided by the passage of time and objective scholarship, has begun to sort the wheat from the chaff. Hitherto embargoed historical archives, new documentation and personal testimony are all confirming that the Lawrence story has solid foundations. In fact, even before the end of the war, accounts of Lawrence's exploits and achievements were doing the rounds of military, intelligence and political circles in both the Middle East and England.

An indication of Lawrence's growing reputation during the war can be had from Hogarth's letters home from Cairo in 1917. He wrote of his protégé in a fatherly way and in language full of personal touches, which stand out all the more when read beside the norm of impersonal wartime communications. He wrote in October: 'Tell his mother he has now four decorations including the CB (to qualify for which he had to be promoted Major) and despises and ignores the lot. Says he does not mind what they give him so long as he has not to wear them! He is rather run down but very hard and his reputation has become overpowering.' In mid-December, less than a month after Lawrence's capture and torture at Deraa, Hogarth wrote: 'T.E.L. was with me at Gaza and is here now for a day and is looking much fitter and better than when I saw him last! He still looks absolutely boyish for 29! He is off again soon on another and bigger, but less perilous, adventure. I hope he has written to his mother!' In a Christmas letter, clearly amused by Lawrence's behaviour, Hogarth said: 'It was a refreshing contrast to have T.E.L. about for a week. He anyhow only lives for one thing. They put him up at the Residency this time and made much of him. He went about happily in a 2nd Lieutenant's tunic with badges somewhere between a Lieutenant and a Captain, and no decorations and no belt.' And in early 1918: 'Tell Mrs Lawrence that her blessed boy is all right, but his hair has got very long again.'[33] The reminiscences of others offer similar proof of how widespread Lawrence's reputation was during the war, let alone after it. One memoir commented: 'Lawrence and his prodigies made me early into a true disciple. During the rest of the war I earnestly cross-examined all who came from the Near East as to the latest exploits of our modern crusader. My best informant was Sir Henry McMahon himself, who was enthralling about Lawrence, and gave me in full measure the epic story … But I had many other friends fighting in Palestine; and from time to time they came home on leave, and brought more and more fantastic tales of the doings of this strange young man'.[34]

There is one particularly significant confirmation of the importance of Lawrence's role with the Arabs and of its vital contribution to General Allenby's success in Palestine, which, in my view, all but settles any debate. The French Military Mission to the Arabs, often preoccupied with what they saw as France's historical claims on Syria, did their utmost to influence Feisal and the ashraf and to prevent the burgeoning Arab Revolt from spreading north. With the capture of Aqaba a *fait accompli*, the French then tried to ensure that Lawrence's activities were confined to the Ma'an-Aqaba region. General Allenby insisted to London, who were clearly getting jittery at the problematic political issues arising from increasing Arab involvement in the Middle-East campaign, that Lawrence's operations were military and not politically sensitive because, in the terms of the Sykes-Picot Agreement, they were 'outside the French sphere'. Allenby kept the French – always suspicious of British geopolitical ambitions – at arm's length by largely confining his communications with them to military considerations. He promised London that if Lawrence ever did act in the French zone (i.e. north of Jerusalem), the French would 'be informed as fully as military exigencies permit'.

In October 1917 he wrote to General Sir William Robertson, the Chief of the Imperial General Staff: 'Lawrence must not be hampered while engaged on delicate and dangerous tasks which are purely tactical, which may be of great importance to the success of my operations, and which he alone can carry through.'[35] Needless to say, Lawrence had his own political and territorial agenda that went well beyond the tactical and envisaged a wholly Arab Syria to the exclusion of the French.

The Revolt, with its hair-raising skirmishes and dynamiting raids on the Hejaz railway, its gruelling marches and rare set-piece battles, moved in stop-start stages northward, drawing in ever more tribal and British support. Lawrence was trusted by the sherifs and admired by the bedouin and was, by common consent of the British officers and men, together with Feisal the inspiring and driving force of the Revolt with its culmination the final advance on Damascus and the capture of the city on 1 October 1918 so evocatively described by Lawrence in *Seven Pillars*.

There followed the cynical political manoeuvrings of the Paris Peace Conference in 1919 (where, at Feisal's side, Lawrence was a vocal, and purposely very visible proponent of Arab autonomy, supplementing his advocacy with innumerable proselytizing articles in national newspapers); and then the Cairo Conference of 1921, after which he pronounced himself satisfied that an equitable settlement for the Arabs had been secured. But he surely knew that the settlement was fundamentally a compromise contrived to accommodate the needs (including oil) of British Imperial policy and what France rather ambitiously insisted were her claims on Syria.

No wonder that half a century later David Lean wanted to make a blockbuster film about the Arabian war. It had all the ingredients for resounding cinematic success. Crystallized into legend, the Arab Revolt was seen by the cinema-going public of the 1960s as a thrilling adventure, an old-world trial of arms in the desert, with awe-inspiring backdrops, withering heat, numbing cold, fiery sheikhs with daggers in their belts, fierce, camel-mounted bedouin toting their ancient rifles, British Staff officers with their polished boots and stiff upper lips, a French Mission with its own covert imperialist agenda; warships, field guns, armoured cars, biplanes, and bombers; and the regular forces of the Imperial Camel Corps, the Desert Mounted Corps, the Australian Light Horse, the Gurkhas, and Indian cavalry and infantry. Woven into it too were comradeship, betrayal, loneliness, despair, triumph, loss and love – and at its heart, attired in flowing white robes like some latter-day prophet, an extraordinary Englishman orchestrating the whole kaleidoscopic cavalcade. Here was the full panoply of a medieval crusade played out on a twentieth-century stage. Lean must have been hugely excited at the prospect of transforming this unique saga of arms and individual heroism into an epic of the silver screen.

What Lean didn't know was that the stirring finale of the Revolt at Damascus hid a very different Lawrence from the public figure of the triumphant conqueror. The film does end with Lawrence looking tired and disenchanted, but the truth was that he was physically and mentally shattered and had lost so much weight that he was down to below eight stone. In the portrait of him by the official war artist, James McBey, painted just after the capture of the city, his face is gaunt and he stares blankly out spent and indifferent, a hint of sadness behind the eyes. He later commented on the picture: 'It is shockingly strange to me.'[36]

I had now researched as thoroughly as I could into these early stages of the Revolt in the hope that what I found would clearly establish whether the favourable claims made for Lawrence in a plethora of biographies really were true. Now convinced that they were, that the legendary Lawrence of Arabia had indeed real foundation in fact, I returned to my original objective – to discover what had made him the extraordinary person he was. This urge kept pulling me back to his youth and beyond, an urge to uncover the heavily disguised private man, a scarcely visible figure standing in the shadow of the celebrated hero. I wanted to wind the reel back to the very beginning. What had made Lawrence so unusual, so different in the eyes of the friends of his youth long before the Arab Revolt transfigured him into legend? Was he quite simply an exceptional person from birth, or had some traumatic experiences been stirred into the childhood mix and affected him for the rest of his life? Wordsworth's adage 'the Child is father of the man' constantly came to mind.

Lawrence was gradually becoming a sort of champion for me: I saw a loner who was misunderstood, sometimes denigrated, but who triumphed despite everything. Some may hear faint biblical echoes in all this, and, having had the regulation Church of England schooling until the age of about seventeen, I felt, if unconsciously, that there were some Christ-like qualities about Lawrence. Jesus, according to Christian theologians, is referred to prophetically in Isaiah as 'despised and rejected of men; a man of sorrows, and acquainted with grief.' I perhaps saw Lawrence, to a much lesser extent of course, as an updated version of such a troubled prophet figure, a sort of Colin Wilson 'Outsider'. By and large materialism held no attraction for Lawrence; neither, it seemed, did status, sex, marriage, or religion. There were demarcations too in his intellectual pursuits. He devoured books by the dozen but in his youth immersed himself totally in all things medieval – history, literature, sculpture, church and military architecture, armour, chivalry and Provençal poetry. After the war he remained a voracious and eclectic reader, reserving a special place for English poetry and poets of the day and becoming friends with contemporary novelists, poets and artists. However, heavyweight, analytic subjects such as politics, economics and philosophy held little interest for him. In his voluminous, post-war correspondence there is scant mention of either society or major political events. You will find no gossip about the social gallivanting of the 'Roaring Twenties', no talk of the mass unemployment and the General Strike of 1926, no comment on the Wall Street crash of 1929 which led to the Great Depression of the 1930s.

In the post-war years Lawrence turned himself into a down-to-earth, busily practical man, a mechanic and a do-it-yourself aficionado both at work and privately: he had experimented with explosives and all sorts of technical improvisations in the desert war; now in his later life he worked creatively on air-sea rescue boats in the RAF, developed modifications for his motorbikes, and made improvements to his little cottage. A very private person and someone often thought to be more interested in things and places than in people, he nevertheless liked – and wanted to be accepted by – the ordinary man, and he had the kindest of hearts. He cared about people, quietly offering a helping hand to friends, even acquaintances, who were suffering financial hardship. He demanded very little for himself, suffered much privately, and, perhaps most significantly, he seemed to speak powerfully to the ascetic, to the solitary hidden inside many people. What increases that appeal is that he could resist material temptations when most of us surrender to them. Such conspicuous self-control, self-denial, even otherworldliness (which he sometimes attributed to a tyrannical will) has offered an intoxicating cup to those in search of a role model and a greater moral purpose that they do not find elsewhere.

The year 1922 was one of several important watersheds in Lawrence's life. After the 1921 Cairo Conference and a four-month mission to the Hejaz and Transjordan as an adviser to the Colonial Office, he returned to civilian life and became preoccupied with the urge to write his account of the Revolt, *Seven Pillars of Wisdom*. He also wanted to shed his 'Lawrence' skin, to become someone else, anyone but Lawrence. In addition, he resolutely turned his back on the conventional and on his middle-class background – a volte-face encapsulated in the almost monastic existence he embraced by enlisting in the ranks of the RAF in 1922. This renunciation of a so-called normal life only increased public interest in 'the Uncrowned King of Arabia'. Yet he undoubtedly did have a strange numinous power of attraction, which was not simply an illusion of the popular imagination or an inevitable accretion to a legendary name. It was always in him and just as evident before the war as after. People from all walks of life were drawn to him, and those who got to know him testified to the profound impression he made on them. And as a young man his golden hair and hypnotic blue eyes only added to the arresting figure he cut.

A.E. 'Jock' Chambers, who met Lawrence in 1922 when they were both aircraftmen at RAF Farnborough and became a close and loyal friend, told John Mack, the Pulitzer-Prize-winning American biographer of Lawrence and Professor of Psychiatry at Harvard Medical School, that Lawrence was 'my only real friend, the only one I've ever had. He was one of the finest men who've ever trod the globe, better than Christ or any of them. He hated injustice.'[37] A similar comparison was made by Lawrence's literary agent, Raymond Savage, who said: 'He was simple and sincere to a degree; he was a generous and magnificent friend, and in his Christ-like character supreme.'[38]

A cursory leaf through that hymn of praise, the eclectic miscellany *T.E. Lawrence by his Friends* (published as a collective tribute in 1937), leaves the reader with more than a whiff of beatification. There is a sense of being in the presence of a sort of secular saint, or, for the cynical, of having read a cleverly orchestrated piece of hagiography intended to sow the seeds of legend in fertile ground. A few examples from this encomium and other reminiscences give some idea of the impact Lawrence made on people. Francis Yeats-Brown had been in the Royal Flying Corps in Mesopotamia in 1915, was captured and later escaped from Turkey. After the war he became literary editor of the *Spectator* and author of *Bengal Lancer*, among other books. He met Lawrence after commissioning some book reviews from him and wrote: 'He possessed a radiant physical awareness … an Irish sense of humour, a cool, clear sparkling wit and had a power of giving happiness such as I have never known another man to possess … His mind, so critical of himself, so charitable to others, had more bright facets than any other I have known. To be with him was to feel that one had bathed in some mountain spring'.[39]

The metaphor of Lawrence somehow expressing the life-giving properties of water, the true elixir of life, was also used by the classicist, polymath and diplomat Sir Ronald Storrs in whose company Lawrence first went down to the Hejaz in 1916 to promote the Arab Revolt, and who was to become Governor of Jerusalem. He said that only twice had he felt 'close to the springs of life' and that one of these moments was 'under the "deep questionings that probe to endless dole" of T.E. Lawrence.'[40] Then there was the assessment of Lieutenant-Colonel W.F. Stirling, who was with Lawrence the night before the entry into Damascus: 'In my considered opinion, Lawrence was the greatest genius whom England has produced in the last two centuries, and I do not believe that there is anyone who has known him who will not agree with me. If ever a genius, a scholar, an artist, and an imp of Shaitan were rolled into one personality, it was Lawrence.'[41]

Architect Sir Herbert Baker (Lawrence wrote much of *Seven Pillars of Wisdom* in the attic above Baker's office in the quiet of Barton Street in Westminster) said: 'To me it was love at first sight; he radiated some magnetic influence, such as long ago I experienced in the presence of Cecil Rhodes. I felt I would have followed him, had I been younger, in any adventurous quest.'[42] The writer Henry Williamson eulogized: 'Never before and never since have I felt so free from myself, so without body: happiness beyond the consciousness of happiness. This man understood a thought before it was uttered.'[43] John Buchan, who had a distinguished career as a novelist, historian and Imperial administrator crowned by a term as Governor-General of Canada, wrote: 'There is no brush fine enough to catch the subtleties of his mind, no aerial viewpoint high enough to bring into one picture the manifold of his character'. He ended his memoir:

I am not a very tractable person or much of a hero-worshipper, but I could have followed Lawrence over the edge of the world. I loved him for himself, and also because there seemed to be reborn in him all the lost friends of my youth. If genius be, in Emerson's phrase, a 'stellar and undiminishable something', whose origin is a mystery and whose essence cannot be defined, then he was the only man of genius I have ever known.[44]

This unstinting praise continued in the many reminiscences that rained down on the reading public after Lawrence's death. That is to be expected. After all, when a man dies, especially a man as famous as Lawrence, those close to him may have a tendency to exaggerate his virtues and underplay his faults. In Lawrence's case, however, there is a difference in degree from the average eulogy amounting almost to a difference in kind. All the tributes to him, whether from ordinary people or major public figures, are effusive, often unconditional, in their admiration, any cited faults or weaknesses amounting to little more than peccadilloes. It has been said before that if Lawrence had been an impostor, he would have been found out long ago. The spotlight trained on him during his lifetime and ever since has been far too glaring not to expose falsehood. You can't pull the wool over the eyes of a huge range of friends and contacts spanning the whole social spectrum and expect to get away with it. Of course, there were puzzling – even occasionally glaring – inconsistencies in his behaviour and his statements, which have led some hostile critics (the most relentless being the biographer Richard Aldington) to conclude that Lawrence was a charlatan and a liar whose writings and recorded utterances should be taken with a large grain of salt or even dismissed as pure invention. Yet we all tell white lies to protect ourselves from unwanted intrusion and Lawrence has nearly always eventually proved to be telling the truth in really important matters. As Ralph Waldo Emerson, the nineteenth-century American writer quoted by John Buchan, put it: 'A foolish consistency is the hobgoblin of little minds.'

The sceptical have tended to distrust the printed panegyrics like those in *Friends* as irredeemably biased. But some of these glowing tributes, despite being now almost commemorative clichés, still strike right to the heart of the matter. Brigadier-General Clayton, who was not a close friend of Lawrence but who, as his Intelligence chief in Cairo, had known him and his value well from the very early days of the war, was a man not easily taken in. He wrote of Lawrence to a young relative: 'He was a truly great man and don't let anybody tell you different.'[45] Another admirer was Colonel Archibald Wavell (A.P. Wavell), later Field Marshal Earl Wavell of Cyrenaica, who had been Chief of Staff of XXth

Corps in Allenby's Palestine and Syria campaigns and had met Lawrence in December 1917 at the official entry into Jerusalem. The two became friends in the post-war years. Wavell wrote:

> He will always have his detractors, those who sneer at the 'Lawrence legend'; who ascribe his successes with the Arabs to gold; who view the man as a charlatan in search of notoriety by seeming to seek obscurity; who regard his descent from colonel to private as evidence of some morbid nostalgie de la boue. They knew not the man. Those who did, even casually and sporadically, like myself, can answer for his greatness. The complexity of his character, the 'mystery' of Lawrence, on which so much has been written, seems to lie mainly in the fact that he transcended the ordinary heights in so many qualities: in courage, in knowledge, in self-discipline, in skill with his hands, in artistry of words, in sympathy with the common working man and with the scholar, in demanding so little from life for his body and so much – too much perhaps – for his mind. But I am not competent to analyse the man: all I can say is that he was cast in heroic but very human mould, and that it was good to know him.[46]

There is one especially revealing insight into the mystical aura that seemed to envelop Lawrence. It takes the form of a spontaneous but thoughtfully worded comment by his youngest brother, Arnold (A.W. Lawrence, or Arnie, as he was known in the family) that came near the end of a penetrating 1986 television documentary. For someone like me – who by accident of birth could never have had the chance, however unlikely, of meeting or knowing Lawrence – to watch and listen to his brother on film provoked, for a fleeting moment, the strange feeling that I was suddenly in Lawrence's presence. A.W. Lawrence was known to have been at times an awkward and difficult man who could be bluntly, even unkindly, dismissive if the urge took him, but here, on film, he radiated a shy, childlike charm which was instantly engaging. He seemed to be wrapped in a kind of quietude. This, and an arresting juxtaposition of firm self-assurance and gentle resignation, compelled attention and reminded me forcefully of the image of his brother I had built up over the years from much reading and from meeting people who had known him. There was the strong family jawline and that endearing diffidence suffused with quiet authority. Arnold's delivery was punctuated by short, telling silences and a disarming smile. His manner and voice had a luminosity about them that was like a glimmering reflection of his brother's magnetic personality. For me Arnold's attempt to provide a real understanding of his brother's appeal was both true and moving. He said: 'He seems to have answered some requirement ... it's almost religious. In fact it is a religion. I had great difficulty in not allowing myself to be used as the St Paul of it. I had, I should think, something like five hundred letters soon after his death, the majority wanting me to take up … his mantle. I suppose it was partly his disdain for worldly success. He had wanted it when he was young. He got it … and despised it'.[47]

Indeed, there is about Lawrence's life a powerful sense of the messianic; but this 'messiah' was in disguise, his message there only for those who could decipher it. Running through his post-war years is a strong leitmotiv of self-sacrifice, of being nailed to a cross of his own making, of atoning not for the sins of the world but for his own failure to live up to the articles of an impossibly elevated idealism, and for what he thought was his arrogant assumption that he could. Most lives, when measured against their original hopes, ambitions and standards, are failures. The realization that someone like Lawrence – by common consent a remarkable person – believed his own life to have been a failure can bring unexpected solace to some. Nine months before his death he wrote: 'One of the sorest things in life is to come to realize that one is just not good enough. Better perhaps than some, than many, almost – but I do not care for relatives, for matching myself against my kind. There is an ideal standard somewhere and only that matters: and I cannot find it. Hence this aimlessness.'[48]

Before I escaped to Ireland to become an undergraduate at Trinity College, Dublin my loneliness as a boy at boarding school had been made tolerable by long bicycle rides far up on the Downs, remote, inviolate and little frequented. There was a still heat and a high, solitary peace there in July, which somehow comforted me, and the wide open skies and lark song, the waving grasses and lone trees, were my loyal companions. Later I thought I had found a kindred spirit in a solitary Lawrence, and made him a part of a kind of romantic mysticism into which I had poured the sense of alienation of my schooldays. Initially he was simply an unconventional hero figure; I knew little of consequence about his life before or after the war, or even much about the war. I love poetry and had read some of the war poets (Siegfried Sassoon, Wilfred Owen and Robert Graves, who was to make a more important impression on me later) and they had given me some shocking insights into that vast tragedy that was the First World War. But Lawrence's true origins and deepest motivations were still unknown quantities to me.

All this was about to change, because what I didn't know was that Lawrence would be where I least expected to find him: in Ireland. My return for a new term at Trinity would be not just to my studies but to the beginning of an extraordinary journey into the past and to the start of a quest that would change my life.

TWO

Irish Initiations

AS FAR AS my academic endeavours in Dublin went, and they didn't go far, I flitted from course to course over five years before ending up in the non-honours faculty of General Studies. I played truant and secretly enrolled instead on the far more engaging if imaginary course of T.E. Lawrence Studies.

Trinity College in those days was a playground of riotous fun-and-games, new friendships, sudden passions, nightly parties, daily pranks, and carefree penniless-ness. It was like most undergraduate worlds, but with one crucial difference – it was Irish and it was in Ireland, and Ireland has always been inviolably different for me. It answered some deep longing and does still.

Now, Lawrence's father had been an Anglo-Irish aristocrat who had deserted his wife and daughters, eloped with their governess, and left Ireland. That much was known, but little else of consequence about him and his Irish background was. I couldn't stop myself feeling that the unknown Irish Lawrence and his lost Anglo-Irish family were beckoning to me to tell their story, to make a fully rounded family portrait out of a picture that had always remained dark and two-dimensional. At Trinity our social cocktail included the sons and daughters of many of the remaining Anglo-Irish families, whose ancestors would have moved in the same exclusive circles as Lawrence's. The Ascendancy, as they were known, were endearingly Irish in both thought and attitude, if not behaviour, their accent

– the hallmark of their class and original social and political allegiance – by now delightfully modulated by gentle Irish resonance and inflection. They had known wealthier days and their Victorian forbears had crossed the Irish Sea for their education at Eton and Oxbridge.

Dublin was the ideal place to understand the long-gone world of Lawrence's lost ancestry; an incredible place where perfect parades of Georgian architecture seemed to march grandly on forever; square after square of decaying history that made you want to stand and applaud. Noisy, scruffy, dirty Dublin, with her pubs and coffee houses and bookshops bulging with people, an infectious devilment in her grubby children and a soft poetry in every street-corner conversation. This busy, vibrant city was the springboard that launched me into my obsessive quest for Lawrence's secret Anglo-Irish heritage.

In the Dublin of my student days Victorian times seemed always just round the corner. There were still a few flamboyantly dressed gentlemen with silver-topped canes and colourful buttonholes strolling the fashionable walks. These last representatives of a dying breed – their exaggerated courtesies mimicking the manners and mannerisms of yesteryear – comingled easily with the indigenous Dubliners with their garrulous irrepressibility. I remember being in St Stephen's Green and looking across at the Kildare Street Club, that bastion of the gentry, Woodward's splendid Venetian palace with its great sash windows and quiet gloom. I was certain that, if I just waited long enough, Lawrence's father would emerge, cane in hand, stand grandly for a moment at the head of the steps surveying the promenading throng below, glance at his fob watch, then walk imperiously away towards Grafton Street.

The past mingled with the present in my Dublin. What differentiated Ireland from England, what does still, is the definite and true, but instinctive and unformulated, philosophy of its people. To them, as to the peoples of the Mediterranean, old age is respected as the embodiment of experience, wisdom and family continuity, and death is as much a fixture in life as a pint of stout or the Cheltenham Gold Cup. The Irish have an uncanny ability to recall past experiences in vivid detail or to daydream themselves into an exciting, imaginary future. You will find echoes of these half-mystic inner worlds in the hidden Lawrence too. He once wrote to his mother: 'One can only live in the future or the past, in Utopia or the Wood Beyond the World.'[1]

In the brave new Europe of today, of course, the Irish on the surface are as materialistic as any, but they still retain a highly tuned sense of the absurdity of life and our tenuous hold on it, and that is a marvellous corrective to some of the more ludicrous secular tyrannies of our society and age. It soon became clear to me that this attitude to life informed Lawrence's personal psychology and behaviour too. As my research into his heritage deepened, I realized just how Irish in nature he was and how, after his life-changing experiences in the war, he began again to question his identity, to try to establish it on an acceptable foundation – acceptable not so much to others, but to himself. By the mid-1920s the public saw him as a romantic, if rather mysterious hero, but he disliked the adulation. It made him question himself. Yes, he had done something extraordinary in Arabia; yes, he had been blessed with great abilities and gifts; yes, he was charming, attractive, brilliant, enigmatic. Yet deep down he seemed always to have doubts about himself, about where he truly belonged, who he really was; and these doubts seemed to grow with the passing years and his increasing lionization, which had created a person more chameleon than man. A myriad Lawrences were walking abroad, mythical doppelgängers over whom he had no control. And there were several actual impersonations too. He wrote to Charlotte Shaw: 'Often I fancy that Colonel Lawrence still goes on, and that it is only me who has stepped out of the way.'[2] The existence of these multiple selves provoked the kind of responses from the public which it does to this day. People either thought of him as a British Imperial hero worthy to sit in the national pantheon beside Drake, Nelson and Wellington, or found his post-war life bizarre and regarded him as a perplexing, slightly suspect oddity. We tend to like our heroes clearly packaged, understandable and not too unconventional. Lawrence's unpredictable lifestyle poses uncomfortable questions about human nature and about our own identities and purpose.

I was by now beginning to feel a little uneasy from the realization that my own lifestyle was revolving more and more around Lawrence. I had an insatiable hunger for more information about him. When one door opened and I had enthusiastically explored the room inside, there was always another door and another room beyond. With all my bits and pieces of research lying scattered round me, I would sit down in the middle of the floor and try to make sense of them, to assemble them into a shape that my intellect as well as my emotions could accept. If it was an obsession, it was an oddly satisfying one. Lawrence seemed to represent for me a triumphant redemption of imagined failure. My own shortcomings made me feel that I could identify with a man who seemed to believe that he had failed on an incomparably grander stage than any in my life could ever be, and had tried to redeem himself by casting off his mantle of heroic man-of-action and transforming his life into a kind of pilgrimage into humility and anonymity – a kind of private salvation. It is arguable that his true greatness lies in his post-war years in the RAF and not in the desert. During his time in the ranks you will find a man who had in his small, spare frame a vast reservoir of concern and love – 'esteem' was the word he preferred – for his fellow man and the ability to dispense this in little, unobtrusive ways which were of real, practical help. It is a commonplace, but worth repeating, that Lawrence was at heart a giver not a taker, a man of almost painful honesty and integrity, but who was nevertheless quite capable of dissembling if it served his ultimate purpose. John Buchan said of him: 'I can imagine him, though the possessor of an austere conscience, crashing through all the minor moralities to win his end.'[3] He was, when he wished to be, an almost irresistible force, a man of immense presence and character; and yet he could turn it off like a tap and go unnoticed, a shadowy, almost drab figure, reserved, enigmatic, shyly observant.

Francis Yeats-Brown wrote: 'On another occasion, when another person was in my flat, T.E. sat very quiet: there was a riddling smile on his lips and a cruel look in his eyes: he was always the soul of courtesy, but he had no small talk, and an immense capacity for silence. Presently he seemed to fade away like the Cheshire cat: he was no longer there: instead of T.E. I saw a small, polite man, inclined to wring his hands, sitting stiffly on the edge of my sofa'.[4] Sir Ronald Storrs, remembering the Lawrence he had known in the Middle East, wrote: 'He had Shelley's trick of noiselessly vanishing and reappearing. We would be sitting reading on my only sofa: I would look up, and Lawrence was not only not in the room, he was not in the house, he was not in Jerusalem. He was in the train on his way to Egypt.'[5]

THREE

A Lost Heritage

BY NOW I was reading everything I could find about Lawrence. I had stumbled first on Aldington's notorious 1955 biography, *Lawrence of Arabia, a Biographical Enquiry*. Aldington (who felt that Lawrence was a dilettante playing around in skirts in the desert pretending to be a sheikh while much worthier young men were dying in their thousands on the Western Front) did about the best demolition job on him anyone has ever attempted. It seemed to be such a powerfully sustained onslaught that it must surely be true. But a nagging doubt still remained. I had always found that childhood heroes had, on deeper investigation, proved to have had feet of clay, to have been very human indeed, some of them taking along as baggage some nasty personal traits too. Lawrence was apparently another such. I didn't want humans when I was very young, I wanted gods. However, I soon discovered that there weren't many of them about – that is, until David Lean's Lawrence, courtesy of Columbia Pictures and the Richmond Odeon, appeared with his motorbike in the summer sunlight of a Dorset farmyard.

Aldington's book, which was so sensational in its day that it went helter-skelter into paperback, has a frontispiece quotation from Oscar Wilde: 'Untruthful! My nephew Algernon? Impossible! He is an Oxonian.' It is an ironic intimation of what's to come. The core of the book concerns Lawrence's origins, which on his father's side were solidly Irish. Lawrence's father was an Irish gentleman called

Thomas Chapman, who had deserted a wife and family, run away to England with his children's governess-nursemaid, changed his name to Lawrence and produced five sons with his new love, the first in Ireland, the other four successively in Wales (T.E. Lawrence), Scotland, the Channel Islands and England. To the public in Aldington's day this was news; to Lawrence admirers, rather shocking news; but to Lawrence's close friends it was nothing to make a big fuss about. They had known the facts for some years. Aldington points to Lawrence's illegitimacy as the source of all his woes and worries and of all his enigmatic behaviour, secrecy and 'lies'. However, time in its remorseless way has exposed Aldington as a knowing corrupter of the truth. After reading the book I felt profoundly let down. I decided, nevertheless, to give it one last shot and went to the apologias of Basil Liddell Hart and Flora Armitage, and these largely restored my faith in Lawrence. I was mollified, but the doubts sown by Aldington lingered. And so began my search for the hidden T.E. Lawrence. It was far from scholarly at the start (and may not conform to orthodox biographical canons even now) but it was certainly a fervent investigation and I was determined to leave no stone unturned. I met many generous individuals with absorbing or primary information on their subject, some of whom had known him and were only too ready to share their cherished memories.

I had found a holy grail in Lawrence's lost family, a family about which neither he (as a young boy) nor anyone else at the time knew anything. Roots and family origins play a significant role in the shaping of a person's life, but what if you don't seem to have any roots and don't know where to start looking for them? Your family background would resemble an iceberg – the tip, the known part, clearly visible above the water, the much greater part, its true shape and foundation, lying hidden below the surface. On the research front, the realization that Aldington's early chapters had dealt laboriously but thinly with Lawrence's Irish family, and that no one else had discovered anything of real consequence on the subject, came as an exciting shock. Now here were Ireland, which I loved, and Lawrence, whom I admired, inextricably bound together; and I had friends who could open doors for me into the heart of what was left of the Anglo-Irish establishment. This was indeed serendipity!

These old Anglo-Irish Protestant families lived in a strange, half-forgotten world. Medieval cartographers often marked those parts of a map on which they had sparse information with the phrase 'Here be dragons'. I was now going into what my imagination had already pencilled in as dragon country, which with luck would yield something to breathe fire into the adventure. An unlikely trio now came together to launch my search for the Irish Lawrence: a married Englishwoman with Scottish blood who ran a hotel in the Irish Midlands; a middle-aged Irish gentleman who exuded that well-intentioned hauteur and gentle aloofness usually associated with the best of the English squirearchy; and an auburn-haired, Anglo-Irish girl. Susie Kindersley – the Englishwoman – was in her late thirties, with a quick wit, a twinkle in her eye and a smile that could light up a room like sudden sunlight. She had come into a legacy through an English family connection and had been able to acquire acreage as well as property in Ireland because of her husband Nick's Fitzgerald antecedents. The Kindersleys ran the rambling Newcastle House near Ballymahon, once the home of the Earls of Rosse, in the depths of rural County Longford. Susie was an uproar on two feet: wherever she was, wherever she went, others followed.

Dark-haired, strong-featured and attractive, she could turn her hand to almost anything and frequently did. A woman with the robust, fearless, no-nonsense approach of the *grandes dames* of the British Empire, she nevertheless had a quite post-Imperial outlook. Sadly, she died suddenly in the early 1990s.

Then there was Johnny Bellingham, a bachelor in his early forties whom I had met in Baghdad, a humorous academic who had become a reluctant 'squire' in County Westmeath. But he was no absentee landlord despite having pieds-à-terre in both London and Paris. Eton- and Oxford-educated, he was a bibliophile, linguist, traveller, amateur archaeologist, spare-time Arabist with a good knowledge and love of the Levant in general and Iraq in particular, a kind and generous host, and master of a draughty Georgian house called Glencara in the heart of the county. Glencara was visited in the 1940s by John Betjeman, a favourite poet of mine who had preceded me at my boarding school and didn't enjoy it much either. He wove Glencara into his poem about the callous Sir John Piers of nearby Tristernagh Abbey: 'Hear how the beech trees roar above Glencara'; and they bent and roared in the wind too when I lived there at Johnny's invitation, trying to write. I hope they still do. Tall, whimsical, charming, generous, fastidious, mannered and well-mannered, Johnny Bellingham had many facets. He was not altogether unlike Lawrence in protecting his private life, deflecting curiosity about it without losing a friendship. A born aristocrat, he had the common touch and was equally at ease with the Arab of the desert or the town, but he didn't suffer fools gladly and tended to judge others by his own class and mores. He opened doors for me to some influential Anglo-Irish contacts and effected introductions that he thought might prove productive, as indeed some of them did.

When he was away in London, Paris or the Middle East, I would sit working in his study just off the upstairs landing at the top of the wide staircase, whose walls were lined with family portraits and mementos of generations of service to the British Empire. From Johnny's large, cluttered desk with its faded leather top I would gaze out over the long grass of the demesne with its two lovely copper beeches like twin sentinels on either side, out across the ha-ha and the meadowland to where racehorses elegantly grazed the far fields below a gently sloping hill – the Hill of Uisneach, which marks the centre of ancient Erin and was the seat of the High Kings before the coming of Christianity. I was at the very heart of Ireland. My hours of Lawrence writing were relieved by the extraordinary Somerville-and-Ross lifestyle of the small Glencara household. During Johnny's frequent absences I would usurp his role of Master of Glencara and, on his behalf, entertain members of the Anglo-Irish gentry, many of them in reduced circumstances yet full of character and quirky humour. Johnny would spring the dinners on me at the last moment and, in turn, I had to spring them on the housekeeper, poor Mrs Urell. She would come briskly out of the big, warm kitchen with its uneven wooden floor, old range and rows of pots and pans, look at me like a startled owl and half-heartedly scold me with: 'Now, tell me, Master Richard, what am I to find for the dinner? There's no meat in the house; there's no beef, no lamb, not a bit of meat in it! Mr Johnny has said nothing to me at all now! I don't know, really I don't; Lord bless us and save us, Master Richard, where will it all end?'

Finally there was Audrey Naper, an undergraduate I had met at Trinity. (An earlier Naper relation had been an aide-de-camp to General Allenby in Palestine, and had met Lawrence.) Audrey had long, silky hair and dark pools of eyes. She was sweet-natured almost to the point of humility, quick to blush but possessed of a clipped and commanding voice. Well educated, witty and socially assured, she had an indefinable attraction, which grew on you slowly but inexorably. The Naper family seat was Loughcrew House in County Meath, a Palladian mansion near Oldcastle and yet one more Anglo-Irish house that had burned down mysteriously, no less than three times! She was to become a loyal and delightful friend and knew everyone worth knowing, from the premier Earl of the Irish Realm down to the humblest Church of Ireland curate helping to minister to a tiny congregation in some remote parish in the fastnesses of Connemara.

These three people opened the door to what remained of the world in which Lawrence would have lived had his father not been such an unlikely romantic and uprooted himself so finally from the old, fading society of County Westmeath. I was far too uncritically enthusiastic about my new status as biographer-in-waiting. I thought that all I had to do was knock on the doors of a few grand Westmeath houses and an owner would say: 'Certainly, come in, all the Lawrence stuff is catalogued and filed in my study.' However, I didn't know any such people, or even where they lived. Nevertheless, I had four key advantages: my all-consuming interest in Lawrence, and Susie, Johnny and Audrey. Within days of being infected with my proselytizing ardour, friends like Audrey were happy to lay their own hobbies aside to join my hunt for the Irish Lawrence. In the main line Lawrence's father's family, the Chapmans, were long gone from Ireland, but some of the families they had known and with whom they had intermarried were still living in Meath and Westmeath. Audrey paved the way: 'Did I know Barbara Casey at Rockview? Had I met the Nugents of Bracklyn, and Ballinlough? Perhaps Major Ogle at Dysart might help. They probably know something.' And so they did.

Audrey used her family clout enthusiastically, recruiting her father, Captain Nigel Naper, to the search, and blowing the cobwebs off the local entries in Burke's *Landed Gentry of Ireland*. It was eventually to pay quite a dividend. On summer afternoons the two of us, instead of sitting down in Trinity Library to write essays, would set off eagerly for the promised land thirty miles west of Dublin. We wandered this secret countryside where tourists seldom went, raising the dust of many a private avenue whose verges, once manicured borders tended by numerous gardeners, were peopled now only by dandelion, cow-parsley and nettle. With the unmetalled avenue crunching and popping under our wheels, we would drive up to what in the old days was always called 'The Big House', behind whose great front door usually lay dim quietude and faded grandeur, and, occasionally, vivid memories and memorabilia of the heyday of the Ascendancy families. Some of these *parvenu* Protestant landlords of Meath and Westmeath who had usurped the lands and livelihoods of the old established gentry in the 1650s after Oliver Cromwell's brutal subjugation of Ireland, did their best to integrate. They tried to respect local traditions, customs and sensibilities and, as a result, eventually developed amicable working relationships with their tenants and with the Catholic population in general. Others, though, made little effort to establish an enduring *modus vivendi*, charged punitive rents and, as an imposed ruling class, were never fully accepted by the native Irish.

Yet some of these Ascendancy families had over the years become 'more Irish than the Irish' themselves and had been gradually, if perhaps grudgingly, accepted by rural Ireland. In fact, the anomaly of their position, their very incongruity, had been yet another rich ingredient in that colourful social mix that was Irish country life in the mid-nineteenth century. It is a world long vanished but perfectly evoked in the stories of Edith Somerville and Violet Martin in *The Experiences of an Irish R.M.* The authors, one from West Cork, the other from Connemara, were Anglo-Irish themselves and knew intimately the world they fictionalized. Their breezy, heart-warming humour was the perfect medium for chronicling that gossip-filled, laughter-led, parochial parade of incident and accident which was the very stuff of their own lives at the turn of the century. I realized later that much of Lawrence's social eccentricity and unpredictable behaviour was very Irish. Had he been brought up in Ireland as one of the gentry, no one would have noticed anything out of the ordinary. Nearly everyone of character in Ireland was, and still is, colourfully individual and very much 'his own man.'

The ambivalence of nature so evident in Lawrence is mirrored in the divided loyalty that Anglo-Irish families like the Chapmans felt from the moment they established themselves by force. They became Irish yet they were also loyal to England. Even their use of English, influenced daily by local usage, had a quality of its own. The native Irishman's marvellously renegade treatment of the language created a vividly arresting vernacular and imagery, which inevitably rubbed off on the Anglo-Irish. Yet there was a tragic pathos about them all, and Lawrence's family were no exception. They were entrenched in their class, almost marooned, prey to an unconscious urge to declare by their behaviour and attitude a kind of exclusive Irishness, which at root was a Protestant Englishness that prolonged geographical isolation had turned into an odd social mutation destined ultimately to fade away. Many Anglo-Irishmen were born with the conviction of their inalienable right to govern; they had great character, were hard-headed, fond of their port and porter, rode full-bloodedly to hounds, and had a roving eye. The Chapmans were a colourful example, with Lawrence's father reputed to have been a conspicuous carouser.

However, their once vast lands had shrunk to little by the 1960s. Many had become withdrawn, stuck in a past others tried to forget, their divided allegiance still pulling them between an England long gone and an Ireland new-minted, an adopted country they made little real effort truly to understand and which many could not bring themselves to embrace unconditionally. Yet they had become in their detached way an integral part of their communities and the locals either had a soft spot for them or accepted them with a kind of reluctant fealty. The Anglo-Irish had, and have, great character, and at the height of their power boasted political acumen and literary skills as well as wealth and influence. The more prominent of these families, today in a social and political no-man's-land, were among the founders of the British Empire. The top brass of Queen Victoria's army were regularly drawn from the ranks of the Anglo-Irish. That tradition, in the upper echelons of the officer class, runs right through to the 1939–45 war and beyond: the Duke of Wellington, the Napiers, Wolseley, Roberts, Kitchener, Montgomery – all British generals, all from Ireland. Lawrence's family background was fittingly warrior caste.

The Catholic Daniel O'Connell, The Liberator, paved the way for Irish independence, but great Ascendancy names also had major roles in the movements for political freedom and the establishment of a sovereign state, and they too nurtured the nationalism that found its ultimate expression in the 1916 Rising. Grattan, Burke, Wolfe Tone, Emmet, Parnell, and the writers and artists: Swift, Goldsmith, Sheridan, Farquhar, AE (George Russell), W.B. and Jack Yeats, Somerville and Ross, Wilde, and Synge, even Douglas Hyde, the Gaelic-speaking first President of Ireland, were all Protestant.

The Anglo-Irish as a social elite and a political force are almost a thing of the past, their great houses dotting the landscape like forlorn memorials to a forgotten tribe. Yet I used to tingle with excitement at the thought of what I might stumble upon behind the portals of those crumbling bastions of privilege. I found the search addictive. The sense of being among the ghosts of a grand past, in the presence of the attractively eccentric doyens of a lost ruling order, the last of their kind, was mesmerizing. I was a time traveller. To walk through Ireland with open eyes and an open mind is to learn the secrets of the past and to know the present for the evanescent thing it is. The ambience of those old Irish houses I visited with Audrey, at a time when everyone else was besotted with the present and clamouring for the future, was irresistible. Most of them were not grand stately piles or great manorial estates, just modest Georgian or mock-Gothic country seats set in shrunken demesnes that their owners struggled to maintain. What had once been small Ascendancy residences, social and political statements in stone, were now little-known yet oddly moving places of rundown charm and rarefied nostalgia, living museums of a forgotten world. I gleaned tantalizing titbits of Lawrenciana and gradually built up a picture of the Chapmans' nineteenth-century world. The many allusions in his voluminous correspondence strongly suggest that Lawrence had made a point of looking into his Irish family history in some depth.

I had by now got to know many of the local people who had Lawrence connections or reminiscences and I certainly had enough information to write a lively if short thesis on the Chapmans. Then, as I completed my university course with a spectacularly poor degree, I was unexpectedly compensated with spectacularly rich Lawrence material. It was probably inevitable that I would eventually stumble across something original, given the time and effort I was devoting to that end in Westmeath and among historical and family records in Dublin. One day Susie Kindersley suggested casually, 'You ought to meet Walter Armytage at Moyvore; he collects all sorts of literary things; his study is chock-a-block with books, all over the floor right up to the ceiling. You can't move for books. I think he said he'd got an album or something on Lawrence's family.' I was in due course invited over to Halston, Walter's neat little Georgian home, its silent interior a model of classical good taste. Somewhere a clock ticked quietly, accentuating the silence. His study *was* extraordinary. There were books of every sort and condition on the shelves including an astonishing section of pre-sixteenth-century works, and many more lying about on tables and chairs cheek by jowl with the miscellanea of a literary life. Sitting almost buried in the middle of this gloriously untidy temple to the written word was Walter.

A model of the retired gentleman-academic, he wore a happily rumpled, ginger-brown tweed suit and a red tie, which jarred wonderfully with everything else. He was charmingly imperious and exuded a casual resignation, as though nothing could surprise him, as though he had wearied of all the world's traps and traumas and finally settled for the least troublesome life: a solitary existence relieved by the company of his wife, his Labrador, books, and publishers' lists.

'Yes,' said Walter, waving his spectacles about, 'the photograph album over there, by the dictionaries; got it by private purchase before the 1955 contents sale at South Hill … you know, Lawrence's father's place in Delvin. Never know, might be something of interest.' I couldn't believe my eyes. It was a typical Victorian family photograph album with a worn, olive-green and scroll-embossed cover. To my knowledge there had never been a published photograph of Lawrence's father, Thomas Chapman. I was afraid that the album would start too late, perhaps in the 1890s, and would include no picture of Thomas. I was, therefore, astonished to find that, if anything, the reverse might be true – that the family sequence would end too early. I opened the album and there in their slots were the expected sepia-toned, self-consciously posed family portraits. I turned the first stiff-boarded page and saw a photograph of Lawrence' great-uncle, Sir Benjamin Chapman, taken in 1861, and next to him one of 1864 of Louisa Chapman (née Vansittart), Lawrence's grandmother. I was delighted but also now worried that the collection might finish before I'd reached Thomas Chapman's generation.

I turned over page after page of Chapmans. No Thomas. Then, on the very last folio, there he was, staring out at me. His expression was striking: haunting, wistful, hinting of melancholy and an elusive reserve. 'Thomas Chapman, 1864'. Aged eighteen and looking very boyish, just like his famous son, he was seated at a desk, his face one of delicate sensitivity with penetrating eyes and a sculpted upper lip, again just like his son's. It was a real find. On the same page were pictures of his brothers and sister, Lawrence's uncles and aunt: William Eden, Francis Vansittart, Caroline Margaret. 'Any good?' ventured Walter, tapping his pipe. 'It has every-thing,' I replied. 'Oh good, there we are then,' he said with a patrician smile evincing little surprise or, for that matter, personal interest. He betrayed no sign of awareness of the significance of the album. It was there because he just had this delightful magpie urge to collect, to have old family and literary curiosities about him. He simply seemed pleased to have been of help and was perfectly agreeable to letting me use the photographs. It was another milestone.

More discovery was to come. Audrey and I went to see Major Nick Ogle at Dysart, a lovely old house and demesne near Delvin, where the Ogles had lived since the days of Cromwell. Overlooking boggy land with a thin surround of trees and a little lough and river close by, Dysart seems in the distance from the road like some great white ship. Mary, the Major's wife, ushered us into a large, bright study with an apse at one end and one wall lined floor to ceiling with books. The room had all the faded attractiveness of the Irish country house at its best: a great open fireplace, big windows flooding the room with light, the beguiling smell of old chair leather, and worn, casually laid Turkish carpets striped with gold by rays of early spring sunshine. There were a few family oil portraits, clutters of memorabilia, a desk chock-a-block with odds and ends, and copies of *The Field* in a rickety pile; and at the heart of it all an occupant of character and quiet charm. For a while Major Ogle talked of Middle-East matters, then he suddenly said: 'Would you like to see a photograph of ... I suppose you'd call her Lawrence's step-mother ... Lady Chapman?' I nodded an eager assent and he added: 'In fact, I think I've got some of Lawrence's half-sisters too.' He rummaged about in a back room and returned smiling with the photographs. There on a summer's day demurely seated in a social grouping in front of Dysart were Lady Chapman and two of Lawrence's half-sisters, Rose and Mabel; there was also a portrait of Eva, the eldest Chapman girl.

The County of Westmeath, hidden away and self-contained on the great central limestone plain of the Irish Midlands, has an indefinable remoteness about it. It also has very good farming land, a fact not lost on Protestant planters like the Chapmans. It keeps itself to itself and gives up its secrets grudgingly. I have always loved it: a landscape of small, proud hills and little hollows and rivers, and loughs of every size and shape strewn across the land like giant raindrops. The sensation, when you reach the core of it, of being forgotten, of being unaccountably and happily lost, is almost tangible. Everywhere there is a strong sense of antiquity. It is no surprise that Uisneach lies in this county. In the larger geographical context Westmeath is in the province of Leinster with its western border the great River Shannon and the historical crossing-point of Athlone, the largest conurbation in the county but too far west to lay claim to the title of county town. That honour is reserved for attractive, bustling Mullingar, the marketing heart of Westmeath. The rest is little, out-of-the-way towns and villages whose way of life has changed little down the years.

In Ireland's rural wilds the country byroads, running through undulating farmland forged by the ice age, are bordered by ash and alder and hawthorn and by watery ditches rich with every shade of green and brown; everywhere is ancient, open bogland with its dark turf trenches and its wild purple orchises and yellow flags and mosses and little white heads of bog-cotton nodding to the wind. Ireland is water, water which is a great fragmented mirror to huge, ever-changing skies, alternately bruise-blue with heavy raincloud or luminously white with great galleons of cumulus sailing grandly eastward. The hallmark of these mystical Westmeath heavens is movement, an endless parade of light and shade. Lawrence's ancestors lived in a land of unspoiled, pastoral perfection that he would have loved. The little up-and-down roads wander like ribbons thrown haphazardly over the terrain. They lead past quiet villages and lone farms and isolated modern bungalows with absurd classical columns or pseudo-Spanish arches, and those once-great houses, glimpsed through trees at the end of potholed avenues.

Across the road from Dysart stands Rockview House, the seat of the Fetherstonhaughs, collateral relations of the Chapmans, and home to Barbara Casey. The last of the Irish line, she had raised an eyebrow or two among the local Protestant community by marrying a Catholic late in life, but he had died suddenly and she had become 'old Mrs Casey up at Rockview'. Like many of the Anglo-Irish she was a person of great if eccentric character. Born Barbara Rosetta Frances Fetherstonhaugh in 1898, she was the only daughter of Colonel John David Fetherstonhaugh, who had inherited Rockview while his elder brother, Major-General Richard Steele Rupert Fetherstonhaugh, had lived at Killulagh and Milltown in Westmeath before settling in England. Barbara's father had been a typical Anglo-Irishman, his military career with the Argyll and Sutherland Highlanders devoted to the service of Britain in the far-flung outposts of Empire, where he saw action on the North-West Frontier.

Barbara now lived a life of solitary gentility at Rockview, surrounded by the dusty artefacts of a grander life and another age. In the early nineteenth century her great-grandfather, Richard Steele Fetherstonhaugh, of Rockview House, Killucan, second son of James Fetherston of Bracklyn, had had five children, three of them sons. In 1855 the youngest of these sons, Rupert Pennefather, had married Louisa Mary Frampton, daughter of Henry Frampton of Moreton, Dorset, and had assumed the arms of Frampton and the name of Fetherstonhaugh-Frampton. In 1849 Rupert's eldest sister, Maria, had married Lawrence's great-uncle, Sir Benjamin James Chapman, fourth baronet, of Killua Castle. It was this distant family link that facilitated Lawrence's purchase of his Dorset cottage, Clouds Hill, from the family at Moreton.

Barbara was in her late sixties, short, grey-haired, endearingly dumpy and – typical of the gentry – quite indifferent to her appearance, dressed in a much used, old cardigan and a maroon skirt. She had bird-sharp eyes that didn't miss a crumb and a quick, shy smile, which would disconcertingly appear a good five seconds after the comment that had provoked it. There was a hint of vintage Bette Davis about her. She was quietly spoken with a wonderfully dry sense of humour, her pithy conversation delivered in a deep gravelly rasp, the result of years of chain-smoking. Rockview (a bit of Georgian, a bit of everything) was falling down. Valuable family china was dispersed all round the house on the floors, priceless bowls casually placed to catch the rain dripping in through the great leaking roof. Barbara didn't seem to mind. 'Well, I mean, you know, what can one do these days, it's only a bit of water,' she would chuckle, almost to herself, coughing and lighting another cigarette.

On the landing, staring down the wide Spartan staircase and badly in need of a clean, was a large, lugubrious oil painting of a Victorian gentleman. He was posed à la mode, seated with one hand resting on a table, fashionably bearded and gazing vacantly forth. This was Lawrence's grandfather, William Chapman. 'Yes, he's been up there for as long as I can remember. Doesn't look up to much, does he?' chuckled Barbara, tapping her cigarette ash onto the threadbare hall carpet, 'Can't see him on a camel! Would you like some tea?' And she was off without waiting for a reply. Audrey and I sat perched on the edge of an ancient, well-worn sofa as the high drawing-room windows drew in the soft, glowing light of the summer evening, investing the room with that deep stillness peculiar to old Irish country houses. Barbara, with a little coaxing, regaled us from cigarette to cigarette, the blue smoke rising lazily up across one constantly half-closed eye, with tales of Rockview and South Hill and Killua Castle, the main Chapman seat four miles away at Clonmellon. She told of her great-cousin, Lawrence's odd, lanky, bibulous uncle, Francis Chapman, and of Lawrence's imposing aunt Lina, and of the slow disintegration and disappearance from Westmeath of this increasingly eccentric family. I drank it all in as she recreated a society that had been doomed to extinction. I half expected Francis Chapman to walk into the room at any moment and pour himself a whiskey.

FOUR

A Territorial Root in the Proper Place

THE VISITS to Halston, Dysart and Rockview were the first of many to the big houses of Westmeath and Meath, and the story of the Chapmans in their nine-teenth-century heyday began to unfold – a rich, colourful history of a now largely forgotten but once prominent Anglo-Irish dynasty: T.E. Lawrence's lost family.

> 16.iii.27. If money ever offers me itself in an attractive shape, I shall take some of it, and buy myself some yards of County Meath (why Meath of all places, you'll say? Well, for historical reasons, to keep some of Walter Raleigh's gift in the family of which I have the honour to be not the least active member!) and squat on it for a while. Not for ever, that being contrary to instinct: but it will warm my diaphragm, to feel that I've got a territorial root in the proper place. At present I feel as though my exile was not voluntary: whereas when I have that square yard, it will be deliberate. Also I want it for its own sake. I like England so much as I do because I am not English: whenever the point crops up succinctly I know that I am Irish. Odd, isn't it? Sentimental, I suppose. Let's be sentimental then.[1]

This is an excerpt from a letter Lawrence wrote to Charlotte Shaw, a letter from one Irish expatriate to another, from an emotional orphan to a surrogate mother. It is certainly more than the confession of a closet patriot, or a genealogical carrot dangled in front of the noses of future biographers. Lawrence's identification with

Ireland had deep roots. There are too many incidences in correspondence and memoirs of his proudly asserting his Irishness (they increase as he grew older) for such an association not to be both true and heartfelt. What initially encouraged a degree of intimacy between Lawrence and Charlotte was undoubtedly their common Anglo-Irish heritage. To be able to discuss his Irishness freely with such a kindred spirit would have strengthened his fragile sense of identity and allowed him to allude to his grand, aristocratic pedigree that the need for family security and social taboo prevented him from declaring openly. The problem of his identity certainly troubled him. He had created Lawrence of Arabia and was condemned to live with the unrelenting hero-worship this alter ego attracted. As Bernard Shaw wrote to him in a critical but avuncular way: 'You masqueraded as Lawrence and didn't keep quiet; and now Lawrence you will be to the end of your days.'[2]

Side by side with his fascination with his fame went an abiding need to hide his inner self. He would never allow anyone close enough to get more than a glimpse of it. The mask only rarely slips. In fact, he claimed that even he did not understand himself much of the time. For Lawrence the price of this psychic imperative, which demanded enigmatic behaviour and the laying of false trails, was ultimately to be a tragic loneliness. This compulsion to both hide and advertise himself was evident well before the war years. In the 1986 TV documentary, Canon Edgar Hall (a close boyhood friend of Lawrence's usually referred to as Canon E.F. Hall, or by his nickname of Midge) accurately discerned this odd dichotomy in Lawrence's character. Speaking in short, considered phrases as though thinking aloud, he said of the schoolboy Lawrence: 'There was a sort of dual personality … there was … the boy …and there was also … I think he called it a mask. That's rather crude … but it is … the boy in the mask. We all liked him … but he began to be quite different.'[3]

It would be a triumph of understatement to say that Lawrence has never been understood. He is like a blank sheet of paper onto which people would confidently inscribe 'this is the real Lawrence' only to find such 'insights' had merely been mirror reflections of their own prejudices and presumptions. He once wrote of such confidently possessive pronouncements: 'Lots of people go about saying that they alone understand me. They do not see how little they see, each of them separately. My name is Legion!'[4] Yet, just occasionally, a judgement on him carries the mark of a curiously penetrating insight. One such came from an old mystic schoolmaster called Bowhay, who had taught Eric Kennington, the sculptor and

Seven Pillars of Wisdom illustrator who was to become a close friend of Lawrence. Kennington had shown Bowhay one or two chapters of *Seven Pillars* and the teacher had commented:

> Reading this book has made me suffer. The writer is infinitely the greatest man I have known, but he is terribly wrong. He is not himself. He has found an I, but it is not his true I, so I tremble to think of what may happen. He is never alive in what he does. There is no exchange. He is only a pipe through which life flows. He seems to have been a very good pipe, but to live truly, one must be more than that. He has told you his colour is black. It would be so, for all colours melt into black.[5]

Public fascination with a Lawrence of Arabia manufactured to appeal to everyman had initially intrigued, even amused Lawrence, but as the years passed he came more and more to resent his celebrity self. The American journalist Lowell Thomas, who had briefly visited Lawrence in Aqaba in 1918, had loosed this created figure onto the world in 1919 with his lavish Illustrated Travelogue *With Allenby in Palestine* (to which *and Lawrence in Arabia* was soon added). It was first shown at the Royal Opera House in Covent Garden but popular demand saw its run extended at the Royal Albert Hall, the Philharmonic Hall and finally the Queen's Hall. Thomas's show had been virtually guaranteed success. 750,000 soldiers from Britain died in the Great War, mostly in France, one in eight of all those who went out carefree and confident to fight for King and country in a war they expected would be over and won by Christmas 1914. But for four years the public had been bludgeoned by disasters and starved of good news. Now, in stark contrast to the horrors of the Western Front, here was this dramatized presentation of a medieval conflict in the desert, an Arabian romance, hot, sunlit and exciting. No waterlogged, mud-filled trenches here; no days of endless rain; no scything down of a nation's youth. Seen by more than a million people, including royalty and leading establishment figures, Thomas's picture-show launched the 'Lawrence of Arabia' legend into what seems to be permanent orbit. A resigned Lawrence wrote to a friend in 1920 that the American promoter had turned him into 'a kind of matinee idol'.[6] Yet he had tiptoed into Thomas's show more than once to stand incognito at the back, intrigued, flattered and horrified, as he witnessed his apotheosis taking place in front of him. He later went out of his way to help the impresario with his *Boys-Own*-hero biography of Lawrence, the first of an endless succession.

Initially Lawrence seemed to consider all the attention good fun, a game of hide-and-seek. To say that on occasion he told the world to count to a hundred while he ran off like an excited child and hid in a cupboard is not far from the truth. He wanted them to find him and he didn't want them to find him, or, as Lowell Thomas aptly commented, quoting an old Turkish adage, 'He had a genius for backing into the limelight.'[7]

However, by 1925 he was writing to Charlotte Shaw that this larger-than-life Lawrence, hero-worshipped by the public and courted by the great and the good, was not someone he recognized, or wanted to recognize, any more. He said: '… The Lawrence who used to go about and be friendly and familiar with that sort of people is dead. He's worse than dead. He is a stranger I once knew.'[8] The novelty had worn off. He was tired of the public's obsession with him. But the adulation persisted. Four years after his 1925 comment to Charlotte Shaw he was writing to Jock Chambers: 'Jock, I'm very weary of being stared at and discussed and praised. What can one do to be forgotten? After I'm dead they'll rattle my bones about, in their curiosity'.[9] Bernard Shaw's prophecy was proving true.

There would have been one particular concern lurking behind his wish for anonymity: namely the fear that his increasing fame might lead to the exposure of his real family history and cause his mother deep distress and embarrassment. There was too the press attention that would inevitably descend on Lady Chapman and her daughters in Ireland, were the facts to become publicly known. These reasons for Lawrence's suppression of the truth were made clear in a letter he wrote in 1927 to his solicitor Edward Eliot about changing his name to Thomas Edward Shaw: 'Perhaps, though, you won't require parents' names, for my deed-poll. Better not, if possible, for I don't want anyone to know about it, while my mother and step-mother are both alive.'[10] He put it another way, and with a hint of sadness, when writing that same year to a Royal Tank Corps friend, Regimental Sergeant-Major Harry Banbury: 'Original family began with "C", but is not to be used, because the authentic family does not approve of me.'[11]

In 1927 Lawrence was stationed with the RAF in India. *Revolt in the Desert*, his popular and acclaimed abridgement of *Seven Pillars of Wisdom*, would be published in 1927. Also poised for publication this same year would be the first serious biography of him, by Robert Graves. Lawrence would have wanted to avoid the surge of renewed interest in him, which would inevitably have followed the books' release, and so a posting abroad, for which he volunteered, proved welcome. 1927 was to be an important year for his revaluation of his life. Certainly for his sense of identity and family origin it seemed to be a key period. In his letters he now spoke more often about his Anglo-Irish family background and of his desire to visit the home of his forefathers and perhaps to buy land or property on or near the family estate. To Charlotte Shaw he was particularly expansive on the subject. It seems clear that his enforced inability to establish a real self, to claim and declare his true heritage, caused Lawrence more than a little anguish. Ireland's history is complex and bound symbiotically to England's, and there has always been a shifting ambivalence in each country's attempts to understand the other. This, in turn, is a metaphor for an abiding, if hidden, ambiguity in Lawrence's life too: the need to maintain his false identity and a recurring urge to reclaim his genuine one. In his own mind he was publicly an English somebody but privately an Irish nobody. At a post-war party in London he told the Anglo-Irish poet W.B. Yeats, with melodramatic pauses between each phrase: 'I was an Irish nobody … I did something … it was a failure … and I became an Irish nobody again.'[12]

The more you collate and compare Lawrence's allusions to his antecedents – their importance to him often masked by a kind of throwaway, self-deprecating humour – the clearer it becomes that the problem of trying to establish his true identity puzzled and disturbed him. It was in part to discover this identity that he became such a prolific letter-writer and was after the war so ready to be portrayed in print, paint and clay. The Greek adage 'know thyself' was one he liked, but for him it posed the additional, troubling question of who he really was – a disinherited aristocrat or an illegitimate upstart. Fate had combined in his ancestry the very top and the very bottom of the social order. At the top was his father, an Irish baronet, at the bottom his mother, the illegitimate daughter of an alcoholic housemaid. However, there is no need to turn any search for Lawrence's paternal antecedents into a melodramatic whodunnit full of damning brushstrokes of condemnation in the manner of an Aldington, because Aldington's revelations, if they came as a shock to the public, were nothing new to those close to Lawrence. They had known the truth long before the appearance of Aldington's merciless tract of denigration. A group of Lawrence's friends, later dubbed the Lawrence Bureau, had closed ranks and rushed to defend his name as soon as the damaging biography hit the stands. The main planks of Aldington's arguments have since proved to be unsafe, if not rotten. His biggest plank was that the shock discovery of his illegitimacy and his parents' masquerade turned Lawrence into a pathological liar and a consummate self-promoter who virtually invented his own legend. In his book Aldington discourses briefly on the meaning and mechanics of ancestry and its contribution to the formation of character, which, he says, is considerable. He then devotes his next seven pages to a rather laborious search for the truth about Lawrence's parents, in which, he claims, lies the clue to what he calls Lawrence's abortive career and tortuous character.

Some clue to Lawrence's lack of identity, his disdain for convention and his self-abasement certainly lies in his attitude to his parents and their origins. Their family histories provide a foundation for a sympathetic understanding of his behaviour – that constant oscillation between the persisting need to be considered someone in the social order and the lurking feeling that he was in fact an illegitimate nobody. The facts of Lawrence's background first appeared in a brief mention in a French biography by Léon Boussard, published in 1946. Boussard was helped in his researches by Arnold Lawrence. Called aptly enough *Le Secret du Colonel Lawrence*, the fact that it was not published in English meant that it was little known in the English-speaking world. The details were again mentioned by Thomas Jones in his *Diary with Letters* in 1954, so the extravagant claims made by his publishers for Aldington's book were not altogether true and were presented in relentlessly sensational form.

The 'secret' was of course that Lawrence's father was not Thomas Lawrence, as he appears on his second son's birth certificate, but Thomas Robert Tighe Chapman, seventh and last Baronet Chapman of (if not owner of) Killua Castle in Ireland. Chapman had courted his children's nursemaid, Sarah 'Junner', left Ireland, his wife and their four daughters behind him and changed his name to Lawrence to live with his new love. And love it was for they lived together devotedly for about thirty-two years until Chapman's death in 1919. Sarah was to bear him eight sons, two still-born, one who lived for only a few hours, and five who grew up to become the middle-class, churchgoing Lawrence family of Oxford suburbia.[13]

These 'Lawrences' were as different as chalk and cheese from their true forbears, the aristocratic Chapmans of Westmeath. *Burke's Peerage and Baronetage* for 1917 and 1921 sketch out a pedigree. Far back in the Middle Ages the Chapmans were said to have been merchants, Members of Parliament, and soldiers, with land in Hinckley in Leicestershire in England. The first Irish ancestors of the Westmeath Chapmans were almost certainly brothers John and William Chapman. They benefited from the political clout of Sir Walter Raleigh, whom they claimed as a maternal cousin and whose influence enabled them to buy land in County Kerry in the reign of Elizabeth. So it was more than two hundred years after these first Hinckley Chapmans that the Irish branch arrived in Ireland's far south-west. However, they may have been totally unconnected to the Leicestershire Chapmans and only distantly related to Raleigh by way of a tenuous family link with a cadet branch of the Champernowne family of Modbury in south Devon. In 1580 Spain's Philip II and the Pope despatched seven hundred Spaniards and Italians to Ireland to support Irish insurgents in the Desmond rebellion against English rule. This force landed in Smerwick Harbour on the Dingle peninsula in Ireland's wild and remote far west and occupied and reinforced the fort there. But the English, with Raleigh among their leaders, were much better prepared than the insurgents. They besieged the rebels in the fort, compelled them to surrender and massacred the garrison. It was precisely in this part of the Dingle peninsula that Lawrence's Chapman ancestors were to be made their first abortive grant of lands in Ireland. Lawrence downplayed the role of his swashbuckling forbear in the Smerwick slaughter when he wrote to the literary critic Edward Garnett in 1927: 'The Smerwick massacre was more Grey than Raleigh. R. was picturesque, and a braggart. People ascribed to him more action and less sensibility than the truth. Did you ever read his poem?'[14] Lawrence's father apparently bore a close resemblance to his claimed distant forbear. Lawrence had written to Garnett in 1924: 'Raleigh isn't an ancestor, only the son of one. My father, middle-aged, was his walking image. I'm not like that side of the family though.'[15]

The total land involved in the Elizabethan plantation of the province of Munster, which was to give the Chapmans their foothold in Ireland, amounted to a huge 574,645 acres, and the new recipients, known as 'undertakers', had to be English. The Crown set about planting the province by despatching several Royal Commissions to visit and obtain an exact estimate of forfeited lands. These surveyors had a rough time of it. After a couple of false starts the Queen's men set about their thorny task, working their way westwards towards Kerry and remote areas like the Dingle peninsula, and they were met everywhere with the passive, sullen opposition of 'the Irishry', as they called the native Catholic people. But they were often up against bad weather and at times almost impass-able terrain. Some caught fever while one of their number, Sir Valentine Browne, was always falling into bogs and having to be pulled out. Twice he narrowly escaped drowning, his son broke an arm, and several horses were lost.[16]

T.E. Lawrence's first Anglo-Irish ancestor was William Chapman, but in Elizabethan times, when name-spelling was treated far more cavalierly than it is today, his name was recorded variously as Chapman, Champion, Champen, or

Champernowne. His elder brother, John, and a George Stone were granted the Seignory of Ballymacdonnell, an estate of 1434 acres situated about Dingle and Smerwick that boasted two castles and much other property and land. However, after six months they are on record as selling their new estates to the Earl of Cork for the very large and rather doubtful sum of £26,000. In a letter of 1589 to Lord Burghley, Sir William Herbert, one of the Queen's Commissioners, dismissed 'Mr Stone the Queen's footman and one Champion a man of Sir Walter Ralegh's the one of them worth little, the other worth nothing, neither of them even able to perform what they have undertaken nor the hundreth part thereof.'[17] This derisive comment suggests that Champion must have been relatively low down in the pecking order of Raleigh's retinue and, if a kinsman, not an especially close one, and that he and Stone had been unable to carry out their 'undertaking', because, quite simply, they hadn't enough money. This first association of two Anglo-Irish families, the Earls of Cork (the Boyles) and the Chapmans, was to be renewed three hundred years later in Lawrence's collaboration with Captain 'Ginger' Boyle in the Red Sea naval operations, which marked the early stages of the Arab Revolt.

Today there are branches of this Chapman family living in the USA whose ancestors emigrated from Ireland to Barbados in the mid-seventeenth century and established themselves as sugar planters. They are quite clear about their family origins. Their tree begins with a Rychard Chapman of Husbands Bosworth in Leicestershire, born about 1538. His wife is unknown but it is possible that the connection with the Devon Raleighs stems from this generation. Rychard had four sons: John, William, Thomas and Richard. There was certainly a William Chapman baptized in 1566 in Lutterworth, which is ten miles from Hinckley. This John and William, so the American version goes, became the founders of Lawrence's Irish Chapman family.

To recapitulate, these first Chapman ancestors are said to have had well-connected west-country cousins who were related by marriage to the high-born landed Raleighs of Hayes Barton in East Budleigh in Devon. In the late 1540s Walter, head of this family, married as his third wife Katherine Gilbert, widow of Otto Gilbert but, more significantly, daughter of Sir Philip Champernowne of Modbury. This union produced two sons, the second of whom, born around 1552, was to become the famous Elizabethan, Sir Walter Raleigh. Lawrence had written to Edward Garnett: 'Raleigh isn't an ancestor, only the son of one.' So, if Lawrence is right, the link between Sir Walter Raleigh and the Westmeath

Chapmans' purported Leicestershire roots was through the Modbury Katherine Champernowne. However, although it is possible to establish Champernowne connections between Devon and Leicestershire, the crucial tie between the Irish and Hinckley Chapmans, the Devon Raleighs, and the Champernownes has not been firmly established. There is, nevertheless, one tenuous link. In 1797 a Westmeath Chapman, Maria, had married a Captain Thomas Browne … who came from Hinckley.

That said, Lawrence, with his fascination with all aspects of the medieval, must have been quietly proud to discover family ties with Raleigh, the Elizabethan plantation of Kerry, and the Champernownes – a name which may derive from de Champernon, a corruption of the place name Cambernon in Normandy. The possibility of his being able to claim Norman descent would no doubt have equally delighted him. Katherine Gilbert/Champernowne's mother, also called Katherine, was the daughter of another powerful Devon family, the Carews. Her connections reached right up to the throne. At court she was one of the gentle-women appointed in 1536 to attend the infant Princess Elizabeth. Her sister Joan married Sir Anthony Denny, and a branch of the Denny family were granted land in Kerry in and around the town of Tralee during that same Elizabethan planta-tion in which the Chapmans gained their first landed foothold in Ireland. The Dennys became a prominent and powerful Kerry family, so it seems likely that Lawrence's distant forbears would eventually have established influential connec-tions in Ireland.

After the death of the first Kerry Chapmans, John and William, the Irish side of Lawrence's family might well have faded into obscurity but for the opportunism and vision of William's son, Benjamin. His adventurous spirit and prescience assured its ultimate establishment as a powerful landowning family in the front rank of the Ascendancy's social and political orders. In a way, the Irish beginnings of Lawrence's family in Kerry are a sideshow. The true founda-tion of his Chapman ancestors in Ireland was undoubtedly in Westmeath. It was only with the granting of confiscated estates by Cromwell after 1642 that the Chapmans were able to seize their chance and put down firm roots in the Irish Midlands. Yet, they certainly did have Kerry connections. Richard Kiely, a Killua worker in the 1920s who lived in a small estate house near the Chapmans' grand castle, told me that his home, Glena, had been so called at the suggestion of an earlier Lady Chapman after a family residence of the same name near Killarney in Kerry, where, he said, the Chapmans often took summer holidays.

FIVE

A Huge Grant of County Meath

IN THE 1640s Ireland was in ferment. Established Catholic landowners were once more ranged against planter Protestants like the Chapmans, the old order facing the impending new. In 1641, driven to action by injustice and the constant failure to redress their grievances, the old Irish of the provinces of Ulster and Leinster, and the old English lords of the Pale, rebelled. Eleven years of civil strife followed. These were, of course, also unprecedented times in England with the seismic upheavals of the Civil War culminating in the execution of King Charles I in 1649. Cromwell, having subdued both the Scots and the Welsh, ruled unopposed everywhere but in Ireland. He now set about imposing his will there too, arriving in Dublin in 1649 at the head of an army of 17,000 men. Meanwhile, the ruthless but able military strategist, Murrough 'the Burner' O'Brien, Earl of Inchiquin and Parliamentarian Lord President of Munster, had become a campaigning Protestant of the coming order. He swept through the province crushing the forces of the old Irish. The politically astute Benjamin Chapman had, perhaps predictably, become a cornet-of-horse in a cavalry regiment raised by Inchiquin. It was a shrewd move and was to prove the foundation stone of the Chapman dynasty.

The Adventurers Act of 1642 had declared forfeit the estates of leading Catholic insurgents and offered them to subscribers – the 'adventurers' of the Act (opportunists might have been a more apt title). Of Ireland's total land, half of it (11,000,000 acres) was confiscated and signed over to Protestants and to those who had served Cromwell in his repressive campaigns. The Catholic landowners were reduced to a minority and a totally new Protestant landlord class was firmly imposed on Ireland. History knows them as the Anglo-Irish Ascendancy and Lawrence's ancestors were to rise to their front rank.

After the Restoration, Charles II tried, rather half-heartedly, to redress the wrongs inflicted on the old Irish landed classes, and a third of the estates held by Cromwellians in 1659 were returned to their original Catholic owners. But the *parvenu* Anglo-Irish landlords of Westmeath need not have worried. When the county's ousted Catholic landowners returned from their banishment in the province of Connaught and the far west, hoping to be reinstated in their lands, they found to their dismay that the grants of their former estates to the usurping Protestants – among them the Chapmans – had already been legally ratified. The die had finally been cast. Out of this military and political maelstrom Lawrence's Chapman forbears emerged not only intact but with their name and fortunes considerably enhanced, thanks to Benjamin Chapman. His reward for serving Cromwell's cause was handsome indeed. After Cromwell's conquest of the country, land and estates were handed out like medals. Sometimes they were granted to serving soldiers in lieu of pay, sometimes they were even allocated by lottery. Great Anglo-Norman families were summarily dispossessed, their great estates made over to acquisitive English Protestants eager to assume the mantle of landed Irish gentleman. Recipients of forfeited estates in Westmeath included the Pakenhams (subsequently Earls of Longford) and of course, Captain Benjamin Chapman. The scion of a Protestant family already settled in Ireland, he received a great swathe of land known as Killua, which had been confiscated from Richard Nugent, Earl of Westmeath.

Benjamin Chapman, Lawrence's first real Irish ancestor, now found himself the recipient of the largest grant made in the Parish of Killua, and the Chapman family were henceforward to have a major role in the administration of Westmeath and Meath. The Killua estate was to remain in the family for 250 years, until the death in 1919 of the last Chapman incumbent, Lawrence's aunt, Lady Caroline Chapman. The trail of Lawrence's ancestors across the first forty years of the seventeenth century, which links the family's modest Kerry beginnings to their new estates and status in Westmeath, is hard to follow. The country had been in turmoil and Benjamin Chapman must have been constantly on the move with

Cromwell's forces. This Chapman patriarch's first wife was, of course, Protestant and they had three sons and a daughter. However, Benjamin had married twice, his first wife having presumably died young. The offspring of the second union were to move to Mullaghmeehan in Westmeath and thence westward to County Longford, where Chapman descendants are still living today.

Benjamin's heir, his son William by his first wife, married Ismay Nugent of Clonlost in the local parish of Rathconnell, an estate situated eight miles south-east of Killua. She was a sister of Thomas Nugent, of the Earls of Westmeath branch. The following two generations saw two Benjamins and then a Thomas as Killua heirs. The Chapmans rose to become barristers, Sheriffs, Lord Lieutenants of the county, and Members of Parliament. They also gained titles.

Brothers and heirs, Benjamin, the eldest, and Thomas (the former created baronet in 1782, the latter knighted in 1780), were the fourth generation of Killua Chapmans. They had a younger brother, William, whose descendants subsequently moved to the town of Trim in County Meath and thence to Wicklow, where they broke with genteel tradition to become newspaper proprietors, owning *The Freeman's Journal* – an interesting story in itself. This William's branch of the family moved yet again, this time west to Athlone, and in the late nineteenth century took over the *Westmeath Independent* newspaper, which they owned right up to 1970. It is said that in the time of the notorious Black and Tans (a brutal militia raised by the British to suppress Irish insurrection, which had begun in 1916) the offices of the *Independent* were burned (despite the owner being a Protestant) as punishment for its strong Republican stance. After Ireland achieved independence the first Irish government honoured the Chapman proprietor for his support of Irish nationalism. To find that there had been a nationalist adulteration of the conservative blue veins of the Protestant Chapmans would have brought a wry smile to Lawrence's face. The dissident in him lay always just below the surface.

The titles bestowed on Benjamin and Thomas, deserved though they may have been, were just as likely to have been rewards for political allegiance. In 1782 the Duke of Portland, the new Whig viceroy and Lord Lieutenant, had arrived in Dublin as Henry Grattan's party secured Irish parliamentary independence from England. There would have been busy lobbyings and alignments in yet another turbulent time in Irish politics. Clearly the eldest Chapman had ensured that his political influence was actively wielded in the service of the powerful cabal that surrounded the viceroy, because, despite the substantial euphoria at Ireland's new-found parliamentary autonomy, much of the power in government still lay in his hands and in those of his small junta, who saw as their primary duty the imperative of keeping Ireland firmly in the British interest. Sovereign parliaments could be dangerous things, so the Lord Lieutenant was now exercising a fulsome if calculated patronage, bestowing preferment, pensions, and titles as thinly disguised bribes to ensure ultimate political control.

Lawrence knew that his ancestor's title might well have been conferred as a political reward or inducement and commented in the 1927 letter to his solicitor: 'My father's death wound up the baronetcy (a union title, of all the rubbish!) and one of my brothers is breeding heirs. So the family looks like continuing, in the illegitimate branch!'[1] His disparaging comment was somewhat off the mark: the Chapman baronetage was not an union title but was conferred nineteen years earlier for unnamed services.

On a lighter note, Sir Benjamin Chapman, the first baronet, seems to have exemplified splendidly the colourful eccentricities of the Anglo-Irish of the day. He used to give what he called 'Trumpet Dinners' and kept a bizarre land steward named John 'Jacky' Dalton. Dalton, a small man, had a crooked 'weasel eye' and 'a squint in his mouth,' which together produced the impression that his face was fixed in a disconcerting leer; and one of his legs was shorter than the other, which gave him a gait somewhere between a run and a hop. He wore a yellow wig and a hat pushed far back on his head. When the baronet was not dining to the sound of trumpets, Jacky Dalton used to sit at the foot of his table and play the bagpipes. The baronet was fond of music and Jacky Dalton played rather well. He also deceived rather well, defrauding the baronet out of a lot of money from cattle by substituting his own poor stock for Sir Benjamin's on the way to market in Dublin and keeping the animals belonging to the Master of Killua for himself. In the end he came, as they say, to no good and drowned. His ghost was said to have haunted the castle thereafter. Ireland is full of ghosts, and curses, especially associated with the Ascendancy. There are stories from all over the country of the local Catholic priest cursing the Big House and its family. The most common such imprecation was 'the crows will fly through it' and, in many instances, this ominous prediction did come true. The crows flew through the ruins of Killua Castle for at least forty years after the departure of its last occupant.

The first baronet dying without issue, the title and estates passed to the knighted Thomas. All the while the family married largely into their own – the Protestant Ascendancy and the English establishment – and Thomas was not one to break the mould of class convention. Whether he broke the mould of class morality is another question: At the age of fifty-two he married a woman thirty-two years his junior – the twenty-year-old Margaret Anne Fetherstonhaugh, daughter of James Fetherstonhaugh of Bracklyn Castle. They married in 1808 and in that same year she gave birth to a son – which may have raised an eyebrow or two in Westmeath society! Sir Thomas's mastership of Killua probably marked the height of the family's public distinction and of its fortune too. He began the grand gentrification of Killua, adding the castellations that completed its final form.

Family contribution to the government of the county and the country and to the affairs of an exclusive but not yet moribund society continued unabated for two more generations. However, by the time Lawrence's father left Ireland in the 1880s, the Ascendancy was no longer the dominant political force in Irish life. As the dialogue with England decreased after the Union of Great Britain and Ireland in 1801, so the isolation of the Anglo-Irish increased, and families like the Chapmans, overtaken by political developments, gradually withdrew into themselves and into a world of country pursuits and genteel socializing. Their pre-eminent role in Irish society was becoming redundant, passing inexorably into the shadowland of history.

The next two generations of the family, which preceded that of Lawrence's father, were nevertheless still active in the administrative sphere. However, the second baronet's successor, his eldest son, the bachelor Sir Montague Lowther Chapman, was lost at sea in 1853 at the age of forty-five, shipwrecked off the coast of Australia. He had gone there to purchase a large estate in Adelaide with the purpose of settling on it as many of his Irish tenants as were prepared to emigrate, and, after the terrible depradations of the great Irish famine of 1845-50, many did. To this day the Chapman name survives as a district of the city of Adelaide. Sir Montague's brother, Benjamin James, had now unexpectedly come into both title and estates. Marrying Maria Fetherstonhaugh of Rockview, in 1849, the new and fourth baronet had two sons and died in 1888 – the year T.E. Lawrence was born. It was Benjamin James who built up much of the sumptuous art collection that adorned Killua Castle at the height of its glory. The hugely wealthy baronet made discerning use of the Grand Tour, travelling extensively and bringing home exquisite works of art and superb furniture. When the contents of the Castle were auctioned in 1920, there was an incredible collection of immensely valuable old masters, antiques, antiquities, silver and books (all pre-1900) on display. In the glittering gallery of more than two hundred paintings there were two Caravaggios, a Rubens, a Rembrandt, a Van Dyck, a Holbein and many other works of the great Dutch and Italian Schools. Perhaps not surprisingly, in pride of place was a portrait of Oliver Cromwell.[2]

The Killua estate straddles the old road to the west of Ireland and the Chapmans part-excavated an ancient tumulus near it, unearthing some fine arte-facts, which they added to the family collection. In the end they had enough to create their own museum within the castle. Ultimately the Chapman finds became the so-called 'Killua Hoarde', which today forms a valuable part of the National Museum of Ireland's display of Irish antiquities. Here Lawrence, an archaeologist, would have felt proudly at home. He would have made the perfect curator of the family museum.

The mid-nineteenth century marked the beginnings of the decline of the main branch of the Chapman family, for neither of Sir Benjamin James's sons was to provide an heir. The eldest, Sir Montague Richard, married his cousin, Lawrence's aunt, Caroline Chapman, when they were both in their early forties. They had no children, and Montague's slightly eccentric brother, Sir Benjamin Rupert, the sixth baronet, never married. Thus did the title start its eventual, if unexpected, reversion to Lawrence's father, because the fourth baronet, Sir Benjamin James, had a younger brother, William Chapman of South Hill. William was Thomas's father, and thus Lawrence's grandfather. It was his dim portrait that had stared down at me from the head of the big staircase at Rockview.

From the seventeenth century onwards the Chapman genealogy is littered with earls, barons and baronets from Ireland, England and Scotland, who had helped to grow an impressive and influential family tree. Lawrence knew that by birthright he should have moved in the highest social circles had it not been for that Victorian stumbling block, the bar sinister. He had pieced together the truth about the family background when just a young boy. He didn't confront his parents with his startling discovery or tell any of his brothers at the time. Only many years later, after his father's death in 1919, did he let slip to his mother that he knew, and in 1921 he told his youngest brother, Arnold, some of the story. Lawrence pretended to care little about his illegitimacy, writing in 1926 to an academic friend: 'Bars sinister are rather jolly ornaments. You feel so like a flea in the legitimate prince's bed!'[3] This was typically Lawrencian humour but it cloaked a sense of social disorientation and much hidden hurt. From time to time he would talk to close friends about his illegitimacy 'with great bitterness'.[4] Stumbling on the truth about the family had come as a huge shock. It not only disturbed him but festered like an untreated wound, until eventually it seems to have provoked an emotionally charged reaction from him – to run away from home and join the Royal Artillery.

He supposedly enlisted in late 1905 or early 1906 when he was just seventeen, serving for a short while, perhaps six months, as a boy soldier in the Royal Garrison Artillery at St Mawes Castle close to St Just-in-Roseland on Cornwall's south coast, before his father is said to have bought him out. No records or evidence of this military stint in the far west of England have ever been found. It is possible that he joined up under another name, possibly Gray, but that has not been identified either. His mother and elder brother always denied that it had ever happened, but they would have had compelling reasons for doing so. Lawrence clearly never told his parents why he had run away, and they, in turn, it seems, never let him know that they suspected his absconding was an emotional reaction to his discovery of their secret.

In the final analysis we have only Lawrence's word for this early stint in the Army, which oddly prefigures his later, more permanent life in the ranks of the RAF. However, the incident does chime with what sparse information we do have about his discovery of the family secret. His descriptions of his time in the artillery, given to various correspondents such as Charlotte Shaw and Sir Basil Liddell Hart, and also in his book *The Mint*, are not short on detail; and Lawrence's friend, Colonel Newcombe, told the biographer Flora Armitage that it was Lawrence's discovery of his illegitimacy that led to his running away from home and enlisting.[5] What also supports the belief that something seriously disturbing happened to him in late 1905 is that there are no letters from him – to his family, or to anyone else – recorded in any of the published collections between mid-August, 1905 and August, 1906. He wrote to Charlotte Shaw in 1925: 'I was a garrison gunner for a little in the old castle. My mind was not so peaceful then, for I had not tried everything and made a final choice of the least ill.'[6]

This impulse, at the urging of mounting distress, to enrol at a very young age in a rough, working-class army (which is skated over in many biographies) is, I believe, far more significant than has hitherto been realized. There is little doubt that his shock discovery of the deception being practised by his 'middle-class' father and his pious mother, and of their true identities and unmarried status, caused him considerable psychological damage. It was a hurt that the passage of time never fully healed. His boyhood friend Midge Hall accurately discerned this fissure in Lawrence's nature, sensing that his youthful poses and postures were a front, 'a mask', behind which he hid his real self. Hall had felt that Lawrence had 'a sort of dual personality'.[7] It was almost as though he were trying to lighten the burden of his illegitimacy by turning it into a bizarre game of hide-and-seek, provoking his friends into questioning his identity and behaviour, asking them rhetorically: 'who do you think I am?'

Lawrence's troubling discovery was also partly responsible for his later detachment from society, particularly from its grand upper echelons, and from organizations whose interests and functions implicitly declared a sense of important social class and identity (gentlemen's clubs, regiments, hierarchical institutions); from anything, in fact, which would label or pigeon-hole him, or remind him of his true class, the aristocracy, from which he was forever debarred. In the ranks of the RAF (where he achieved a certain, if uneasy, mental equilibrium and worked productively and happily on projects that engaged his mechanical bent) he had reached social bedrock. Here common identity was extinction of identity – a classless, anonymous uniformity. Here he felt safe. If he and his fellow servicemen knew that he was different from them, he was at the same time respected and accepted by them, and they protected him from the prying eyes of the curious. Deliberately electing to serve as a ranker not as an officer – a choice that puzzled some of his friends and irritated or shocked others – was also his coded way of telling the world that he was prevented by illegitimacy from being who he really was: a Chapman, an Anglo-Irish gentleman. It's as though he were tacitly declaring that if he couldn't be who he should be, then he would go to the other extreme and be a social nonentity, 'an Irish nobody'. And what better way of making the point than becoming a simple serviceman, where the individual is reduced to a name and a number?

Writing to Charlotte Shaw from India in May 1928, Lawrence commented cryptically about reactions to his joining the ranks: 'Only when people tell me I am throwing myself away: or wasting on a few ignorants what I should lavish on the many intelligent ("of my own class": how little they know what my class is!) why then I am only sorry that I cannot share their confident knowledge.'[8] And again from India earlier in 1928 in reply to a letter from Lord Stamfordham, King George V's Private Secretary, Lawrence hinted, with provocative mystification, at his having lowly, even base, origins. To Stamfordham's reproach that he should not be an aircraftman but should take his 'proper place ... at home amongst men & women of intellect and culture' like himself, Lawrence responded: 'I don't agree with your strictures on my present. I wasn't very respectably born, and had to make my own way. The war elevated me too high: and I've reverted. That's all.'[9]

The social class of Lawrence's father and his sons was, of course, not what it seemed. Chapman-Lawrence had always desperately hoped for a legal separation from his wife. In a confessional letter to his sons, which none of them – with the possible exception of Lawrence himself ('Ned' to his family) – ever saw, he wrote: 'There was no divorce between my wife & myself. How often have I wished there had been!'[10] According to Eric Kennington's wife, Celandine, the Killua Chapmans had urged Mrs Chapman to have her marriage annulled, but she remained obdurate in her refusal to do so.[11] It was an enormous tragedy for everyone involved. If 'Mr Lawrence' *had* managed to secure a divorce (which would have been very difficult in Victorian times with the Matrimonial Causes Act of 1857 demanding infidelity by the petitioner's spouse as a legal requirement for annulment – and Mrs Chapman had, of course, committed none), he might well have been able to reclaim his suppressed Chapman name and remarry, this time to Sarah, the woman who in all but legality and the eyes of the Church was already his wife. However, the consequences of his coming out of hiding and re-establishing his true identity might not have been all happy.

The sons (except probably Ned) would have been stunned; scandalized friends and neighbours might have distanced themselves from the startlingly metamorphosed 'Lawrences'; the new and no doubt suspect 'English' Chapmans could have found themselves the butt of malicious local gossip; and the Chapmans in Ireland might have been temporarily embarrassed. For Thomas Chapman, however, such hurtful alienation would surely have been a price worth paying for the relief of being able to legalize his family and rid himself of the lie he had been living and the anxieties that had accompanied it. In the event of a divorce there would, theoretically, have been one further and much more far-reaching consequence for Chapman: the alluring possibility of his being reinstated as heir to the castle, the estate and great wealth, in addition to the title, if his two baronet cousins of the main line, Montague and Benjamin, were to die without issue – as in fact they did. Given this improbable scenario, the sons of the resurrected Thomas Chapman would also suddenly have found themselves in the Chapman inheritance line. How different their world might then have become: Bob 'Lawrence', the eldest son, would have been heir to the title, and perhaps even to the estates, and found himself a very wealthy man. Yet it is almost impossible to envisage the very unworldly, very proper, very religious, and very English Bob as the baronet master of Killua Castle. The mere idea of such a stratospheric social elevation of the quiet, strait-laced Bob much amused his brothers, Ned and Arnold.[12]

Next in line, with an immense learning in history, a fascination with his Irish forbears, the wish to be considered Irish, an Irish nature – unpredictable, independent, impishly humorous – and a great sensibility and empathy, Ned Lawrence might have made the ideal heir. However, the picture this conjures up of T.E. Lawrence as a daredevil aristocrat who survives countless ordeals in the service of Empire like some John-Buchan adventurer, and then retires to his estate to live the quiet life of a country squire, somehow doesn't really fit the man. The image of Lawrence as an Anglo-Irish landlord in a tweed suit, complete with polished brogues, hat and cane, being driven grandly round Killua in his carriage graciously acknowledging the cap-doffings of his tenants and workers does seem, if not ludicrous, somehow a little fanciful. And yet, had he ever succeeded to the estate and achieved further fame of some different kind, we might today be familiar with the title Chapman of Killua, a man who would undoubtedly have been just as fascinating as his alter ego, Lawrence of Arabia.

SIX

Ancestral Voices

THE GENEALOGY of Lawrence's Anglo-Irish ancestors depicts a distinguished and well-established family. However, to appreciate the world into which Lawrence's father was born and to which Lawrence might have been heir, consideration should be given to the real position of the Anglo-Irish and to the historical events in nineteenth-century Ireland that irreversibly undermined the dominance of the Protestant Ascendancy. This position was one of active discontent among the tenant farmers and growing insecurity in the ranks of the gentry. With the Union of 1801 the separate Kingdom of Ireland had disappeared and with it its independent ruling aristocracy and Parliament. Thus was the Protestant Ascendancy of Ireland shorn of its political power. Leading up to the Union, the Dublin administration was still strongly against Catholic emancipation. John Fitzgibbon, Lord Chancellor and first Earl of Clare, succinctly and evocatively summarized the foundations of Anglo-Irish rule in his Union speech:

> The whole property of this country has been conferred by successive monarchs of England upon an English colony composed of three sets of English adventurers who poured into this country at the termination of three successive rebellions. Confiscation is their common title, and from their first settlement they have been hemmed in on every side by the old inhabitants of Ireland, brooding over their discontents in sullen indignation.[1]

The Protestant Ascendancy had lost its political independence. Several decades later its ownership of lands was to be hugely reduced too. The 1840s in Ireland had brought the potato blight and the famine, which followed the failure of the crop (Lawrence's kinsman Sir Walter Raleigh is said to have planted the first potato in Ireland. Still standing today in the grounds of Killua Castle is an obelisk erected by the second baronet, Sir Thomas Chapman, to commemorate his illustrious forbear). The famine was a watershed between an old and a new history. Well over a million people died and a flow of emigration to America and the colonies began, a great and terrible uprooting in such appalling conditions aboard the vessels of passage that they became known as coffin ships. This desperate exodus was to continue for the next sixty years almost unabated until the population of Ireland, which before the famine had been eight million, was halved. It was a barely disguised mass deportation that burned itself indelibly into the Irish psyche. And yet, amazingly, by the 1860s Ireland appeared reasonably prosperous again. Most of the landed families had been seriously affected by the famine and its terrible human toll, despite some, the Chapmans among them, having done their best for tenants who were now living on the breadline or worse – hence the humanitarian attempts of Sir Montague Lowther Chapman, the third baronet, to encourage his tenants to re-settle in Australia. The genteel life of the wealthiest Anglo-Irish families continued but the famine and mass emigration had taken the shine off their gilded social world. Some landowners who had tried to alleviate the sufferings of their tenants ended up in ruin themselves, to be replaced by new landlords who had little sympathy with the plight of tenants. However, in the higher echelons of the Ascendancy it did not take very long for the tragedy of the famine and the decimation of the peasantry to be consigned to the past. Nevertheless, the grounds for grievance and anger among an ill-treated people were many and genuine; life for the native rural Irish did not substantially improve.

With the earlier Union not only had the centre of political life transferred to England but so, gradually, had 'society', or 'high life' as contemporary columnists dubbed it. As a result, the wealthier Anglo-Irish families found Ireland becoming a social as well as a political backwater and began to move across the Irish Sea to England – sometimes just for 'the season', sometimes more permanently – to be closer to the heart of social and political influence. They also sent their sons to school in England, many of whom, including Lawrence's father, went to Eton. These families, who now saw London rather than Dublin as the hub of their world, became the notorious 'absentee landlords' of history. They left behind them estates that they put in the hands of land agents charged with wringing as much money as they could from an already exploited peasantry.

As already stated, Lawrence's ancestors remained in Westmeath throughout these troubled times, surviving the vicissitudes of the years of agrarian struggle and doing their best to support their tenants and the local economy. Another half century would pass before the family's final decline. Then failure to produce an heir in both the main and collateral lines, combined with the diminishing importance of the gentry, would see the Chapmans more and more isolated from national affairs in a new Ireland which was slowly and painfully emerging. After the disaster of the famine the social mortars of the old Ireland were beginning, imperceptibly but irreparably, to crumble.

In 1849 the Imperial Parliament passed an Encumbered Estates Act, which allowed for the sale of the lands and property of ruined owners. A radical revision of the land laws was urgently needed but powerful vested interests resisted change. A fundamental reordering of land tenure was against the convention and precept of the age that sanctified property and favoured the landowner. In 1867 there was a limited armed revolt by the Fenian movement. Lawrence's father recalled these days to a friend in Oxford, remembering the clang of bullets on the shuttered windows of the Big Houses during the time of the Land League.[2] Many of the estate owners now felt deserted by England and allowed their lands to be appropriated by the state under Land Purchase. A series of further enactments accelerated the process of division of the land among the Irish farmers, which in turn heralded the final transfer of control from the few to the many. Most of the Anglo-Irish families in Ireland today, whose ancestors once exercised great power and owned thousands of acres, now only claim their houses, their modest demesnes, their pedigrees and their memories, and many of them – like Lawrence's family in Westmeath – no longer exist at all, at least not in the main line. The tragedy is that the majority were devoted to Ireland without being culturally a part of her. They remained at heart expatriates whose ultimate loyalty lay with Britain. Yet over the centuries they had become anything but English in manner and outlook.

Lady Fingall, a senior member of the Ascendancy, evoked with a strange poignancy that indefinable sense of not wholly belonging, that reluctance by the Anglo-Irish to acknowledge the truth about their anomalous place in the history of Ireland. Writing of her family's lost home, Danesfield, in County Galway, she said:

'The front of the house seems to have had a blank look, the windows staring across the country, like blind eyes. It is a look that the windows of Irish country houses often have, as though indeed that was the spirit of the colonists and conquerors, looking out across the country, which they possessed, but never owned'.[3]

The Chapmans typified the Anglo-Irish way of life in the Ireland of the mid-nineteenth century: they hunted, shot, rode, fished, held and attended balls, and spent most of their time mingling with the influential in a society to which their birthright gave them an automatic entrée. *The History of the Westmeath Hunt* gives an artlessly accurate insight into the exclusive carousals of 'the quality', as the rural Catholic Irish referred to the gentry.[4] From 1876–81 the mastership of the Hunt was held by Lawrence's great-cousin, Montague Richard Chapman. Just down from Oxford, in his twenties and living at Killua with his mother and father (the fourth baronet, Sir Benjamin James), he was elected Master, a position for which, apparently:

> No better selection could have been made … as Mr Chapman would do nothing by halves, he took rooms in Mullingar for the hunting season, and was on the spot to direct operations, and to look after the many details of the hunt establishment. He was a big man, riding over fourteen stone, always usefully mounted and generally in the first flight, taking more note of his hounds than did some of the scatter-brained thrusters in front of him.

During Montague's mastership most of the Chapmans were active in hunt affairs. Montague, who later as the fifth baronet liked to stride round his estate with a sturdy walking-stick, organized the first point-to-point races in the county, and during his fourth season as Master, he, and Lawrence's father, a keen huntsman, were mingling with the cream of society. The Hunt history proudly records that 'Westmeath was now honoured by Vice-Royalty; the Duke of Marlborough, then Lord Lieutenant of Ireland, occupied Knockdrin' and 'Lord and Lady Randolph Churchill constantly graced the field with their presence.'

The whole Chapman family were actively involved in the maintenance of not just the estates but also of the village of Clonmellon, which was developed in the 1770s by the first baronet. He also built ten almshouses for old and sick labourers – who were given an acre of land and £2 each per annum – founded and endowed the local school, and established the little Protestant church of St Lucy's. A record of 1837 describes Clonmellon as 'a market and post town in the Parish of Killua, Barony of Delvin, County Westmeath and Province of Leinster, four-and-three-quarter miles West North West of Athboy, on the road to Oldcastle containing

960 inhabitants. This is a neat little town consisting of 183 houses.'⁵ Clonmellon today – situated thirty-seven miles north-west of Dublin – is a sleepy little place with a wide, empty main street and retains vestiges of a rural Ireland that is fast disappearing. Killua Castle stands less than a mile away to the east and was, until 2003, just an impressive ruin. In the late nineteenth century, however, it was hugely grand, a perfect example of the romantic neo-Gothic ideal which was all the rage in Victorian times; and the estate, across three counties, matched it for size and value, amounting to nearly 10,000 acres with a further 4000 of moor-land and bog in the west of Ireland for shooting and fishing. Together these were worth nearly £7000 a year, a lot of money in those days. Lawrence's Chapman ancestors were enormously wealthy.

The castle overlooked an extensive demesne, a small park, an artificial lake, a maze, and 250 square feet of greenhouses. Then there were five stylized lodges, once offering beautiful vistas of the turreted castle, two further houses, and exten-sive, undulating pasture-land. In the grounds there was a Lord Nelson obelisk, now collapsed, while the lovely pleasure gardens and landscaped woods long ago disappeared.⁶ During the family's heyday there was an old stone barn on the edge of the estate where Chapman scions of yesteryear are said to have made assigna-tions with local girls.

From the rear of the castle, in the distance across the lake, you can see Killua churchyard topped by its graveyard folly – a contrived ruin of a church created from the stones of a local church long redundant. The graveyard is a melan-choly place now, forgotten and unkempt. John Betjeman's lines from 'Ireland with Emily' fit it perfectly: 'There in pinnacled protection / One extinguished family waits / A Church of Ireland resurrection / By the broken, rusty gates.' In this large, walled enclosure lie the untended graves of thirty-nine local people and estate workers. Buried here too are six of Lawrence's Chapman ancestors: Lady Maria (wife of the fourth baronet); Sir Montague, Sir Benjamin (fifth and sixth baronets) and their spinster sister, Dora Marguerite; Lady Caroline (Lawrence's aunt); and, the earliest of all, Katherine Copeland, née Chapman (1672–1728), daughter of that very first Benjamin Chapman whose grant of Killua from Cromwell re-launched the family and its fortunes in its new seat in 1667.

I have often stood alone in that churchyard with its rioting nettles, box trees run wild and graves lost among tall grasses, and am always taken by a *poignant* awareness of the evanescence of human affairs. Nowhere on the Killua estate is the feeling so depressingly strong of grandeur and wealth and privilege come to naught. It was hard to believe, looking at the shell of Killua, silent and empty but for the chattering jackdaws nesting in the ivy-clad tower-tops, that this was once a great house alive with voices – liveried servants, grandees and their ladies promenading the landscaped walks, carriages rumbling along the main avenue, thronging balls, genteel conversation, song and dance and laughter.

At the turn of the nineteenth century the isolated Irish gentry, though in decline, didn't see their impending demise on the horizon and carried on much as they had always done. The fourth baronet, Sir Benjamin James, died in 1888 to be succeeded by his fox-hunting elder son, the 35-year-old Montague Richard, a graduate of Christ Church College, Oxford and a former Captain in the Rifle Brigade. As the twentieth century and the Edwardian decade loomed, the Castle still looked as though it had always been there in perfect harmony with its perfect setting, but the writing, if not yet the graffiti, was on the wall. The major part of Killua was Georgian, a three-storey, bow-fronted house built in 1780 by Benjamin, the first baronet, and extended by his brother, Thomas. Benjamin had pulled down the original house on the site and had initially decided to call his seat St Lucy's. He then began enlarging the estate holdings, adding new outbuildings and the pleasure gardens. There was also fine variegated woodland, its initial planting begun prior to 1750 and thereafter continually augmented. Names survive that evoke these extensive plantations: Larch Hill, Alder Grove, Limetree Walk, Silver Fir Avenue. Gothic tower and castellation were added to the castle in about 1825, probably designed by James Shiel. The rambling shape of the property reflects a family tradition that each incumbent should make some structural addition.

Yet by the mid-twentieth century the only part of the estate left intact was the obelisk commemorating Sir Walter Raleigh. Killua Castle, the home of Lawrence's ancestors, had joined the hundreds of other ruined houses scattered across the Irish countryside, unintended memorials to the genteel families of an age whose splendours and extravagances are gone forever. In 2003 there were twenty-nine Anglo-Irish houses in Westmeath either in ruins or demolished. Until the 1990s these properties, some stunningly beautiful, were to many Irish merely reviled symbols of Ascendancy rule. Those that weren't burned down in The Troubles were thereafter treated with indifference or, if abandoned, pillaged, as at Killua, for marble fireplaces and other fittings. Others were simply left to fall to pieces. Only in the 1990s did the new, booming Ireland begin to see these languishing properties as important to her architectural heritage and start to do something about their preservation. Those that had not already been turned into golf clubhouses or quaintly individual country house hotels were at last, with government aid, renovated and promoted as treasuries of Irish artistic talent. In 2002 an inspired and cultured financier bought Killua with ten acres for a figure believed to be more than €500,000 and bravely took on the challenge of restoring it to its former glory. When he purchased the property the new owner was believed to have been unaware that it had been the home of Lawrence of Arabia's ancestors. By 2012 a fine and full restoration was well under way.

The early years of the twentieth century had seen the Chapman dynasty in terminal decline. The fifth baronet, Sir Montague Richard, died from acute pneumonia in 1907, aged fifty-four. He was a good and popular administrator. A death notice in the *Westmeath Guardian* commented: 'His demise is much lamented, as he was a kind and indulgent resident landlord, and took a keen interest in every movement concerning the welfare of the county.'[7] He was the last of the title to reside in any style at Killua, although after his death his widow and cousin, Lady Caroline (Lawrence's aunt), lived on there, initially in the company of her other cousins, Montague's brother (the bachelor sixth baronet, Sir Benjamin Rupert, who died in Dublin aged forty-nine in 1914) and his sister, Dora Marguerite. By the eve of the Great War the big estates were embroiled in dispute and politicking. After her husband's death, Lady Caroline took over the management of Killua and was at the forefront of the confrontations with the local tenantry and political activists who were agitating ceaselessly for land reform. She led all the negotiations with the Estate Commissioners about the ultimate breaking up of the Killua estate.

The childless Sir Montague Richard, knowing that his heir, his brother Benjamin, was erratic and eccentric, had arranged with his wife, Lady Caroline, that Killua would be entailed to his mother's grand-nephews, Richard and George Fetherstonhaugh, should he predecease her. However, these joint heirs were killed in the Great War and their father, Major-General Richard Steele Rupert Fetherstonhaugh, who was living on England's south coast, unexpectedly came into possession after Caroline's death in 1919. He had no wish to remove to Killua and sold the property to a Colonel William Hackett from County Laois. Killua Castle had passed finally out of the Chapman family. The Colonel died before the Second World War and his widow sold the castle to an auctioneer, who in turn sold it to a scrap dealer, who dismantled the roof. The demesne was bought by a publican; and finally, in 1967, the estate was acquired by the Land Commission, whose remit was to break up former great estates into smaller parcels of land for reallocation among local smallholders. Then for nearly fifty years Killua remained a Gothic shell, its décor the graffiti of the philistine passer-by, its sole visitors indifferent, grazing cattle. Still head-turning and romantic from the distant roadway, it was now just a long-abandoned mansion inhabited only by the ghosts of a bygone age. Time and history had turned Lawrence's imposing ancestral home into a monumental folly.

Killua in its heyday, however, was a splendid, neo-baronial castle with the original Georgian building still discernible behind Shiel's battlemented parapets, mock-Tudor entrance and added towers. The interior was luxury itself. Delicate mouldings and cornices with classical motifs everywhere vyed for attention, and arched corridors patterned with shallow coffering linked innumerable communal rooms, including a grand ballroom, the museum and the magnificent, white-and-gold, oval drawing-room; and on the upper floors were at least nineteen bedrooms.[8]

To Lawrence Killua perfectly embodied his dreams of his lost heritage. If the complications of the bar sinister and his ambivalent nature had permitted, he might have fulfilled his onetime ambition, mentioned in a letter of 1924 to Thomas Hardy's wife, Florence, to buy Killua and settle there. During that year she had visited Lawrence's cottage in Dorset and left a painting of the castle for him. He wrote with a touching deference to thank her: 'Am I to think of it as a gift (once I meant to earn money and buy the place: now I'm wiser and want only to buy Clouds Hill…): it's one I'd value very much, but I hardly like to assume it, when it may be only a loan. If it's a gift, then please whose gift – for I'd owe a letter of thanks. Will you be good enough to lighten my darkness?'[9] Three months after the letter to Mrs Hardy he wrote to his mother about the Irish family connection with the Fetherstonhaugh-Framptons of the Moreton estate in Dorset: 'The Fetherstonhaugh people want to give me this little cottage (quaint how these people are settled all about here. The daughter of the rector (?) of South Hill parish it was who knew all about us. She had kept in touch with affairs, and is living in camp, being the mother-in-law of one of our officers).'[10]

If Lawrence had managed to buy Killua, and even perhaps to live there, it might still be widely known and visited today, its grandeur enhanced by the fame of its one-time incumbent. Instead Lawrence had to settle for something rather more humble – Clouds Hill, which he eventually bought from the Moreton estate.

SEVEN

Fashionable Marriage

SOUTH HILL – the other Chapman seat and the home of Lawrence's direct ancestors – was acquired through marriage with the Fetherstonhaughs and the Tighe family, who built it. It lies a mile from the village of Delvin and four from Killua. This three-storey Queen Anne house boasted marble fireplaces and lavish décor. It had an avenue of Irish yews, a landscaped park, great trees, gardens lovingly laid out with an extensive variety of rare flowers, three acres of kitchen gardens and a small river. The property was maintained reasonably well until Lawrence's half-sisters finally moved to Dublin in 1952. In the 1880s the house was the home of Lawrence's grandparents, William and Louisa Chapman, and was to witness the final, official phase of the family history. William was a typical Irish grandee: a graduate of Trinity College Dublin and a High Sheriff and Deputy Lord Lieutenant of Westmeath, his clubs the Kildare Street in Dublin and the Reform in London. His side of the family was as wealthy as the main branch, owning thousands of acres in Westmeath, Meath and Mayo. Like most of the Chapmans he was tall, his expression verging on the supercilious but also quizzical and not unkind, and he sported the statutory beard.

At the time Lawrence's father left Ireland for a new life, the Anglo-Irish must have been feeling under siege. In 1879 the potato crop had again failed, resulting in famine and near-starvation across the country. Now a decade later disgruntled tenants on the big estates were agitating for land reform through the Land League, using boycott and the withholding of rent as weapons. The landlords responded with innumerable evictions, the tenants' restraint broke, and there were shootings. As early as 1868 a relation of the Chapmans was shot dead.[1] By 1887 Lawrence's grandfather's extensive estates were in the thick of the land battle. The *Westmeath Examiner* commented: 'The tenants on the Auburn Estate of Mr. W. Chapman received ugly Christmas cards in the shape of civil bill eject-ments per post – what Mr. Gladstone was pleased to call "Death Sentences." Certainly very bad treatment for the poor people on his property, who have been rent-producers for him for over forty or fifty years.'[2] (Auburn, real name Lissoy, is famous as 'the loveliest village of the plain' from the poem 'The Deserted Village' by Oliver Goldsmith, whose father had been Rector there.)

Acts of Parliament and the tenants' agitation ultimately brought landlordism to its knees. William Chapman, a widower since 1877 when his wife, Louisa, had died, had in fact come to a generous accommodation with his tenants, but the settlement didn't last and he was reported to be 'again on the warpath' and 'again evicting' by 1888.[3] However, within a year, at the age of seventy-eight, he was dead, perhaps driven to despair by seeing his estates under threat but equally likely by the scandal involving his eldest son and heir, Thomas, which was becoming a topic of excited gossip in Westmeath.

Lawrence's grandfather had three sons (the second being Lawrence's father) and a daughter by Caroline Eden Louisa Vansittart, whose family were English landed gentry, originally from Holland. However, if they were rich, this final generation of Chapmans – represented by the offspring of the fourth baronet Sir Benjamin James and his brother William – were, with the probable exception of the fifth baronet, Sir Montague Richard, to lead largely anonymous, parochial lives. The social destabilization following all the political upheaval spread like a slow cancer among the Anglo-Irish, but with the Chapmans there was possibly another factor at work too. The Anglo-Irish, perhaps more than any other social grouping in the British Isles, had been knit together over the centuries by a complex web of intermarriage. The Chapmans exemplified this. Sir Thomas, the second baronet, had married Margaret Fetherstonhaugh and their second son, Sir Benjamin James, was to link the families again by marrying Maria Fetherstonhaugh of Rockview, his first cousin. Marriage of close cousins has been thought medically to encourage a higher incidence of recessive genes, which can sometimes lead to weak or slow-going offspring, although it can also perhaps produce genius.

Certainly the last generation of Chapmans in the main line had some decided peculiarities. Several did hold public office but such appointments were almost automatic for gentlemen of established standing. The sixth baronet, Sir Benjamin Rupert, was, to say the least, odd. Richard Kiely told me that he lived 'hard and fast' and was an inveterate philanderer, ending his days as an invalid living in Kingstown (now Dún Laoghaire) just south of Dublin; and his sister, Dora Marguerite, was thought to be a bit unbalanced. Sir Benjamin Rupert was, however, a sporting enthusiast and founded the Killua cricket team. The collateral branch of the family was hardly blessed with distinction either. Lawrence's uncles, father and aunt – William Eden, Francis Vansittart, Thomas Robert Tighe, and Caroline Margaret – represented the end of the line for the Chapman dynasty and, with the exception of Lawrence's father, led relatively uneventful lives.

William Eden, the eldest, might have inherited the baronetcy had he not died suddenly at South Hill in 1870, unmarried, at the early age of twenty-six. There was a rumour of suicide or foul play, and even today some locals can point out a hollow just inside the Killua estate boundary where it was said there had been an incident, or accident, involving William Eden and a firearm. A major in the Fifteenth Hussars, he was in command of a squadron in the garrison town of Athlone, when, like his cousin Sir Montague years later, he was said publicly to have suffered an acute attack of pneumonia and never recovered. There is a photograph of him in England leaning languidly against a balustrade on the Brighton promenade dressed impeccably in the fashion of the day, silver-topped cane in one hand – almost a caricature of the Victorian dandy. Lawrence's other uncle, Francis Chapman, would inherit South Hill (by arrangement with his elder brother, the runaway Thomas) and was typical of the later Chapmans both in behaviour and physical appearance. Tall, long-legged, reticent but haughty, he drank heavily and made frequent trips to England with women of casual acquaintance, who, Barbara Casey said, were subsequently rewarded with a gift of a thousand pounds each. When he died at South Hill in 1915 aged sixty-four, he was extremely wealthy. The gross value of his estate would now be worth more than €25,000,000. He bequeathed most of his effects to his eldest niece, Lawrence's half-sister, Eva Jane Louisa Chapman. More importantly, he left his brother Thomas £25,000, a sum equivalent today to about €10,000,000, with a similar amount to be divided equally between Thomas's four daughters.

Another and perhaps more important article of Francis's 1912 will stated that on 30 March 1888, in return for an annuity of £200 a year for life, Thomas had assigned to Francis certain lands that he, Thomas, had acquired as part of his marriage settlement of 1873. The 1888 date is significant. It supports the likelihood that, with the birth of his second son, Thomas Edward 'Lawrence', imminent, Thomas Chapman was hurriedly settling his affairs, divesting himself of most of his landed ties with Ireland preparatory to a flight to Britain. This probability is further underlined by the absence of his name from the listings of the Westmeath Grand Jury after March, 1888.

Francis Chapman brought the first motor car to Delvin, parading it through the little town to the incredulity of the inhabitants. He would often walk over to Rockview from South Hill and could frequently be seen sitting on a wall drinking whiskey from a flask. He was also perpetually troubled by the conviction that he ought to get married, a preoccupation he often confided to his aunt at Rockview and which was given a comical twist by a speech impediment that prevented him pronouncing the letters 'L' and 'R' normally. 'Do you think I ought to get mawwied, aunt?', he was always asking her, and she finally replied: 'I don't think anyone would have you now, Francis – you're too odd'; to which the dismayed Francis retorted: 'O, aunt, do you think so? I'm not weewwy that odd, just a bit pecuwia!'[4]

But it was his sister, Lawrence's aunt Caroline (aunt Lina), who was the impressive relation. She was very close to her favourite brother, the fugitive Thomas, and sympathized with his predicament in the years after he left Ireland. Wife to her cousin Montague, the fifth baronet, she had agreed to marry him only when past childbearing, believing that the dangers of further intermarriage morally obliged her not to add to a family, which, in any case, she had always considered at the best eccentric and at the worst unstable. This opinion was reinforced by the unpredictable behaviour of her other cousin, Benjamin Rupert, who once took her up onto the parapets of Killua and in a vein of uncertain humour threatened to throw her off the top: 'You'd look a fine mess down there!' he said to her, whereupon she locked him in the tower and fled.[5] Caroline, who hunted and often wore black, was impressive in both appearance and character, but in her later years she became an invalid; she died in her late sixties in 1919 in Queenstown (now Cobh) in County Cork, unable, it appeared, even to put her name to documents.

Eccentric some of these Chapmans perhaps were but in mid-nineteenth century Ireland their privileged lives at the top of the social order seemed as firmly established as ever. For Lawrence's father, however, this social grandeur was to undergo a dramatic change which he could not have foreseen in his wildest imaginings. Thomas Chapman, William Chapman's second son and his heir, was a very different man in Ireland from the one who later built a second life in England under an assumed name. The Irish Thomas Chapman and the 'English' Thomas Lawrence were a Jekyll and Hyde, an Irish somebody and an English nobody. As a Westmeath aristocrat, he was, in Lawrence's words: '… on the large scale, tolerant, experienced, grand, rash, humoursome, skilled to speak and naturally lord-like. He had been 35 years in the larger life, and a spendthrift, a sportsman, and a hard rider and drinker.'[6] Some, remembering the self-effacing 'Mr Lawrence' of his Oxford days, have doubted this and prefer to think it a romanticized image dreamt up by his son to preserve an illusion of a father who was once a raffish aristocrat cutting a social dash in elegant Ascendancy drawing-rooms. Nevertheless, those few in Ireland to whom I talked and who had distant family recollections of 'Tommy Chapman' all endorsed the picture of the man painted by Lawrence in the letter to Charlotte Shaw. He was tall, slim and elegant and at times could seem withdrawn. But he had another side. He could be wild, wayward, attractive to women, charismatic, revelling in the social life of the Big Houses and the excitement of the hunt, with little concern for the future other than that it would one day see him Master of South Hill and its considerable estates. He was educated at Eton from September 1860 until December 1865, then took a course in agriculture at Cirencester in the west of England and spent some time travelling. He was also a keen mountaineer and cyclist and took an active interest in church architecture. Later he and his son Ned would go on long cycling trips, like the one to East Anglia in August 1905, searching out churches and buildings of antiquarian interest. He was also a pioneer photographer. He infected his second son with all these enthusiasms at a very early age. Add to this a keenness for yachting in later years, golf (he was still winning competitions at the age of sixty-seven) and shooting (he was reputedly one of the best snipe shots in Ireland and his second son was to become equally proficient with firearms), and you have a man of substantial character and considerable talent in the sporting field. Happily buoyant on a private income, he threw himself into life with confident abandon, carousing through the social calendar, taking his exercise on horseback, mountain and bicycle, and indulging a predictable taste for wine, women and song. And he clearly enjoyed being centre-stage at social functions too. An example of this occurred at a farewell dinner held for a retiring member of the Hunt in 1871 when he gave the speech of reply to the toast 'to the health of the ladies who hunted in Westmeath'.[7] In fact, Thomas Chapman seems to have personified perfectly the colourfulness, social charm and personal whimsy of the Irish gentry.

Then, two years later, came the event that was to sow the seeds of a complete transformation of his life as astonishing as it was unforeseeable – a lavish Victorian marriage that was to turn into a fatal mismatch. Unbeknown to the bride and bridegroom, that day would mark the peak of the grand life that Lawrence's father's family had led for generations. As he prepared for his much-trumpeted wedding, little did the twenty-seven-year-old Thomas Chapman know that fifteen years later he would throw up this privileged world of inherited titles and fortunes, change his name and see his life descend into middle class anonymity in an Oxford suburb.

Thursday, 24 July 1873 at the village of Tyrrellspass in the parish of Clonfadforan was a big day in Westmeath's social calendar, when 'was solemnized in Tyrrellspass Church the marriage of Thomas Tighe Chapman, Esq., eldest son of William Chapman, Esq., D.L., of South Hill, and Miss Rochfort-Boyd, only daughter of G.A. Rochfort-Boyd, Esq., of Middleton Park.'[8] Edith Sarah Hamilton Rochfort-Boyd was the only surviving daughter of George Augustus Rochfort-Boyd, who had assumed the additional name of Rochfort by Royal Licence in 1867 and inherited his Westmeath estates and a considerable fortune from his mother, the last Countess Belvedere.

Edith was certainly a woman of character and was not unattractive; she had a sense of humour, if infrequently manifested, dressed well in the fashion of the day and had a strong will. However, she is remembered by local families as someone for whom social standing, rank and title were what mattered and who was obstinate, strait-laced and set in her ways. In that respect, ironically, she was not unlike Lawrence's mother, whom years later she would come to hate with an implacable virulence. Edith's family, 'the Boyds', as the locals called them, were out of the top social drawer, but some of them were stuffy and snobbish, in stark contrast to the Chapmans, who, while aristocratic, were charming and often easy-going.

Thomas Chapman's wedding was the last word in aristocratic ostentation. The *Daily Express* wrote enthusiastically and deferentially: 'Perhaps no event in the memory of the present generation has caused such interest in Westmeath as this union of two of the most influential families in the county.'[9] And a local newspaper reported at effusive length under the customary heading, 'Fashionable Marriage':

So seldom does it happen that scions of Westmeath marry ladies in their own county that we do not wonder at additional interest being added to the union of two highly influential and popular families. From Castletown Station to Middleton Park the road was spanned at intervals by arches erected by the tenants, and on entering Middleton Park by the Castletown gate the house appeared decked out with flags and appropriate mottoes. The guests invited were so numerous that Middleton, though probably one of the largest houses in the county, was unequal to the task, and was supplemented by an encampment which, while it afforded accommodation to batchelors, added greatly to the picturesque, as viewed from the terrace …

On arriving at the Church (rebuilt by the bride's grandfather in 1818), a charming scene presented itself. The children of the Belvedere Orphan Schools (munificently endowed by the bride's grandmother, Jane, Countess of Belvedere, in 1836), were ranged in front of the building, and strewed flowers as the bride entered, leaning on her father's arm, preceded by her mother, leaning on the arm of her eldest son, Mr R.H Rochfort-Boyd (15th Hussars), and attended by her eight bridesmaids, who, attired in white dresses, with pink and blue trimmings, were greatly admired … The bridegroom was attended by his brother, Francis Chapman, Esq., as best man. The service was performed by the Very Rev. the Dean of Kilmore, assisted by the Rev. Richard Dowse, Incumbent of the Parish, and the Rev. John Battersby, Rector of Vastina, in the presence of a vast number of friends and spectators, while the space outside the church was filled by a dense crowd. The ceremony concluded, the happy couple left amidst the blessings and cheers of all present for Middleton Park, where a sumptuous dejeuner was given to the relations of the bride and bridegroom, and to the elite of the county …[10]

Guests included, of course, many of the Province's aristocrats: the Earl and Countess of Longford, the Earl of Granard, Lord and Lady Harrowden, Lord Kilmaine, together with the whole retinue of the Westmeath and Meath gentry. Family gifts to the bride reflected the affluent world they inhabited: a profusion of tiaras, brooches, bracelets, lockets and rings, in diamonds, emeralds, rubies and pearls. The local press, dutifully chronicling the extravagances and love of lavish spectacle of the wealthiest of the Anglo-Irish, continued: 'During the repast the band of the Westmeath Rifles played an appropriate selection of music. The *dejeuner* over, Mr. and Mrs. Thomas Chapman left in a carriage and four for Castletown Station, where a special train awaited to convey them to Dublin, *en route* for the Continent.'[11] What a far cry this grand Victorian wedding was from the bourgeois life of Lawrence's youth. Such prodigal expenditure was a world away from the relatively modest outgoings of Thomas Chapman's later existence and the carefully fostered middle-class image that he chose to present to unsuspecting neighbours in Polstead Road.

There must have been some degree of physical attraction between Thomas Chapman and his wife, because the fifteen-year union produced four daughters, born between 1874 and 1881: the eldest, Eva Jane Louisa, followed by Rose Isobel, Florence Lina and Mabel Cecile. There would be no further children, and so, significantly, no legitimate Chapman heir. It was not a happy union and Thomas and Edith became more and more estranged, their marriage marked by mounting tension and increasing incompatibility. Mrs Chapman grew into a strict social conformist and religious martinet, while her husband had all the attributes of the gay cavalier. In retrospect it is hard to imagine how two such different people could have found anything in common beyond their heritage. A marriage considered a good match based on caste tradition and the solid principle of agrarian consolidation was to prove disastrous. Mrs Chapman became by all accounts a difficult and tragic figure and is described by people who remembered her as 'that frightful woman'. Intensely religious, she ruled her household with martial austerity. Inculcating her convictions in her daughters, she attempted a similar domination of her husband, who quietly ignored her, salting his circumspection with humour whenever possible. A story describing him going into the Kildare Street Club wearing, at her command, the blue sweater of the Salvation Army, illustrates not so much her dominant character and his cowed will as the absurdity of her religious fanaticism and his sense of fun – a characteristic much evident later in his famous son. Chapman saw the humorous potential and the joke was much enjoyed by his fellow club members.[12]

If Edith Chapman was rather puritanical, she was nonetheless a woman of genuine religious conviction, her private letters littered with Biblical quotation. However, in Dublin society she earned herself the uncomplimentary nicknames of Vinegar Queen and Holy Viper. Two anecdotes show well how she earned her titles. If she thought one of her daughters had told a lie, she would punish the unfortunate girl by pricking her tongue with a pin. And on one occasion when Chapman had taken his eldest daughter, Eva, to the theatre in Dublin, on their return she locked them both out of the house and accused him of giving their daughter to the devil.[13] Tommy Chapman was a man who liked his drink and convivial socializing. The clinical atmosphere of religious observance and strict temperance at home merely encouraged him to seek more congenial company elsewhere. While his wife was haranguing the 'Papist' servants with evangelical polemic, Chapman was out enjoying the high life, with a taste for good claret, an eye for a pretty face and a dislike of anything that restricted his freedom. His increasingly rocky marriage survived into the early 1880s but it was to be irretrievably doomed. By 1881 he and his family were renting Clonhugh, a large Georgian mansion five miles north of Mullingar. His daughters, Eva, Rose and Florence, were then aged seven, three and one, while the youngest, Mabel, would not be born until 19 October that year.

With three young children to look after and a fourth on the way, the Chapmans would have felt a pressing need to engage a nanny to help with the growing family. Apparently recommended by a Scottish Episcopalian minister on a visit to Westmeath in 1882, a Sarah Lawrence was engaged by Chapman as nursemaid-governess. She was brought from Scotland – according to some sources by an Andrew Balfour, an agent for the Chapman estate – to take up her post in the unfamiliar Anglo-Irish household. Petite, blonde, neat and dignified, with blue eyes and 'pretty as a bird,' as an old Chapman family retainer recalled, Sarah Lawrence clearly impressed her prospective employers. When her Evangelical upbringing, likely to stand up to the cold appraisal of the lady of the house, and her physical attractions, liable to take the eye of the worldly Tommy Chapman, are taken into account, she must have seemed the ideal choice. Her arrival in Westmeath would have gone largely unnoticed but six years later its consequence was to become one of the county's most romantic scandals.

Sarah fitted in to the growing Chapman household extremely well and was very good at her job. According to Lily Montgomery – a spinster from an Anglo-Irish family who lived with the adult Chapman daughters for ten years at South Hill as a companion – Mrs Chapman was delighted with Sarah; but so, ominously, was her husband. Lily Montgomery said that the daughters told her that when their father came into the nursery at Clonhugh and saw the governess, his face would light up with pleasure. Normally round the house he tended to look rather glum. A relationship developed between the bibulous aristocrat and the pretty working-class nursemaid, which then, fatefully, grew into a genuine love-match. The scene was set for marital disaster and for Thomas Chapman's world to be turned upside down. In 1885, according to Barbara Casey, 'Miss Lawrence', as she was always called by the family, gave in her notice – much to Mrs Chapman's surprise – claiming she had to return to Scotland because her mother needed her. Mrs Chapman held Sarah in such high regard that she promptly offered to double her wages if she would stay and, when Sarah insisted on leaving, gave her a locket containing a photograph of the Chapman daughters as a farewell gift.[14] The real reason for her determination to go was, of course, that she was pregnant with her first son by Mrs Chapman's husband. Chapman initially lodged Sarah at 33 York Street, off St Stephen's Green in Dublin, where on 27 December 1885 she gave birth to Montague Robert 'Lawrence'. Later Chapman moved her and their son to rooms above a barber's shop opposite the Gaiety Theatre in King Street, also just off the Green.

Lawrence's father was now maintaining a precarious *modus vivendi* between two entirely separate *ménages*: one with his wife and daughters at his grand Westmeath mansion, the other with his mistress and young son in the Dublin lodgings. He managed to sustain this uneasy dual existence until late 1887 when Sarah became pregnant again, this time with Thomas Edward 'Lawrence'. There is a faded rumour alive in Clonmellon to this day that T.E. Lawrence was not in fact born in north Wales but in a bedroom above the smoking-room in Killua Castle itself. Extremely unlikely, of course; but then many unlikely things about Lawrence have ultimately proved to be true.

Chapman was now under mounting pressure from his double life. Matters came to a head when Mrs Chapman, riding down Dublin's Grafton Street in a barouche, was astonished to see Miss Lawrence walking along the pavement. The former Chapman nursemaid saw she had been spotted and disappeared down a side street. A shocked and suspicious Mrs Chapman hired a private detective to investigate. He followed Thomas Chapman to the King Street rooms and, when he inquired of the barber about the occupants above, was told that a Mrs Chapman and her little boy lived there. The real Mrs Chapman was outraged, confronted her husband and demanded he leave Clonhugh.

Chapman is recorded as serving on the Westmeath Grand Jury for the 1888 Spring Assizes in early March. He does not appear, however, on the jury listings for July or thereafter. His second son's birth was expected in August and now, with his wife's ultimatum ringing in his ears and the scandal about to break, he knew the game was up. He would have to leave Ireland and his aristocratic life of luxury and licence behind him forever. As he was to write to his sons twenty-seven years later: 'Yr mother and I unfortunately fell in love with each other & when the expose came, thought only of getting away & hiding ourselves with you Bob, then a baby.'[15]

The moment of truth had come. Local tradition has it that on the day of the elopement a wrought-up Thomas Chapman rose at dawn, mounted his horse, galloped to Delvin and rode round the boundaries of his father's estate one last time, knowing that he would now never inherit it, nor perhaps ever see it again.[16] On that same day, sometime between March and August 1888, he would stand with Sarah and their two-year-old son on board the *City of Dublin* steam packet bound from Kingstown Harbour across the Irish Sea to Britain and north Wales. As he watched Dublin and the dark contours of the Wicklow Mountains dissolve into the horizon, he must have been churning with conflicting emotions – elation at starting a new life with Sarah, relief at escaping from an impossible marriage, and a deep and abiding sense of loss at the abandonment of a much-loved lifestyle and native land.

When the scandal broke and it became known that the middle-aged Thomas Chapman had left his wife and young daughters and run off with their twenty-seven-year-old governess and a two-year-old son, it was hardly surprising that it created an even bigger stir in the county than his grand wedding at Middleton Park. In late Victorian times family indiscretions and marital misdemeanours were hushed up, so when the Thomas Chapman affair burst upon Westmeath society, it reverberated round the dinner parties of the Big Houses for months. The abandoned Mrs Chapman was left feeling outraged, embittered and foolish, while her wholly innocent young daughters were distraught and bewildered. One wonders how Thomas Chapman reconciled his actions with his conscience. His independently wealthy wife was not, of course, left short of money, yet he must have known that money is no substitute for a husband and father's presence and support. Mrs Chapman has always been caricatured and vilified in accounts of her husband's desertion but in many ways she had every right to feel that she and her daughters had been cruelly wronged. However, her snobbery and religiosity ensured that she remained an object of both pity and ridicule in the county.

On the other hand, Chapman – now posing as Mr Lawrence, a married man with sons – was thenceforward forced to maintain a deception, burdened with the constant fear of exposure. It must have taken its toll on him. Yet it is also clear that before and after 1896, when he and Sarah ceased their fugitive roamings and settled in Oxford for the sake of their sons' education, he regularly returned to Ireland to visit relations and friends and to attend to matters concerning the Chapman estates. Many years later, referring to his father's covertly maintained links with his native land, A.W. Lawrence was to tell Celandine Kennington: 'I know my father used to go away for quite considerable visits; I believe he used to stay at his club.'[17]

EIGHT

The Abandoned Sisters

LOVE DROVE Thomas Chapman from his home, his children, his siblings, his friends, his privileged life, his inheritance and his country. Lack of love turned his deserted daughters into social misfits dominated by a sanctimonious, disciplinarian mother who rigidly controlled their increasingly isolated lives.

For a while Lawrence's sisters maintained a façade of social gentility. They liked to dress well and were ferried about in a chauffeur-driven Rolls-Royce. Eva was the only one to have any social pretensions and these often had comic consequences. One evening after a dinner at the Fetherstonhaughs of Rockview, draped in a white fox fur, she offered to sing accompanied at the piano – a common post-dinner entertainment in those days. Her rendition of Puccini's *Tosca* was so melodramatic and so distorted that the two little girls of the house (one of whom was Barbara Casey) had hysterics and were promptly packed off to bed.[1] Rose, who is said to have borne a marked facial resemblance to her half-brother Ned Lawrence, appears to have been the most outspoken of the four sisters, and tried to take the lead in managing the affairs of South Hill after her mother's death, without too much success.

According to the sisters' rather uncharitable companion, Lily Montgomery, they 'hadn't the brain of a rabbit between them' and the estate and attendant business and agricultural concerns were not viably maintained. A solicitor sold an outlying farm, pocketed the proceeds and never mentioned the transaction to his clients; the stewards, of whom there was a succession, embezzled at every opportunity, and the servants and gardeners were allowed to behave virtually as they pleased. 'O, we mustn't interfere' was the oft-heard response when friends tactfully suggested to the sisters that this or that servant seemed to have been given rather too free a hand.[2] Clearly, the absence of a strong male figure at the head of the family had contributed to advantage being taken of the guileless and fatherless daughters.

Their Dublin town house in Northumberland Road, Ballsbridge, latterly used by Florence and Rose but in the early years occupied by the youngest sister, Mabel, served as a base for charitable activities. Mabel busied herself among the poor and sick but her inheritance was lost to opportunists eager to relieve an eccentric spinster of her wealth.

She bizarrely invested a lot of money in a Turkish baths enterprise, which failed, and bought a house and took in lodgers, which offended the caste pride of her sisters. For most of her later life she walked with an odd stoop. Rose too was philanthropic and opened up South Hill for dances in aid of such organizations as the Lifeboat Institution, and at Christmas she toured Delvin distributing money and blankets to the needy. The sisters' genuine concern for the less fortunate (a quality shared by their half-brother T.E. Lawrence) did not extend to an understanding or tolerance of the Lawrence side of the family. Mrs Chapman decreed this a taboo subject. Yet later, according to Barbara Casey, Eva, Rose, and particularly Florence, covertly took a keen interest in the achievements of their half-brother and after his death – and their mother's – the sisters were said to have bought copies of *Seven Pillars of Wisdom* and kept them by their bedsides. However, they seem later to have contradicted this. They also apparently had a scrapbook into which they had pasted serialized sections of Lowell Thomas's biography of Lawrence. Rose often discussed Lawrence with close friends and it is believed that Florence was present at her father's funeral in Oxford and actually met her famous brother, although neither of them ever admitted as much.

The Chapmans remained extremely wealthy. In their aunt Caroline's 1911 will the sisters were jointly bequeathed her more valuable personal effects. She left her brother Thomas £20,000 and her youngest brother Francis the famous Killua diamond necklace and brooch, which, after his death were to go to Eva Chapman. Much of the rest of Caroline's property was in trust for Francis for life and after his death for her nieces. Francis died in 1915 and Caroline added a

'Irish House of Commons', 1780, by Francis Wheatley RA (1747–1801).
Benjamin Chapman, 1st baronet, barrister and Member of Parliament
for Fore (1772–6) and County Westmeath (1776–83), visible *centre
foreground* above the red box on the table. (Bridgeman Art Library,
Leeds City Museum)

Sir Benjamin Chapman,
4th baronet.

The 4th baronet in phaeton outside Killua Castle,
Westmeath.

Dowager Lady Chapman, wife of above,
née Maria Fetherstonhaugh of Rockview,
Westmeath.

Sir Montague Chapman 5th
baronet, as a boy.

Sir Montague Chapman,
5th baronet.

Caroline Margaret Chapman,
TEL's aunt Lina, daughter
of William Chapman of
South Hill, wife and cousin
of Sir Montague.

Sir Benjamin Chapman,
6th baronet, as a boy.

Sir Benjamin Chapman,
6th baronet.

William Chapman of South Hill, TEL's grandfather; photograph of oil painting.

Louisa Chapman, *née* Vansittart, TEL's grandmother, at South Hill.

William Eden Chapman, William Chapman's eldest son, TEL's uncle.

Thomas Robert Tighe Chapman, his second son, aged eighteen in 1864. The earliest known photograph of Lawrence's father.

Thomas Robert Tighe Chapman aged *c.* forty. (Imperial War Museum, London)

Francis Vansittart Chapman, Thomas Chapman's younger brother, TEL's uncle, as a boy.

Lady Chapman (wearing hat), probably at South Hill.

Eva Louisa Chapman, TEL's half sister, Thomas Chapman's eldest daughter.

Lady Edith Chapman (seated centre left) with Eva (far right), at South Hill.

Mabel Chapman, TEL's youngest half-sister (standing left), with her mother, Lady Chapman (seated with parasol), at Dysart.

Rose Chapman (seated far left), TEL's other half-sister, at Dysart.

Killua Castle, Clonmellon, Westmeath, in the 1890s.

Interior: the gold-and-white oval drawing-room.

The staff at Killua Castle in the 1880s.

The rear garden-front of South Hill, Delvin, Westmeath, in the 1950s – the home of TEL's grandfather William Chapman, and his wife, Louisa, and of his son Francis and daughter-in-law Edith Chapman, and her four daughters.

St Sinian's Church, Tyrrellspass, Westmeath – where TEL's father and Sarah Edith Hamilton Rochfort-Boyd were married in 1873.

Clonhugh, Westmeath, in the 1880s, rented by TEL's father – where the governess Sarah Laurence (*sic*) came in 1882–3.

codicil to her will in 1916 leaving virtually everything, including the monies and rents from various land holdings, to three of her nieces.

When South Hill was sold to a Belgian order of nuns in 1952, Rose and Florence, the two surviving sisters, moved to the Dublin house. Rose died in the early 1960s and Florence, who died in 1966, spent her twilight years in the care of a County Meath family who received a handsome sum in her will, believed to have been £23,000. The lady of the house turned away anyone who came hoping to speak to Florence, including Audrey and me. I still find it difficult to forgive this refusal because Florence was the one person who could have given a detailed account of the Irish side of the Chapman-Lawrence story. When we asked why we couldn't speak to the last of the Chapmans, we were told: 'Florence naturally takes her mother's side.' There is good reason to believe this to be untrue.

With the death of Florence, the last Westmeath Chapman, at the age of 86, the official history of the main branch of the Chapman family in Ireland came to an end. The absurdly puritanical Lady Chapman drummed her virulent dislike of male sexuality into her daughters. They never married. It was as though, like some modern Medea, she perversely took her husband's desertion out on them, exceeding her duty as their moral guardian to control their friendships and their social life and to deprive them of courtship, marriage, children. Strictly monitored by their mother, Lawrence's sisters lived apart in a social no-man's-land. Their life together, controlled by a draconian mother and lacking a father, was as tragic in its emotional and social deprivation as that of their famous brother in its private loneliness and spiritual angst.

A glimpse into the characters and lives of Lawrence's forsaken sisters is contained in an account of a visit to Ireland made in 1954 by Celandine Kennington and a friend.[3] She travelled to Ireland with the express purpose of finding out about Lawrence's forbears and meeting his half-sisters in the hope of using whatever information she gleaned to counter the sensational and damning revelations about Lawrence's family background that were about to break upon the world in Aldington's biography. Celandine visited Delvin and talked to a Mrs Sherwin, who ran a small shop in the village. This outgoing woman, who was clearly fond of the Chapman girls, told Mrs Kennington that after their father's elopement his daughters had withdrawn and 'did not take their place in society', and that much later when their father died, 'they went into quiet mourning' at South Hill. After further conversation of little real consequence Mrs Kennington and her companion then drove fourteen miles south to Killyon

Manor, the ancestral home of the Magan family. Opposite the main gates to the manor stands Killyon Lodge, which was the home of a dear friend of mine, Niall Fallon. A writer and newspaper editor and a man of hugely impressive character, he was a pillar of support and a source of valuable information and penetrating insights throughout my quest for the Irish Lawrence. I could not help feeling that his living next to the manor visited by Celandine Kennington was just one more strange Jungian synchronicity on a journey strewn with such unlikely coincidences.

Mrs Kennington was ushered into the manor to meet Colonel Magan, who was almost a caricature of the eccentric Irish gentleman, and she recorded his memories of the Chapman daughters in diary form:

> … Colonel Magan breezed in. About 75, long, lean, very voluble, charming: started off at once, 'You want to know all about the Lawrence family and the Chapmans. I'll tell you all I know … I knew T.E. myself quite well, saw a lot of him at the War Office Q.M.G's dept.' Col. Magan said he was most careful not to tell T.E. what part of Ireland he came from and the fact that he knew anything about the family history. I had the impression that he didn't know T.E. very well personally, but that T.E. used to come in and out of a room where he worked to see someone else. He specially stressed T.E.'s high sense of honour and integrity, his brilliance, his sense of humour, but kept on saying 'A queer fellow, a queer fellow, you never knew how he would take anything.' He spoke of T.E.'s sense of humour as being second to none and spoke with delight of marvellous verbal sparring matches between T.E. and old Smuts.[*]

Colonel Magan told Celandine that he and his wife had known Lady Chapman and her daughters very well, adding that the daughters 'only just about ticked over, in fact they hardly ticked at all'. In 1954 only two of the four sisters, Florence and Rose, were still alive. The Colonel continued, 'Florrie is the brightest of the bunch, she ticks quite well, she worked in a canteen during the war … Rose? Well Rose can hardly be said to tick at all!' Of Lady Chapman he commented caustically that she was, 'the sort of woman who was terribly pious, and would go to church at all hours of the day, and then if a wretched kitchen maid got into trouble, would cast her out without a character. Where did Christianity come in in that?' He added that she was narrow, stupid and rigid: 'impossible'.

---

[*] This must have been General Jan Christiaan Smuts, who had been a member of the British War Cabinet in 1917 and whom Lawrence would probably have met in London, on 5 December 1918, when the Cabinet's Eastern Committee convened to discuss the future of Palestine.

The Colonel's father had told him all about the elopement and said that it was, 'The only sensible thing Tommy Chapman ever did in his life … can't think why he didn't do it sooner.' In the Colonel's opinion Thomas Chapman was 'a good fellow, but hadn't a brain in his head,' but had been liked by 'the county' who were not censorious of his doings and in no way felt that he had behaved badly by absconding. It should, of course, be borne in mind that Magan was unlikely to have known Chapman, who had left Ireland in 1888 when Magan was just a boy.

The Colonel claimed to have worked with Lawrence in the War Office, presumably just after the war, but almost certainly had no first-hand knowledge of these Chapman family upheavals of long ago. So some of his reminiscences should be treated with caution. A few of his comments to Celandine Kennington are quite obviously inaccurate. For example, he said that Sarah Lawrence's father had been a factor on a huge estate in County Galway belonging to the Pollock family. On the other hand, his recollections of the main branch of the Chapmans are vivid and clearly genuine. He spoke of Sir Montague with delight, saying that when the fifth baronet was Master of the Westmeath Hounds his (Magan's) father had been his deputy for three seasons when the baronet was away, probably in America. Magan added: 'Old Montague Chapman … grand fellow … but mad … mad as bedlam.' He also said that the Chapman family had been 'enormously rich … pots of money.'

The highlight of Mrs Kennington's Irish visit was the almost surreal meeting with the two surviving Chapman daughters. She called on them one afternoon in their Victorian house in Dublin. In her own words: 'We went up, rather tremblingly I must admit, and rang. The door was opened: a very good-looking woman, aristocratic aquiline face, smooth silver hair, very charming manner, dressed in a very good pale blue tweed suit which toned with her especially beautiful blue eyes. I said, 'Are you Miss Chapman' and she said, 'Yes, Miss Florence Chapman.' I introduced myself as a friend of Colonel and Mrs Magan, and received a charming welcome … and we all went into the drawing room. This was a perfect 'period piece' – a biggish room with a large bow window and all the Victoriana you can imagine, low shell-shaped armchairs, a beadwork screen, curved shelves loaded with China, footstools, a very unusual Victorian lacquer cabinet, smallish family pictures, and miniatures. You felt nothing had been touched for generations … and would not be'.

Mrs Kennington explained that her husband had done the illustrations for *Seven Pillars of Wisdom* and that she had been travelling in Ireland and felt that she must call on the sisters. Florence, who showed both surprise and interest and no caution or reserve, said: 'My sister has just been doing the flowers, I'm afraid the room is rather a mess, let us go and join my sister in the garden.' Florence led her down an ornamental outside staircase to where her sister was gardening. She introduced Mrs Kennington and made it quite clear who she was. Rose, according to Mrs Kennington, was completely different from Florence.

She got the impression of: 'A terribly rigid personality, but yet a curiously vague manner. Thick pebble glasses, and scratley, unbrushed-looking hair … she was dressed in a very good tweed suit, which she somehow managed to make look shabby, her whole manner was markedly unbecoming, but conventionally polite; I wondered whether this was particularly for us, or if she always resented unexpected strangers. A curious mixture of being apprehensive and gentle and yet a very dominant personality … She was a strange mixture of gentleness, vagueness and determination. I think the word "batty" is what really fits her … she very obviously completely dominates Miss Florrie.'

It is clear from the Kennington account that Rose distrusted the visitors and was not going to disclose any information about the family. Florence, on the other hand, once alone again with Mrs Kennington, was only too keen to talk and gave a tantalizing and unexpected glimpse into that first major crisis in Lawrence's life, a glimpse that would seem to provide indirect proof that the Lawrence and Chapman families had once, if only briefly, been in close touch in pursuit of a solution to a mutual family problem. Mrs Kennington broached the tale of how around 1904 Ned Lawrence had found out about his illegitimacy and his Irish family and was terribly shocked: 'I don't know how T.E. came to know the story, but I know he did come to know it when he was about sixteen.' Florence immediately broke in excitedly: 'Oh I can tell you about that, it was because of an examination he had to take when he was about sixteen and he had to produce his birth certificate, and it was then that it all came out, and he had to know. And he was in such a way about it, such a terrible way that they sent over to my uncles to know what they were to do with him, and it was my uncles who suggested he should go out digging with … with …' Florence hesitated. 'Hogarth?' interpolated Mrs Kennington. 'No, no, that wasn't it … Wo … Wo', said Florence. 'Woolley?' volunteered Mrs Kennington. 'Yes,' said Florence, 'that was the name; he was to go out with him and be kind of out of the way for a while, and that was the beginning of his work among the Arabs.'

This seems to be a muddled collage of hearsay and half-truth and, of course, Lawrence did not go out to Syria until 1909, when he was twenty-one. Nevertheless, how, in 1954, could these sheltered spinsters possibly have known anything about Lawrence's crisis of identity far away in Oxford all those years before – unless Thomas Chapman had been in touch with the family in Ireland in 1904 or 1905? The Chapman sisters were not great readers and anyway little if anything had appeared in print until 1955 – indeed the story and the facts had for obvious reasons always been firmly suppressed by Mrs Chapman, the Lawrence parents, and by Lawrence himself. So it seems clear that during his son Ned's emotional crisis Thomas Chapman had been in close touch not only with his siblings, Caroline and Francis, but also with his cousins, Florence's 'uncles', the fifth baronet Sir Montague Chapman and his brother Benjamin. In 1904, when Lawrence was sixteen, his sisters had only one uncle, Francis Chapman. Since Florence said 'uncles' plural she almost certainly meant her great-uncles, the fifty-one-year-old baronet and his thirty-nine-year-old brother. There is another possible flaw in Florence's story. T.E. Lawrence's birth certificate gives his father as Thomas Lawrence and his mother as Sarah Lawrence, formerly Maden, so there is no reason why this should have aroused any suspicion in him. Also he once claimed never to have seen his birth certificate.[4] Nevertheless, it does certainly look as though around the year 1904 or 1905, Florence Chapman, then in her early twenties, and perhaps her sisters too, had overheard their mother talking about the fact that Thomas Chapman's son Ned Lawrence had managed to find the cupboard containing the family skeleton. The fact that Florence knew anything about it at all suggests that Thomas Chapman had concluded that his son, Ned, had somehow discovered the family secret and had reacted by running away and joining the Artillery. As a precaution Chapman may have forewarned his Irish relations in case Ned, in his disturbed mental state, were to do something rash and somehow reignite the family scandal in Ireland. The revelation that the errant Thomas Chapman had surfaced in England with five sons by his daughters' former nursemaid-governess would have been relished by the gossip-mongers of Westmeath. It would also have made the Chapman sisters feel more foolish and abandoned than they already did and have embarrassed their mother and the Irish Chapmans. Either way it does seem that Thomas Chapman kept in closer contact with his relations in Ireland than has been thought.

Mrs Kennington then raised the subject of *Seven Pillars of Wisdom*, asking Florence whether she had ever seen a copy. Florence replied that they hadn't and were hurt not to have been offered one. She said: 'We thought Mrs Fetherstonhaugh might have either got us one or left or lent us one.' Mrs Kennington then asked her: 'Do you remember Miss Lawrence?' Her whole face lit up. 'Oh, yes, we all loved her so much, she was so gay and pretty. She gave me a lovely present but I wasn't allowed to keep it. It was a scent bottle, such a lovely twisty shape, with a silver top, but they took it away from me.' Mrs Kennington asked her whether by 'they' she meant her mother. Florence replied: 'Yes, they took it away, I wasn't allowed to keep it. They gave me another in its place, but it wasn't at all the same thing. Oh, not at all … I can remember how terribly I cried.'

For a while she reflected wistfully over this before Mrs Kennington continued: 'Your father was a very jolly kind of man, wasn't he?' Her face lit up again and she said: 'Oh yes, he was a lovely person with children.' The conversation then slipped away and Florence began to put questions to *her*: 'Was the missionary brother still a practising missionary? What did the youngest brother do? She didn't know Mrs L was still alive, and who lived with her, and Mrs Kennington described how Bob was both a son and a daughter to her.'

Mrs Kennington then told Florence that a book was about to be published, which would make these family matters public and that she (Mrs Kennington) was trying to stop it and wanted to get the true facts about the family. Florence said: 'I hope you do stop it.' Florence then told her that her mother and sisters had had several residences, moving between South Hill, London, the south coast of England, and sometimes France. Bob Lawrence had once said to Mrs Kennington: 'I know my father's people lived on the South Coast.' Then, surprisingly, Florence suddenly said: 'The old uncles (again, this must mean Montague and Benjamin Chapman) wanted to bring us up, were most anxious to, but my Mother wouldn't hear of it.'

This raises an interesting point. Thomas Chapman's favourite sibling, who had sympathized so much with his marital problems and had kept in touch with him throughout their lives, was his sister Caroline, and in 1894 she had married her cousin Montague Chapman, the fifth baronet. It could well have been she, in consultation with her perhaps guilt-ridden brother, Thomas (who must at times have been concerned about the uncertain future of his fatherless daughters) who had encouraged the fifth baronet to take them under his wing.

By now Rose was keen to be rid of the inquisitive guests and engineered their departure. Before they left, Mrs Kennington had told Florence that the eldest Lawrence son, Bob, had no idea about the irregular family history. Florence was amazed. Bob Lawrence was indeed totally ignorant of the truth about his parents and remained in denial until it was impossible for him to be so any longer. He refused to admit the truth until it was staring him in the face. How stubbornly he clung to what he believed despite the accumulating evidence to the contrary is clear from a letter he wrote to Basil Liddell Hart in 1955 after the publication of Aldington's biography with all its damaging fallout. Bob's confident refutation of Aldington's claims was tragically self-deceiving:

> I do not believe this story of Ned being illegitimate. I know father and mother too well. They are both very decided Evangelical Christians. Father went to no end of trouble in dividing up the money he was leaving us so that we should have exactly the same amount each to avoid quarrelling and there has been none. He would not be less careful about his marriage to make Mother's way correct. Aldington is sure to have heaps of mistakes about this in the rest of the book. Mother told me some years ago that my birth certificate could never be produced because it was destroyed when the Law Courts in Dublin were burnt by the mob (IRA) and I have wondered if the marriage certificate was destroyed at the same time? ... My point is that father was in close personal touch with (his) solicitors, they were bound to have seen that his marriage was correct. Could all the Dublin registers of Church of Ireland churches be searched from 1880-1881 for a note of the marriage? I was born on 27 Dec 1885 in Dublin. I think Mother ought to be told Aldington has attacked her as well as Ned. Everyone else knows it; it concerns her more than anyone else and she knows nothing about this wicked story. She cannot see to read at all but her mind is perfectly clear and she is bound to know all about her marriage. It is very hard on me not telling her and I think she would expect me to do so. I have been hindered by my fear she might be greatly upset if she hears of Ned and Mrs Shaw's letters. I wish they had been destroyed. Do you know what is in them?[5]

If Bob *had* undertaken a search of the Church of Ireland registers for proof of his parents' marriage, it would, of course, have proved barren. In fact, Thomas Chapman did, on one occasion, record a fictitious marriage on an official document. On the birth certificate of his third son, Will, Chapman had entered under 'Date and Place of Marriage': '1883 September 6th St Peter's – Dublin'.

The reason Sarah Lawrence told Bob that his birth certificate was unobtainable was not because it had been destroyed. It exists. I have a copy. What his mother must have been desperate to conceal from him was that no birth certificate for him existed under the name of Lawrence. It is the only one of the five boys' certificates in which their father gives his real name. So the true certificate, if Bob had somehow stumbled upon it and worked out that it had to be his, would have revealed to him that his real surname was Chapman. On this Irish document his father is recorded as 'Thomas Chapman', occupation 'Gentleman', while Sarah is entered as 'Sarah Chapman formerly Laurence' [sic]. What on earth would Bob have made of this? The parents' deception would now surely have begun to unravel, and his mother would have had enormous difficulty in explaining it away.

Bob, who revered his parents and almost worshipped his mother, would have been jolted to the roots to discover that the paragon of virtue he fondly believed her to be didn't really exist. Her moral position was flawed at the most fundamental level. Whichever way he looked at it, he would have been faced with the fact that his mother, and his father, had lied to him and his brothers. He would have been forced to admit to himself too that his mother must have colluded in his father's abandonment of his wife. Poor saintly Bob. The shock to his system when he could no longer deny the truth must have been considerable. Initially it had been Celandine Kennington who, at the home of T.E. Lawrence's friend Colonel Newcombe and his wife, Elizabeth (Elsie), had taken him aside and told him. Celandine said that when she told Bob, 'He roared with laughter, rejected it.'[6] After that A.W. Lawrence wasted no time in disabusing his brother of his self-deception. Finally convinced, a sadly chastened Bob wrote to Liddell Hart, whom he had asked to combat what he thought were Aldington's cruel falsehoods: 'Arnie has sent me a private note today which alters matters considerably. Please take no action about the letter I sent you on 1st March, written on 28th Feb. and do not allude to it in writing to us both.'[7]

Mrs Kennington, still in Ireland, then wrote to Florence Chapman trying to arrange a second visit but, undoubtedly because of Rose's disapproval, was refused. The two English women then returned to Delvin and talked to a Mr FitzSimmonds. This garrulous man, very much an admirer of T.E. Lawrence, confirmed the prevailing view of Lady Chapman as 'strict, very strict'. Mrs Kennington asked him whether Thomas Chapman was 'very wild'. He replied, 'Och, it's not that I'd be saying ... I'd be saying he was just a real Chapman, and she was always trying to make a preacher of him. I'm telling ye she had an allarrum bell in their bedroom to wake them o' nights, for him to have to read the Bible to her.' He spoke very highly of Florence but said that, 'Miss Rose was very stiff, you could say she was a regular Boyd.' Mrs Sherwin, the shopkeeper, was also fond of Florence, saying, 'Miss Florrie was so sweet, but she was always treated as being very much the baby of the family.' Asked again how Thomas Chapman was regarded in the neighbourhood, FitzSimmonds smiled and said, 'He was a regular Chapman ... full of charm.'

Mrs Kennington then met an unkempt old man called Paddy Mangan, whose father had been steward to both Sir Montague and Sir Benjamin and who had himself worked for the family and knew the Chapman daughters. He spoke highly of Sir Montague but thought that Sir Benjamin was 'soft in the head'. He said of Rose and Florence, 'They were like two families. Miss Florrie is a Chapman, but Miss Rose … Miss Rose is a Boyd all right.'

NINE

A Double Life

MIDWAY through the Edwardian decade Chapman's sons, ignorant of the truth about their parents, were growing up in suburban Oxford and leading happy, secure, comfortable lives. For the sake of their children's future, Mr 'Lawrence' and his 'wife' now had to be more careful than ever to safeguard their conventional, middle-class façade.

For eight years they had fled all over Britain and farther to avoid discovery, but now that they had stopped running and settled down, they must have wondered whether the past might catch up with them and expose what they always thought of as their shameful secret. That said, the Lawrences couldn't have chosen a better place in which to maintain their disguise. Polstead Road in those days was part of a fairly new suburb, its architectural hallmark Ruskinian Gothic. John Betjeman later wrote of it: 'The inner North Oxford is a life in itself, a home of married dons, dons' widows, retired clergymen, retired dons, preparatory schools, theological seminaries, bicycle sheds, ladies' colleges, tea parties, perambulators and peace' – in other words, the perfect place to hide and to maintain an image of respectability.[1]

None of the sons, except, of course, Ned, had the remotest idea that all was not what it seemed, that their charming, caring father was living two lives, one English, the other Irish. Barbara Casey told me that his loyal sister, Lady Caroline Chapman, accompanied by her maid, Jane Evans, would take rooms for a month annually in the Queen's Hotel in Queenstown in County Cork, where she would be visited by both her brother Thomas and Lawrence's mother. This concurs with a curiously critical comment made by Lawrence writing home from Baron's Hotel in Aleppo in Syria at the end of September 1913: 'Another letter has just come from Cork from Mother. I am glad she has found Ireland unfortunate. I think that what we cannot help knowing of its history, that it is a sort of duty of English people to avoid it.'[2]

The Irish visit is confirmed by Lawrence's brother Will on board ship en route to India writing to his mother, also in September 1913, saying, 'you must be enjoying yourself grandly in Ireland.'[3] Two days later he writes: 'I wonder how you are getting on in Ireland.'[4] And again, this time from Port Said: 'And what a good time you seem to have had in Ireland.'[5] A month later Ned Lawrence, with quite opposite sentiments to his brother's, is writing home from Carchemish and yet again inveighing against Ireland: 'Don't go to Ireland, even to play golf. I think the whole place repulsive historically: they should not like English people, and we certainly cannot like them.'[6] Further indication of Lawrence's father's continuing link with Ireland and of his son Ned's disapproval of it can be found in a letter home four months earlier. Lawrence asks: 'By the way, what meant an isolated sentence in Will's letter that "Father was still in Ireland?" Why go … to such a place: perhaps he had desires to sign a covenant.'[7] (Lawrence must have been referring here to the 1912 Ulster Covenant, a declaration, mainly by Ulster Protestants, against the proposed Third Ireland Home Rule Bill).

I came across yet more evidence of Lawrence's father's sustained links with his homeland when I was at Rockview, where I discovered an entry in a handwritten ledger of contributions to the County Westmeath Motor Ambulance Fund, which seemed to show that Thomas Chapman in person had donated £1 on 15 March 1916. His younger brother, Francis, had died nine months before and it is possible that there were matters of probate requiring Thomas's presence. A world away, his son Ned, a member of the newly titled Medforce Intelligence, was in his office in Cairo and shortly to travel to Basra to help in the negotiations with the Turks for the release of British prisoners at Kut al Amara.

As well as disapproving of his parents' visits to Ireland Lawrence was clearly disturbed by them. This is plain from those comments in his letters home. Reading between the lines, they are further indirect proof that, unlike his brothers, he knew the truth of his parents' life of masquerade. For the young Lawrence any mention of Ireland was a painful reminder of his illegitimacy and it stirred up a mixture of emotions – anger and also probably shame and social insecurity. He hated the fact that his parents had to lie to him and his brothers about the main purpose of the Irish trips and that his father and mother weren't who they said they were. He felt entangled in the subterfuge and deceit in which their relationship was mired. He couldn't talk to his parents about it because it could have destroyed family unity. Only in the years after the war and after his father's death did he start to come to terms with his hidden Irish origins, eventually solving the problem by accepting them with pride – if only privately.

Back in their safe, sedate Oxford suburb Lawrence's parents would still have been constantly aware of their Achilles heel – the Irish connection. Polstead Road might have been a perfect place to hide but chinks in the armour occasionally appeared. A friend of Ned Lawrence's varsity days claimed that the Lawrences had been ostracized and that his fellow undergraduates had sensed that there was something 'odd' about the family who, even by the very correct social standards of the day, were always 'so punctilious, churchgoing and water-drinking.'[8] It seems likely that to cover their tracks and avert any danger of discovery, Thomas Chapman and Sarah had concocted a sketchy and fictitious family background, which had been accepted by all the sons, except, of course, by Ned. Chapman also invented plausible reasons, sometimes involving his health, for his extended absences from his English family when he was clearly in Ireland.

Inevitably there were times when the secret became suddenly vulnerable, such as the artless interest in Ireland and his father's visits there shown by his son Will. Writing to his mother in December 1913, Will said: 'Is Father going to go away at all this Winter? That will be lonely for you; I hope he'll keep fit and not have to'; and two weeks later, again to his mother: 'Father will be bound to be the better for the sea-baths. I wish I had seen something of Ireland before I came away. And it will be jolly if you can get over there and join him for awhile.'[9][10] There is real pathos in all this make-believe, in the ignorance in which the innocent Lawrence boys had to be kept by their parents. Thomas Chapman and Sarah never escaped the guilt and fear they felt about the lie they were living and the double life they were forced to lead. As Chapman wrote in his 1915 letter to his sons: 'You can imagine or try to imagine how yr Mother & I have suffered all these years, not knowing what day we might be recognized by someone and our sad history published far and wide.'[11]

It troubled them deeply to have to maintain this charade unremittingly, to have to deceive sons who looked up to them as models of Christian virtue and social probity. It is surprising, nevertheless, that the sons never questioned the absence not only of grandparents but also of uncles, aunts, cousins, or, for that matter, relations of any kind. There is no indication that this struck Bob, Will or Frank as very odd. However, it obviously struck Ned. The Lawrences were officially a family without an ancestry. Family connections mattered in late Victorian times. To have none was most peculiar. It would perhaps have felt a bit like having no memory. People with amnesia are troubled by the loss of the past. Such a gap in recollection and in the continuity of their lives gnaws away at them. Despite the wonderful support and love they received from their parents, the Lawrence sons must occasionally have felt that they were living in a perplexing genealogical limbo.

Back in Ireland, as the Chapmans' reign at Killua began to stutter to a halt, monies, which Lawrence's father, the last baronet, thought would pass to him from a considerable estate, were not forthcoming. His brother Francis, the last male Chapman to live at South Hill, had left his brother £25,000. This was a considerable sum in those days but fell short of the legacy Lawrence's father must have expected. He was soon to be financially frustrated a second time. His sister Caroline had bequeathed him £20,000 in the will of 1911, clearly wishing his sons – her nephews – to benefit too. However, Thomas Chapman died from pneumonia on 8 April 1919 at the age of seventy-two, a victim of the Spanish influenza pandemic that had swept across Europe. Just eight months later his cherished sister also died and, from the point of view of her legacy, the crucial and cruel fact was that he had predeceased her and in that event her bequest to him would go not to her Lawrence nephews but to residuary legatees: her brother's four daughters in Ireland. Chapman's daughters had inadvertently thwarted their father's sons by depriving them of what was arguably their due from the Killua estate. This diverted legacy, surely intended originally for T.E. Lawrence and his two surviving brothers, may well have been in Lawrence's mind when he wrote in 1921 to his devoted friend Eric Kennington: 'A lump of money I was expecting has not (probably will not) come.'[12]

In 1927, when Robert Graves was researching his biography, Lawrence wrote to him about his background:

> My father didn't like his wife: so he left her for my mother. No divorce. Wife took all property, by agreement, and title, when succession eventually fell due. You'll find him in Debrett's Baronetage, under Chapman, of Killua and South Hill. Father took name of Lawrence (not even my mother's name) when he left Ireland. As widow and mother are both yet alive this story is not for publication.[13]

In this same key year, in the letter to his solicitor, he wrote of his mother's origins: 'I believe Lawrence was the name of her supposed father: but her mother (called Jenner) was not married to the original Lawrence.' Further on he remarked: 'I suppose we were an odd family, because it never struck me to ask him [his father] the facts of the name Lawrence. His will might solve the question.'[14]

Mrs Chapman, and publicly her daughters too, always refused to acknowledge the existence of Thomas Chapman's sons. Ned Lawrence had underlined this in his 1927 letter to Sergeant-Major Banbury in which he had teasingly disclosed the initial letter of his real Irish family name. He later interpolated a gloss into an early draft of Sir Basil Liddell Hart's biography of him: 'T.E.'s father's family seemed unconscious of his sons, even when after his death recognition of their achievement might have done honour to the name.'[15]

Contrary to the impression that Lawrence rather curiously liked to give to friends in the early post-war period that he had little money and was always scrimping and saving, he had in fact more than adequate financial provision. In a letter of 8 March 1916 to Lawrence, then in the Intelligence Department in Cairo, his father gives details of some securities that he had assigned to his son: 'As the income of yr securities amount to about £270 per annum I shld think there wld be no difficulty with most Banks in opening an acct.' He added the proviso: 'There is a condition I must put before you strongly ... that if our Will shld prove to be alive, that you & Bob & Arnie shld each return me what I wld ask you for of yr capital, so that Will may have the same Capital as you others.'[16] (£270 in 1916 would today be worth something in the region of £11,200, or £215 a week).

In another wartime letter 'Mr Lawrence' touchingly tells his son, Ned, of the confirmation of his brother's death:

> We have at length received such news which I am sorry to say leave to us no doubt of Will's death ... Poor Will, as you know, left everything he had to you and made you sole executor ... I gather from a letter of yrs that you do not intend to benefit personally from his Will but nevertheless you will have to prove it when the Court gives you Probate. How I wish this war wld end & that we might meet again.[17]

Although, as his friend Sir Ronald Storrs said, it is about as easy to visualize Lawrence in hunting pink as wearing an old school tie, there is equally no doubt that if he could not be constrained by the dictates of class he nevertheless felt excluded from what he knew to be his own. Biographer Malcolm Brown put it another way:

To Lawrence, who had rubbed shoulders over years with so many of the nation's elite while concealing his own pathetic illegitimacy, it must have seemed galling to think how near he was to being one of them – In fact, a mere 'bend sinister' away. Yet that gap was enough. In literature and history (and we are discussing a widely read and deeply cultured man) the bastard was always the villain, the malcontent in the wings: Edmund, not Edgar, in Shakespeare's King Lear. That he should be doomed to this role – ever the lowly outsider, the woodcutter, never the prince – must have bitten hard into his psyche.[18]

Unlike his brothers, Lawrence knew the history of his parents' life together long before he was twenty. Debarred from his true inheritance, he could only dream of the life he might have led as a wealthy Irish gentleman moving in elite circles. He must at times have felt like a pariah, and the example of the damaging marital upheaval in his father's life seems to have determined him never to get emotionally carried away, never to lose self-control. When he had stumbled on the truth, it is clear that his innate reaction was to distance himself from his parents, if only temporarily. (Their building of the little bungalow at the bottom of the Polstead Road garden for his exclusive use, ostensibly to give him peace and quiet for his studies, was perhaps in part a belated parental response to an agitated recoil from family life.) If his parents were hiding behind a mask of respectability, then why shouldn't he too wear a mask and hide his true self? If they had dangerous secrets, well then, he too would have his secrets. If his parents kept the truth hidden, even from their children, then why shouldn't he too keep the inner sanctum of his life locked away from a prying world? After all, weren't secrecy and duplicity endemic to the family? Lawrence was by nature shy but after the traumatic discovery about his parents when he was just a boy, his natural inclination to keep his feelings and his personal life to himself had been considerably reinforced. He had been handed a shock justification for dissimulation and disguise. In many ways he was thenceforward to spend his life in disguise, from the fancy-dress parading of his carefree, pre-war years at Carchemish, to the donning of an Arab headdress, then rich robes for the Arab Revolt, and on through his various names and incarnations as army private, aircraftman, simple working man among working men, and friend to the unexceptional, the disaffected and the lonely.

Lawrence's illegitimacy would also have created a more immediately damaging exclusion – preventing him from following any career where social status and family standing were important (and in the early-twentieth century that meant most careers of any consequence), or where his ancestry might come under scrutiny. Ned Lawrence would have known that to him the doors to preferment normally open to the sons of upper-class families were firmly shut, and he may have harboured, even if unconsciously, some resentment towards his parents, (and towards his father's wife) for placing him in this predicament, a predicament which was a source of constant anxiety and remorse to his father and mother too. As A.W. Lawrence put it: 'The children's illegitimacy mattered desperately to their parents, who were convinced of sin. It had the practical effect of depriving the children of their due place in society, as T.E. soon became aware.'[19]

Inevitably, the presence of this social and professional barrier frustrated and embittered Lawrence. A.W. Lawrence summed up his brother's painful dilemma: 'If my own experience is a reliable analogy T.E. was happy at home till he developed ideas incompatible with his parents', particularly his mother's, when mutual affection increased the inevitable strain. But in his case the strain must have been greater because he knew and hated the position they had got into through their inability to marry.' [20]

His parents' sad pretence clearly played a significant part in turning Lawrence into an outsider, almost into a rebel, forced to watch from the sidelines as his peers effortlessly claimed their roles in society and confidently stepped onto the first rungs of pre-ordained careers. He would have to fight his own way up the ladder of success.

TEN

A Standing Civil War

THE CHAPMAN line died out with the demise of T.E. Lawrence's father, the last official heir, on 8 April 1919. Lawrence preserved both the telegram and the letter informing him of his father's illness and death and they were found amongst his papers after his own death sixteen years later. The Genealogical Office in Dublin Castle held the pedigree of the Chapman family, which was drawn up and signed by Edith Chapman in 1914 when her husband succeeded to the title. At the foot of the document in pencil was appended the note 'extinct 9.4.1919.'

Edith Chapman's bitterness, resentment and obduracy ensured that she would never grant Thomas Chapman a divorce, a solution that would have saved Ned Lawrence's family from fear of social disgrace and might have injected a new vigour and intellectual life into the moribund baronetcy. It might also have brought Lawrence's unfortunate sisters some measure of release from the strain imposed on them by their mother's continual denial of the marital break-down. When her husband succeeded to the baronetcy, having lived apart from her in England for over twenty-five years, she insisted on being addressed as Lady Chapman, an ironical stipulation that prompted Barbara Casey's father to comment caustically, 'Who on earth cares what she calls herself?' Her pride ruled out any hope of divorce, or, as her daughter Rose put it, 'O, but mother had to think of us!'[1]

In Victorian times both the Church and the conventional middle class would have regarded an unmarried, cohabiting couple like the Lawrences as living in sin and as a social outrage. So to live together 'Mr and Mrs Lawrence' had to maintain the pretence of being married. Their antidote to the guilt they felt about this necessary deception was religion. Sarah Lawrence was the driving force behind the family's earnest religiousness, which was to affect three of her sons, Bob, Will and Frank, who were brought up to be models of church-going propriety. She tried to ensure that they lived godly, chaste lives at a time when such a 'happy band of brothers' (their mother's words) should have been socializing, if very respectably, with young women, going to college balls, and enjoying that wonderful, if short-lived, sense of freedom and immortality that is life's gift to early manhood. She clearly disapproved of close relations between young men and women and seems to have been watchful for any such liaisons involving her sons. She once told Robert Graves: 'We could never be bothered with girls in our house.'[2] She also undoubtedly tried, not always successfully of course, to put a moral brake on youthful over-exuberance and on indulgence in racy but largely harmless social pursuits enjoyed by most young men of spirit.

Her strict religious observance was in large measure an attempt to redress what she believed was the serious sin she had committed in stealing another woman's husband. The concept of 'Sin' was writ large in Mrs Lawrence's life and included a strong disapproval of 'drink' as well as of anything remotely hinting of sex. Her moral rigidity probably derived not only from her guilt at 'living in sin' but also from the shame of her own illegitimacy, from painful memories of an insecure and poverty-stricken early childhood blighted by her mother's alcoholism, and from recollection of Thomas Chapman's bibulous carousing among the Irish gentry. Lawrence's mother lived a life of never-ending atonement and tried to turn her 'husband' and sons into paragons of Christian virtue as a sort of peace offering to God for her sinfulness. In her old age during an illness she was heard to murmur, 'God hates the sin but loves the sinner.'[3]

Arnold Lawrence, noting how his mother constantly mounted assaults on his elder brother's life, on his privacy of thought and feeling and action, conceived a lifelong animosity towards her. He was quite certain that, 'their mother had seriously damaged T.E. and that was something he could not find in himself to forgive.'[4] The depth of that animosity is reflected in a startlingly damning judgement on her he made late in life to a friend: 'she was an abominable woman.'[5]

Sarah Lawrence may have been a woman of iron will but Thomas Chapman was not subservient to her, as some have suggested. She was in charge of the household and of domestic affairs, even, sometimes, of the disciplining of the boys, but it was Chapman who took control where major family matters were concerned. In an interview with John Mack, A.W. Lawrence said he felt that his father's role in the family had been distorted by writers who had depicted Mr Lawrence as weak in comparison with Sarah. Arnold was impressed with his father's quiet authority. Mack commented:

> Although Mr Lawrence tended to be gentle, quiet and reserved, and reluctant to show his feelings, he could be very firm when necessary. At times of family crisis he was the one who stepped in and made the basic decisions. Arnold Lawrence also feels that his father was an understanding person who had a considerable capacity to make peace: he could often find the right words to ease family tensions. Also, through his knowledge of people and skill in handling social situations, he was able to make others feel better, an ability T.E. grew up to possess as well. Although most of the time he left the handling of the children and the household to Sarah, on occasion he would raise his voice to intervene when he felt that she was being unduly harsh, and she would subside.[6]

T.E. Lawrence wrote of his mother to Charlotte Shaw from India in 1927:

> To justify herself she remodelled my father, making him a teetotaller, a domestic man, a careful spender of pence. They had us five children, and never more than £400 a year: and such pride against gain, and such pride in saving, as you cannot imagine. Father had, to keep with mother, to drop all his old life, and all his friends. She by dint of will raised herself to be his companion: social things meant much to him: but they never went calling or on visits together. They thought always that they were living in sin, and that we would some day find it out. Whereas I knew it before I was ten, and they never told me: till after my Father's death something I said showed mother that I knew, and didn't care a straw.[7]

Later in his life Lawrence would intermittently reveal the truth to carefully chosen friends. In 1924 he wrote to Hogarth: 'I don't think my elder brother knows anything of that story of our origins, which I sent you. I told A. [Arnold] a little of it, three years ago, when I had an opportunity.'[8] The following year, again discussing his mother, he told Charlotte:

> Yet I do not think you are right in seeing her suffering from honesty: for she had never any money before she married. It was my father who was wonderful in throwing up all his comforts to go away with her: and I never remember him being sorry at having so little, as we grew bigger. Mother was always caring (to my mind) too much about such inessentials as food and clothes. Life itself

doesn't seem to me to matter, in comparison with thought and desire. That was how my Father acted. Our pinched life was very hard on him – or would have been, if he had pinched: only he didn't. He was pinched, instead, and that's a mere trifle.[9]

This is a classic example of how Lawrence could weave truth and untruth seamlessly together to create his desired image of himself. In fact, by the social standards of the time his father had more than enough money to keep his family, if not in luxury, certainly in comfort – and comfort that included two live-in servants. In the 1901 population census the entries for 2 Polstead Road, Oxford, record, in addition to the Lawrence family, two women, both single, both aged twenty-three: Rose Betteridge, a housemaid, and Annie Ivings, a cook.

On 13 March 1888, shortly before his flight from Ireland, Thomas Chapman had signed an indenture, the terms of which assigned his life interest in the family estates to his brother Francis and gave Thomas an annuity of £200 a year for life. By 1916 he had also inherited other capital amounting to £20,000. This should have yielded an annual income of about £1000 and allowed a very indulgent lifestyle – in stark contrast to the image of his family life that Lawrence liked to promote.[10] When Thomas Chapman died in 1919, his estate after probate was given as worth £17,828. Today that would be the equivalent of anything from £700,000 upwards to £1 million. Money was not a problem for the Lawrences. T.E. Lawrence's exaggerated picture of a family with limited means is another example of the boy in the mask. If his parents were presenting a false image of themselves, why shouldn't he too be cavalier with the truth? After all, it created a rather heroic picture of a family struggling valiantly with straitened finances.

In 1933 Lawrence subtly retouched the family story again, this time by revising a draft of Basil Liddell Hart's forthcoming biography of him. Lawrence wrote: 'Your p.1. The second paragraph. There are (as I hinted at Hindhead) things not quite desirable in this. Without wanting to censor I suggest alternatives – written with the allusiveness that hints at knowledge refusing to betray itself except between the lines'.[11] There is a studied coyness about this advice which smacks of Lawrence's habit of 'backing into the limelight'. Nevertheless, his concern here to tone down details of his family origins is justified in one respect: he had to protect his mother. Yet he still couldn't resist a chance to leave the tantalized reader wondering. Either way, such 'allusiveness' would hardly divert attention from sensitive family matters; on the contrary, it would tend to do the opposite. It is, in fact, typically Lawrence. His revision for Liddell Hart went as follows:

He was of mixed race. His father's family were Elizabethan settlers from England, favoured in gaining land in County Meath by Walter Raleigh, a connection. During three hundred years of Irish domicile they never married into Ireland, but chose their wives from intruders such as themselves, from England, from Holland even. His mother was Island Scottish in feeling and education, but her parentage was part English, part Scandinavian. The sympathy of his home was Irish, all the stronger for being exiled. Wales of the Atlantic coast had no share in him, after his first year.

The friends of his manhood called him 'T.E.', for convenience and to show him that they recognized how his adopted surnames – Lawrence, Ross, Shaw, whatever they were – did not belong. The father's self-appointed exile reduced his means to a craftsman's income, which the landowning pride of caste forbade him to increase by labour. As five sons came, one after the other, the family's very necessaries of life were straitened. They existed only by the father's denying himself every amenity, and the mother's serving her household "like a drudge". Observers noted a difference in social attitude between the courtly but abrupt and large father, and the laborious mother. The father shot, fished, rode, sailed with the certainty of birthright experience. He never touched a book or wrote a cheque. The mother kept to herself, and kept her children jealously from meeting or knowing their neighbours. She was a Calvinist and ascetic', though a wonderful housewife, a woman of character and keen intelligence, with iron decision and charming, when she wished.[12]

Here, what initially seems to be an honest, straight-talking account is another example of Lawrence's yarn-spinning rather than a frank attempt to assist a biographer. Arnold Lawrence vehemently rejected this picture painted by his elder brother, commenting that the family had, 'a vast number of holidays, mostly in expensive hotels. There was never the least shortage of excellent food. My father denied himself no amenities (except drink, and that because he had become teetotal).' Arnold claimed his brother had completely misrepresented their mother's lifestyle: 'I emphatically deny that my mother served 'like a drudge'; she kept two maids, a charwoman, a gardener; spent the mornings shopping (mainly for food) and seldom did any housework. She did not attempt to keep her children from the neighbours, and met them herself freely. She was neither a Calvinist nor ascetic.[13]

This revision of Liddell Hart's biographical draft is another example of Lawrence being cavalier with the truth and quite untroubled by moral qualms. He neatly mixes fact with fiction so that it's hard to work out where one ends and the other begins. His rewrite is totally accurate until you reach the words 'did not belong', referring to his name changes. Thereafter it is largely fabrication.

Whatever has been said about the remarkable qualities of Lawrence's mother
– and she could be kind and affectionate – she was at times tyrannical and opin-
ionated, a person of iron will and rigid principle. She could also be very difficult.
In her later years she lived for a short while in the country with Robert Falcon
Scott's widow, the sculptress Lady Kathleen Scott, who at one time had a 'crush'
on Lawrence.

Lady Scott was ill and in bed. She described Lawrence's mother as 'like a
figure in the Old Testament', who, when the national anthem came on the radio,
would stand bolt upright with Lady Scott lying to attention in bed to keep her
company. Eventually she found living with Mrs Lawrence so trying that, rather
than ask her to leave, she herself left and went to stay with someone else.[14]

For Thomas Chapman his low social profile and role as model husband and
father were merely necessary disguises. In Ireland in the 1880s he was presented
with a stark choice: to renounce his passion for his children's governess and try
to repair the damage done to his marriage, or to desert his wife and family and
run away with his new love. He chose the latter and it must have taken considerable courage to do so. Yet he never lost his longing for his native land and for the
rolling acres of his father's estates in Westmeath and suffered frequent bouts of
nostalgia for the carefree life of gentility he had left behind.[15] Lawrence explained
the repercussions of his father's decision in one of the most important letters he
ever wrote. Penned to Charlotte Shaw from India in that key year of 1927, it bears
the stamp of truth:

> Mother is rather wonderful: not very exciting [this has always been misread as
> 'but very exciting']. She is so set, so assured in mind. I think she 'set' many years
> ago: perhaps before I was born. I have a terror of her knowing anything about
> my feelings, or convictions, or way of life. If she knew they would be damaged:
> violated: no longer mine. You see, she would not hesitate to understand them:
> and I do not understand them, and do not want to. Nor has she ever seen any of
> us growing: because I think she has not grown since we began. She was wholly
> wrapped up in my father, whom she carried away jealously from his former life
> and country, against great odds: and whom she kept as her trophy of power.
> Also she was a fanatical housewife, who would rather do her own work than
> not, to the total neglect of herself. And now two of my brothers are dead, and
> Arnie (the youngest) and I have left her, and avoid her as our first rule of exis-
> tence: while my eldest brother is hardly her peer or natural companion. It is a
> dreadful position for her, and yet I see no alternative. While she remains herself,
> and I remain myself it must happen. In all her letters she tells me she is old and
> lonely, and loves only us: and she begs us to love her, back again, and points us

to Christ, in whom, she says, is the only happiness and truth. Not that she finds happiness herself.

Of course I shouldn't tell you all this: but she makes Arnie and me profoundly unhappy. We are so helpless: we feel we would never give another human being the pain she gives us, by her impossible demands: and yet we give her the pain, because we cannot turn on love to her in our letters, like a water-tap: and Christ to us is not a symbol, but a personality spoiled by accretions of such believers as herself. If you saw her, you whose mind has not grown a shell-case, perhaps you could show her other sides and things of which she does not dream. If only she would be content to loose hold of us.

His mother, he added, had been brought up as, 'a child of sin in the Island of Skye by a bible-thinking Presbyterian, then a nurse-maid, then "guilty" (in her own judgement) of taking my father from his wife...' This candid outpouring about his mother ends with perhaps the most revealing comment of all:

One of the real reasons (there are three or four) why I am in the service is that I may live by myself. She has given me a terror of families and inquisitions. And yet you'll understand she is my mother, and an extraordinary person. Knowledge of her will prevent my ever making any woman a mother, and the cause of children. I think she suspects this: but she does not know that the minor conflict, which makes me a standing civil war, is the inevitable issue of the discordant natures of herself and my father, and the inflammation of strength and weakness which followed the uprooting of their lives and principles. They should not have borne children.[16]

Yet in his book *The Mist Procession* Lord Vansittart, a distant relative, wrote: 'Father knew all about Lawrence long before youth sprang at fame with exuberance and panache. Lawrence had Vansittart blood, though "my people" did not tell about that. His grandmother, Louisa Vansittart, was all right but of his Chapman father mine thought little and nobody else thought at all'.[17] Lawrence knew about the Vansittarts. He wrote to Charlotte Shaw in 1926 about the writer who lived in the Vansittart ancestral home on the River Thames: 'that poor sorrowful person Mary Borden; who lives in Bisham (do you ever see her?) among all sorts of my ancestral Vansittart portraits.'[18] Lord Vansittart may have held a poor opinion of Lawrence's father but this man of whom 'nobody else thought at all' cut a quietly impressive figure to observers in Lawrence's Oxford days: tall, abrupt but courtly, shy but very kind, and considered by L.C. Jane (who coached Lawrence in his last year at school and while he was at the university) to be one of the most charming men he ever met, resembled by his son in many ways.

Like his father, William Chapman, he sported a beard – a red one – partly no doubt to dignify 'Mr Lawrence' with a fashion of Victorian male society and partly, no doubt, to help disguise the fugitive Mr Chapman. This was a thought that had obviously occurred to Arthur Kerry, a school friend of Lawrence's, who commented that Chapman, 'was always waving when we passed him – very friendly looking,' and was 'stately, courtly and friendly, an obvious aristocrat in hiding.'[19] Kerry described Chapman in Oxford as often to be seen wearing a Norfolk jacket and breeches.

Lawrence and his brothers were closer to their father than has sometimes been thought. Arnold talked of him as 'our ever-considerate and loving father' and is also on record as saying of him: 'T.E.'s words "I liked him so much," apply to me too.'[20][21] Arnold also quickly corrected anyone who suggested that his father was weak, commenting emphatically: 'Both parents had strong personalities.'[22]

Their father reciprocated his sons' affection and took great pride in their achievements. During the war, in 1917, T.E. Lawrence's friend, E.T. Leeds, Assistant Keeper of the Ashmolean in Oxford, had come across Lawrence's father sitting in the Oxford Union Society's smoking room and had congratulated him on his son's award by the French of the Croix de Guerre for the capture of Aqaba. Mr Lawrence hadn't heard about it and was visibly moved. Leeds wrote: 'It was news to him and I can see him now shaking with pride, speechless until at last he rose to his feet saying, "I must tell his mother", and hurried away.'[23] Contrary to the received belief that he was a rather insignificant figure always in the background – a contrived impression reinforced by the unquestioning acceptance of some biographers – Thomas Chapman was quite the opposite: courteous and friendly, yet forceful and resolute when necessary, and a man of both attractive personality and considerable character.

He is recorded as 'Thomas Lawrence' on all his sons' birth certificates except the first, Bob's, where he gives his real surname of Chapman. His rank or occupation is entered variously as 'gentleman', 'of independent means' and 'retired merchant.' These certificates are like a synoptic documentation of the life led by Thomas Chapman and Sarah, a nomadic, unsettled and unsettling existence, during which they were always looking over their shoulders, always moving on. From Ireland they went first to remote Tremadoc in north Wales (where T.E. Lawrence was apparently born), then to Kirkcudbright in Scotland, briefly to the Isle of Man, then to Jersey, Dinard in northern France, the New Forest, and finally and permanently to Oxford.

Meanwhile their young sons (in 1896 Bob was eleven, Ned eight, Will seven and Frank three, while Arnie was not born until 1900) had become quite accustomed to an itinerant life, the constant moves bringing them new friends, new experiences, new discoveries. Ned, however, soon made the discovery that rather than engage his intellectual curiosity profoundly shocked him – of his parents' real identities. One can only imagine his feelings on finding that his father was really an Anglo-Irish gentleman living under an assumed name with a woman who wasn't his wife. Of course, before Victorian *mores* were swept away by the First World War such irregular unions risked social disaster, and fear of exposure could turn a family self-protectively in on itself and so, as with the Lawrences, make it more close-knit. A.W. Lawrence told the biographer John Mack that his brother had worked out by the time he was ten that he was illegitimate from remarks he had overheard his father making to a solicitor.[24] In his later youth Lawrence would occasionally drop teasing hints about his Irish roots. On his twentieth birthday in 1908, while on a cycling tour of France, he had written to his boyhood friend 'Scroggs' Beeson back in Oxford, commenting casually: 'My father is Irish you know.'[25] Sometimes, as already mentioned, he would tell trusted friends the truth. In 1914, when he was twenty-six, he confided to Colonel Newcombe that his parents 'were not married.'[26]

There is anecdotal evidence of what Lawrence is supposed to have known before the war about his family origins. The way he reacted to this knowledge offers a rare insight into his mind. In his youth he became a loner; he didn't like group activities such as sports; he liked to be different and this was no doubt partly because he was different, but it was also partly an unspoken declaration. If his parents were forced to live a lie and deceive their sons and their friends, then he would tacitly register his disapproval by distancing himself and purposely developing unusually individual ways.

Canon Edgar Hall, of course, was one who was aware of the quirks of this created persona. He said: 'His eccentricity seemed too pronounced. Or was it that he always wore a mask, the outer covering of which was at school irreverently termed by us his "grin"?'[27] So he would ride his bicycle up hills and walk it down; he would read all night with the curtains drawn; he would even deprive himself of food and sleep just to discover what effect it would have on him. Then there was his claimed stint as a runaway, teenage army gunner with the Royal Artillery in Cornwall; and, of course, the bungalow that his father had had built exclusively for him. When decoded, all these attitudes, affectations and actions can be seen as reactions to an emotional dilemma. They were a cryptic protest, an outward expression of his shock discovery that his family was an invention.

His parents' fears that they would be unmasked are made painfully evident in a revelatory letter from Thomas Chapman to his sons. It was almost certainly written in the unsettling early days of the war and is a straightforward admission of the secret the parents had always kept from their sons. Both Thomas and Sarah were burdened by guilt about the deception. Mrs Lawrence for example, always referred to Mr Lawrence as 'Tom' or 'the boys' father', never as 'my husband.'[28] A.W. Lawrence is on record as saying that T.E. had told him that their parents were 'a genuine love-match', but Arnold added adamantly, and revealingly, that, despite this, both parents 'thought they were damned.' [29]

That in his confessional letter Chapman addresses his sons as 'you all' (which leads one to feel that he was writing to at least three of them and more probably four), and mentions that his brother is dead, shows that he must have written the letter after 19 May 1915, when his brother died at South Hill, and before his third son, Will, who was in the 3rd Battalion, Oxford and Buckinghamshire Light Infantry, was killed in France five months later on 25 October. Thomas's fourth son, Frank, a second lieutenant in the Third Gloucesters, had been leading his men forward preparatory to an assault when he was killed on 9 May, just ten days before the death of Francis Chapman, the uncle of whose existence he never knew. A year earlier on 24 May 1914 Thomas Chapman's cousin, Sir Benjamin Chapman, the unmarried sixth baronet, had died in Dublin. Fate and unexpected genealogical devolution had now, and very likely to his dismay, turned Mr Thomas Lawrence of Polstead Road, Oxford into Sir Thomas Chapman, seventh baronet of Killua Castle.

The demise of close family members may bring with it intimations of one's own mortality. The death of Francis – Thomas's only surviving brother, who had been his best man at his ill-starred marriage in 1873 and had been, in Thomas's words, 'always loving to me' – followed by the loss of a young son in war, within days of each other, must have been a major blow to him. There was death and grief now on two sides of his family and then too there was the danger that the unexpected and unwanted devolution of the title upon him might reawaken in Ireland local curiosity about the whereabouts and doings of the vanished seventh baronet. These family deaths, together with the fact that he was approaching his seventieth year and now had yet another family secret to keep under lock and key – his title – must have worried him and perhaps made him look back with some misgivings at what he had made of his life. It seems to have aroused in him a need to place on record the truth about his and his son's real forbears.

It is probable, therefore, that he wrote the letter in the summer of 1915 to his sons, Bob, Ned, Will and Arnold. On the envelope is written: 'To my Sons, (But not to be opened except Mother & I are dead.) – OR when Mother desires to.':

My dear Sons,

I know this letter will be a cause of great sorrow & sadness to you all, as it is to me to write it. The cruel fact is this, that your mother & I were never married.

When I first met mother, I was already married. An unhappy marriage without love on either side tho' I had four young daughters. Yr mother and I unfortunately fell in love with each other & when the expose came, thought only of getting away & hiding ourselves with you Bob, then a baby. There was no divorce between my wife & myself. How often have I wished there had been! Then I drank & mother had a hard time but happily I was able to cure myself of that. You can imagine or try to imagine how yr Mother & I have suffered all these years, not knowing what day we might be recognized by some one and our sad history published far and wide. You can think with what delight we saw each of you growing up to manhood, for men are valued for themselves & not for their family history, except of course under particular circumstances. My real name when I met yr Mother was Thomas Robert Tighe Chapman (see Burke's Peerage, under Chapman) & by unexpected deaths I am now Sir Thomas Chapman Bart but needless to say I have never taken the Title. There is one little gleam of sunshine in the sad history, namely, that my Sister who married my cousin Sir Montagu Chapman, & my brother Francis Vansittart Chapman of South Hill (my father's place; the life interest of which I agreed to sell) were always loving to me & it is thro' their goodness that I have been enabled to leave you the greater part of the sum I have left. My brother at his death left me £25000, & my sister in her Will has bequeathed me £20000, but owing to the wording of her Will I shall not receive this £20000 if I die before her. She is alive but a great invalid & no fresh Will of hers wld be valid tho' I know she intended and wished this £20000 to go to you all, if I shld die before her. She for many years gave me £300 a year, which, with my own fortune, enabled us all to live fairly comfortably & saved Mother and me great pinching to make ends meet & also kept me from drawing on my Capital for every day expenses. Bob's name was registered in Dublin (near St. Stephen's Green) as 'Chapman'; hence his name in my Will. I shld recommend him retain his name of Lawrence; a man may change his sirname [sic] anytime & need not take legal steps to do so, except he is expecting to inherit places or moneys from others, who know him by his former name.

I can say nothing more, except that there never was a truer saying than "the ways of transgressors are hard." Take warning from the terrible anxieties & sad thoughts endured by both yr Mother and me for now over thirty years!

I know not what God will say to me (yr Mother is the least to be blamed) but I say most distinctly that there is no happiness in this life, except you abide in Him thro' Christ & oh I hope you all will.

Father.[30]

ELEVEN

A Child of Sin

IF LAWRENCE'S father's family history was darkened by illicit liaison in the last generation, it might be expected that Lawrence would have found at least conformity and social respectability on his mother's side to provide an acceptable family origin and orientation. But Lawrence's mother's antecedents were even more of a mystery than his father's, which were not so much mysterious as simply concealed.

When the poles of Lawrence's ancestry are contrasted, it seems obvious why a young man of his sensibility and intellect should have found the lines of his developing character entangled in emotional turmoil. In short, he had had suddenly to come to terms with the fact that his father was an aristocrat in disguise and on the run, and his mother a woman of lowly origin with a questionable family background. There is no doubt, nevertheless, that Lawrence's mother was a remarkable woman, remarkable not so much for anything she did but for what she was, and her influence on her most gifted son has been emphasized by the more perceptive writers and with persuasive authority by biographer John Mack. However, her family origins have remained obscure and controversial, even to Arnold Lawrence, who wrote to me that he would have made the essential facts publicly available long before to prevent idle speculation, had he known them. He told Mack that his mother had told T.E. that her own mother had died of alcoholism. Although Arnold thought his mother never knew who her father was, I shall show that it is probable that she did know, or certainly had an inkling of his identity.

In his article on Lawrence in the Dictionary of National Biography (DNB) for 1931-40, Sir Ronald Storrs gave Lawrence's mother as 'Sarah Madden, the daughter of a Sunderland engineer … brought up in the Highlands and afterwards in Skye.' Storrs was intrigued by the rather romantic mystery of Lawrence's Irish roots and went to Ireland and stayed with the Fetherstonhaughs at Rockview while trying to uncover information about the Chapmans.[1] Roughly the same history as Storrs' DNB entry was given by Lawrence to Charlotte Shaw, except that this time it is not corrupted by half-truth. His account, like most of his utterances on matters he considered genuinely important, is refreshingly simple and frank: 'My mother is very unusual and remarkable. Remember that she was brought up as a charity child in the island of Skye, and then had to fend for herself…'[2]

From this and his comment elsewhere that his mother had been 'a child of sin', it would suggest that she was illegitimate and had been brought up in an orphanage or some similar institution. Lawrence told Basil Liddell Hart that his mother was island Scottish in feeling and education but that her parentage was part English, part Scandinavian. A part Norse ancestry was also given to Robert Graves. But there are other clues. The only publication in which there seems to be some concrete evidence is *T.E. Lawrence by his Friends*, in which his mother's year of birth is given as 1861. On the birth certificates of her five sons her maiden name appears sequentially as 'Laurence' [sic], 'Maden,' 'Jenner,' 'Junner,' and 'Junner.' The 1861 year taken in conjunction with Storrs' reference to Sunderland, narrows the field of inquiry and, as Aldington found, although there was no 'Maden' recorded in the birth records for 1861, there *was* a 'Sarah Junner' and she *was* born in Sunderland. This entry is almost certainly that of T.E. Lawrence's mother.

An attempt to establish the full ancestry of Lawrence's mother presents a problem that reflects Lawrence's own dilemma: how to reconcile the extraordinary contradictions of his parental origins. The pride, or stigma, attached to family antecedent and standing doesn't matter so much these days but in Lawrence's time it mattered a great deal. So who was Lawrence's mother? It seems at first that the conclusion reached by Aldington that she was a Miss Sarah Junner is correct, but the evidence for this is not entirely convincing. Lawrence wrote that his name had no better foundation than his father's whim and was not even his mother's name. Yet, in that 1927 letter to his solicitor about changing his name, he had said of his mother: 'I believe Lawrence was the name of her supposed father: but her mother (called Jenner) was not married to the original Lawrence.'[3] To Charlotte Shaw he implied that his maternal grandmother was Scottish and expanded this in a letter to her husband where he said she was a Gordon. Gordon is a Scottish clan name with a territorial root in Berwick and its dependent family names or septs are Adam, Adie, Crombie, Edie, Huntley, Milne and Todd. Add to these Madden, MacAlister, Maclellan and McCatten, thrown up by rumour and speculation over the years, and the obfuscation is complete.

So I went to Sunderland to try to find Lawrence's mysterious maternal grandparents. He had clearly taken pains to try to establish his parental antecedents, because the general outline he gave his early biographers is a fairly accurate précis of the true histories that emerged from a more thorough investigation.

Lawrence's mother's birth certificate records her as a Sarah Junner, born on 31 August 1861 at 7, William Street, North Bishopwearmouth, Sunderland. Sarah's mother had her baptized at St Michael's Church, Bishopwearmouth on 22 September and registered her birth three days later. That this Sarah 'Junner' was Lawrence's mother is confirmed not only by the Junner maiden name, which occurs on the last two Lawrence boys' birth certificates and in variant form on a third, but also by a home letter of Ned Lawrence's of 1915 expressly written on his mother's birthday and dated 31 August. We now come to the interesting facts. On Sarah's birth certificate her parents are given as 'John Junner', a 'shipwright', and 'Elizabeth Junner, formerly Junner'. Formerly Junner? That seemed odd. By coincidence there was a national population census in 1861 and the returns for Sunderland were completed by May. Lawrence's mother was born four months later but in the census, which is comprehensive, accounting for everyone and anyone in the borough at the time, there was not a single mention of a John Junner. From Sarah's birth certificate it could be deduced that her parents – both seemingly Junners – were related. As a result, there has been speculation over the years that they might have been cousins. This proved unfounded because John Junner clearly never existed; he was an invention, a fictitious father and husband made up by Elizabeth Junner. Lacking family support, socially isolated, and no doubt ashamed at being a single woman with an illegitimate child, she had obviously attempted to disguise her plight by trying to give the impression on the birth certificate that she was married. However, the fact that she entered 'John' as the Christian name of her non-existent husband proved to be highly significant.

As though all this documentation were not confusing enough, there were now further puzzles and complications, arising from census, baptism and marriage certificates, that needed clarification, and which, initially, seemed intractable. In short, there looked to be two Elizabeth Junners. Day after day I was glued to the census microfilm but found only one other Junner family, which was not the one I was looking for. The less likely candidate to be T.E. Lawrence's grandmother was an Elizabeth Junner living in 1861 at 72, Church Street in the township of Monkwearmouth Shore. She appears in the census return as one of two daughters of a shipwright called Christopher Marriner, who had two grandchildren: James A. Junner, aged two, and William Junner, aged two months. The Christian names of both Marriner's daughters are partially obscured by overwriting but both women are given as married, one aged twenty-four, the other twenty-five, both born in Monkwearmouth.

The younger daughter's surname is still given as Marriner (her maiden name) while the elder's is entered as Junner. That the obscured Christian name of the elder woman was Elizabeth, that her married name was Junner, and that she was Christopher Marriner's daughter are all confirmed by both the Monkwearmouth marriage and baptism registers. An Elizabeth Marriner, aged twenty, is recorded as marrying a Walter Junner, a twenty-two-year-old seafarer, at St Peter's Parish Church, Monkwearmouth on 5 September 1853. Baptism records show that Elizabeth and Walter Junner had two sons, James Alexander and Walter (the census entry was probably inaccurate in giving him as William), born in 1858 and 1861 respectively. The date of birth of the second son, Walter, was 7 February 1861. T.E. Lawrence's mother was born on 31 August that year, so it is virtually impossible that this Elizabeth Junner gave birth to Lawrence's mother less than seven months after having a son.

So where was the other far more interesting Elizabeth Junner? After five days in Sunderland Reference Library going through the census returns I had found only the Walter Junner family. Of the elusive Elizabeth there was not a sign. I was beginning to despair and by this time some of the library staff, who had become infected with my eagerness to solve the Junner conundrum, were as disappointed as I was that my research had so far drawn a blank. They would creep up and inquire in a whisper, 'any luck?' or 'found it?' I would shake my head. Then, as I spooled through the very last reel, it suddenly leaped out from the page. 'Roker Terrace', it read, and, at the bottom, the name 'Elizabeth Junner'. To my astonishment, above this entry, inscribed eight times one above the other, was the surname 'Lawrence'. I found myself blurting out 'That's it, that's it!' The library staff gathered round me.

To my amazement the search had come full circle back to the name 'Lawrence'.

The reason that there had been no census entry for an Elizabeth Junner at 7, William Street (where she was to give birth to Lawrence's mother) was because when the census was taken in April, Elizabeth was living at a rather more salubrious address. She was recorded as being in domestic service at 1, Roker Terrace, Monkwearmouth Shore with a family whose head was a man of some means. His household included two domestic staff, of whom an Elizabeth Junner – entered as unmarried, aged twenty-eight, house servant, born in Scotland – was one. Now we come to the really fascinating entry. The name of this family by whom Elizabeth Junner was employed was Lawrence.[4]

The pieces started to fall into place. According to the census, these Sunderland Lawrences – by extraordinary coincidence called Thomas and Sarah – had six children, the one of interest being the eldest son, John, whose birth certificate says he was born on 16 November 1842 in Chepstow, Monmouthshire. In 1861 he was eighteen and, according to the census, unmarried and a 'ship carpenter' by trade. When I placed these facts about John Lawrence side by side with the sparse recorded information about 'John Junner' (the purported identity of 'Sarah Junner's' father as recorded by Elizabeth Junner on her daughter's birth certificate) there was an uncanny similarity. This is almost certainly because the 'John Junner, shipwright' of Sarah's birth certificate and the 'John Lawrence, ship carpenter' of the census were one and the same person. This was surely T.E. Lawrence's maternal grandfather.

I had always had a nagging suspicion that the name Lawrence had not just been plucked out of the air by Lawrence's father when he and Sarah left Ireland, because Barbara Casey and others in Westmeath had told me they were sure the Chapman governess was called Miss Lawrence. It is unlikely that 'Lawrence' would have been one of the first surnames that would have come randomly to Chapman's mind as a cover replacement for his own when he fled Westmeath. It is clear that he had decided to use the surname that Sarah had assumed. So, if my research was substantially correct, then the name of Lawrence had a firm foundation in fact, which both disposed of the mystery surrounding the origins of T.E. Lawrence's mother and established for the first time an accurate, if irregular, maternal genealogy. The evidence strongly points to T.E. Lawrence's mother being the daughter of John Lawrence; and the maiden name of Laurence [sic], which later appeared on the birth certificate of her first son, Robert/Bob, suggests that she probably knew this.

I felt that my discovery had added a new dimension to an hitherto obscure family history, and so in 1988 I published the key facts in a west-country newspaper to mark the centenary of Lawrence's birth. Jeremy Wilson read my article, enlisted an interested genealogist to follow it up, and belatedly incorporated the essential information in an appendix to his authorized biography – but failed to credit me with what surely was a major revelation. However, some years later, on his online 'T.E. Lawrence Studies List', he kindly acknowledged me as the source of what he generously termed 'a remarkable discovery'.

By the late 1920s, if not before, Lawrence himself seemed to have been aware of his mother's 'Lawrence' family connection. In the 1927 letter to his solicitor about his planned name change he had said that he believed Lawrence was the name of his mother's supposed father, but that *her* mother, whom he thought was called Jenner, had not been married to the original Lawrence. He clearly wasn't sure, because in the next paragraph he added that it had never struck him to ask his father 'the facts of the name of Lawrence.'[5] And in the same year he wrote to his American publisher friend, Frank Doubleday, about the Lawrence name, 'my father chose it for me because it meant nothing, to his family.'[6] Two years earlier he had written to Charlotte Shaw, 'The Lawrence thing hasn't any better foundation than my father's whim.'[7] Nonetheless, Lawrence's hints to his two official biographers turn out to be accurate. His mother's parentage *was* part English, part Scandinavian, and her father *did* live in Sunderland where he *did* work as an engineer of sorts. So Lawrence's mother, 'Mrs Lawrence', the illegitimate 'wife' of an Irish aristocrat, began life as a disguised 'Miss Lawrence', the illegitimate daughter of a Sunderland ship's carpenter.

John Lawrence, her probable father, came from a family that would have aspired to membership of the burgeoning middle class of Victorian England: respectable, reasonably comfortably off, with a professional man at its head, and no doubt possessing a strong sense of civic duty and a belief in the virtue of hard work and the importance of social position. However, from Lawrence's mother's birth certificate, where the only true facts about her father are that his Christian name was John and that he was a shipwright journeyman, and from rumours of family secrets and obscure origins which over the years have filled a vacuum created by a lack of information, it could not be guessed that the head of the Lawrence household at Roker Terrace was a Lloyd's Register shipping surveyor. This man, Thomas Lawrence, was born in Swansea, Wales, in 1808. In the 1830s he had married a Sarah Sergeant, a native of Chepstow in Monmouthshire, and while they lived there, between 1838 and 1848, she bore him four children, two boys and two girls – Jane, Fanny, John and Harry. Promotion for Thomas took the family north to Sunderland in 1849, where two more children were born – Sarah in 1850 and Frederick in 1852.

Then, almost a decade later, the respectability and order of the Lawrence household in Sunderland was suddenly threatened with disruption. It looks likely either that John Lawrence and the house servant, Elizabeth Junner, had begun a furtive affair, or that leading up to Christmas, 1860, on a perhaps alcohol-fuelled impulse, John had seduced her (or she him?), because the relationship, whatever it was, had a worrying, unforeseen, and unwanted consequence – Elizabeth became pregnant.

Marriage as a solution would probably have been considered out of the question by both of them, and by John's parents too, if they had known of Elizabeth's condition. At eighteen John was barely more than a youth just starting out in life while Elizabeth, aged thirty-three, was fifteen years his senior and perhaps not altogether inexperienced in the ways of the world. Even if marriage *had* seemed to offer a way out of a potentially damaging family crisis, John's parents would surely not have countenanced their son marrying a woman so much older than him and whom they would probably have regarded as beneath them socially.

So the unfortunate Elizabeth left her job and domicile at Roker Terrace and in August, 1861 gave birth to Sarah in the William Street lodgings. There is one further consideration: If the affair between the teenage Lawrence son and the live-in housemaid had been one of just brief physical attraction, Elizabeth, distraught at her predicament, might well have left Roker Terrace without telling John, or anyone else, that she was pregnant. Or perhaps the truth emerged and the Lawrence parents, outraged or fearing a scandal, brusquely dismissed her and sternly rebuked their son. We shall never know now. However, given the slum where the shamed Elizabeth later gave birth to Sarah, the relationship clearly had one of these tragic, if predictable, outcomes. Elizabeth must have been hinting at the truth when she registered her child's father as John Junner, occupation shipwright, the closest approximation to John Lawrence, ship carpenter, that, presumably, she felt she dared make.

Or could it, just conceivably, have been John's father who was Elizabeth's paramour and Sarah's father? It is within the bounds of possibility. In 1861 Thomas Lawrence was fifty-three and as head of the household would have had considerable power over a resident servant. But he was to live for only seven more years, dying at the age of sixty in 1868 still working for Lloyd's Register in Sunderland. His widow, Sarah, then wrote at least three times to Lloyd's, soliciting work for her son John, who had already served a seven-year apprenticeship at William Pile, the Sunderland shipbuilders, and worked a further four years in the industry in Glasgow. As a result of his mother's importuning, he was taken on by Lloyd's, remaining in their employ for the rest of his working life, first at Liverpool, then London, Leith, Glasgow, Barrow and finally back in Sunderland, where in 1894 he was promoted to principal surveyor. He retired in 1903 and died, aged seventy, in 1912, never having married.[8]

To return to Elizabeth Junner: her surname is of Nordic origin and isn't to be found among traditional Scottish surnames, while you will find Jenner, Joiner, Joyner and Junor – all usually accepted as deriving from the medieval 'engynour', one who operated engines of war. Family tradition has it that the Junners originated in Norway or Denmark, most likely in Norway, and were seafarers. Two of them were said to have been shipwrecked near Elgin in the early seventeenth century and survived to settle in the area, one turning his back on his former calling to become an accountant, the other continuing his life at sea. Colin was one of the favourite family names and is perpetuated by the Junner descendants of today, some of whom are to be found in the Aberdeen area, which is close to the traditional territory of the Gordons – which may, in part, account for Lawrence's belief that his mother's family was of the clan. There is more definite evidence of a Gordon connection, which I shall come to later. After the putative shipwreck of its founders, the Junner family established itself in the general area of Moray Firth and the Black Isle region of Cromarty in Scotland's far north-east. Coincidentally – was it coincidence? – in the 1930s Lawrence took little-known trips to this area with two other men, one of whom was the notorious John Bruce who was central to Lawrence's flagellation complex. These trips were to a fishing village called Collieston on the east coast. They stayed at a house owned by a Mrs Ross, from where Lawrence went out to ride, swim in the sea and generally to subject himself to a harsh, Spartan regime, probably in response to a psychological compulsion linked to the humiliating wartime beating and rape he suffered at Deraa in November 1917.

In summary, Lawrence's grandmother, Elizabeth Junner, had been born and brought up in Cromarty, where her parents, George and Simona Junner, then lived. As a young woman she was to travel south to Sunderland to seek work, perhaps offered support there by Junner relations. She was to work for a time as a live-in servant in the household of the Lawrence family before an unwanted pregnancy virtually destroyed her life. To describe Elizabeth Junner's history as desperate and very sad would be no exaggeration. By the time she gave birth to Sarah she had been reduced to living (surviving would be a more apt word) in conditions which cannot have been far short of wretched. In North Bishopwearmouth, a grindingly poor, run-down part of Sunderland close to the quays of the River Wear and filled with the clamour of the expanding port, the tenement in William Street where the cast-out housemaid had managed to find a lodging was home to no fewer than twenty-three people – four families and three further lodgers; elsewhere the poorest of the poor sometimes slept twenty to a room. By the 1860s appalling overcrowding and waterless houses had made William Street scarcely fit for habitation, and slum clearance was ordered and new streets planned. T.E. Lawrence's mother's early childhood must have been both frighteningly insecure and far from happy.

The major industrial cities of mid-Victorian England were concentrations of poverty, squalor, disease, pollution and crime. Urban rivers were clogged with disease-ridden waste; factory chimneys darkened the skies with toxic smoke which settled on both buildings and people; and the din of production was cease-less. Diseases such as typhoid and cholera were rife. There were child workers in the factories day and night, and half the children living in the densely popu-lated industrial centres died before the age of five. In the 1840s life expectancy in Manchester, home of the great mills, was less than twenty-seven. Sunderland, the site of one of the earliest monastic settlements in the north of England, had been transformed into a major port famous for its coal and shipbuilding (of both sailing and then iron vessels) and known for its manufacture of a burgeoning range of goods such as ropes and bottles. By the mid-nineteenth century rapid growth had seen it become a sprawling industrial complex manifesting many of the props of that dark satanic realm powerfully evoked by the poet William Blake. It was another world altogether from the secure, sedate Edwardian Oxford of T.E. Lawrence's youth.

So the sudden change to a Wordsworthian rural surround must have been both startling and welcome to the young Sarah when, as some have it, she was taken, on the death of her mother from alcoholism (when and where Elizabeth Junner died is unknown), to live on a farm in Scotland with her ageing grandpar-ents, George and Simona Junner, both now in their late sixties.[9] According to Mrs Lawrence's friend, Elsie Newcombe, this was supposed to have been in Blairgowrie in Strathmore, Perthshire.[10] Her grandparents were apparently strict but fair, yet Sarah seems to have had a rather lonely and isolated childhood. She received an elementary education, walking two or three miles to and from school each day, and was tutored in the evangelical tradition. She attained a certain proficiency in French and developed an interest in reading. But by the late 1870s, when it is thought her grandmother died, she had moved again and was now living near Blair Atholl with her uncle, her mother's brother, also called George, and his wife Jane. This George Junner turns out not to have been, as A.W. Lawrence wrote to me, an evangelical Church of Scotland clergyman but successively a servant and a master gardener on two estates in the area owned by aristocrats. George's wife was employed as a cook. Could Elsie Newcombe perhaps have confused Blair Atholl with Blairgowrie? The Junners and Sarah later moved west to the Isle of Skye, where George, now aged fifty-six, was again employed as a gardener at Duisdale Vore on the shores of the Sound of Sleat. Sarah, now in her late teens, worked there as a milliner, assisting in the making and sale of ladies' bonnets and hat trimmings. The 1881 population census confirms her residence on Skye with the Junners, recording her as 'Sarah Laurence' [sic], George Junner's niece, aged nineteen, and born in Sunderland.[11]

What is significant about this entry is that Sarah's surname is given as 'Laurence', which suggests that her mother had at an early stage decided to give her her father's Lawrence surname; or that perhaps the strong-minded Sarah had somehow found out who her father was and had decided to assume his name. Either way, it means that her uncle on Skye must surely have been aware of the circumstances of his niece's birth and knew that her father was called Lawrence. Did Sarah and her father ever meet, or communicate? I could find no evidence for either. As already suggested, it is possible that Sarah's mother had left the Lawrences' employ in Sunderland's Roker Terrace without, tragically, telling John Lawrence that she was pregnant with his child.

The Skye George Junner had been born in Cromarty in 1826 and his younger sister, Elizabeth (Lawrence's grandmother), had been baptized in Cromarty on 9 October 1828. Now, there seemed to be an anomaly here. In the 1861 Sunderland census Elizabeth is given as aged twenty-eight, which would mean she had been born in 1833. But this doesn't agree with her baptism date. This suggests that Elizabeth's age had been incorrectly entered in the census and that there had been a confusion of the 1828 baptism with the age of twenty-eight in the census. If this is so, then in 1861 Elizabeth Junner would have been aged thirty-three.

Although further exploration of the Junner baptism and marriage records takes the genealogical trail right back through the distant reaches of Lawrence's mother's ancestry to the Cromarty of the late-seventeenth century, it doesn't add much more to an understanding of her background. What it does reveal, however, is that T.E. Lawrence clearly knew more about his maternal forbears than has been believed, because among them are those two names which he linked to himself – Gordon and Ross (see Appendix 4).[12] And he would occasionally refer to his 'Scotch grandmother'. It is also clear from his remarks about the Dorset Fetherstonhaughs in his letter to his mother of May 1924 that by the mid-1920s he had let her know that he was aware of the true history of his parents' life together and certainly knew about the Irish Chapmans.[13] Finally, there is an important conclusion that can be drawn from the 1881 census: that Sarah Lawrence did not leave Skye to join Thomas Chapman's household in Ireland until after that year. This is supported by the fact that Chapman, in his confessional letter to his sons, stated that when he and Sarah met, he was already married and had four young daughters.

Growing to womanhood on Skye, Sarah Lawrence began, in T.E. Lawrence's words, 'to fend for herself'. And now chance, in the shape of a Scottish Episcopalian Minister's visit to Westmeath, would herald a completely new life for her. The Scottish cleric clearly knew the Skye Junners and had recommended Sarah to Thomas Chapman and his wife for the post of governess-nursemaid to their young daughters. She was taken on, and the seeds of an extraordinary story were sown.

Sarah's independent spirit, stoicism, iron will, and religiosity were subsequently to affect many lives. Her son Ned would undoubtedly have found it amusing as well as ironic that his domineering mother, who often had the last word in the Lawrence home in Oxford, had even managed to have it here – on which family name would be the one to go down to posterity. After all, it is *her* father's name, not the aristocratic Chapman, which will live in history in her famous son's legendary title, Lawrence of Arabia.

TWELVE

My Native Land

THE CHAPMAN motto, *Crescit sub pondere virtus* (virtue thrives under oppression), is an apt one for any Sisyphus. It is paradoxical that of all members of the family it should be most applicable to Lawrence, whose alienation officially debarred him from its use.*

Eight years after Thomas Chapman's death in 1919 the hidden world of his Irish background was still casting its long shadow across Lawrence's life. As he approached middle age, the lingering ghosts of the family's past began to manifest themselves again. Lawrence's two years in India (January 1927 to January 1929) marked another watershed in his life, in his understanding of who he really was, in his feelings about his future, and his past. It was from India to Charlotte Shaw that some of his most revealing, explicit, and moving letters were written – about his real family history and about his parents. It was the period too when he officially shed his 'Lawrence' surname, which had hung round his neck like a millstone since the war; he changed it to Shaw two weeks after his thirty-ninth birthday, the Deed Poll reading: '… do hereby wholly absolutely and

---

* There is an extraordinary corollary to this mention of the family motto, more particularly to the Chapman escutcheon, which suggests that Lawrence and General Allenby, C-in-C British Forces in Palestine in the First World War, may have been distantly related by marriage (see Appendix 1).

utterly renounce relinquish and abandon the use of my said former surname of Lawrence ...'¹ Also while he was in India, the person who had meant more to him than anyone else as adviser and mentor, Hogarth, died. Lawrence wrote to Charlotte Shaw on 10 November 1927:

> Yesterday Buxton wired me that Hogarth is dead: and that means that the background of my life before I enlisted has gone. Hogarth sponsored my first tramps in Syria – then put me on the staff for Carchemish, which was a golden place – then moved me to Sinai, which led to the War office: which sent me to Cairo on the staff: and there we worked together on the Arab business, until the war ended: and since then whenever I was in a dangerous position I used to make up my mind after coming away from his advice.
>
> He was very wise for others, and very understanding, and comfortable, for he knew all the world's vices and tricks, and shifts and evasions and pretexts, and was kindly towards them all. If I might so put it, he had no knowledge of evil: because everything to him was fit to be looked at, or to touch.
>
> Yet he had his own position and principles, and was unmovable on them. Till I joined up he did everything for me. It was the first thing I did entirely on my own. So lately I have seen little of him: but I always felt that if ever I went back to living I'd be able to link up with him again.²

Three weeks later he was still writing to Charlotte about the loss of his mentor: 'All my letters are still about Hogarth. You were just right when you said he was a parent I could respect. He was so full of understanding, that he did not exact explanations, ever. Nor did he interfere, except by request.'³ He wrote of him again in a letter to Sir Herbert Samuel: 'Hogarth's death put me out of gear. He had been so very much to me: and I liked him more than any man that I'd ever met. I owed to him, too, everything I ever got or did, until I enlisted ... somehow, D.G.H. was riper and better than anybody. Oxford existed for me as the place where he lived.'⁴

And in early December he wrote to H.S. Ede, the Assistant Keeper at the Tate Gallery: 'But I cannot write to-day. This note is only to explain my apparent rudeness. There was a man called Hogarth, who did everything for me for about 12 years, while I was growing up: and he died lately, leaving me with a queer feeling that I had lost it all again. It is like being once more on one's own: and it will take me a few weeks to get square again.'⁵

Hogarth's death clearly hit Lawrence hard. In the ranks of the RAF, marooned in the cultural and social deserts of Drigh Road, Karachi and Miranshah on India's northwest Frontier, and with his lifelong mentor suddenly gone, Lawrence seems to have become preoccupied with the past and with his identity and antecedents. Earlier that year he had written to Charlotte Shaw, 'Also in this colourless place I have more time for speculation than ever before in my life.'[6] While the remoteness and isolation of the posting may have appealed to his need for privacy, its similarity to the landscapes of his war years disturbed him, waking half-buried memories and provoking uneasy reflection. In January 1927 he had written to Charlotte:

> The depot is dreary, to a degree, and its background makes me shiver. It is a desert, very like Arabia: and all sorts of haunting likenesses (pack-donkeys, the colour and cut of men's clothes, an oleander bush in flower in the valley, camel-saddles, tamarisk) try to remind me of what I've been for eight years desperately fighting out of my mind. Even I began to doubt if this coming out here was wise.[7]

Approaching forty and in a far-flung outpost of Empire, with little to occupy him other than to work over the remaining sections of *The Mint* (his stark notes of his harsh experience as Aircraftman Ross at RAF Uxbridge in 1922), start a commissioned translation of *The Odyssey*, write letters, read, and walk about the periphery of the camp homesick for England, he seems to have become unusually reflective, even at times brooding. This seems to have provoked both introspection and retrospection and made him question again who he was and where he truly belonged. It seems to have triggered too a kind of romantic nostalgia for his ancestral home, a wish for what he had described to Charlotte Shaw as 'a territorial root in the proper place'. As late as November 1934, six months before his death, he was still writing to her about Ireland: 'I have been wondering of late if I dare try to go back there, or go there, rather. I feel always that it would be "back", and it would be bad if it proved to be strange, after all. Wiser perhaps to keep a fiction in reserve.'[8] Some people in Westmeath claim that he did not leave it to his imagination and covertly visited both Killua and South Hill, but was too shy to intrude himself any further than the estate boundaries. One of the local gentry who had heard the rumour of Lawrence's coming to see the home of his forefathers was Colonel Magan's wife, Irene. She commented: 'It was said that Lawrence came to South Hill incognito and had a good look round.'[9] This visit could well have taken place in the early 1930s, after Lady Chapman's death.

For more than seven years Lawrence had clearly had this urge to go to Ireland and perhaps to buy some land there. From 1927 onwards he was to talk several times about it. In March of that year he wrote to the Hon Robert Butler (a son of Baron Dunboyne of Knappogue Castle in County Clare in Ireland), who had been in Egypt for some of the war and who lived in Wool, only a few miles from Lawrence's Clouds Hill cottage:

> Lady Chapman has kept South Hill, my father's own house, near Killua. But I'm told she and the daughters generally live in Earl's Court or some such place! I have the fancy, if money ever comes my way, to buy some square yards of Ireland for myself, and dig myself in there: after the old lady dies. The daughters will not bear me malice, probably. Having experienced a mother, they will not lament the absence of a father![10]

Two years on, in March, 1929, Lawrence was writing to his friend from the Arab Revolt days, fellow Irishman Colonel Pierce Joyce: 'How is Ireland? I dream of spending my next month's leave (autumn perhaps) partly there. Are there roads in Ireland, fit for motorbikes?'[11]

Further evidence supporting Irene Magan's comment that local people believed Lawrence had visited Westmeath came from Niall Fallon. He had had several long talks with a local author, Jim Reynolds, who told him that Lawrence had indeed visited Ireland, and Westmeath. According to Reynolds, a Major McVeigh, master of Drewstown House just over a mile from Killua, was a friend of Lawrence's from the war years. Reynolds said that a local man who had been McVeigh's butler claimed that Lawrence had stayed at Drewstown and that he had twice served him at dinner.

The picture of a slight, unobtrusive figure on a motorcycle gazing at Killua Castle, the modern working-man contemplating the wealthy, privileged world of his ancestors, might seem a fitting one. Lawrence was at times genuinely more at home with the ordinary man and the unemotional machine, both of which he had found in his RAF career. Yet with his sense of history and his youthful dreams of honour, chivalry and knighthood, perfectly embodied in the medieval fantasies of his favourite author, William Morris, his thoughts, as he looked at the Castle, must have lingered on the romantic ideal of inherited nobility and aristocratic derring-do symbolized by his father's grand ancestral seat. He would surely have reflected wistfully on what might have been.

In the 1927 letter to his solicitor about the legalities of changing his name, he outlined some of what he knew of his Irish family: 'Of course if Father registered me as Chapman, that will do, and there's no need to have the intermediate stage of Shaw, between Lawrence and it: for eventually, I suppose, Chapman it will have to be. There is a lot of land in that name knocking about: and I don't want to chuck it away, as Walter Raleigh, for whom I have a certain regard, gave it to my father's first Irish ancestor. I have a feeling that it should be kept in the line.'[12] He expanded on this in the same letter: 'My father was a younger son of an Irish family called Chapman, of Killua, in Co. Meath. His own place was called South Hill, also in Meath. His widow, Lady Chapman, and her daughters still live there: but Killua has been sold.'[13] However, writing to John Buchan, again in 1927, he wrongly stated that the family land received through the Raleigh connection was in Meath not Kerry:

> My father's people were merchants in the Middle Ages: then squires in Leicestershire. In Tudor times they had promoted themselves to soldiering, and had married with a Devon family: by favour of one of these cousins (Sir Walter Raleigh) they got a huge grant of County Meath in Ireland, from Queen Elizabeth: and there they lived till the Irish Land Acts did away with most of the estate. … My father had other troubles too, which made him change his name & live abroad, in Wales and England, the latter half of his life. So there weren't any Lawrence ancestors or relations: but it's not my line to say so, since the fiction is less trouble than the truth.

Unbeknown to him, he did, of course, have a Lawrence genealogy, but one again complicated by illegitimacy.

There is further persuasive evidence in his letters that Lawrence wanted one day to reclaim his lost Chapman name and at least to write under it. In that key year of 1927 he wrote to Dr Arthur Cowley, Librarian of the Bodleian Library, Oxford, whom he had known since before the war, 'I've published as Lawrence, as Shaw, as Ross: and will, probably eventually publish as C.'[15] His Irish ancestry had come to mean a lot to him, even if he knew that the Anglo-Irish (the Chapmans among them) only infrequently intermarried with the indigenous population. He told the novelist E.M. Forster that the Chapmans were 'without a drop of Irish blood in us, ever'[16]. (This is not, in fact, strictly true. At the end of the seventeenth century William, heir of the first Killua Chapman, had married Ismay Nugent, who came of Norman stock, which went right back to the twelfth century in Ireland – long before the Elizabethan and Cromwellian plantations.) Yet when the poet and Irish national icon W.B. Yeats wrote to Lawrence to tell him that he had been nominated to the Irish Academy of Letters, qualifying as the son of an Irishman, Lawrence wrote to Charlotte Shaw, 'I would like it, because it is a gesture on my part, that I am Irish: and I would like to think that.'[17]

Lawrence's interest in his Irish antecedents was an abiding one. When he was engaged on his translation of Homer's *Odyssey*, he joked to the literary critic

David Garnett, with Keats's poem in mind, that his own version ought to be called *Chapman's Homer*. His letters are dotted with allusions to what he felt were his true origins. Writing in 1929 to the Labour MP Ernest Thurtle, he said: 'I have assured myself (so certainly that all the print in the world won't shake my conviction) that I'm a very normal sort of Anglo-Irishman.'[18] He wrote thanking W.B. Yeats for nominating him to the Academy: 'I am Irish, and it has been a chance to admit it publicly,'[19] and he reproached Bernard Shaw, 'You've forgotten that I'm Irish.'[20]

In 1934 at a Christmas dinner at the painter Augustus John's house, the seating plan had put Lawrence next to one of Lady Pansy Lamb's younger sisters (two of four daughters of Westmeath's Lord Longford) and he had picked up his place-name and said, 'Ah ... Shaw ... I wondered what name they would put.' Lady Lamb's sister, thinking Lawrence was joking, asked him: 'Have you many aliases?' Lawrence replied, 'Quite a few.' But when she then quipped, 'And many nationalities?' Lawrence answered firmly, 'Always Irish.'[21] He even liked to think that his Irishness betrayed itself in his writing, telling Edward Garnett (in 1927): 'I thought my native land exuded its brogue all over my prose!'[22] He certainly liked to believe that he *sounded* Irish, referring in a letter to Lady Astor in 1931 to his 'anglo-irish tongue.'[23] Yet this Irish accent seems only to have become evident in these later years and was again probably a part of the unconscious urge to recover his Irish roots. Only a few years earlier the artist and writer Wyndham Lewis had observed that Lawrence, 'Had no brogue, only a modest little Oxford accent.'[24] In contrast Robert Graves in 1930 said that Lawrence's 'speaking intonation had changed from Oxford University to garage-English'.[25]

During his early twenties, still disturbed by his discoveries about his family, Lawrence had distanced himself from, even derided, Ireland and things Irish whenever any suggestion of a family connection inadvertently arose. Those deceptively casual criticisms in his 1913 letters home are proof enough of his need to repress a troubling and unresolved problem: how to come to terms with his illegitimacy and with his parents' secret family backgrounds. But the balm of time had brought a new perspective. His wartime achievements had ensured that he was known and respected for himself. He was a self-made man with friends and admirers everywhere, and this in turn gave him the confidence to view the Irish hinterland of his life with less anxiety and with a growing interest and pride. Certainly the compulsion towards self-denigration was always in him, but that had wider and more complex origins. By 1927 Ireland was no longer psychologically off limits to him and he wanted to reclaim his lost Irishness.

In fact, his rapprochement with his Irish homeland had begun in startling fashion even earlier. Lawrence flirted momentarily with the idea of joining the Irish Army under the charismatic rebel leader Michael Collins. In December 1920 Lawrence and Collins apparently met in London during the Anglo-Irish Treaty negotiations when Lawrence is said to have 'conveyed his support for the cause of Irish independence.'[26] He was about to start work with Churchill at the Colonial Office and deep down was still uneasy about the way the British were treating the Arabs, even when later, in 1921 at the Cairo Conference, an honourable settlement seemed to have been reached.

Lawrence finally left the Colonial Office on 1 July 1922 and in that same month was approached by Collins and offered the position of colonel in the newly formed Irish Free State Army. He must have felt both flattered and intrigued by Collins's overtures and may have been tempted by the exciting challenge – which would have been guaranteed to lift him out of his post-war doldrums – to return to his ancestral homeland and become a military midwife at the birth of a wholly new and perhaps totally independent Ireland.

The irony of the erstwhile liberator of the Arabs lending his unique expertise in irregular warfare to the armed forces of a fledgling Irish Free State would not have escaped Lawrence. It didn't escape Churchill either. The alarming prospect and potential political embarrassment of the newly dubbed 'uncrowned King of Arabia', an English national hero, becoming embroiled in a possible Irish civil war as one of Collins's officers was more than Churchill and other senior members of the British establishment could bear to contemplate. Fortunately for them, Lawrence chose instead to join the ranks of the RAF. In any case, by the end of August Collins was dead, ambushed in what to this day remain mysterious circumstances.[27]

The beginnings of the change in Lawrence's mind from dislike and rejection of his Irish ancestry to an affectionate reclamation of it can be seen if we contrast his pre- and post-war attitudes to it. When his dismissive jibes about Ireland in those home letters of 1913 are compared with his warm enthusiasm for the country and the Irish family homes in his correspondence with Charlotte Shaw and others fourteen years later, the contrast could hardly be more marked. There was a powerful longing in him, certainly from the late 1920s onward, to feel himself a part of his true family history and genealogy. The term 'my native land', which he called Ireland in the 1927 letter to Edward Garnett, is an unambiguous declaration of emotional as well as territorial allegiance. Lawrence's continual linking of himself with Ireland in personal correspondence was his private way, perhaps his only way, of reclaiming his proper identity, of being a Chapman without attracting unwanted publicity and the disapproval of the family in Ireland – not to mention the slur of illegitimacy on himself and his two remaining brothers, and the humiliation for his mother, which would undoubtedly have followed had he revealed the truth to the public. This is reflected in a letter he wrote from India in 1928 to Colonel Joyce, who had written to thank him for the gift of a copy of *Seven Pillars of Wisdom* and to invite him to stay at his home in Galway in Ireland. In his reply Lawrence mentioned his own Irish origins in Killua, but added the postscript: 'Don't tell of this. I hate having my real roots dragged up for inspection.'[28]

To some of his friends Lawrence seemed almost quintessentially Irish. 'Irish he undoubtedly was,' said Robert Graves, who, being of Anglo-Irish extraction himself, had a particular insight into the Irish character: 'He had all the marks of the Irishman: the rhetoric of freedom, the rhetoric of chastity, the rhetoric of honour, the power to excite sudden deep affections, loyalty to the long-buried past, high aims qualified by too mocking a sense of humour, serenity clouded by petulance and broken by occasional black despairs, playboy charm and theatricality, imagination that over-runs itself and tires, extreme generosity, serpent cunning, lion courage, diabolic intuition, and the curse of self-doubt which becomes enmity to self and sometimes renouncement of all that is most loved and esteemed'.[29]

A crucially important part of Lawrence's complex internal struggle undoubtedly lay in his difficulty in reconciling the artificial, illegitimate 'T.E. Lawrence' with the ideal Irish gentleman, 'Thomas Edward Chapman'. He told Frank Doubleday that 'The only authentic part of my name is the initials T.E.', adding that most people who knew him wrote to him as 'Dear T.E.' because they felt safe at that, remarking with wry humour: 'There aren't many things safe about what are beautifully called "natural" children!'[30] He peremptorily dismissed his Lawrence name in a letter of 1923 to Bernard Shaw: 'I'm going to wash out that old name, which has too many war associations to please me: and which isn't my real name, any more than Ross!'[31] Two years later at RAF Cranwell he said something similar to a young Frank Whittle, later to become the famous Sir Frank Whittle but then an aircraft apprentice. A friend of Whittle's, a young girl, had asked him if he could get Lawrence's autograph for her. Lawrence, so often kind to children, happily if uncharacteristically consented but wanted to know which name Whittle would like. Whittle replied, 'the real one, please,' to which Lawrence responded, 'I am afraid you cannot have that.' Whittle then asked, 'won't you write "T.E. Lawrence"?' Lawrence said 'certainly' but then signed with three names, Lawrence, Ross and Shaw, and mystified Whittle by adding that none of these was his real name.[32]

He commented to the writer Harley Granville-Barker that his genuine birthday initials were T.E.C. and told Robert Graves that Lawrence was a name he heartily rejected. He disparaged it further by publishing *Revolt in the Desert* under the name 'T.E. Lawrence', in single inverted commas; and in a typed letter from RAF Cranwell to Colonel Dyas, the librarian of the British Army's Staff College at Camberley, he signed himself T.E. Shaw, adding the footnote, '"Lawrence" was only a fake name, and I'm sick of it. Hence the change.'[33]

The despair of not belonging is a very real one. Lawrence felt that he was a man without roots and without a name and, if his personal nomenclature served useful purposes and was treated by him intellectually as a bit of a joke, privately it distressed him deeply. This lack of an acceptable identity is perhaps most poignantly expressed by an observation of Frank Doubleday's widow, Florence. In its pathos it conjures up the shadowy presence of Thomas Edward Chapman and evokes the latent sadness of the troubled man who lived uneasily behind the masks of Lawrence, Ross, Smith, and Shaw: 'He asked us to call him T.E., because he said that was the only part of his name which really belonged to him, and people who were fond of him should call him that.'[34]

THIRTEEN

Crazed with the Spell of Far Arabia

THE MORE I reflected on the grand world of Lawrence's lost Irish ancestry, and on its concomitant – his secret world of invented identity and created middle class image – the clearer it became that he lived simultaneously as two quite separate persons, one a charismatic, much fêted public figure, the other a very private man with a disturbing family secret, resentful of the false position he felt he had been put in by his parents.

While it is a truism that most people have both a public and a private persona, for Lawrence the two had been deeply confused by his discovery about his family and by his own complex psychology. He dealt with the problem by pretending it was something of minor importance and by deflecting the curiosity of anyone who came too close with a defensive screen of half-truths, distracting humour and a kind of manufactured indifference.

The impetuosity of the human heart can have astonishingly unforeseen consequences. Who could have guessed that an illicit, seemingly insignificant love affair in 1880s rural Ireland would trigger a series of events that would affect so many lives in Ireland and England and ultimately give the world the perennially enigmatic Lawrence of Arabia? I had uncovered a privileged Irish world behind Lawrence's self-protective façade and now, to continue an unmasking of the inner man, I set about negotiating a minefield of hunches and half-truths in the hope of establishing what were the hidden relationships that really mattered to him.

For me the key to this conundrum lay in the dedication of *Seven Pillars of Wisdom* to S.A., its enduring mystery a metaphor for both the secret yearnings of his heart and an urge to concealment and disguise engendered by having to mask a true identity with an invented one. In order to ensure that the book's dedicatee would never be discovered, Lawrence gave a number of conflicting and puzzling explanations to keep the curious at bay. Also, his impish nature would have delighted in imagining the knots people would tie themselves into trying to unravel the truth. It was a serious dedication but so typical of Lawrence deliberately to obscure its meaning. The key, I sensed, would be found in his happy, carefree, pre-war years as a young archaeologist at Carchemish. So my quest was now eastward-bound, to the little towns of Syria's hinterland, to the mountains of the Lebanon, and to the desert, which I romantically saw as the borderless, ungovernable land of the bedouin where a tyrannous sun is a constant companion and a profound silence whispers to the soul.

Imagination and research were becoming hopelessly entangled and a world away from the reality of my existence as an undisciplined student in Dublin. But now, after four hedonistic years at Trinity College and my productive wanderings in Westmeath, the east and Carchemish beckoned. Since childhood I had had an inexplicable longing for the unknown and was always drawn to what I felt was a profound if elusive truth at the heart of things. But my feet were now firmly on the ground. I was preoccupied with down-to-earth considerations, with the all-consuming practicalities of the journey to Syria. And yet I daydreamed of the gates of Arabia opening before me and spiriting me fifty-five years back into the Edwardian springtime of 1909 when Lawrence 'went singing southward when all the world was young' on his fateful journey to Syria and his destiny.

In England the Edwardian decade before the Great War was a golden time for the social élite who had the wherewithal to enjoy it; in France, and in England, this was the height of the period later dubbed the Belle Époque, with its flamboyant celebration of a confident new society and its exciting innovations and advances in the arts, science and fashion. And when in 1911 George V was crowned Emperor of India at a great durbar in Delhi, it seemed to many Englishmen to confirm Britain in her divine right and duty to preside benignly over the world forever. Yet it was in fact the watershed of Empire. Outbreaks of industrial unrest among workers such as the London dockers, poverty and malnutrition in the working class, nationalist agitation in Ireland, the suffragettes, and ominous rumblings in the distance presaging the First World War, were all warning signs that, unbeknown to many, the end of an era was imminent. Yet in those early years of the new century it must have seemed to comfortably-off, middle-class families like the Lawrences that the future would be a never-ending summer's day. A line from James Elroy Flecker's *Golden Journey to Samarkand*, a poem that Lawrence liked, 'All that calm Sunday that goes on and on', for me encapsulated it perfectly.

At home in Richmond in Surrey I went out down to the banks of the River Thames to ponder an enticing future. As the warm summer's day closed, the distances blurred and dimmed and became strangely transfigured. I strained my eyes. Where there should have been the smudged grey silhouette of trees I saw a hazed horizon dancing with heat. There was a faint, Protean figure of someone waving, and somewhere, far off, the siren sound of recitation. Fond imagining it all was but my mind raced, my heart quickened: 'Far are the shades of Arabia, where the Princes ride at noon, 'mid the verdurous vales and thickets, under the ghost of the moon...' As stillness settled like sleep over the evening river, I seemed to hear it again: 'Still eyes look coldly upon me, cold voices whisper and say – "he is crazed with the spell of far Arabia, they have stolen his wits away."'[1]

In the late summer I found myself with a variety of rather ragged baggage at Victoria Station set to board the Orient Express to journey to Paris and then on to the warm south and the parched east. Six days on the rails lay ahead, four to Istanbul's Sirkechi station, two from Hydarapasha station on the Asian side of the Bosphorus via Konia and down through the Taurus mountains and the Cilician Gates to Iskenderun, ancient Alexandretta. It was historically and geographically a part of Syria but since 1938, when the French allowed the Turks to annex it, had lain politically in modern Turkey. From here I planned a *dolmus* ride (a shared taxi) up across the border into Syria and down to Aleppo and Baron's Hotel, where Lawrence had stayed all those years ago. This was to be an oasis of rest and recuperation before travelling on south through Syria to Jordan, and to Aqaba to look at what might be left of the old fort that Lawrence and the Arabs had captured in 1917. I would then go up the Barada Gorge from Damascus and over into the Lebanon to stay with friends in Chemlan on the heights above Beirut.

The proud train with its gleaming blue *wagons-lit* steaming quietly at its London terminus bore no resemblance to the raggle-taggle collection of ancient, creaking wagons and bizarre eastern European rolling stock that would eventually puff wearily into Sirkechi station four incident-packed days and a continent later. The train clattered through the night and at dawn was crawling round the outskirts of Paris before gathering speed for Dijon, Switzerland and Lucerne, the

Simplon Tunnel, Domodossola and down onto the Lombardy plain to Milan, and thence to Venice and Trieste.

The countryside and the towns passing by seemed now less European and had hints of the east and of other cultures, other religions, other ways. We hastened through Yugoslavia and crawled through Bulgaria, minarets not spires now standing sentinel at the heart of dusty, sun-baked villages. I fretted in the stagnant, smothering heat of the late afternoon after days in a train that had wound its sluggish way through the deep, forested gorges of the Balkans and down across the tip of northern Greece to Edirne and into European Turkey. The magical part of the journey was beginning. The crumbling remains of the huge, antique walls of Constantinople and the great minarets and domes of the capital of the Caliphs came into view round the last corner of the last stretch of line in Europe, and I was suddenly alert. Before me in the deepening orange glow of twilight lay Istanbul, one of the great cities of the world, and across the Golden Horn, over the waters of the Bosphorus, Asia and the Levant. I look back on myself then with a smile and an odd affection, like a father quietly proud of the youthful adventures of an exuberant, ingenuous son full of optimistic expectation.

I remember that I found it hard to believe I was there, standing at my own small frontier of discovery and about to set foot in a world where Lawrence was to know perhaps the greatest happiness, the greatest triumph, and the greatest disillusionment of his life. The maelstrom of thought and anticipation tumbling through my mind was a heady cocktail. I arrived in Iskenderun tired, dusty and happy and was invited to stay by a kind Arab librarian I had met on the train, a slight, balding, earnest man with a moustache and wearing a shiny, pale-grey suit. It was my first experience of Arab hospitality and I found his anxious concern for my welfare touching. He couldn't do enough for me. Mahmoud took me proudly round his small library, the detached spines of some of the worn books hanging loose like hinges, insisted on my meeting his family, feeding me and giving me a bed for the night. I took some photographs of the harbour under the suspicious gaze of the Turkish naval sentries and then waited all day to get a *dolmus* or a little bus over the hills to Syria.

It seemed that no one travelled by that road to the border any more. Eventually I was on my way. The driver, a sharp-eyed, unshaven man, was irrepressibly talkative: 'You know Chicago? Yes, big, yes? Many car; I work there many year; good money; now I come back. Why you go to Halep, may be problem this way? But I take you near to border, OK?' On and on at an alarming speed we bumped and rocked along the unmetalled roads, winding up into the bare hill country, the tyres spitting dust and stones into the roadside. First came the village of Kirikhan and then on to Reyhanli. Someone started to recite an Arab poem about his horse in a singsong voice. Despite the dust and discomfort and heat everyone was unfailingly good humoured. Poor but proud, these villagers laughed and joked and gossiped away, some of them eyeing me curiously, puzzled at why I was using such basic transport when I could surely have afforded to travel in comfort. The battered little bus was constantly screeching to a halt and then abruptly taking off again, people clambering on and off almost, it seemed, on a whim, sometimes in a straggling village, sometimes in what appeared to be the middle of nowhere.

After three hours of reckless driving I was dropped in no-man's-land and in the warm dusk walked the three miles to the border post. The frontier officials eyed me up, half with suspicion, half with incredulity, because, they said, no one came to Syria along this road. Lawrence was not a name to drop into the conversation – he had long been cast in the role of Imperialist agent by many Arabs. So I said I wanted to see the little-known Syria, which was true, and that to go by shared taxi and on foot was the best way to meet the people and understand the country, which was also true. They seemed to take this as an unexpected compliment and from then on did their best to help me.

The only way down to Aleppo apparently was by a more expensive taxi on my own. They had to make a telephone call to summon it. It finally arrived, an old American car, a whorl of dust zigzagging up from the Syrian side of the border. The ride cost me more than I had budgeted for but there was no other way. I was tired and wanted to reach my destination before dark. Down through the wild, rocky scrubland we drove until, a dot in the distance, there was Aleppo with its famous citadel. Baron's Hotel was almost as I hoped it would be, its parochial grandeur speaking of older, more gracious times. There was a deliciously cool atrium with grandiose columns and a beautifully tiled floor, and tall rooms, their quietness broken only by the hypnotic swish of a fan high above. The Armenian owners, an Anglophile husband and wife, couldn't have been more welcoming. Civilization: a bath, a meal and then up to my room. I lay on the bed in the warm darkness with the distant evening sounds of the old Arab town rising up like a soothing lullaby through the open window, as my mind wandered back and forth, wondering whether tomorrow, or the day after, or the day after that, I would find what I had dreamed of finding, a journey's end that would justify all the reading and letter-writing, all the planning and hoping.

Journey's end was, in large part, S.A. Simple attribution, complicated theory and outlandish hypothesis have all been confidently put forward as the true explanations of the dedication ever since Lawrence enshrined in it his unremitting efforts to gift the Arabs freedom through the Arab Revolt. But to attempt an immediate analysis of the known evidence about S.A. was to put the cart before the horse. The right approach, I thought, was to try to understand Lawrence's mental and emotional condition just after the war – a war during which his body and mind had suffered visceral assaults – and to look at the subliminal factors underlying his need to create a deliberately cryptic dedication to *Seven Pillars of Wisdom*. What was his motivation? What kind of mind in what state of mind would make such a dedication?

When Lawrence returned to England after the war, exhausted and played-out, he must have felt like a foreigner in his own land. He had gone out to Egypt an anonymous, eager young man known for his intelligence and his specialist knowledge of Syria. He was just one of many young wartime army officers who found themselves in the eastern theatre at the start of the Great War. By its end he had become almost a celebrity and certainly a changed man. He could never be anonymous again. His state of mind was disturbed and volatile, his constitution at times almost at meltdown.

As for myself, I was simply an eager stranger in a strange land, a keen researcher on a quest, excited at being somewhere where Lawrence had once been. I was really a tourist in thin disguise, albeit a reasonably well-informed one, someone who hoped to explore as much desert and town life as his resolve and budget would allow, and so hopefully acquire some understanding and insight. Perhaps too I might briefly experience something of native life and get just a flavour of what Lawrence had so loved all those years ago. For the next few days I wandered about Aleppo – the home in Lawrence's happy, archaeological years of his great friend, Dr Ernest Altounyan. I tried to make sense of the ancient citadel with its layer upon layer of history – Hittite, Egyptian, Byzantine, Arab – and lost myself in the cool, alluring labyrinth of the suq with its constant chatter and intimate charm and its shafts of sunlight piercing the high roof and alighting here or there to illuminate a dusty corner or a half-hidden doorway. I pondered Lawrence conundrums in between sipping sweet tea mixed with cardamom seeds from little waisted glasses, as I sat with this proprietor or that outside his colourful emporium, chock-a-block with jewellery, silks, carpets or 'antiquities', amid the clamour and seductive, spicy smells of the bazaar and the hammerings of the copper suq further down the way. All about me was the busy cacophony of bargain-hunter and shop-owner settling their transactions with laughter, a handshake and the obligatory and stylized ceremony of the glass of tea. What I liked so much about this ancient Arab market of ceaseless movement and colour was its occupants' delight in giving hospitality, in observing the little rituals of good manners and simple courtesy, and in the enjoyment of exchanging news and tittle-tattle. These were the strong, binding mortars of an age-old society where Arab, Turk, Kurd and Armenian, Jew and European, Sunni and Shia Muslim, Syriac rite and Greek Orthodox Christian, all lived harmoniously together, exhibiting a civilized social behaviour and a tolerance that even in those days were becoming a thing of the past in the west.* It was a faint but clearly audible echo of what Lawrence himself had found so engaging in his pre-war years in Syria. For me it was oddly almost like being back in a packed, friendly pub in some busy, gossipy little town in Westmeath.

After four days I set off by *dolmus* for the south and Damascus, crammed into the back of a big old car with two talkative, young Damascene men who were intrigued by my using this unorthodox method of travel. We spoke in halting English punctuated by a lot of warm laughter, and the 190-mile trip to Damascus seemed to take no time at all. I was sitting on the left-hand side of the car and after a time my neck began to ache from craning to see the huge landscape to the east, barren, exposed, with no features visible to variegate the never-ending flinty terrain – a vast desert beckoning to infinity, lying captive and cowed under the relentless dominance of the sun, its little tells and dry, sunken wadis lost in a universal flatness. Somewhere over the far horizon lay the meandering Euphrates river, and hundreds of miles beyond, Iraq, and then, way off to the south, the silent, searing sand-wastes of the great Arabian peninsula.

Hidden over to the west, running north-south along the cosmopolitan Mediterranean coastline and, as though craving a cultivated security as far removed as possible from a dangerous, unknown hinterland, were Alexandretta, Antioch, Latakia, Tripoli, Beirut, Haifa, Tel Aviv, Gaza. Rising to protect them from the sweeping march of the desert were the magnificent, snow-capped mountains of the Anti-Lebanon. Over on their eastern flanks south of Aleppo lay in succession Hama, Homs, Damascus, Deraa, Amman, Maan, Aqaba, and farther

---

* At the time of writing, this historic, picturesque, enchanting Aleppo had tragically been all but obliterated, imploded into sectarian conflict, religious polarization and violent destruction.

out again the sparse settlements of the wilderness and the evocative tents of the bedouin dotted like little black smudges in the sun-trembling distances. Even now, so many years later, the memory of those places, those days, remains as fresh as summer air after rain.

Our big car bumped and rocked ever onward, past the pretty town of Hama on the Orontes River with its house-high water wheels made entirely of wood and on to Homs, with a hundred miles away to the east the romantic, Romano-Arab ruins of Queen Zenobia's doomed Palmyra, and then the final leg of the journey down to Damascus. I strained my eyes westward towards the distant Bekaa valley cradled in a fold of the mountains where there was even grander testimony to long-forgotten dynasties lost in time – the great temple of Baalbek-Heliopolis exuding grandeur from every one of its huge columns. Scattered across the desert barrenness were the remains of an astonishing continuum of civilizations and cultures and kingdoms reaching back into the dawn of history. No surprise then that to Lawrence Syria was an archaeological wonderland where youth and youthful adventure, freed of stuffy English conformity and respectability, looked set fair to go on forever.

Damascus was a cliché come true. The contrasts were stunning: characterless concrete blocks of flats and offices, then around a corner, down crazy, wandering walkways, another world – the old city. I was suddenly back in Biblical times. Crumbling adobe buildings, their plaster rendering flaking off, and an endless maze of narrow little streets where ancient Arab houses with mysterious latticed windows leaned perilously over the alleyways dappling their powdery surfaces with cool, dark shadow. Two veiled women hurrying by; a donkey standing motionless and vacant-eyed weighed down by its top-heavy burden; and here and there, recessed in a wall almost unseen, a beautifully carved wooden door behind which lay an intimate Eden – a family home with ornate arches and curtained rooms ranged round a small, flagged courtyard with palm trees, vines and decorative greenery, all silent and still in the heat of the midday sun, the only sound the plash of water tumbling from a fountain. I made friends with two Arab university students, Georges and Fouad, who were tirelessly upbeat about everything, despite the fact that they were living in a police state. They took me proudly into the history of their jewel of a city in the desert. Look, there was the site of the Victoria Hotel where Allenby and Lawrence had met on 1 October 1918! And now we were in the great Ummayyad mosque gazing upon the reputed tomb of John the Baptist, and now on a visit, through one of those wonderfully carved doorways, to Georges's family home, where kindness was a byword and hospitality embarrassingly generous.

Then another *dolmus* to the far south, through the controversial Deraa to Amman in King Hussein's Hashemite Kingdom of Jordan, the last derisory vestige of the territories created by the 1916 Arab Revolt. Then on down to Guweira and the heart-pounding experience of being invited to ride for six hours with the Howeitat tribesman through a withering heat to Wadi Rumm – that breathtaking wonder of stone in the wilderness, which so moved Lawrence – and on to the wild, remote borders of Saudi Arabia, joyously if very briefly sharing a simple nobility of existence that would soon be all but gone, overtaken by the materialism of an advancing modern world.

Rumm's huge processional way and towering sandstone walls made me want to sing in praise that such stupendous grandeur could exist at all. Moving silently – apart from the grumbling throats of the camels – through this magnificent natural architecture that would have put a cathedral to shame, with around me the lithe, gnarled bedouin with their dark, burning eyes, and, high above, a roof of motionless, pale-blue sky traumatized with heat, proved the nearest I have ever come to mystical experience. I was so moved by this other-worldly place that years later, in hospital in Dublin, coming round from a general anaesthetic after breaking my wrist, the doctors told me I had shot up in bed wide-eyed and shouted 'Wadi Rumm!'

In the glow of the dying day we shrank to dots swallowed up between the great walls of Rumm blushing pale pink in the sunset. As we sat round a brushwood fire drinking bitter coffee from little cups, without a word one of the bedu produced a rubaba, a one-stringed musical instrument. In total self-absorption he drew his bow ceaselessly across the string in a repetitive yet hauntingly hypnotic lament that perfectly complemented the great desert spaces far out in the darkness.

Finally, days later by car, I reached Aqaba and the sea. It was small, rundown, dusty and poor with ruined buildings scattered about and little sign that it had ever been anything more than a sleepy, little-used port at the tip of a finger of water pointing northward from the Red Sea. To my delight the remains of the old fort were still there. I stood in front of one of the intact stone arches and asked a puzzled, passing Arab clad in a pristine white jelabiya to take a picture of me with my little Kodak camera. Then in the dead heat of the midday sun I stood still and closed my eyes and drifted in my imagination into a past I had read about so many times before. Was it hotter than this all those years ago? Did the Turks, the handful that had been left to defend Aqaba, stare in alarm to the north at the appearance of a raggle-taggle bedouin force coming suddenly out of a sandstorm and advancing on them? Was there the muffled thunder of hundreds of charging camels and the sound of war cries spreading along an irregular line of tribesmen as Lawrence's strategic vision was fulfilled?

I was convinced that quantum leaps were simply made, that time was an impostor, and that in the distance up the valley I saw the unseeable: camel-mounted fighters advancing like a mirage through the storm of sand and dust at a headlong gallop, their rifles thrust victoriously aloft, and in their scattered midst the medieval figure of a standard-bearer holding high an Arab flag tattered and torn from the assaults of wind and sand. It was 6 July 1917 and a thousand-strong Arab force was sweeping down on Aqaba. I opened my eyes and coming slowly towards me, probably returning from some journey upcountry, was a solitary, rather drab, semi-settled tribesman on an ageing camel. There was no Arab force, no storm, no standard-bearer. And yet the spell was not broken. I could feel Auda abu Tayi's Howeitat riders milling about me, I could hear the cries of triumph, and, spreading like a ripple through the gathering of fighting men, a shared delight at the realization that hopes and dreams had been, at least in part, fulfilled, that a great adventure had begun. Aqaba, when I saw it, had relapsed into a forgotten backwater where nothing much ever happened. And yet for me on that day it had become again, just for a strange moment, the vibrant heart of a great endeavour, the epicentre of a growing revolt, the seeding-ground of self-belief. I was glad I had come. I had not been disappointed.

I returned to Damascus and then headed up the Barada and over into the Lebanon, skirting along the heights to Chemlan to stay with friends, the Joyces – Jack, a Scot, and Gudrun, his Swedish wife. Jack was an executive with the Iraq Petroleum Company and was studying Arabic at MECAS, the Middle East Centre for Arab Studies. Their friendship, generous hospitality and enlivening company relaxed me and gave me the time to contemplate again the research I had gathered over the years about the dedication to *Seven Pillars of Wisdom*. In the evenings at dusk we sat on the balcony of their house drinking Ksara rosé from the Bekaa Valley, with, far below us, Beirut, the coastal settlements in a necklace of glimmering lights, and the Mediterranean, an infinite expanse of darkness now and then momentarily lit by the phosphorescence of gently rolling surf. The world seemed full of promise, around us the enveloping warmth of the evening air, above us the deep blue of the night-skies and a vast shimmering of stars.

FOURTEEN

The Last and Lingering Troubadour

I WAS CERTAIN that for Lawrence the one place where reality and his romantic dreams of the ideal medieval life coalesced was the home of his archaeological years, the Hittite site of Carchemish at Jerablus in northern Syria. Days passed seamlessly as I sat in the sun-filled living room of the Joyces' mountain eyrie, the thronging little coastal ports marooned in a silent haze hundreds of feet below me. I laid out all my dog-eared papers on the floor and began again to try to find the clues I knew were hidden somewhere in their midst. The key surely lay in decoding and under-standing the unspoiled, pre-war Lawrence – Lawrence of Carchemish.

He was twenty-two when he took up his archaeological post there and his four years in Syria were undoubtedly the happiest of his life, only ended by the Great War. He wrote to Charlotte Shaw in 1927 that Carchemish had been 'a wonderful place and time: as golden as Haroun al Raschid's in Tennyson.'[1] He told Robert Graves, 'Till the war swallowed up everything I wanted nothing better than Carchemish, which was a perfect life.'[2] He also annotated a draft of Liddell Hart's biography (where Hart had quoted him as saying that Carchemish 'was the best life I ever lived') with the comment 'better even than the R.A.F. which was the refuge of his maturity.'[3]

Whenever I imagine Lawrence at Carchemish I see a confident, ebullient, young man released from the bourgeois restrictions of suburban Oxford, a highly intelligent romantic bursting with knowledge and curiosity. This carefree, adventurous Lawrence on the brink of amazing achievement is somehow encapsulated for me in a verse from a poem by G.K. Chesterton:

> Dim drums throbbing, in the hills half heard,
> Where only on a nameless throne a crownless prince has stirred,
> Where, risen from a doubtful seat and half-attainted stall,
> The last knight of Europe takes weapons from the wall,
> The last and lingering troubadour to whom the bird has sung,
> That once went singing southward when all the world was young.[4]

Here at Carchemish with the British Museum expedition was his medieval world brought to life again in the twentieth century: proud, independent and sometimes warlike tribesmen owing unquestioned allegiance to sheikhs in colourful robes who dispensed an arbitrary justice sanctioned by tradition. It was a benevolent autocracy, a kind of noble but barely regulated anarchy, a feudal society in the desert. Lawrence loved it all. Here you would have found a delightful, impish Lawrence, a person who has been neglected and often overshadowed by the tortured, introspective caricature of some biographical studies. Where this Lawrence is best reflected is in his letters to E.T. Leeds, first published in 1988. In the Carchemish years he wrote more letters to Leeds than to anyone outside his immediate family.[5] In 1908 Leeds had taken over from Leonard Woolley as assistant keeper of the Ashmolean in Oxford under keepers Sir Arthur Evans and then Hogarth.

These letters to Leeds overflow with enthusiasm; they are provocative, teasing, and full of the incident and gossip of Lawrence's adventures in the wide Syrian hinterland and of his visits down to Aleppo to see friends and to buy provisions and artefacts. The correspondence is a lively and infectious mélange of local news and scholarship – stories of day-to-day life on the dig, colourful descriptions of the country people and their lives, topics of archaeological interest, obvious pleasure in the life he is leading, and a gleeful indulgence in fun and games of all sorts. The letters perfectly evoke the character of a man who is fully engaged in his life and his work and is clearly happy. In light-hearted mood he would often begin and end a letter with a humorous salute: 'O Leeds!' and sign off 'salaams to' or 'salaamat'.

It is also worth mentioning that all the while Lawrence had the vital support of a loving and close-knit family. The book that gives a special insight into this, and to what he was like until the war changed him irreversibly, is the often-neglected *Home Letters of T.E. Lawrence and his Brothers*. Over the years and through the innumerable biographical portraits Lawrence has become a larger-than-life, almost unreal person. So it is sometimes forgotten that he was once able to be simply a very likeable and attractive member, if a precociously intelligent and adventurous one, of a relatively normal, comfortably off family. He was of course moulded by the influences and constraints of his class, family and time, and lurking in the background were the guilt-ridden, religious fervour of his mother and the stigma of illegitimacy. But he was not then the tormented soul he was later to become. On the Carchemish excavations he proved to be an extremely practical and professionally competent man, as the records of his work amply illustrate, while privately his inner romanticism clearly remained an intact and motivating force. He threw himself into the colourful local life and enjoyed adventures of all sorts.

A further complicating factor when trying to assess Lawrence's personality and behaviour is that his life encompassed a major turning-point in British social history – the Great War, which over-arched two quite different worlds: one, almost over, of conspicuous assurance in an ordered, hierarchical England anchored on the power of Empire, and another, being ushered in, where a peaceful but irreversible social revolution was gathering pace. The first of these worlds, the pre-war one of order, stability and confidence, comes evocatively to life through the Lawrence boys' letters home. Many people seem to tear out from these what they have decided is the important information about Lawrence, and then largely ignore the letters of his brothers. This is surely a mistake. A more rounded portrait comes from placing the person in the revealing context of family and society. The value of the *Home Letters* lies in reading all of them, Will's and Frank's as well as Ned's. After you have finished the book you come to realize what a remarkably close family the Lawrences were and what the intellectual pecking order of these three brothers was. Ned was in front, then Will, and, some way behind, Frank. The eldest, Bob, compiled and published the *Letters* and is not represented in them, while Arnold was only a boy at the time they were written.

Ned is the giant, but Will, who was the nearest in age and affinity to him, is no intellectual slouch. Obviously imbued with Christianity and, unlike his more agnostic elder brother, Ned, driven by its precepts, Will comes across as a loving and lovable personality, as charming as he is intelligent. Frank's intellectual aspirations seem less ambitious. He is very likeable and kind but a more straightforward, down-to-earth person, endowed with a very good but less powerful mind. Unlike his brothers he loved and was good at sports, yet, like his brothers, he was out of the top drawer academically and gained an Exhibition in mathematics to Jesus College, Oxford. In his letters he uses the word 'nice' a lot: so-and-so was very nice, such-and-such a place was nice; while a favourite epithet of Will's in summing up events and experiences is 'jolly'.

In Frank, as in Will, his mother's religious influence is very apparent, certainly in his early youth, with Christ then at the centre of his life. Her influence is evident in other ways too, such as in Frank's obvious belief that alcohol was a dangerous tool of the devil – shades of Thomas Chapman's drinking in Ireland and Mrs Lawrence's later efforts to eliminate it. Perhaps what appeals about him is that he is artless and seems quite happy not being notably bookish like Ned and Will; but in common with his brothers he was very sensitive about the feelings of others and the two letters he wrote to his parents in 1914 and 1915, in anticipation of his death at the Front, have a self-effacement that is very moving.

Will, on the other hand, was closest to Ned in interests and intellect. Also an Exhibitioner (of John's College, Oxford), he was widely read, with a special love of the Classics and, like Ned, Provençal poetry. There is a warmth, a charity, an unselfish interest in others about Will, as well as a sharp intellect and a breadth of vision, and, as in his brothers too, a touching loyalty to and care for his family, which permeate all his letters home. He must have been a delightful person to know. Writing to his father in September 1913 en route to see Ned in Carchemish, Will said: 'I was quite sorry to leave Damascus. It's the most beautiful town I've ever seen, with its black and white doves for ever fluttering over it and its ever-green trees round it, and the great desert beyond with towers of dust circling about like columns of smoke. And the fruit and the flowers of it. Peaches and nectarines and apples and grapes were the main fruits, with all manner of others I could not name, and sunflowers and roses the flowers. Also coming away a girl in the train gave me a little white flower like a buttonhole rose on a lilac stem, smelling sweeter than any flower I know.'[6]

Five realizations emerge from reading the *Home Letters*: the clearly dominant role of the boys' mother and the high esteem in which they all hold her; the exceptionally close-knit nature of the Lawrence family, reflected here by the incredible number of letters they all write to their parents and to each other; their care for one another; the pre-eminence of Ned among this unusual brood of siblings; and an overflowing enthusiasm for life and a delight in discovery, which imbued them all. Will wrote to his mother from Carchemish five days after the Damascus letter to his father, 'So far Ned has not heard from you since he left home. That means your letter of August 16 has gone astray, and no doubt others, which is usual but very annoying. Ned was very anxious for news when I saw him.'[7] And in July 1914, again to his mother, he said, 'The mail came last evening, letters from Father, Mother Ned and Frank.'[8]

The boys' letters home, with the occasional exception of Ned's, always mention their last and next communications to their parents, particularly to their mother, and their most recent and next expected news from them. These young men wanted to share all their experiences with their parents. Letters flew back and forth like despatches. When in December Will wrote from India to his mother from St Stephen's College in Delhi, where he taught, he included the text of an article he had written for the College magazine. Entitled 'A Turkish Soldier', it is subtly informative and very well crafted. Ned's letters are chock-a-block with comment about what he has been doing, where he has gone, who he has met, and what he has been reading and wants to read – a crowded and eclectic portfolio of literature from the classical to the modern. In his undergraduate days he had read voraciously, sometimes lying on the floor in his bungalow and reading two or three books simultaneously, turning the pages alternately.

Of course, letter-writing was far more common in the early twentieth century than it is today. The first municipal telephone exchange was inaugurated in Glasgow in 1901 but it wasn't until 1912 that the first unified system became available throughout much of Britain. Apart from telegrams then, letters were the only means of communication from a distance. Despite this, the Lawrences were unusual in the sheer volume of their family correspondence. It reflects their closeness, a closeness probably engendered by the parents' ever-present fear of exposure. They would have been protective of their sons, ever vigilant, ready to divert any prying questions, innocently intended or otherwise, about the family's origins. The Chapmans could be hidden away behind a screen but they were always there, a worrying, shadowy presence. That said, before the war Lawrence was out of harm's way at Carchemish and enjoying himself hugely. What's more, his four pre-war years in Syria were the foundation of his intimate knowledge of the Arabs, particularly the desert Arabs, and of his uncanny insight into the mentality and nature of the bedouin.

Lawrence was back in England from Syria in the summer of 1914, but with the outbreak of war that same year he soon found himself returning to the Middle

East, first to Cairo and then, from 1916 to 1918, with the Arab revolt. The war was to change him irrevocably, with perhaps his sexual violation at Deraa in 1917 and his sense of having betrayed the Arabs to keep them in the British interest, causing him the most anguish. The war over, back home in Oxford and in a state of extreme depression and nervous exhaustion, Lawrence was to start writing *Seven Pillars of Wisdom*. His mother told David Garnett, who edited *The Letters of T.E. Lawrence*, that, when he returned from the Peace Conference in Paris in 1919, Lawrence 'would sometimes sit the entire morning between breakfast and lunch in the same position, without moving, and with the same expression on his face.'[9]

It should also be remembered that his 72-year-old father died unexpectedly in April, 1919. Lawrence was very fond of him so his sudden demise from pneumonia must have been a considerable blow to Lawrence and only have deepened his depression. He had hurried home from Paris in response to a telegram from his brother Arnold but arrived too late to see his father alive. Two of his brothers had been killed in the war and now his father had gone.

In death Lawrence's father was fated to remain as anonymous as he had contrived to be during his later life. Sir Thomas Chapman, seventh baronet of Killua Castle, born into a family at the top of the Ascendancy's social order, lies forgotten in an unmarked grave in Oxford's Wolvercote Cemetery. For years he had concealed his true identity and origins behind the false name of Lawrence. In death he was to keep his secret. He is interred, unidentified, in the quietude of the spacious, landscaped burial-ground in north Oxford. His plain rectangular grave, part-shaded by fir trees near the junction of two paths, is overlaid with stone chips and contained within granite kerbstones. There is nothing, not even a headstone, to tell the curious observer that buried here is the father of one of the world's most legendary figures. The only clue is a puzzling dedication carved along the sides of the granite enclosure: 'In memory of F.H. and W.G.Lawrence killed in action 1915, and of their father who died, April 8 1919. Also of T.E.Lawrence who died May 19, 1935. And of their mother, who died November 15, 1959, aged 98'. More puzzling still is a small metal plaque stuck in the ground at the foot of the grave bearing the fading inscription: 'T.E.Lawrence'. It is said to have been put there by Cemetery officials for the benefit of people looking for the family grave – the grave in which Lawrence's mother also lies, her coffin placed two feet above Thomas Chapman's. Lawrence himself is, of course, buried near his cottage in Moreton in Dorset. His brothers, Will and Frank, were killed on active service in France. Frank was buried there in a war cemetery, while Will's body was never found.

TEL with his nurse Margo
in Tremadoc, north Wales,
1889. (Imperial War Museum,
London)

John Lawrence, Sarah's father,
in 1884 aged forty-two.
(Lloyd's Register)

Sarah Lawrence with her four sons – Ned, Will,
Frank in arms, Bob – at Langley Lodge, Fawley,
Hampshire, 1894–5. (Bodleian Library, Oxford)

TEL (left) with his four brothers, Frank,
Arnold, Robert and Will, in 1910.
(Bodleian Library, Oxford)

Graeco-Roman ruins at Jebail (ancient Byblos) on the Lebanese coast.

Farida al Akle (centre front) seated cross-legged with child.

Farida al Akle; she and TEL had met at the American
Mission School at Jebail, north of Beirut, in 1909.

Mrs Emily Rieder, *c.* 1912,
a language teacher at the
Jebail Mission School,
where TEL learned Arabic.

TEL in Areya, Mount Lebanon,
c. 1912, visiting the poet and British
Çonsul James Elroy Flecker.

TEL (seated on a Roorkhee, or portable campaign chair) and his fellow officers outside tent at Aqaba in 1918. (Standing left to right) Sub-Lt H.W. Langbein, Captain H.C. Hornby and Major W.E. Marshall; (seated left to right) Major P.G.W. Maynard, Major R.H. Scott, and Captain R.G. Goslett. (Marist College Collections, USA)

Ali Rida Pasha al-Rikabi, military governor of Damascus, but covertly leader of the Arab Secret Society in Syria. TEL met him in Damascus at the end of his secret ride in June 1917.

TEL in foreground with George Lloyd, on a raid at Batra, south of Maan, late October 1917. (Imperial War Museum, London)

ADC William Lennox Naper (left) with General Sir
Edmund Allenby, Commander-in-Chief, Egyptian
Expeditionary Force, by the sea in Palestine, 1917–18.

TEL enters Damascus in
Rolls-Royce tender, 1 October 1918.
(Rolls-Royce Ltd)

TEL on the balcony of Victoria
Hotel, Damascus, 2 October 1918.
(Imperial War Museum, London)

Portrait of TEL by war artist James McBey, Damascus, October 1918. (Imperial War Museum, London)

Portrait of TEL by Augustus John, 1919. (Tate Gallery, London)

TEL at the Paris Peace Conference, 1919, photographed by Harris & Ewing of Washington DC.

Portrait of TEL in RAF as John Hume Ross, by William Roberts. 1922. (Ashmolean Museum, Oxford)

Unofficial squadron photograph of Number 4 Hut, RAF Uxbridge, January 1923. TEL, or AC2 Ross, was then calling himself John Hume Ross. He asked to be excluded but can be seen peering through the window (left). Three of the servicemen described by Lawrence in *The Mint* are included: Drill-Sgt 'Taffy' DavIes (centre with stick), 'Sailor' (front row of four, second left), and 'China' (extreme right with leg raised).

'A nice cup of tea.' TEL (left) on a speedboat in the Tamar estuary, near Plymouth, *c.* 1930.

Clare Sydney Smith, wife of Wing-Commander Sydney Smith, TEL's commanding officer at RAF Mountbatten, Plymouth, TEL and Robert Eliot (younger son of the Earl of St Germans), on a jetty at Port Eliot, Cornwall, early 1930s.

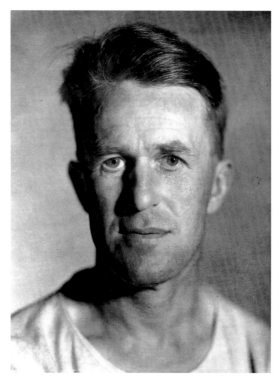

TEL photographed by Howard Coster, 1931.
(National Portrait Gallery, London)

Mystic painting of TEL
by Howard Gurschner, 1934.
(National Gallery of Ireland,
Dublin)

TEL photographed by
Wing-Commander Reggie Sims at
Hornsea, Yorkshire, winter 1934–5.
(John Sims)

This barren plot in Wolvercote Cemetery is all there is to mark the close of Sir Thomas Chapman's undistinguished yet somehow extraordinary life. There is something touchingly sad about his final, anonymous resting-place. Once he had been heir to great wealth and estates, scion of a notable Irish family and born into the grandeur of the great houses of the gentry – Killua Castle, South Hill, Clonhugh, Middleton Park. Yet he had turned his back on this world of privilege and chosen instead an existence of bourgeois conformity and disguise in a quiet Oxford suburb, and had ended his days in a neglected grave lost in a crowded municipal cemetery. Chapman's 'wife', Sarah Lawrence, is buried with her 'husband', but she had died in Swanage in Dorset, as in 1971 aged 86 had his eldest son, Dr. Robert (Bob) Lawrence, who was probably responsible for some if not all of the inscription round his parents' grave. Although he bought his own separate burial-plot nearby in the 1960s, there is no indication of its location. Bob Lawrence's remains lie beneath the uncut grass separating the two graves immediately above and to the left of that of his parents. There is nothing to identify him – no defined grave, no headstone, no name – only a patch of grass. The youngest of Chapman's sons, Arnold, who died in Wiltshire in 1991 aged 90, disliked memorials. He was cremated and it is believed that his ashes were scattered anonymously. But there is a twist in this tale: the line, if not the Chapman name, did not die out with Arnold's demise. He had two grand-children, but, like their great-grandfather, Thomas Chapman, they avoid the limelight. I visited Wolvercote. It was on a still, warm spring day and as I stood looking at the Chapman graves, I felt, sadly, that it was almost as though this family, secretly so different from normal families of their day, had somehow wanted to be forgotten.

But to return to T.E. Lawrence, and to another secret identity: Armed with the knowledge of his likely state of mind immediately after the war, I felt better placed to consider in detail the mysterious dedication of his book to S.A. Despite his depression, the urge to write his personal account of the Arab Revolt preoccupied Lawrence, and he began to turn his attention to the dedicatory poem between 1920 and 1922, although his first tentative deliberations on it may have begun as early as 1919. It would seem reasonable to list all Lawrence's known statements and utterances on S.A. in chronological order. This order is significant:

To S.A.
I loved you, so I drew these tides of men into my hands
And wrote my will across the sky in stars

To earn you Freedom, the seven-pillared worthy house,
that your eyes might be shining for me
When we came.

Death seemed my servant on the road, till we were near
And saw you waiting:
When you smiled, and in sorrowful envy he outran me
And took you apart:
Into his quietness.

Love, the way-weary, groped to your body, our brief wage
ours for the moment
Before earth's soft hand explored your shape, and the blind
worms grew fat upon
Your substance.

Men prayed me that I set our work, the inviolate house,
as a memory of you.
But for fit monument I shattered it, unfinished: and now
The little things creep out to patch themselves hovels
in the marred shadow
Of your gift.

Lawrence made five known written references to S.A. in the early post-war years, between 1919 and 1923, when his memories of the Revolt would still have loomed large. The first was found among his papers in the Bodleian Library. This is a copy of a pencilled note he wrote in 1919, in a tiny hand, across a blank flyleaf at the end of a copy of the book *The Singing Caravan* by Sir Robert Vansittart, which had been a gift to Lawrence from the author. It is the only time the sex of a dedicatee might *seem* to be identified: 'A (?) I wrought for him freedom to lighten his sad eyes: but he had died waiting for me. So I threw my gift away and now not anywhere will I find rest and peace. Written between Paris and Lyons in Handley Page.'[10] The coda detailing the place where (and, in fact, when) Lawrence had written the note seems just a trifle odd. Since it would appear to have been scribbled in flight as an aide-memoire for his personal use only and could perhaps be a first attempt at an outline of the dedicatory poem, why would Lawrence record where he had written it, *unless* he knew that some day scholars might stumble across it and that, when taken in conjunction with all his other references to S.A., it would add to the obfuscation with which he clearly wished to surround the dedication?

Authorized biographer Jeremy Wilson also feels that Lawrence's recording of the note's provenance was out of character, commenting, 'He was not given to noting where he had written things.'[11] There is a further anomaly. Until very recently the Bodleian version of the note has been the one to appear in the few published examples. However, it is a typed transcript. In the original (which is in the Kilgour Collection in the Houghton Library at Harvard) there is no question-mark after the letter 'A'. The anonymous transcriber seems to have found the character not clearly discernible and, perhaps in an attempt to indicate this, may have interpolated the bracketed question-mark, thereby confusing matters further. Was this the only tampering with the note? In the original the lone initial figure could conceivably be a triangle but under magnification looks to be the letter 'A'. For those whose researchings have taught them to be careful about accepting some of Lawrence's written comments and retailed utterances verbatim, these anomalies may counsel caution in attaching undue significance to the note.

Such confusing problems of interpretation as this are, of course, typically Lawrencian. Rarely does anything about Lawrence turn out to be straightforward and clear-cut, and that's the way he liked it. Teasing all and sundry was fun, and ambivalence also served a serious psychological purpose in his life.

It disconcerted and sometimes irritated people too – which would have pleased him even more. He would have chuckled at any perplexity or debate provoked by his in-flight jottings. Elsie Newcombe wrote to me of *Seven Pillars'* dedication, 'My husband maintained it was just a "leg pull" to keep people guessing and when we told that to T.E. he just laughed!'[12]

The second reference to S.A. comes in a letter of November 1919 to J.G. Kidston, a member of the Eastern Section of the Foreign Office, in response to his request to know what Lawrence's motives were for his involvement in the Arab Revolt. Lawrence listed four 'in order of strength', as he put it. He described the first as follows: '(i) Personal. I liked a particular Arab very much, and I thought that freedom for the race would be an acceptable present.' When he enlarged on this in the same letter, he said: 'Motive (i) I found had died some weeks before: so my gift was wasted, and my future doings indifferent on that count.'[13] The third reference is in a personal letter of 22 November 1923 to Major Robin Buxton, who had been with Lawrence in the Arab Revolt as commander of two companies of the Imperial Camel Corps. He later became a banker and Lawrence's financial adviser. Lawrence wrote to him, 'S.A. was a person, now dead, regard for whom lay beneath my labour for the Arabic peoples. I don't propose to go further into detail thereupon.'[14] The fourth comment was in a letter to a young aircraftman friend, Robert Guy, written on Christmas Day 1923: 'People aren't friends till they have said all they can say, and are able to sit together, at work or rest, hour-long without speaking. We never got quite to that, but were nearer it daily … and since S.A. died I haven't experienced any risk of that's happening.'[15]

Together, all these references would suggest an Arab dedicatee, probably male, who was now dead. There is no intimation here of a dedication to a person still living, or of one which is symbolic of an idea, a place or an experience. However, there is what I consider to be a highly significant fifth attribution from this earlier period that does not chime at all with the previous four. It appears in a letter Lawrence wrote to Robert Graves in 1922 when both men were at Oxford. Graves's evidence, and his perceptive understanding of the private Lawrence, deserve more serious consideration than they have hitherto had. Graves's interpretation of S.A. is worth laying out in full, because it shows that as a poet he may have had a telling insight into Lawrence's dedicatory inspiration:

> [Graves wrote:] Lawrence idealized masculinity, partly perhaps because he knew that he was not conventionally masculine himself, in spite of his great physical strength and habitual knight-errantry. I do not mean that he was homosexual – he was not. But he could never squarely face the fact of the existence of women; he placed them in general on a romantic plane remote from reality, in which their actual presence made him rather uncomfortable. He seems to have felt at home only with practical not-very-young women of the good-wife-and-mother type; and had a peculiar sympathy for childless married women: He was afraid of women who thought for themselves.
>
> In the winter of 1921–1922 Lawrence was in a very nervous condition, did not eat or sleep enough, and worked over Seven Pillars again, destroying the second text which I had seen on his table at All Souls. He wrote by night; his days were largely spent in work at the Colonial Office. Late in January he came to see me at Islip, and looked so bad that I told him that he must take himself in hand. I asked why he didn't try to find some appropriate woman who would help him to a settled life; because if he went on experimenting with solitariness like this there would be a collapse. He said that he had never been able to fall in love: and the hysterical pursuit of him by women who, after listening to Lowell Thomas's lectures, had fallen in love with his fame had made him avoid the society of women even more than he usually did. As a boy he had never had much to do with women, having had no sisters, only brothers, and the habit had stuck. He said, jokingly, that the only settling down he could contemplate was

enlistment in the Army or Air Force, where he would be compelled to eat and sleep normally, and have no time to think … A few days later he wrote me the following (undated) letter:

Sunday
Lord,

What I told you last week about my likes was not altogether true. There was an exception who provided a disproportionate share of the motive for the Arabian adventure, and who after it was over dictated the enclosed as preface to the story of it.

I turned it out a day ago when preparing for a printer: and I don't know – It's hardly a literary question of good or bad (nearer the address to a letter) but is it prose or verse?

> *à toi*
> *Jourdain.*
> *Will you return the outburst?*
> *L.*[16]

Graves continued:

This letter and the one that follows are in minute hand-writing – about the size of Charlotte Brontë's. When Lawrence was feeling low his handwriting shrank; when he was pleased it sometimes grew enormous. The enclosure was the dedication to 'S.A.' which appears at the beginning of Seven Pillars. I did not take the word 'dictated' literally, for he seemed to regard the thing as his own. Who 'S.A.' was I do not know, and the dedication affords no help; though it suggests that S.A. was someone who would have benefited by Arab freedom and who had indeed inspired Lawrence to his leadership of the Arab Revolt … One of his oldest friends told me, in 1927, that he believed S.A. to have been a certain Sheikh Achmed, an Arab with whom Lawrence had a sort of blood-brotherhood before the War; and that Sheikh Achmed died of typhus in 1918. I hinted at this in the first draft of my biography: "Shortly before he captured Damascus there came news of a death by typhus, and this is one explanation, I believe, of his coming immediately away from the scene of his triumph and of much that has happened to him since". But Lawrence commented in the margin: "You have taken me too literally. S.A. still exists: but out of my reach, because I have changed." This is difficult to square with the words of the dedication:

> …ours for the moment
> Before earth's soft hand explored your shape, and the blind

worms grew fat upon
Your substance.

and with his remark to Liddell Hart on May 7, 1933, that S.A. "croaked" in 1918.[17]

Graves told me that the Sheikh Achmed identification had been suggested to him by A.W. Lawrence, who later wrote, 'It is believed that his personality supplied the largest element to the figure of S.A., to whom the *Seven Pillars* is dedicated.'[18] Graves's analysis continued:

> My impression is that S.A. was a woman; else the foregoing letter was unnecessarily misleading. Lawrence had told me that he had never been in love with a woman, not that he had never loved anyone; and the confession that he had not been frank with me about his "likes" meant to me, at the time, that S.A. was a woman, as it does still. It is likely, in view of his temperament, to have been ideal love in the mediaeval poetic tradition of knightly love for some impossibly removed lady; and it is likely too that the news that came to him shortly before the capture of Damascus spelt not the death of S.A. herself, but the death of the idea she had represented. 'The marred shadow of your gift' suggests disillusion rather than physical loss. I cannot agree with Mr Vyvyan Richards's suggestion that S.A. was a lay figure of literary passion. S.A. was clearly of outstanding personal importance to Lawrence during the Revolt.[19]

Lawrence confirmed that S.A. and the personal motive of *Seven Pillars'* epilogue were one and the same. In this postscript he wrote: 'Throughout, my strongest motive had been a personal one, omitted from the body of the book, but not absent, I think, from my mind, waking or sleeping, for an hour in all those years. Active pains and joys flung themselves up among my days like towers: but always, refluent as air, this persisting hidden urge re-formed and became a very element of life: till near the end. It was dead before we reached the town.'[20] It is worth noting that Lawrence says that it is 'the motive', the 'persisting hidden urge', that 'was dead' – not a person.

All further known references by Lawrence to S.A. were made four years later, during or after 1927, in response to queries from his biographers Graves and Basil Liddell Hart. His explanations by then had less of the immediately personal about them. Some have seen this as an attempt by Lawrence to dissemble, to put people off the track. I don't agree. His earlier references may well support the view of those who want to believe that S.A. was a man, perhaps Dahoum – the name of the young Arab worker who was a friend of Lawrence's at Carchemish and whose real name might, just conceivably, have been Sheikh Achmed, a title of which there is only one known, pre-war, written example, and that in an almost illegible note to Lawrence's Arabic teacher Farida al Akle; and even this identification has been considered doubtful by some experts.

The later S.A. evidence tends to support the views of those who feel that the dedication is more complex, perhaps multi-layered, including a person or persons, an idea, a dream, a personification. Lawrence wrote to Graves in 1927 that, 'S.A., the subject of the dedication, is rather an idea than a person.'[21] And at the top of his own private, handwritten record of the writing, printing and distribution of *Seven Pillars of Wisdom,* made yet again in 1927, Lawrence had written in a tiny, cramped hand, as though interpolated almost as an afterthought: 'Dedication of book is to an imaginary person of neutral sex.'[22]

Then in 1933, during the preparation of his biography, Liddell Hart arranged a number of question-and-answer sessions with Lawrence, jotting down his replies; he also had several informal talks with him, making notes of them from memory later. During one of the sessions Liddell Hart asked: 'Who is "S.A." of the dedication to *SPW*?' Lawrence replied 'One is a person and one is a place.'[23] Liddell Hart wrote the word 'vague' after this entry; and, recalling a talk in which the topic of *Seven Pillars* arose, Liddell Hart entered in his diary: 'The "personal" motive mentioned first in the concluding bit was the "S.A." of the opening poem. But S.A. "croaked" in 1918.'[24] In another informal conversation, the content of which he again recorded only later in note form, Liddell Hart wrote: 'Talked of his dedicatory poem in *Seven Pillars* to "S.A." Asked him was there any real person or only symbolical. He said partly geographical. S. and A. were two different things, "S" a village in Syria, or property in it, and "A" personal.'[25] This is clearly an expansion of Lawrence's earlier comment: 'One is a person and one is a place'. However, the order of this shorter version logically suggests that S was the personal element and A the village or property. Liddell Hart's record of Lawrence's second, more detailed explanation of the two letters may be accurate, but, because of the time that elapsed between the conversation in which it occurred and Liddell Hart's written recollection of it, it should be regarded as the less reliable of the two references. Given these uncertainties, it is not unreasonable to believe that the attributions had been confused in the memory and that S was the personal element and A the village or property.

In 1963 Robert Graves wrote an article in an American periodical about Lawrence's *Seven Pillars'* dedication and again introduced the idea of medieval knightly love into the S.A. conundrum. Considerable weight is lent to the credibility of Graves's explanation when it is borne in mind that Lawrence told him in 1927 that at Jesus College he spent nearly three years reading Provençal poetry and mediaeval French *chansons de geste* when he should have been concentrating on his history degree. Graves wrote:

> Lawrence had immersed himself in the Medieval French troubadour love poems, the spirit of which had been brought to Provence by Arab lute players. The troubadour fixed his devotion on a lady and won from her love a mystical power that he claimed would overcome every conceivable obstacle; the bond acquired a peculiarly sacred character. This would wholly explain both the S.A. dedication and Lawrence's fantastic feats in the desert; for he wrote that the image of S.A. was omnipresent with him throughout the campaign.[26]

You could not devote three years to studying Provençal poetry without becoming something of an expert on it and on the convention of love which was its driving force. More importantly in Lawrence's case, he would not have become so deeply absorbed in such esoteric poetry unless it had struck a powerful chord in him. It might be objected that there is only the one known written reference by Lawrence to a preoccupation with Provençal poetry; but this can be countered by the fact that not only was secrecy a vital principle of the troubadour convention, it was also an essential part of Lawrence's inner nature. When something had a profound, emotional effect on him, he kept it strictly to himself.

Graves told me that he and Lawrence frequently discussed Provençal poetry and that Lawrence was extremely knowledgeable on the subject. One of the many topics they debated was whether troubadour love was always honourable and whether lovers ever pretended to a mystical bond as a cover for sexual adventure. Lawrence told Graves that he didn't think so, because the validity of their mystical union would have been challenged by other men and women who had experienced the ennobling and empowering effect of true love.[27]

To return to his 1963 article, Graves goes on to say that Lawrence's brutal assault by the Turks at Deraa had made him impotent: 'The clue to his story is given by a confession he once made to me in a letter: "I lost my nerve at Deraa."' Graves maintained that Lawrence had not lost his nerve in the usual sense of the word because he continued to show amazing courage in battle. He was using the word 'nerve' in its archaic sense – 'nervus' (from Horace's *Epodes*, 12.19.) – to mean that the flogging he had endured at Deraa had made him permanently impotent. He cites Lawrence's words in *Seven Pillars*: 'The passing days confirmed that the citadel of my integrity had been irrevocably lost'. Graves added 'This was how he had changed, and this alone could account for his apparent desertion of S.A., to whom he could no longer honestly offer himself as a lover.'

There is a curious corollary to this. Graves once presented a letter of Lawrence's to a handwriting expert and wrote about his analysis: 'I showed a letter of his to the most gifted graphologist I know – 100 per cent accurate – who came to me in a flutter and said: "I may be wrong or mad or off-colour, or something, but this writing is that of a man who has been made impotent by some great shock and, instead, enjoys fantastic sexual orgies in his mind!"'[28] Eric Kennington also seemed to be of the opinion that the Deraa incident had made Lawrence impotent.[29]

Graves's article then reveals what could well be the most important part of his explanation of S.A.: 'At Oxford Lawrence forced two books on my attention in a way which I thought a little odd, and which made no sense to me for many years. The first was Maurice Hewlett's *Richard Yea-and-Nay*, a historical novel about the Crusades in which a Christian knight is passionately in love with a lady named Jehane who has fallen into Saracen hands. The other was a collection of short naval stories by (I think) Henry Morley, called *Strange Cargoes*. Lawrence told me, "There's one good story there; never mind the others." One certainly stood out. It concerned a ship that had been thrown by a huge tropical storm over the reef of a coral island and beached high inland. Her captain had felt an obsessive love for the vessel and, although she could never sail again, continued to haunt her rotting timbers through which the jungle grew green.'

Graves went on to surmise that this was Lawrence's way of telling him that 'he could not rid himself of his obsessive love for S.A., even when it had lost its relevance.' (The name of the author of the short stories was in fact Morley Roberts). In 1927 Graves was hurriedly preparing his biography of Lawrence, who was helping him. Lawrence, now in India, asked him to tear up any fan letters in women's handwriting addressed to him. Graves wrote: 'I did so with one exception. A letter came from the south of England written in a small, neat, educated handwriting. The very first sentence told me that this was not fan mail but a letter from someone curiously close to him.' Graves did not read on but he did glance at the signature, which seemed to be Jehanne. He forwarded the letter to Lawrence and, as he expected, received no acknowledgement. However, this letter looks to have been a red herring. Many years later in the USA Graves's account seems to have been the inspiration for two volumes of rather pedestrian poetry 'by Jehanne', which are almost certainly bogus.

FIFTEEN

I'd Rather Morris Than the World

TIME SEEMED suspended in the Joyces' house high above Beirut; there was an exhilaration in the procession of sun-washed days and star-studded nights, the daytime spent poring over my notes, the evenings passed in earnest discussion of Lawrence far into the early hours.

My image of the Carchemish Lawrence began to take increasingly tangible shape. The emerging figure was a romantic one but one concealed behind a mask of intellectual bravura and boyish fun-and-games. My belief that the private Lawrence inhabited a medieval world of his own devising became virtually a conviction. I was certain too that for him such an imaginary existence would have to have a literary counterpart, as a kind of justification for what was essentially emotional predilection. This literature was two-fold: Provençal poetry, and its Victorian reinvention in the Gothic novels of William Morris.

Few people allow their emotional lives to be unduly influenced by a literary convention, or, put another way, few people have such impenetrably complex responses to emotional attraction that they seek a literary precedent by which to justify these responses to themselves. Lawrence, I believe, was one such a person. The strands from which one's relations with people are woven are often hard to disentangle, especially in Lawrence's case. Despite the views of scientific reductionists, the origins of being and motivation remain mysterious. Lawrence once told Robert Graves 'I'd wish every man to be an everlasting question-mark.'[1]

When you are trying to plumb the wellsprings of someone as complicated, and at times as devious, as Lawrence, you are presented with a challenging task. However, I am convinced that the key can be found in significant part in his literary preferences, preferences that reflected his emotions as much as his intellect, and this key is in the end not too hard to identify. There is no doubt that Lawrence was different, and caution should be the byword in analyzing his character. He was like a fish in its element, always elusive, always gliding silently in and out of view, a momentary, refracted shape in the water.

To many who knew him, even to those who knew him well, Lawrence always remained a Protean figure, someone who managed the feat of being at once a mischievous, irresponsible boy and a precociously intelligent, morally driven adult.

To Charlotte Shaw he could be both 'the strangest contact of my life' and an infuriating tease, because of the half-truths and white lies he would tell. Charlotte's husband once asked her whether the fact that they had not seen Lawrence for some time was due to 'any quarrel … any unpleasantness.' She replied: 'No. No quarrel. No unpleasantness. But he is such an infernal liar.'[2] There is not much in Lawrence's life that he was prepared to declare a constant, or to subscribe to unequivocally. He refused to nail his colours to any mast. 'There is no absolute for me,' he told Graves.[3] In literature, however, there was one figure who was like a lodestar to him, a lifelong love and admiration from which he never wavered, and that was William Morris, whose life spanned Queen Victoria's reign.

Known during his life as an arbiter of artistic taste, a writer, and a political radical, Morris is remembered more today as a visionary typographer, the founder of the Kelmscott Press, and as a gifted designer. But he was also a prolific poet (not very much read these days but extremely popular in his time), a writer of folklore-ish 'Gothic' romances (even less read now than his poetry), and a master-craftsman of Victorian-Gothic furniture. In his younger days he was a strong sympathizer with the Pre-Raphaelite Brotherhood, formed in 1848 by John Everett Millais, Dante Gabriel Rossetti and Holman Hunt (Lawrence in his teens crafted a brass lantern copied from the one in Holman Hunt's picture 'The Light of the World', an engraving of which hung in the drawing room of the Lawrence family home). In 1856 Morris, aged twenty-two, and Edward Burne-Jones, both lately Oxford undergraduates, had met Rossetti, who was already an established poet and painter, and had fallen under his spell. He in turn took an instant liking to the two younger men, calling Morris 'Topsy' and Burne-Jones

'Ned'. He would talk earnestly to the two about art and poetry, about the Middle Ages and Arthurian legends, and then at night would take them carousing round Bohemian London.

Morris identified closely with the Pre-Raphaelites' rejection of the materialism of the age and with their artistic credo 'Truth to Nature', which in painting meant pure, bright colour and meticulous faith with realistic delineation and detail. He was also much drawn to their championing of a medieval 'Gothic' ideal, which celebrated and promoted a culture of honest yeoman artistry and craftsmanship. Morris was also attracted, as were many Victorians, to the Arthurian legends. The renewal of interest in Arthurian romance and the dream of an idealized world was in part a reaction to the squalor and poverty that were the by-products of Britain's ever-increasing industrialization; but it was also given momentum by the re-publication in 1816 of Thomas Malory's *Morte d'Arthur*, which, it should be remembered, was one of the books Lawrence carried with him in the Arab campaign, the others being the plays of Aristophanes and the *Oxford Book of English Verse*.[4]

Then there was the poet Tennyson's abiding interest in the Arthurian legends, which saw him produce *The Lady of Shalott* in 1832 and the *Morte d'Arthur* and *Sir Galahad* in 1842. This in turn led to *The Idylls of the King* in 1859 and their completion in twelve books in 1882. In fact, the Arthurian cycle was frequently the chosen subject of many a Victorian writer and painter. It seems to have held a special appeal at a time of unprecedented change, a reassuring dream of a past where noble values permeated an unchanging world of honour, courage and decency.

Lawrence was clearly of a like mind with Morris about the drab, dirty, mean world they felt was being ushered in by a new age of factories and machines that was precipitating the irreversible disappearance of a pastoral England epitomized for Morris, and for Lawrence, by their romanticized conception of the Middle Ages. As late as 1912, at the age of twenty-four, Lawrence was writing home from Cairo that he had bought nothing during his short stay in the city but the 1911 novel *The Centaur* by Algernon Blackwood. He intended sending the book home for his family to read and said that it would interest Will, adding, 'very good, though not "all the way" enough for me: but at the same time more reasoned and definite as an attack on the modern world than anything I've read – bar Morris.'[5]

This imagined medieval simplicity and nobility of spirit found in many of Morris's prose romances is expressed in the form of an epic society of knightly heroism and villainous skulduggery, which curiously prefigures J.R.R. Tolkien's

The Lord of the Rings; a quasi-mystical world where all things are starkly polarized – black or white, good or evil – and destiny is a major integer in the lives of the knights as they go from adventure to adventure through otherworldly landscapes and lost, legendary realms where mysterious powers hold sway. Here men and women exist either as knights and ladies or serfs and peasants, while the central characters, the heroes, are ranged against the stereotypical villains of the piece – evil kings, knights gone to the bad, dangerous witches, sorcerers and magicians.

In Morris's medieval world the real and the surreal happily coexist, as they did of, course, in the minds of the denizens of the actual Middle Ages. It should be noted too that a vital element in almost every tale is the elusive lady, the hero's true love and the inspiration for and enabler of great deeds of bravery and endeavour. After epic journeys and battles the knight errant returns to his noble family and seat to settle down to a long and happy life of domestic bliss and communal harmony. Bringing peace and prosperity to his newly reclaimed fiefdom, he is finally united, or reunited, with his love – the aristocratic woman central to the story.

It reveals a lot about his hidden emotions that the young Lawrence should subscribe to this simplistically romantic and roseate philosophy of life, which found its literary expression in Morris's idealistic parables of selfless heroism battling the forces of greed and self-aggrandizement. It was a wonderful dream-world where emotional bonds and mystical revelations would be created in abundance. It also provided an escape into a world whose realities were not circumscribed by Victorian middle-class mores and restrictions, a world of limit-less spiritual vistas and physical challenges, a world with the power to elevate the individual to undreamt-of heights of achievement and fulfilment. It was a world too in which there would have been more than faint evocations of Lawrence's lost knightly Chapman heritage in Ireland.

Later, after the war, Lawrence seemed to have sloughed off his early adherence to this rarefied model of personal conduct and social behaviour and his belief in its power to motivate. But he didn't – not entirely. He transmuted it into intense friendship and the unconditional offering of a helping hand to those in need. Romantic dreams, the ethic of chivalry, and the resurgent optimism of youth may have been compromised for him by his war experiences, but they re-emerged in the form of an active and pragmatic championing of right and the rights of the under-privileged, and in a forceful exposure of wrong. Lawrence's literary agent, Raymond Savage, commented on 'his utter selflessness and unbounded kindness and generosity' and added, 'His thoughts were always for others. I knew of a number of cases in which his unbounded generosity saved individuals and even families from disaster...'[6] It is not well-known, for example, that Lawrence created an Educational Fund under the aegis of the Royal Air Force Benevolent Fund and at the time of his death was helping to educate thirteen children.[7]

The men who knew Lawrence from the intimate, communal, warts-and-all environment of an RAF barrack room have also vouched for his kindness and concern for others. Robert Graves, who was quite close to Lawrence for a time in the early 1920s, said that Lawrence kept his friendships separated by bulkheads. He was also capable of coexisting in two quite different worlds, as are many creative people. He certainly knew how to handle men and how to lead them, and was at home, if not happily, dabbling and intriguing in politics and the affairs of men. His successes in the Arab Revolt and at the Colonial Office amply testify to this. You need only read his wartime *Twenty-Seven Articles* on how to operate with bedouin to know that Lawrence was both extremely subtle and thoroughly pragmatic when it came to influencing and leading others.[8] He knew too how to play his hand effectively in the counsels of state and of a cynical establishment where intelligence services, politicians and the military exploited the idealism and ambitions of others to their own advantage.

David Hogarth, the man whom Lawrence considered to be almost a surrogate father, perhaps the one person he trusted more than anyone else implicitly to understand his inner nature, penned one of the most pithily perceptive and authoritative summaries of Lawrence's character. This revealing portrait, from which I quoted earlier, is worth recalling. Its form, its compact and provocative prose, is almost as impressive as the penetrating insight of its content. It was written at about the time of the Peace Conference in 1919 and was published in 1920 when Lawrence had taken up a fellowship at All Souls College, Oxford and his name was about to explode onto the world stage:

> He is not so young as he looks and he is hardly anything that he is popularly supposed to be – not Daredevil for example, nor Knight-errant nor Visionary nor Romantic. The things he wants not to be are quite numerous; but things he could be, if he wanted, are more numerous still. He is not fond of being anything, and official categories do not fit him. He can do most things and does some; but to expect him to do a particular thing is rash.
>
> Besides being anti-official, he dislikes fighting and Arab clothes, Arab ways, and social functions, civilized or uncivilized. He takes a good deal of trouble about all things but quite a great deal about repelling the people whom he

attracts, including all sorts and conditions of men and some sorts and conditions of women; but he is beginning to be discouraged by consistent failure, which now and then he does not regret. He has as much interest as faith in himself: but those who share the last are not asked to share the first. He makes fun of others or kings of them, but if anyone tries to make either one or the other of him he runs away. Pushing (not himself) he finds more congenial than leading and he loves to push the unsuspecting body: but if it does not get on as fast as he thinks it should, he pushes it into the gutter and steps to the front. What he thinks is his Law. To think as fast or as far as he thinks is not easy, and still less easy is it to follow up with such swift action. He can be as persuasive as positive; and the tale of those he has hocussed into doing something they never meant to do and are not aware that they are doing, is long. It is better to be his partner than his opponent, for when he is not bluffing, he has a way of holding the aces: and he can be ruthless, caring little what eggs he breaks to make his omelettes and ignoring responsibility either for the shells or for the digestion of the mess. Altogether a force felt by many but not yet fully gauged either by others or by himself. He should go far; but it may be in driving lonely furrows where at present few expect him to plough.[9]

While Lawrence was a busy, prominent and effective actor in the theatre of real life, his secret imagination walked on a quite different stage, a stage peopled by brave knights in quest of grails of all sorts. Here the romantic hero strode larger than life in a world in which Lawrence would probably have much preferred to live. After all, there were knights and castles in his father's Irish family. Typically, he seldom talked of this Morrisean dreamworld. Of course, he was well aware of the differences between a real and an imaginary world, but he also knew that when the imagination usurps reality, strange doors open and many things become possible – as poets are also aware, and he was almost in awe of poets. He wrote to his mother from France in the summer of 1910: 'Imagination should be put into the most precious caskets.'[10] Daydreams are the woken unconscious loosed into the conscious mind and they can be powerful transforming agents. Lawrence wrote in the originally suppressed Introductory Chapter to *Seven Pillars of Wisdom*: 'All men dream: but not equally. Those who dream by night in the dusty recesses of their minds wake in the day to find that it was vanity: but the dreamers of the day are dangerous men, for they may act their dream with open eyes, to make it possible. This I did.'[11]

For Lawrence this powerful dreamworld clearly existed and there were certainly some who knew of it. Occasionally, if only briefly, the mask slips to reveal a glimpse of this private place, Lawrence's secret habitat. Vyvyan Richards, with whom at one time he had planned a printing press project to publish rare books, Edgar Hall, David Hogarth, perhaps Edward Leeds too, probably knew of, or sensed, its existence.

It was the literary heart, the spiritual core of Morris that had attracted the young Lawrence: chivalry, valour, knightly deeds, comradeship, honour, romantic love, honest, hands-on art, and their expression in story form as allegories for living. It was these fundamental components of Morris's literary credo that informed Lawrence's lifelong love of his poetry and prose. There is definitely a window into the inner working of Lawrence's mind and heart in Morris's work. This seems, however, to have gone mostly unremarked, because the values and qualities expressed and promoted in Morris's writings have long been out of both literary favour and intellectual fashion and have been regarded as elements of a rather outdated ethic. And there is in Lawrence's championing of Morris another and vital motivation, which has gone largely unheeded – ideal love of a woman and the concomitant poetic belief that such love has the power to inspire a man to achievements to which he would otherwise never remotely aspire.

In relation to Lawrence this theory has not so much been rejected as never seriously considered, except by Robert Graves. Graves, however, has tended to be dismissed lightly as a well-intentioned prisoner of a slightly absurd idealism who would tend to fudge facts if they didn't fit in with his poetic preconceptions. This view has sometimes been the verdict on him too when it comes to assessing his overall judgements on Lawrence. Graves deserves better and has deeper insights into Lawrence than people have hitherto realized. The poet sees; he doesn't just look.

The later twentieth century was, among other things, an age of obsession with sex. A man who lived a celibate life because he had never found his ideal mate or companion in life, or who wasn't much interested in sex, or was simply just extremely shy, was often considered suspect. The public, bombarded by a constant stream of sexual imagery and allusion in ubiquitous advertisements, were seduced into believing that if you didn't engage in sexual activity there was probably something a bit odd about you. Lawrence, certainly after his shattering ordeal at Deraa, never seemed willing, or perhaps able, to give anything more to another human being than intense friendship. He was repelled by the physical, several close friends considering him virtually asexual. Some contemporary 'sex experts' do not seem to be able to accept this. They say he must nevertheless have indulged in some sort of sexual activity, or perhaps have been a closet homosexual. This is pure speculation.

Times were very different when Lawrence was a young man in the Edwardian decade. Among the growing middle class sexual intercourse between unmarried men and women of respectable family and conventional upbringing was considered immoral and ungodly. When it was discovered, it often resulted in scandal and family disgrace. Lawrence's elder brother, Bob, never married, and, so far as we know, never contracted a serious involvement with either a woman or a man, and yet it has never been suggested that he was either misogynist or homosexual. In his case the reason for what must ultimately have become a rather solitary existence was the powerful and intrusive influence of his mother and her controlling nature. Bob never got away from her, becoming a doctor and a missionary, propagating the gospel by her side in China, and living with her until her death. T.E. Lawrence and his brother Arnold, while being the first to acknowledge that their mother was in her own way a remarkable woman, kept well clear of her, and what they saw as her stifling religiosity and unyielding will. Arnold was to marry and have a daughter, who in turn had two children, while T.E. would, apparently, occasionally muse privately on whether a wife might have been, might still be, the best way out of an increasing sense of emotional isolation.

Why then didn't he marry or appear to have any deep involvement with a woman? The answer is complicated. Firstly, his mother, all too aware of what the consequences of an all-consuming passion could be, clearly discouraged her sons from inviting girls to the house and, with rare exceptions, they were only infrequently seen in the Lawrence household. As a result, the sons seem to have had hardly any knowledge or experience at all of relationships with young women. Secondly, T.E. was always excruciatingly shy, particularly when he felt emotionally vulnerable. In addition he was noticeably short, which affected him more than people have realized, particularly in comparison with his tall, handsome brother, Will, who was almost like his twin, being just sixteen months younger than him. T.E. quite often (though not always) avoided shaking hands and was occasionally even reluctant to look a person in the eye. However, before the war he enjoyed women's company very much. There were the ladies of the American Mission School at Jebail, the ancient Byblos, twenty miles north of Beirut on the Syrian coast, where he was tutored in Arabic. Then there was Winifred Fontana, wife of the British Consul in Aleppo, who wrote of those days:

> I have seen Lawrence quoted as saying that he had 'no time for women' and – though I feel sceptical about his use of such a hackneyed phrase – he may have said something acid to express his dislike of being socially vamped. At Jerablus

he spared himself no pains for this woman's comfort and happiness – nor for that of other women who stayed there. When the tents blew down in a storm it was Lawrence who emptied the room used as a woodstore by the diggers: carrying out the blocks at furious speed to have ready a dry place for my bedding and that of my children before the rain fell. It was Lawrence, remembering my love of music, who enticed a band of Kurdish musicians to play and sing for us; Lawrence who knew without being told, that happy domesticity does not kill a woman's love of adventure, and who took me across the swirling Euphrates in his Oxford canoe to gather wild flowers (so rare a joy on Syrian Plains) on an island which lay towards the Mesopotamian bank of the river – paddling the difficult and dangerous return journey against the current with a coolness and skill that fired my admiration.[12]

After the war and the increasing lionizing by the public Lawrence found it much easier to mix mostly with his own sex, and after his elevation to celebrity status became so weary, and wary, of the continual protestations of love, sometimes carnal love, from men as well as women, that he tended to avoid some women's, and some men's, company. He wrote to Lady Astor:

> People seem to my judgement to lose their heads rather than their hearts. Over the Christmas season two men and four women have sent me fervent messages of love. Love carnal, not love rarefied, you know: and I am uncomfortable towards six more of the people I meet, therefore.[13]

The exceptions were a few favoured women (and not always older women) who posed no sexual threat and whom he could treat simply as people and friends. He wrote to Charlotte Shaw, 'Incidentally these words man and woman are out of date. I have no more use for a man's guide to cookery than for a woman's ditto: do invent a word for a human being, qua entity.'[14] Among these women were Charlotte Shaw, Nancy Astor and Celandine Kennington. And when he visited Augustus John's home at Fordingbridge in Hampshire he would talk for hours at a time to John's second wife, Dorelia.[15]

However, Clare Sydney Smith, the wife of Wing-Commander Sydney Smith, Lawrence's commanding officer in Plymouth, needs separate consideration. Lawrence's service in northern India at the small frontier outpost of RAF Miranshah in Waziristan had been cut short in January 1929, and he had been posted to Plymouth in south-west England. From March 1929–33 he was based there at RAF Cattewater (subsequently changed, partly at his suggestion, to RAF Mountbatten) under Sydney Smith, whom he had first met at the Cairo Conference in 1921. Lawrence became a close family friend of Smith, his wife and their daughter Maureen – nicknamed Squeak – and dubbed this happy period of his life 'The Golden Reign'.[16] During Lawrence's time in Plymouth a Major Colin Cooper made a joint gift of a fast American speedboat to Smith and Lawrence, who renamed it *The Biscuit*. Lawrence immensely enjoyed the exhilaration that manning *The Biscuit* gave him, and he explored the picturesque little inlets up and down the lovely river Tamar estuary, often with Clare, sometimes with other friends, sometimes alone. In her book *The Golden Reign*, her story of her relationship with Lawrence, Clare is careful not to cross the line between friendship and love, yet the hint that there was more to it than met the eye certainly hovers between the lines. The suggestion is there early on in the form of a full-plate, posed photograph of her in soft focus, obviously intended to show her attractions off to best advantage. And she clearly was attractive. Jeremy Wilson knew all about Clare's true feelings for Lawrence. He wrote:

> I don't think it would be an exaggeration to say that Clare S.S. was infatuated with him. Biffy Borton, who knew both Lawrence and the Smiths, once commented … that Lawrence's skilful handling of the situation had saved the Smiths' marriage. Prior to the release of the T.E. Lawrence papers in the Bodleian, biographers who were aware of this (myself included) refrained from public comment in order to spare the late 'Squeak' Smith, Clare's daughter, needless embarrassment.[17]

Lawrence was certainly fond of Clare and much enjoyed her company, but he clearly did not reciprocate her love (if love it was) and was always careful not to respond with more than warm friendship. You can almost feel Clare's controlled frustration and disappointment coming through her prose. In the Malcolm Brown edition of Lawrence *Letters* there is one of November 1934 from Bridlington to Lady Astor. In it a woman's name has been edited out. The relevant sentence reads, 'Mrs – 2 wrote to me ever so often at first. I have sent two notes back. Am I a beast? But she wants something which I want to keep, and she ought to understand it. There are Untouchables thank Heaven, still, despite the Ghandi's of this world.' Note 2 at the bottom of the page reads, 'Name omitted: the wife of an R.A.F. officer.'[18] Brown later explained that the withheld name was that of Clare Sydney Smith:

> Instinctively I felt I didn't wish to divulge her name, as though it were too soon to do so, as though it would be breaking an implicit trust, … If Clare Sydney Smith, as is widely believed to be the case, became to some extent infatuated with Lawrence, fell in love with him, even dared to hope for a closer relationship than

that allowed by the normal rules of friendship, why should this not be admitted? It is surely a matter of considerable interest that she appears to have found him sexually attractive and that he, so often the solitary hiding from the world, in both war and peace a man among men, could suddenly find himself arousing conventional physical affection in a spirited and handsome woman. If nothing else this adds another element to the much discussed matter of his sexuality.[19]

Another reason why Lawrence didn't seem able, or willing, to have a deep involvement with a woman was that after the trauma of the sexual assault on him at Deraa his masculinity and sexuality were permanently damaged, which in turn reinforced his need to keep his self, particularly his physical self, inviolate. When this was coupled with his emotional difficulties and social gaucherie, it would inevitably have made expressing his feelings to a woman all the more difficult. It is sometimes not realized in our own far more liberal times that a century ago courtship, with its moral taboos and family involvement, would have held issues that would have loomed much larger, almost insurmountably large in Lawrence's case, to young, middle class Edwardian men than they do to their counterparts today. When you also had a mother who didn't encourage her young sons to mix with girls or bring them to the house, ignorance and apprehension about relations with the opposite sex must have been all the greater.

Yet, paradoxically, Lawrence seemed to possess an intuitive, almost psychic understanding of a woman's emotions and thinking. The oft-cited example of this is the help and comfort he gave to Celandine Kennington when she had a miscarriage and was desperately ill, becoming at one point almost suicidal. Lawrence came to see her in hospital. She wrote of this meeting:

> He sat on a hard stool leaning forward and gripping it with his hands; he fixed his eyes on me and began, 'Of course you must be feeling very miserable, you feel you have failed in your job, and it's about the most important job in the world, … you must be feeling you are utterly no good and nothing can ever be worth while …' On and on he went, describing me to myself, clarifying all the nightmare fears by defining them, and doing it all from the woman's point of view, not the man's. He seemed to know everything that miscarriage could mean, even down to the shame of being laughed at for it, and as he talked warmth began to come into me, instead of flooding out of me for, besides putting things as they were, he brought a power to re-make them all afresh.[20]

Her husband remembered the occasion and wrote of it: 'He asked if he could have five minutes with my wife, critically ill and despondent. He talked with her for fifteen minutes and left saying nothing. Upstairs I found a joyful person, who from that day had her face turned towards health.'[21] This anecdote has become over the years something of a commemorative cliché, perhaps an expression of disproportionate hero-worship and an attribution to Lawrence of saintly qualities and powers. Yet, given consideration and bearing in mind that the Kenningtons were not gullible dupes but intelligent, sensitive people, the reminiscence gives a telling insight into the real Lawrence.

Side by side with his gift for understanding others went Lawrence's inability to understand women as sexual beings, and his obvious fear of the sexual. This stumbling block to intimacy meant, sadly, that he seemed incapable of forming any relationship with a woman that threatened to involve the physical. Here again the example of his mother's life seems to have been a powerful integer in his attitude to both sex and marriage. In recent years there has been an at times vituperative debate about whether Lawrence's horror of sex was a reaction against his brutal defilement at Deraa, or whether it was always in him, or was a by-product of his love-hate relationship with his domineering mother. In this context there was her tacit disapproval of her sons' forming serious relationships with girls. However, it is likely too that Lawrence's dislike of what he saw as women's seductive powers derived in part from the conviction that his mother had taken his father away from his normal life, limited his freedom, uprooted him from his friends, his country and his inheritance, and prevented him from claiming his rightful place in Anglo-Irish society. Seen from this standpoint, women were dangerous threats to a man's personal freedom. Lawrence confided this view of what he saw as his mother's influence over his father quite unambiguously in that emotive letter to Charlotte Shaw from India in 1927.

There is, however, a certain irrationality about this, because, despite Lawrence's outpouring to Charlotte Shaw and the degree of responsibility he seemed to attribute to his mother for the family upheaval, he must have known that his father (despite the judgement of some Lawrence biographers) was no effete, weak-willed aristocrat and was largely answerable for the decision to run off and start a new, fugitive life. This is reinforced by his father's comment in the confessional wartime letter he wrote to his sons exonerating Lawrence's mother from blame in the matter. His poignant exhortation bears repeating, 'Take warning from the terrible anxieties & sad thoughts endured by both yr Mother and me for now over thirty years! … I know not what God will say to me (yr Mother is the least to be blamed) …'. There is arguably a further possibility, that Lawrence had an innate dislike of the opposite sex; but there is no credible evidence to support this.

Then there is the part played by the so-called 'Deraa incident'. This traumatic experience is a vexed subject and has taken up reams of biographical space. Some commentators even believe it to be fictitious, a dramatic or literary effect introduced by Lawrence into the *Seven Pillars* as a coded admission of his sexuality, or for some unfathomable reason linked to his complicated psychology. Among these sceptics are the more recent biographers Lawrence James, Michael Asher and James Barr, but their attempts to debunk the incident as untrue, while showing some ingenuity and deserving of consideration, smack of being made primarily for sensational effect to promote sales. Their theories have either been convincingly disproved, are inconsistent with key facts, or can be shown to have knowingly attributed a disproportionate significance to some small anomaly. Doubt, disbelief, misinterpretation and misrepresentation have been compounded by the fact that there were no traceable witnesses to the event. However, there are compelling reasons for believing that Lawrence did indeed suffer a brutal sexual assault at Deraa and that it blighted his life thereafter.

The drawn-out intensity of his few written accounts of the event is considered by some to be indicative of masochism, or of homosexuality. This theory, though, can be seen as yet one more example of the twentieth century's obsession with sex and fails to see a more simple truth – that Lawrence had a good reason for writing about the incident in such meticulous detail and with such painful frankness. He drafted it, probably as many as nine times, because his desperate state drove him to do so, in the vain hope that in the process he might in some unaccountable way achieve a kind of resolution and closure. He wrote to Charlotte Shaw in 1925 about working on the Deraa chapter, part of 'the bad book', as he dubbed Book VI of *Seven Pillars*: 'Working on it always makes me sick. The two impulses fight so upon it. Self-respect would close it: self-expression seeks to open it. It's a case in which you can't let yourself write as well as you could.'[22]

A lot of writing is confessional, sometimes in obvious disguise, sometimes, as in the Deraa incident in *Seven Pillars*, starkly and brutally honest. Deeply embedded within him, the recollection of his degradation may well have played a significant role in Lawrence's depression during the period 1919-22 when he was at All Souls College, where he had been elected to a research fellowship worth £200 a year. It was a seven-year award and entitled him to live in rooms in College, where it was intended he should write his very personal account of the Arab Revolt. It would appear that Lawrence hoped that by reliving the agony of such a shattering experience as Deraa by writing about it, catharsis and self-forgiveness might result, that he might finally have cut out the dark incubus that infested his psyche like a tumour. Guilt is a lingering and corrosive emotion. In exposing himself so nakedly in his driven account of what happened at Deraa, Lawrence was confessing his secret guilt and pain at having, so he believed, given in to the sexual brutalities of the Turkish soldiery. It is a tragic paradox that it is the raped not the rapist who is consumed with guilt, and who is often seen, by himself as well as by others, as responsible for the assault.

And what has this to do with S.A., literary convention, idealistic love and Lawrence's emotional life? Let me return to William Morris and Lawrence's state of mind before the war at Carchemish. It was, by his own acknowledgement, a very productive and happy period for him, a 'golden' time. Those who are convinced that Lawrence had always been tortured by self-doubt, plagued by introspection and petrified of sex, women and things bodily, are somewhat deluded.

Before the war Lawrence was certainly different and stood out among many of his contemporaries, but in other ways he was typical of most intelligent, well-educated young men of his age and time. He was excited by everything that challenged or engaged his intellect and he certainly had the power to command loyalty, even unconditional devotion from some. You have only to read the memoirs of his friend Vyvyan Richards to discover how easily people fell under his spell. And he knew they did but – typically Lawrence – he affected to be unaware of such obvious hero-worship. Robert Graves noticed this, commenting that he had 'the power to excite sudden deep affections'.[23] And he loved fun, liked to tease, delighted in adventures and always took the lead.

Yet it is always difficult to pin Lawrence down when it comes to his beliefs, his true passions and how much his friendships really mattered to him. In fact, he seemed to like places more than people. He wrote, partially tongue-in-cheek, to Lady Astor: 'Probably it would be wholesome for me to lose my heart – if that monstrous piece of machinery is capable of losing itself: for till now it has never cared for anyone, though much for places and things.'[24] Nevertheless, there are a few areas where it is possible to feel reasonably certain about his commitment. Literature, history, poetry, and church and military architecture: these were real loves. His Oxford finals and his thesis on crusader castles had won him a notable First Class degree, and the one interest that dominated his intellectual pursuits was medieval history and everything to do with the Middle Ages. John Mack, in his penetrating study of Lawrence, cites A.W. Lawrence as a source of evidence for his brother's medieval preoccupations: 'Although Lawrence read widely, his reading was dominated by medieval romantic works, especially French, and the ideas of medieval romanticism came to fill his consciousness. Arnold Lawrence is of the opinion that his brother's medieval researches were "a dream way of escape from Bourgeois England" …'[25]

From his early youth he had immersed himself deeply in all things medieval: castles, churches, armour, chivalry, and Provençal poetry, the poetry of the troubadours. This disproportionate fascination with the Middle Ages fulfilled the needs of a vivid imagination, but it also reflected a strong urge to escape both from a modern world he found in many ways uncongenial and from his parents' hypocritical concealments, which he hated and which disturbed him, inculcating an abiding sense of alienation. So his journeyings deep into a rich, romantic past, with their secret assumption of the noblest values and virtues of another more colourful, more heroic age, freed him from the present.

In his teenage years he studied the Middle Ages with what his friend and companion on many a youthful adventure, 'Scroggs' Beeson, called 'a passionate absorption'.[26] Beeson recalled: 'At the age of fifteen he was well versed in monumental brasses and had acquired a fine series of rubbings from churches in the eastern and southern counties. Cut out and pasted on the walls of his bedroom were life-size figures of knights and priests', and 'There was much searching in libraries for the histories of those priests and knights and ladies.'[27]

In 1927, in a letter written in note form to provide some essential detail of his youthful preoccupations, Lawrence told his biographer Robert Graves: 'Spare time spent books: and studying mediaeval art, especially sculpture. Later collected mediaeval pottery. At 18, specialised mediaeval military architecture: visited every XIIth Cent. castle England and France. 3) Oxford. At Jesus read history, officially: actually spent nearly three years reading Provençal poetry, and Mediaeval French chansons de geste.'[28] This admission that he had seriously neglected his history degree studies and had instead devoted three years to immersing himself in such an esoteric subject as Provençal troubadour poetry, has a significance easily overlooked. He later enlarged on this to Liddell Hart, 'I also read nearly every manual of chivalry. Remember that my "period" was the Middle Ages, always.'[29] Vyvyan Richards recounts how in his third year at Jesus College 'it was reported that there was a queer stranger among us, who walked solitary at all hours of the night in the still quadrangles of the college. I went to call on him: he was out and the only signs of him were a few strange books – of early French poetry chiefly.' And again: 'I would hunt him out in the Bodleian and find him squatting on the floor in a remote corner with some large medieval volume on his knees.'[30]

In early August 1908, while on his bicycling grand tour of France seeking out early castles, fortifications, cathedrals and churches, Lawrence wrote to his mother detailing his itinerary: '& passed thence through Tarascon to Beaucaire, which I saluted for the sake of Nicolette',...[31] Nicolette, the heroine of the medieval romance *Aucassin and Nicolette*, was a Mohammedan slave while Aucassin was an aristocrat. Note that it is Nicolette, not Aucassin, whom Lawrence salutes. In this thirteenth-century fable the two lovers fight against parental and social interference and experience the bliss of extramarital love long before the story ends, with, for once, a happy marriage. The story contains arguably one of the most remarkable passages of medieval literature: Aucassin is warned that hell not paradise awaits him if he persists in his passion.

He responds with a robust disdain, defiantly insisting that he cares nothing for paradise and only wants Nicolette whom he so loves, and if he has to go to hell, he wants to be in the company of all the great troubadours, minstrels and beautiful ladies of courtly love who will also be there; but, above all, he is adamant that he must have Nicolette with him. If Lawrence disliked women, let alone men's romantic involvement with them, why would he have had a soft spot for Nicolette? Lawrence's letter of August 1908 to his mother is one of the most romantic he ever wrote and is peppered with lyrical Victorian and 1890s poetic quotations. At one point, describing a swim he had had in the warm waters of the Mediterranean, 'the great sea, the greatest in the world', he writes: 'I felt that at last I had reached the way to the South, and all the glorious East; Greece, Carthage, Egypt, Tyre, Syria, Italy, Spain, Sicily, Crete ... they were all there, and all within reach ... of me. I fancy I know now better than Keats what Cortes felt like, "silent upon a peak in Darien." Oh I must get down here, – farther out – again! Really this getting to the sea has almost overturned my mental balance.'[32]

Returning to Lawrence's medieval predilections, J.G. Edwards, a Jesus College contemporary, wrote: 'I remember a rare occasion when he came to a meeting of the College Literary Society: a paper was read on the *Chanson de Roland*. When it was over Lawrence spoke for about twenty minutes in his clear, quiet voice, ranging serenely about the epic poetry of several languages. It was all first hand: you felt that he had 'been there'.[33] Another College friend of Lawrence's, A.T.P. Williams, who went on to have a highly distinguished career as a don, a headmaster, and a bishop, also testified to Lawrence's interest in Provençal poetry and to the indelible impression Lawrence's knowledge of it made on him as an undergraduate. They both had rooms off the same V4 staircase at Jesus. Williams wrote of his colleague: 'I have never since felt anything like the extraordinary fascination which Lawrence's curious, penetrating knowledge of medieval poetry and buildings, and a multitude of strange places, had for me.'[34] Winifred Fontana, with whom Lawrence shared adventures around Carchemish, recorded an anecdote about him that again shows the depth of his knowledge of the Middle Ages. She wrote: 'I have had it said to me by a frenchman who afterwards made a distinguished diplomatic career: "Ma foi, Madame! I thought I knew something about medieval french history and architecture, but your compatriot Lawrence's knowledge is profound."'[35]

It is clear that Lawrence had a deep and detailed knowledge of the real Middle Ages, a world of extremes that contained battles, brutality, licentiousness and treachery side by side with a refined culture of chivalry, troubadour poetry and courts of love. However, what is interesting is that Lawrence was able to reconcile the down-to-earth evidence of dry historical scholarship with the idealistic vision of his imagination, which transformed a brutish world into an ideal one of knightly heroism, comradeship under arms, and poetry inspired by noble ladies in faraway castles. This was Lawrence's secret world. A glimpse into it can be got from a 1910 letter he wrote to his mother from France about the joys of reading through the night at home in Oxford: 'And it is lovely too, after you have been wandering for hours in the forest with Percivale or Sagramors le desirous, to open the door, and from over the Cherwell to look at the sun glowering through the valley mists.' And from the same letter, 'And that is why one can only live in the future or the past, in Utopia or the Wood Beyond the World.'[36] *The Wood Beyond the World* is a William Morris novel and Morris's work was, of course, the perfect literary vehicle for transporting Lawrence from a mundane existence into a mystical one. In some ways Lawrence was a Pre-Raphaelite manqué. If he was a realist when it came to action and getting things done, his true life was an internal, very private, very romantic one typified by Morris's writings. Lawrence wrote to Charlotte Shaw from India in 1927:

> Morris was a great poet: and I'd rather have written The Well at the World's End or The Roots of the Mountains or John Ball or The Hollow Land than anything of the 19th cent. except War and Peace or Moby Dick. Sigurd and The Dynasts and Paradise Lost and Samson and Adam Cast Forth are the best long poems in English. And Morris wrote 50 perfect short poems. Why the man is among the very great! I suppose everybody loves one writer, unreasonably. I'd rather Morris than the world.[37]

Again from India he wrote to her:

> We admire the very great, but love the less: perhaps that is why I would choose to live with the works of William Morris, if I had to make a single choice. My reason tells me that he isn't a very great writer: but then, he wrote just the stuff I like. Your 'Well at the World's End,' here in front of me, comforts me even when I do not open it.[38]

He considered *The Well at the World's End*, *The Hollow Land*, *The Roots of the Mountains* and *Journals in Iceland* 'very marvellous'.[39] He seems to have had a particularly soft spot for *The Well at the World's End*, writing to Charlotte Shaw, 'I sleep for two or three hours at a time in its pages. It is like a river of quietness over my head. Morris had a secret depth in him, from which came such strengths as Sigurd.'[40] In a letter to her, just a week before, he had again talked of Morris: 'I'm reading, one by one, the early prose stories of that master man. They are glorious.'[41] He had a copy of *The Well* at Carchemish in 1911.[42] Eighteen years later, in the RAF in India in 1929, he still had the book with him.[43] Towards the end of the war he wrote to Vyvyan Richards: 'This is a very long porch to explain why I'm always trying to blow up railway trains and bridges instead of looking for the *Well at the World's End*.'[44]

SIXTEEN

The Well at the World's End

WHILE I WAS in the high hills of the Lebanon I would walk up onto the plateau, the no-man's-land between Lebanon and Syria, its bald terrain of haphazardly strewn rocks and stones relieved here and there by a bush or a lone, stunted tree. Sitting in a rare shaded spot, I carefully re-read the material I had gathered about Provençal poetry and Lawrence's self-declared attraction to it. When I placed this alongside the compelling evidence of his abiding love of William Morris, it seemed overwhelmingly clear to me that in combination they were the powerful literary justification for his rarefied feelings, the wellsprings of an intensely private and carefully guarded emotional life, a sort of secret credo of the heart – and that they were almost certainly the key to S.A.

In England the later nineteenth century and the Edwardian decade saw a renewed scholarly interest in the poetry of the troubadours. This literary topicality wouldn't have escaped Lawrence's notice. Nevertheless, why would a seven-hundred-year-old esoteric poetic convention have held such appeal for him? What was it that made him spend so much time studying Provençal poetry with its convention of idealistic love? The reason that immediately springs to mind is that not only did it appeal to his poetic taste and love of the medieval but, more significantly, it fitted his own psychology like a glove. It was the power of literature justifying emotional predilection. By embracing the convention of troubadour love as a kind of template for his own emotional life Lawrence could love secretly, even from a distance, and the physical did not have to be involved. He could dream, he could long, without having to do anything about it other than experience the emotions and acknowledge them to himself. In other words, he could dispense with the bodily and live in the heart and soul.

Since troubadour poetry clearly held more than purely intellectual interest for Lawrence, a brief exposition of its core values and principles may be revealing. A scholar and near-contemporary of Lawrence commented on Provençal poetry and the secret love it expressed:

> The pastime of chivalrous love was carried on under certain well-understood rules and conventions. The first and most important was that the identity of the object of the poet's love and homage should not be disclosed, under the stress of whatsoever temptation. This is very clearly explained by the troubadour Bernart de Ventadour: 'For a man is always fearful of failing in his duty to his beloved; wherefore I dare not be bold to speak. As to one point, my understanding helps me; namely, that no one ever questioned me concerning my joy without my readily lying to him about it.'[1]

This rule of secrecy (the Provençal *celar*) is of key importance in the context of Lawrence's dedication. A true Provençal poet hid his muse's real name behind a *senhal*, or pseudonym, such as Bon Vezi (beautiful face – 'Garati' in the Arabic convention). He would go to great lengths to prevent the discovery of her identity, sometimes disguising it, as did de Ventadour, with a *senhal* of neutral, or even of male, gender, such as 'Midons' or 'Tristan', or with a descriptive one such as *conort* (comfort or consolation) or *aziman* (magnet).

The troubadour Giraud de Bornelle wrote, 'Among lovers the highest praise is secrecy and constancy.' De Bornelle frequented the courts of the sovereigns of Navarre, Castile and Aragon and took part with Richard Coeur de Lion in the Third Crusade (1189–92). Richard was one of Lawrence's favourite historical figures, while another favourite (and like Coeur de Lion a troubadour) was Bertrand de Born, who was a close friend of Richard's. It is said that all royal and noble titles were dropped between the two men. It was de Born who coined the nickname Richard Yea-and-Nay.[2] Richard Coeur de Lion's parents were Eleanor of Aquitaine and her second husband, Henry II of England. Richard was her favourite son. Aquitaine encompassed a swathe of south-west France, with Poitiers as its literary heart, and had close links to Provence, the traditional home of the troubadours. Eleanor's grandfather, Guillem, the seventh Count of Poitiers and ninth Duke of Aquitaine, is credited with being the first troubadour of the West. In 1137 Eleanor had married Louis VII of France and a decade later accompanied him on the Second Crusade to Outremer, taking her troubadours with her. They stayed for a while in Antioch in Syria, where earlier crusaders had settled and intermarried with the local Saracen aristocracy, and where her uncle, Raymond, was the current ruler. Much drawn to Raymond and enamoured of Antioch's sophisticated society where western Christian, Greek and Moslem seemed to live in civilized harmony, she decided to stay on.

Louis forced her to return to France and she is reputed to have brought back with her many elements of the exotic courtly culture that she had found in Syria, including our orders of chivalry. This further enriched the troubadour culture of southern France, which a significant number of scholars now believe may have derived in considerable measure from the long-established Arab culture of Moorish Spain. They would argue that this Moorish-Arabic literary culture and poetic convention had developed over centuries in Arabia and had then spread with Arab conquest along north Africa and into Spain. Thence it was carried through Catalonia into Provence by the *raouis*, gifted itinerants whose performances of songs and poetry are often praised in the *Arabian Nights*. Again their main theme was love.[3]

The Provençals would therefore have been receptive to the even more copious infusions of this eastern culture which poured in on the acquisition of their crown by Raymond Berenger, Count of Barcelona, who had married the heiress of the Provençal kings in 1112. Indeed, the word 'troubadour' could conceivably have Arabic not French origins. The most commonly given etymology is the Provençal 'trobar', meaning 'to invent', thus 'inventor' or 'maker', but an equally plausible derivation is that it is a composite, a corruption of a word or words which originally came from Arabic, namely, *tarrabyadour* 'the joy (or music) maker'.

It may be said in objection to the claimed idealism of troubadour love that it was – like many ideals – corrupted by human nature and that behind the poet's exalting of the unrivalled beauty and virtue of his lady lay a more base motivation, namely sexual desire. Certainly some troubadour poems and poets did express a longing for physical consummation, but such longings mostly remained just that – longings. Nevertheless, it could be argued that the cryptic nature of Provençal poetry was dictated not so much by poetic convention as by the fact that the object of a troubadour's worship was often the wife of his patron, the nobleman in whose court the poet plied his trade as itinerant bard and on whose favours he depended for his subsistence. Such a liege-lord could be boorish, bellicose and jealous and would not take kindly to a dalliance between his wife, the chatelaine, and a court poet, especially if the poet's devotion were reciprocated. So, the argument would run, the need for secrecy would be paramount and would account for the poets' cryptic dedications.

Such an interpretation misses the key point. The core principles of the troubadour convention (certainly as understood by the scholars of Lawrence's day) were not intended as a cover for intimate assignation or lascivious adventure but rather embodied an almost sacred belief in the power of secret ideal love of a woman to transfigure, ennoble and enable. Such a muse could often be unobtainable, sometimes remote and referred to as *La Dame Lointaine* (the distant lady) worshipped from afar. Indeed, for the Pre-Raphaelites this *amor de lonh* (faraway love) typified the essence of courtly love. It is this mystical, spiritual interpretation of Provençal poetry that would have held a strong psychological appeal for Lawrence. In England the fin-de-siècle, scholarly fascination with a poetic concept as noble as the transforming power of ideal troubadour love would have given it a degree of social respectability and legitimacy. More signally, this fresh exploration and acclamation of the quasi-mystical source of western poetry appeared at exactly the right moment to attract a young and idealistic T.E. Lawrence, a Lawrence who always accorded a disproportionate importance to poetry, especially poetry and literature which championed a romantic and elevating ideal.

In his study of Provençal poetry Lawrence would have gone back to original sources where they were available, as in archives like the Bodleian Library, but he would certainly have been familiar with the new appreciations of the poetry by the scholars of his day. I have tried to summarize the essential ethos and beliefs of troubadour poetry to show just what a compelling influence they would have had on a highly intelligent, romantic, emotionally repressed but receptive young man like Lawrence, who – he said so himself – had applied himself over a three-year period to learning all he could about them. The fact that he claimed to have studied Provençal poetry in such depth is in itself an indication of its attraction for him. When Lawrence studied, he studied exhaustively, so he would certainly have known the history, precepts, poetic forms, conceits, and inner meanings of troubadour culture intimately, especially its claim to have the mystical capacity to engage the emotions deeply and to motivate action at the noblest level.

So what are the essential elements of this poetry that attracted Lawrence? The purest troubadour poetry had three key principles, which perfectly complemented his own sensibilities: an insistence on secrecy; a spiritual core and sublimation of the physical; and the power to activate a man's noblest motivations. For the true troubadour love was pure and ideal. Courtly love – or *fin' amors, bon' amors, veraia amors,* or *amors valens* – was not a love of physical possession but one of unconsummated longing, which was seen as a means to an end: progress and growth in virtue, merit and worth.[4] Put another way, in ideal troubadour love sexual intercourse was forbidden as impure, hideous and abominable, the desire for it arising from the animal nature of man. Love was pure only when such animal desires were subdued. Pure love consisted of the union of the souls and hearts of the lovers.[5] The emphasis on this mystical union of hearts and souls would have had a crucial significance for Lawrence's feelings. Of course, in parallel with his Provençal preoccupations went his championing of William Morris, whose tales were in many ways a Victorian reworking of troubadour ideals.

Here is an example of the storytelling and dialogue that characterize the medieval quest that is Morris's *The Well at the World's End,* which, as already shown, was one of Lawrence's favourite books. It depicts the moment when the hero and heroine reach the mystical well:

> Now that level place, or bench-table went up to the very gushing and green bow of the water, so Ralph took Ursula's hand and led her along, she going a little after him, till he was close to the Well, and stood amidst the spray-bow thereof, so that he looked verily like one of the painted angels on the choir wall of St. Lawrence of Upmeads. Then he reached forth his hand and thrust the cup into the water, holding it stoutly because the gush of the stream was strong, so that the water of the Well splashed all over him, wetting Ursula's face and breast withal: and he felt that the water was sweet without any saltness of the sea. But he turned to Ursula and reached out the full cup to her, and said: 'Sweetling, call a health over the cup!'
>
> She took it and said: 'To thy life, beloved!' and drank withal, and her eyes looked out of the cup the while, like a child's when he drinketh. Then she gave him the cup again and said: 'Drink, and tarry not, lest thou die and I live.' Then Ralph plunged the cup into the waters again, and he held the cup aloft, and cried out: 'To the Earth, and the World of Manfolk!' and therewith he drank. For a minute then they clung together within the spray-bow of the Well, and then she took his hand and led him back to the midst of the bench-table, and he put the cup into the ambrye, and shut it up again, and then they sat them down on the widest of the platform under the shadow of a jutting rock; for the sun was hot; and therewithal a sweet weariness began to steal over them, though there was speech betwixt them for a little, and Ralph said: 'How is it with thee, beloved?'
>
> 'O well, indeed,' she said.

Quoth he: 'And how tasteth to thee the water of the Well?'

Slowly she spake and sleepily: 'It tasted good, and as if thy love were blended with it.'[6]

There are pages of this rather contrived, pseudo-medieval language and it does become a taxing read. How many people read William Morris's curious Gothic sagas today? But Lawrence feasted on them. Why? Because beneath their narrative of knightly quests and battles and damsels in distress lay an oddly mystical core, which captured Lawrence's imagination and swept him up into a fantasy world he found far more engrossing and affecting than the real one. Lawrence studied real medieval history in great depth and could talk and write knowledgeably on the subject, and yet for pleasure he preferred immersing himself in Morris's highly romanticized and largely imagined Middle Ages. Why? because it answered a deep need in him: to escape from mundane everyday reality and to live in the limitless imagination.

His love of *The Well at the World's End* is a perfect example of this and provides a real insight into the inner Lawrence. In this hidden sanctum Lawrence would, for example, have seen the Arab Revolt almost as literature-in-action, an epic romance – heroic, noble, challenging and exhilarating. He wrote of the Revolt in *Seven Pillars* as, 'a chronicle in the spirit of the old men who marched with Bohemond or Coeur de Lion.'[7] However, where Lawrence *was* perhaps unusual was that he was able to see the Revolt on two levels simultaneously: a medieval quest and also a bloody conflict where the belligerents were often treacherous and self-seeking, and where the politicians behind the scenes were marked by duplicity and dissimulation, motivated largely by imperial ambition and territorial greed.

The harsh realities of Lawrence's war experience may eventually have dissipated his romantic ideals, but they were certainly firmly in place during the Revolt and would have included that central element: ideal troubadour love. There have, however, been attempts to question Lawrence's interest in Provençal poetry. One of these objectors was M.D. Allen, Assistant Professor of English at the University of Wisconsin Center in the USA. He said: 'Lawrence's claim of immersion in the poetry of the Provençal troubadours is indeed puzzling, and not only because of the paucity of references to it, or the absence of texts at Clouds Hill. It is true that Lawrence was at Oxford (1907–10) when Provençal literature was nearer the forefront of the educated consciousness than it is now.' Professor Allen here acknowledges that there was a considerable resurgence of interest in the troubadours in the literary establishment of the day but then goes on to emphasize what he claims is Lawrence's lack of interest in troubadour love in particular and heterosexual love in general: '… one searches in vain for any interest in or reference to the one subject commonly associated with the Provençal poets … courtly love. Lawrence is not interested in the relations between the sexes, and is most certainly not interested in the perfection of one particular woman or the nature of true love.'

Allen then remarks that in *Seven Pillars of Wisdom* Lawrence seldom mentions women and when he does it is in a pejorative context. To illustrate what he claims is Lawrence's distaste for women he quotes several passages from Wilfred Scawen Blunt and his wife's 1903 translation of *The Seven Golden Odes of Pagan Arabia*, also known as the *Moallakat*, which describes the chivalrous courts of Arabia where the ideal love of women played a major role. Allen quotes Blunt to underline the pre-eminent theme of the *Moallakat*: '"Devotion to a woman nobly born," writes the elder man "of their own noble race and people, is the theme their poets love to dwell on, and always stands foremost in their scheme of romance. It is the keynote initially struck of every poem of the Moallakat."'

Allen, again quoting Blunt, continues, '"It is always the woman loved and lost that is mourned by them with the most passionate longing, for whom they perform their most glorious deeds, and whom they celebrate in their most enduring songs."'[8] Allen then notes at the bottom of a page that Lawrence had a copy of the *Moallakat* with him in Cairo during the war. In fact, Lawrence wrote home in February 1915 asking his family to send him out a copy of the book. So if 'devotion to a woman nobly born of their own noble race and people' is 'the keynote initially struck of every poem of the *Moallakat*', why would Lawrence, whom Allen maintains is almost repelled by heterosexual love, ideal or otherwise, want a copy of these love-centred poems sent out to him? As for Allen's comments that *Seven Pillars* contains very few references to women and even fewer complimentary ones, surely he must have known that war is largely the province of men. Would Allen find many detailed references to women in the plethora of soldiers' memoirs of life on the Western Front?

In further refutation of Allen's views, it should also be emphasized that Lawrence made it almost a self-imposed ordinance never to reveal anything that might expose his deepest feelings. As he wrote to his mother from Cairo in 1915, 'If you only knew that if one thinks deeply about anything one would rather die than say anything about it.'[9] Lawrence wrote in similarly revealing vein to Edward Garnett in that all-important year of 1927: 'The "fear of showing my feelings" is my real self.'[10] This emotional embargo is again reflected in the recollections of his fellow archaeologist at Carchemish, Leonard Woolley, who wrote of him: 'The best of companions, he was frightfully reserved about himself and in all our long talks seemed detached from what he said; if he showed signs of sentiment, as very occasionally he did, he would at once turn them to ridicule. I do not remember his ever admitting to any affection for anybody, though I knew perfectly well that in the case of certain people the affection was there and was deeply felt; in all matters of the emotions he seemed to have a peculiar distrust of himself.'[11]

It is clear that Allen's assertion that one searches in vain for any reference to courtly love in Lawrence's life is in the broadest sense untrue. I would again draw attention to the evidence of Vyvyan Richards's visit to Lawrence's rooms in Jesus College when he noticed a number of books 'of early French poetry chiefly,' and often found Lawrence in the Bodleian with a medieval tome on his knees. Early French poetry is Provençal, troubadour poetry.

At this stage the recurring dilemma of Lawrence's sexuality ought to be addressed. Several biographers, notable among them Allen and Jeffrey Meyers, have been persuaded of Lawrence's homosexuality, largely, I would suggest, because there would appear to be little evidence of heterosexual involvement in Lawrence's life. These biographers ignore the opinions of all his friends and of his fellow aircraftmen in the RAF. Whenever they were asked about whether Shaw (Lawrence) was homosexual, they rejected the possibility out of hand. To give an idea of the nature of some of these suggestions that Lawrence was homosexual, it is worth quoting from Meyers's book, *The Wounded Spirit*, which was published in 1973, three years before John Mack's milestone biography was to treat the subject with much greater insight and illumination.

In pursuit of his argument, Meyers was even prepared to doctor quotations. One example will suffice. Discussing Lawrence's sexuality, he commented: 'Lawrence told Lionel Curtis that his masochism remains and will remain.'[12] Lawrence's actual words were, 'for my masochism remains and will remain, only moral.'[13] Meyers's knowing omission of the crucial qualification 'only moral' alters the meaning completely. Meyers also claimed that 'there is continual evidence of homosexuality, especially with Sheik Ahmed.'[14] This assertion, clearly intended to give the impression that it was an accepted fact, is totally untrue. There is no evidence whatsoever of a homosexual relationship between Lawrence and Dahoum – or for that matter between Lawrence and the young aircraftman, Robert Guy (who met Lawrence in 1923 at the RAF School of Photography at Farnborough), who is also cited by Meyers in support of his arguments.

Guy was about to be married and nicknames, such as those with which Lawrence *and* his fellow aircraftmen, dubbed Guy – 'Poppet' and 'Rabbit' – were commonly given by the servicemen to each other and were a part of the intimacy born of a cramped communal life. Most of the servicemen had nicknames that evoked something in their physical appearance.

Lawrence found himself labelled with the unflattering sobriquet of 'Shortarse'.[15] Guy, in fact, seemed to have become one of the many people who exploited Lawrence's fulsome generosity. Jeremy Wilson has commented of Guy's letters to Lawrence that 'they show that Guy wrote repeatedly about his various difficulties, asking Lawrence for financial help. A number of Lawrence's contemporaries in the ranks have told me that some individuals took advantage of his generosity, and it is difficult to avoid the conclusion that Guy was one of these "spongers".'[16]

The arguments of Allen and Meyers are disingenuous. Firstly, it is probably true, as they point out, that not many girls saw the inside of the Lawrences' home in Polstead Road, Oxford, but there was one particular girl who did, and who turns out to have been very significant in terms of Lawrence's sexuality and of his immersion in Provençal love poetry. I shall discuss her in more detail later. Secondly, when Lawrence mentioned homosexual relationships in *Seven Pillars*, he was simply describing in frank detail what the privations of desert life and the dictates of Arab celibate youth culture imposed on its young men. Lawrence's accounts of such male congresses merely record, objectively and without judgement, the facts of desert life in wartime.

We come now to Vyvyan Richards and Ernest Altounyan. Richards confessed in a biography (*The Secret Lives of Lawrence of Arabia*) many years after Lawrence's death that he had been in love with Lawrence but that Lawrence had found such ardent devotion quite incomprehensible. In return, Richards said, he had received only heartbreaking affection. He wrote:

> Quite frankly, for me it was love at first sight … He had neither flesh nor carnality of any kind; he just did not understand. He received my affection, my sacrifice, in fact, eventually my total subservience, as though it was his due. He never gave the slightest sign that he understood my motives or fathomed my desire. In return for all I offered him – with admittedly ulterior motives – he gave me the purest affection, love and respect that I have ever received from anyone … a love and respect that was spiritual in quality. I realise now that he was sexless – at least that he was unaware of sex.[17]

It was with Richards, the friend of his undergraduate days, that Lawrence explored the Arts and Crafts movement. They spent a lot of their time together preoccupied with the movement's founder, William Morris. They visited the Cotswolds to see Morris's house and view the Kelmscott Chaucer and had planned to put up a building at Pole Hill in Epping Forest (where as a child Morris had ridden about playing at medieval knights) in keeping with the principles of the movement. They had even acquired some old, carved oak king posts, rafters and purlins for the purpose. The building was to be a sort of Pre-Raphaelite hall with all its medieval associations of knights and tourneys and quests. Here they had hoped to produce their own hand-printed books. Richards was to get a rare glimpse of Lawrence's struggle to come to terms with his own oddity, his being somehow set apart from others, and into the self-denigration that was a part of it. The young Lawrence enthused to Richards about Christina Rossetti's poetry, particularly her mystical, self-immolating poem 'A Martyr – The Vigil of the Feast'.[18] It didn't appeal to Richards at all but Lawrence kept pressing it on him, urging him especially to read the stanza: 'Now am I tired, too tired to strive or smile; I sit alone, my mouth is in the dust: Look thou upon me, Lord, for I am vile.'[19] This despairing exhortation certainly evokes a sense of low self-worth, of isolation, and for Lawrence it evoked perhaps too the abiding stigma of his illegitimacy.

Ernest Altounyan, an Armenian with an Irish mother and a father who was a celebrated surgeon, lived in Aleppo and became a doctor. He and Lawrence were close friends during Lawrence's Carchemish years and thereafter. Altounyan was to marry happily but as a young man he too was said to have been in love with Lawrence. But Lawrence again carefully distanced himself, dealing kindly with the matter and gently deflecting it. He once wrote to Altounyan, 'I have never loved anyone, or hardly ever; lands and peoples – yes.'[20] And in a 1933 Christmastime letter, written in response to a request for criticism of some love poetry Altounyan had composed to a woman, Lawrence said: 'The matter puzzles me: you must be patient there with my inadequacy. I do not love anybody and have not, I think, ever – or hardly ever. It is difficult to share with people what one gives wholeheartedly to places or peoples or things. Nor have ever, I think, except momentarily-and–with-the-eye lusted. Altogether I am a bad subject for feeling.'[21]

There exists a prolific and passionate series of letters from Altounyan to Lawrence, now in a private collection, and after Lawrence's death Altounyan wrote a long memorial poem to him in the form of a book of sonnets. Entitled *Ornament of Honour*, the first four lines of stanza forty-six read:

Thou, who didst ever count thyself for nought,
Hast nothing lost in losing all of thee;
While I, who found in thyself all I sought,
Am now made bankrupt by thy loss and me.[22]

SEVENTEEN

Body and Soul

SO, WHAT can be deduced about Lawrence's sexuality? For a man who was often very reticent about discussing bodily functions there are a surprisingly large number of comments from him in correspondence, or detailed in books, about his own sexuality, which make it reasonably clear what his feelings about it were.

He replied to a letter from Robert Graves, which had talked about sex: 'Your last page, about fucking, defeats me wholly. As I wrote (with some courage, I think: few people admit the damaging ignorance) I haven't ever: and don't much want to …' He added that in not indulging he didn't feel he missed much and that 'it must leave a dirty feeling, too.'[1] In correspondence with the Cambridge don F.L. Lucas he repeated that he had never had sexual intercourse and hoped not to.[2] He also betrayed an almost complete lack of knowledge and understanding of the sexual act and of the fact that it could be much more than just a physical congress. He had come to believe that the act was 'transient' and made it clear that it disgusted him. Such was his ignorance that he had to ask his fellow aircraftmen about the act itself; he then deduced from what they told him that, among other things, it was 'all over in ten minutes.'[3]

To Lawrence sex was something mechanical and distasteful, its only justification and purpose being procreation, certainly not pleasure or enjoyment. And yet he believed that it *was* pleasure not procreation that made most men seek out sexual activity. He wrote to Charlotte Shaw: 'The motive which brings the sexes together is 99% sensual pleasure, and only 1% the desire for children, in men, so far as I can learn. As I told you, I haven't ever been carried away in that sense, so that I'm a bad subject to treat of it. Perhaps the possibility of a child relieves sometimes what otherwise must seem an unbearable humiliation to the woman: – for I presume it's unbearable. However here I'm trenching on dangerous ground, with my own ache coming to life again.'[4] This last comment is perhaps an oblique reference to his rape at Deraa.

Again he wrote to Charlotte Shaw, talking of his RAF life:

> From henceforward my way will lie with these fellows here, degrading myself (for in their eyes and your eyes and Winterton's eyes I see that it is a degradation) in the hope that some day I will really feel degraded, to their level. I long for people to look down upon me and despise me, and I'm too shy to take the filthy steps which would publicly shame me, and put me into their contempt. I want to dirty myself outwardly, so that my person may properly reflect the dirtiness which it conceals … and I shrink from dirtying the outside, while I've eaten, avidly eaten, every filthy morsel which chance threw in my way. I'm too shy to go looking for dirt. I'd be afraid of seeming a novice in it, when I found it. That's why I can't go off stewing into the Lincoln or Navenby brothels with the fellows. They think it's because I'm superior, proud, or peculiar, or 'posh', as they say: and it's because I wouldn't know what to do, how to carry myself, where to stop. Fear again: fear everywhere.'[5]

It is clear that Lawrence was in denial about the value of sex within a loving relationship, and probably, deep down, knew that he was; yet his abhorrence of the physical prevented him from any voluntary indulgence, even more so after his rape at Deraa. To Lawrence the bodily, particularly the sexual, is always synonymous with 'filth' and 'dirt'. When he was at a very low ebb in the Tank Corps in 1923 he wrote to Lionel Curtis, an historian and a Fellow of All Souls College, about the coarseness of his fellow soldiers:

> These are foul-mouthed, and behind their mouths is a pervading animality of spirit, whose unmixed bestiality frightens and hurts me. There is no criticism, indeed it's taken for granted as natural, that you should job a woman's body, or hire yourself out, or abuse yourself in any way. I cried out against it, partly in self-pity because I've condemned myself to grow like them, and partly in premonition of failure, for my masochism remains and will remain, only moral. Physically I can't do it: indeed I get in denial the gratification they get in indulgence. I react against their example into an abstention even more rigorous than

of old. Everything bodily is now hateful to me (and in my case hateful is the same as impossible).[6]

In another letter of 1923 to Curtis, written six weeks before, Lawrence had said:

I lie in bed night after night with this cat-calling carnality seething up and down the hut, fed by streams of fresh matter from twenty lecherous mouths … and my mind aches with the rawness of it … We are all guilty alike, you know. You wouldn't exist, I wouldn't exist, without this carnality. Everything with flesh in its mixture is the achievement of a moment when the lusty thought of Hut 12 has passed to action and conceived: and isn't it true that the fault of birth rests somewhat on the child? I believe it's we who led our parents on to bear us, and it's our unborn children who make our flesh itch. A filthy business all of it, and yet Hut 12 shows me the truth behind Freud. Sex is an integer in all of us, and the nearer nature we are, the more constantly, the more completely a product of that integer. These fellows are the reality, and you and I, the selves who used to meet in London and talk of fleshless things, are only the outward wrappings of a core like these fellows.[7]

Hector Bolitho, a journalist and author, recounted an anecdote that illustrates Lawrence's dislike and fear of being in any way confronted or pestered by women. His way of dealing with such approaches was to be brusquely dismissive, which had the desired effect but often, and wrongly, gave the impression that he had no time for women at all. The facts show otherwise. Bolitho described Lawrence's reaction to a woman who had been too intrusive at a weekend house party in 1933: 'The crowded drawing-room made him shy, especially when one of the women guests asked him, "Why don't you marry?" He answered, "I am not interested in women. I have never found one that interested me."'[8]

Yet many who knew Lawrence well have testified that he certainly didn't dislike women. In fact, he could be very fond of them and really enjoy their company. One thinks of Winifred Fontana, Celandine Kennington, Clare Sydney Smith, Dorelia John, and Margot Hill, all attractive and all far from old. Hill, whom he had first met during the Cairo Conference of 1921, recalled: 'My relations with him were on an easy, almost childish plane. We delighted in practical jokes and terrible puns. Occasionally he teased, criticized, or scolded me as might an elder brother.' After the war he used to visit her at her home in London: 'Occasionally he would roll up on the settee for the night or what was left of it. If I were out he would leave little notes: "Took the last apple"; "Your Bovary translation is rotten." Once a catafalque of cushions, books, and oddments was built up in the middle of the room, topped by a penny and the note, "Used your telephone." He would never speak of what was happening to him. I was not going to start it and he never did.'⁹

The idea of marriage *per se* did not repel him. In 1919 during the Peace Conference in Paris Lawrence sometimes visited Colonel Richard Meinertzhagen in his hotel rooms and their conversation ranged far and wide and encompassed Lawrence's personal life. Meinertzhagen (who in other contexts has been shown to have been guilty of fabrication) should be read with some caution, but his comments here ring true.

He wrote:

> To imply any sort of sex-perversion or uncleanness to Laurens [sic] is grossly inaccurate and libellous. He admired virility, energy; he often told me how he admired the figure of a young boy or girl, the most wonderful example of beauty. But his mind was pure as gold. Indelicacy, indecency, any form of coarseness or vulgarity repelled him physically. He frequently discussed marriage and women with me. He was not a woman hater, but loathed the false type, the decorated hussy, the noisy strumpet, the flattering society woman. His objection to matrimony was physical contact. He could not bear even being touched on the sleeve and shaking hands was an effort.¹⁰

And Dr Altounyan wrote: 'He was never married because he never happened to meet the right person; and nothing short of that would do: a bald statement of fact which cannot hope to convince the perverse intricacy of the public mind.'¹¹ The day after Lawrence's death diarist Thomas Jones told a Lady Grigg that Lawrence, 'had sometimes thought of marriage in general but not, so far as I know, in particular.'¹² As early as 1911 in a letter home Lawrence had quipped about his and his brothers' unsuitability for a normal family life: 'Poor Father! His sons are not going to support his years by the gain of their profession & trades. One a missionary: one an artist of sorts and a wanderer after sensations; one thinking of lay education work: one in the army, & one too small to think. None of us can ever afford to keep a wife.'¹³

Years later he joked to a Royal Tank Corps friend about marriage: 'I suppose I should become bored with her in six months, as with all things. And then where would *she* be?'¹⁴ And he once teased Clare Sydney Smith about her passion for furnishing houses and how she would always reposition any picture her husband had put up, 'Now you know why I don't get married!'¹⁵ His almost atomic repulsion from intimate physical contact would have been greatly exacerbated by his torture and humiliation at Deraa. The importance and effect on Lawrence of the Deraa flogging and sexual defilement can hardly be overstated.

Then what of the rumours that Lawrence was homosexual? They just don't stand up. Lawrence's life has been subjected to intensive scrutiny and has been in an almost blinding spotlight ever since he died, yet there has never been any evidence of homosexuality. There have been innuendo, snide hints, allegations, assertions, even lies, from some who have claimed dubiously to be 'in the know', but never any facts.

In a 1927 letter to E.M. Forster Lawrence commented admiringly on the novelist's curious homosexual ghost story, 'Dr Woolacott', adding: 'The Turks, as you probably know (or have guessed, through the reticences of the *Seven Pillars*) did it to me, by force: and since then I have gone about whimpering to myself Unclean, unclean. Now I don't know. Perhaps there is another side, your side, to the story. I couldn't ever do it, I believe: the impulse strong enough to make me touch another creature has not yet been born in me: but perhaps in surrender to such a figure as your Death there might be a greater realisation – and thereby a more final destruction – of the body than any loneliness can reach.'[16]

And writing to Robert Graves about references to the poet Siegfried Sassoon in Graves's autobiography, *Goodbye to all That*, Lawrence said, 'S.S. comes out very well. I'm glad of that, for I like him: homosex and all.'[17] – hardly the remark of someone who was himself homosexual. Then there is a telling comment made by A.H.R Reiffer, the owner of the Red Garage at Bovington where Lawrence filled up his motorcycle with petrol for the last time before his fatal accident: 'I had known him over a period of twelve years and during this time I was in business in Bovington Camp. Lawrence was news throughout the camp and yet I never heard a word about T.E.L. and homosexuality until I was asked by a reporter covering his accident "whether T.E.L. was a homo." Such things could not have happened over a period of twelve years at Bovington Camp and never have been whispered about in the local garage.'[18]

Perhaps the final comment on Lawrence's sexuality should go to his brother Arnold, even though Arnold could be impatient and a little patronizing and often seemed to arrogate to himself the role of final arbiter in many matters concerning his brother. He wasn't, of course. He was only a boy and a teenager before and during the formative periods of his brother's life – Carchemish and the Arab Revolt. There is also no evidence to support the view that Lawrence ever confided anything of a very personal or intimate nature to Arnold. In fact, on occasions Lawrence could be surprisingly scathing about his youngest brother. He wrote about him to Charlotte Shaw from India, yet again in 1927: 'There is a certain ruthless incuriosity about the first generation after the war, of which my brother always seems to me a fine example. He gets enthusiastic never, except in denunciation: and he has so little patience, so little breadth of judgement. He condemns the man, without asking the circumstances of his home-life, or generation: as if all men were born equal ... I think I'm ripe, and benign and charitable, beside him.'[19]

Nevertheless, having been brought up with Lawrence and being the only brother to have married and to have had a child, Arnold did have some key insights. Talking of his brother's sexuality in a letter of 1963, he said, 'No one who knew him or worked with him ever believed him to be a homosexual. He wasn't, though homosexuality disgusted him far less than the abuse of normal sex and attitude of some of the men in the huts in the R.A.F. or Tanks Corps.'[20] He summed up his brother's attitude and his difficulties in squarely facing the fact of sex and women:

> His friendships were comparable in intensity to sexual love, for which he made them a substitute. He could not compromise easily with Nature but rejected its government as far as was humanly possible; he thought it better to die than submit to growing old, and against sex in particular he rebelled unceasingly. His hatred of sex was an irrational instinct, which went far beyond reason's limits, as he himself recognized. While he may have been endowed in childhood with a realization of sin in this respect, I think its action was seldom perceptible before the War and held dominance only during the following years of ill-health and turmoil. In 1925 he could write half seriously of prostitution being marriage à la carte, as though he admitted no distinction of kind between relationships into which sex entered. It was this horror of the physical intimacies that he never experienced with anyone – we have his word for it – which inspired his abstinent habits. 'A one-man monastery' he has been called by a philosopher who did not know him, and his subjection of the body was achieved by methods advocated by the saints whose lives he had read ... in my opinion he neglected the body's claims unfairly. He maintained this 'balance' at a cost so terrible in waste and suffering, that its author would himself, I believe, have agreed that it was a failure. Towards the end of his life he wrote with tender envy of the happy marriage of a contemporary and there was plainly no fate he would have more gladly accepted for himself.[21]

Finally, there was one other consideration which further complicated Lawrence's attitude to sex and procreation – the tension that existed between him and his mother and his underlying disapproval of her duplicitous life. This life appeared on the surface and publicly to be spotless and virtuous, characterized by impeccable Christian practice and model family conduct, while all the while hiding a suppressed truth – that in her formative years she had run off with another woman's husband and by him given birth to five sons, all out of wedlock. In this context it is worth recalling what Lawrence wrote to Charlotte Shaw about his mother: 'She has given me a terror of families and inquisitions. And yet you'll understand she is my mother, and an extraordinary person. Knowledge of her will prevent my ever making any woman a mother, and the cause of children.'[22]

EIGHTEEN

The Citadel of My Integrity

WHAT INSIGHTS does any of this give into the hidden Lawrence? In isolation his comments don't add anything of groundbreaking significance to an understanding of his sexuality. Cumulatively, however, they reveal quite a lot. He was not an homosexual but an idealistic heterosexual and a celibate who was innately repelled by the physical for complex psychological reasons, a major element of which was undoubtedly his wartime rape. His repulsion by sex was so exaggerated, particularly after the war, that it was almost pathological. To consider the sexual act as 'filthy' or 'dirty' would not in the eyes of most people be considered a reasonable or normal attitude.

However, to be repelled by and afraid of sexual involvement is not the same as to be unable to love, and Lawrence *was* capable of idealistic love, and idealistic love for a woman. We might nonetheless initially ask why after the war did his fear and hatred of sex become so deeply entrenched. This is where his treatment at the hands of the Turks in Deraa assumes a paramount importance. Lawrence wrote two published versions of the incident: in the limited 1926 edition of *Seven Pillars of Wisdom* and in the even more limited 1922 edition, and these, together with his frank admissions in letters to Charlotte Shaw and E.M. Forster, and an explanation in a memorandum to Colonel Stirling, are the known accounts of one of the most traumatic events of his life.

The page of his diary covering the period of his ordeal (November 15–21, 1917) is missing, probably torn out by Lawrence. His first written mention of the incident occurs in the body of the report he wrote in Cairo in late June, 1919 to Colonel Stirling, who was deputy chief political officer in Cairo. The report concerns what Lawrence claims was the treachery and anti-British activity during the war of two Algerian brothers, Mohammed Said and Abd el Kader, and he details how the latter betrayed him to the governor of Deraa. Lawrence's language here, in stark contrast to the disturbingly emotive prose of his drawn-out *Seven Pillars* accounts, is what you would expect from a memorandum: plain and to the point: 'I went in to Deraa in disguise to spy out the defences, was caught, and identified by Hajim Bey the Governor by virtue of Abd el Kader's descriptions of me. (I learnt all about his treachery from Hajim's conversation, and from my guards.) Hajim was an ardent paederast and took a fancy to me. So he kept me under guard till night, and then tried to have me. I was unwilling, and prevailed after some difficulty. Hajim sent me to the hospital, and I escaped before dawn, being not as hurt as he thought. He was so ashamed of the muddle he had made that he hushed the whole thing up, and never reported my capture & escape.'[1]

In mid-November 1917 Lawrence was reconnoitring around Deraa to complete his 'spying out the hollow land of Hauran'. His *Seven Pillars'* accounts claim that he was caught by the Turks, severely beaten and, depending on how you interpret his narrative, probably sexually assaulted. In both versions he recounts his ordeal obliquely:

> To keep my mind in control I numbered the blows, but after twenty lost count, and could feel only the shapeless weight of pain, not tearing claws, for which I had prepared, but a gradual cracking apart of my whole being by some too-great force whose waves rolled up my spine till they were pent within my brain, to clash terribly together. Somewhere in the place a cheap clock ticked loudly, and it distressed me that their beating was not in its time. I writhed and twisted, but was held so tightly that my struggles were useless. After the corporal ceased, the men took up, very deliberately, giving me so many, and then an interval, during which they would squabble for the next turn, ease themselves, and play unspeakably with me. This was repeated often, for what may have been no more than ten minutes.

Several harrowing paragraphs later he writes: 'By the bruises perhaps they beat me further: but I next knew that I was being dragged about by two men, each disputing over a leg as though to split me apart: while a third man rode me astride. It was momently better than more flogging.' (In the 1922 text this reads: 'while a third astride my back rode me like a horse.'). He ultimately managed to escape. His account ends with one of the best-known and most controversial admissions he was ever to make. Recounting how, on his way back to Azrak, a raiding party of Wuld Ali bedouin had let his party go unplundered, he wrote:

> This was an unexpected generosity, the Wuld Ali being not yet of our fellowship. Their consideration (rendered at once, as if we had deserved men's homage) momently stayed me to carry the burden, whose certainty the passing days confirmed: how in Deraa that night the citadel of my integrity had been irrevocably lost.[2]

In the 1922 *Seven Pillars* Lawrence is more expansive. After the words 'not yet of our fellowship' it reads:

> and their action revived me a little. I was feeling very ill, as though some part of me had gone dead that night in Deraa, leaving me maimed, imperfect, only half-myself. It could not have been the defilement, for no one ever held the body in less honour than I did myself: probably it had been the breaking of the spirit by that frenzied nerve-shattering pain which had degraded me to beast-level when it made me grovel to it; and which had journeyed with me since, a fascination and terror and morbid desire, lascivious and vicious perhaps, but like the striving of a moth towards its flame.[3]

(Some proponents of the homosexual or masochist theses have dishonestly left out the words 'and terror' in their use of this quotation).

Lawrence's other revealing account of what happened to him at Deraa is in a letter of 1924 to Charlotte Shaw. Lawrence had been discussing her husband's play, *Saint Joan*, and wrote:

> The trial scene in Joan. Poor Joan, I was thinking of her as a person, not as a moral lesson. The pain meant more to her than the example. You instance my night in Deraa. Well, I'm always afraid of being hurt: and to me, while I live, the force of that night will lie in the agony, which broke me, and made me surrender. It's the individual view. You can't share it. About that night. I shouldn't tell you, because decent men don't talk about such things. I wanted to put it plain in the book, and wrestled for days with my self-respect ... which wouldn't, hasn't, let me. For fear of being hurt, or rather to earn five minutes respite from a pain which drove me mad, I gave away the only possession we are born into the world with – our bodily integrity. It's an unforgivable matter, an irrecoverable position: and it's that which has made me forswear decent living, and the exercise of my not-contemptible wits and talents.

You may call this morbid: but think of the offence, and the intensity of my brooding over it for these years. It will hang about me while I live, and afterwards if our personality survives. Consider wandering among the decent ghosts hereafter, crying 'Unclean, Unclean!'[4]

The testimony of Sir Ronald Storrs should also be considered. He wrote: 'I doubted how far even his nerves could ever be the same after his hideous manhandling at Deraa,' adding in a footnote: 'More than one member of his Staff told me that after Deraa, they felt that something had happened to Lawrence which had changed him.'[5]

And Lawrence told Colonel Meinertzhagen that the incident had 'penetrated his innermost nature.' Meinertzhagen added: 'The two tragedies which weigh most shamefully on his sensitive soul are his illegitimate origin and the utter degradation at the hands of a homosexual monster.'[6]

However, what might turn out to be one of the most telling pieces of evidence in support of the veracity of Lawrence's *Seven Pillars'* accounts of the Deraa incident is contained in two unpublished letters to a friend from a major American collector, the late Theodora Duncan. That evidence is revealed here for the first time. Duncan was considered an important enough source of primary material for biographer John Mack to make plans to consult her in California. She wrote: 'Yes, Dr. Marshall is now dead, but I have the written report of what the Dr. told the chap who drove down from Azrak with him [Lawrence] and asked the Dr. after T.E. had been fixed up as best could be done. He said he would never forget the Dr.'s words. Things like that don't become dimmed with time.' She also wrote:

> You may also discount Arnold's [Arnold Lawrence] belief that TE was not rendered impotent. I have the full story from one of the men who served with him, drove with him from Azrak to Aqaba, for medical treatment and dressing of his injuries, and the practically verbatim conversation this chap had with the doctor afterwards, complete with the gory details: he said he'd never forget it. TE himself said it took several days for him to realize that his integrity – no, the citadel of his integrity had been lost.

In the same letter she went over her story again:

> MY source took him [Lawrence] in an armoured car from Abu el Lissan to Aqaba, and he has that story in his diary. The only thing TE fabricated was that he went all the way via camel – but the journey by camel from Azrak to Abu el Lissal (or Lissan) was bad enough, in his condition … My friend mentioned above said all

the fellows who served closely with TE knew the extent of his injuries and many of his postwar friends, too.[7]

As evidence, the value of these emotive quotations must remain speculative, because the informant is not named and I have not seen his diary, which may be in Duncan's major but, at the time of writing, apparently incompletely catalogued collection in the Huntington Library in San Marino, California. Also the armoured car part of her story is inconsistent with Lawrence's account in *Seven Pillars*.

When Lawrence wrote in *Seven Pillars* of the Deraa rape: 'It could not have been the defilement, for no one ever held the body in less honour than I did myself,' he did not then realize the long-term psychological damage he would suffer. Male rape is still a taboo subject, even today, but its effects are now better understood and it is being more openly discussed and treated. In Lawrence's time there was no such medical help available and he resorted to a harsh solution of his own to combat what was clearly an embedded neurosis.

He was, unknowingly, the victim of a repetition compulsion, which was a direct consequence of his wartime rape. From the mid-1920s to the early 1930s he had himself intermittently beaten, engaging a fellow serviceman, John Bruce (and one or two others), to carry out the punishment. Bruce was Scottish, tough, crude, uneducated, untrustworthy and slightly menacing. Lawrence spun the gullible and initially well-intentioned Scot an elaborate fiction about a grand relation who had demanded Lawrence be punished for bringing his Irish family name into disrepute. Some parts of Bruce's story about the beatings – first published in an English newspaper in 1968 – have been proved to be pure fabrication, with payment the inducement. Nevertheless, it seems entirely credible that the whole sorry series of beatings was a manifestation of Lawrence's neurosis. It was not an expression of masochism, as some have claimed, but a tragic attempt by Lawrence to exorcise the memory of his rape. In fact, the beatings sometimes took place on the anniversary of the Deraa incident.

There exists an extremely perceptive article about Lawrence's ordeal, which is notable for both its insight and its sympathy. Although not written by a medical expert or a clinical psychologist, it nevertheless bears the stamp of a convincing and arresting authority. It is worth giving in full:

> Claims seemingly given credence by newspaper interviews with Privates of the Tanks Corps who confessed to having flogged Lawrence at his solicitation between 1925 and 1934, combined to set the seal on the alleged secret life of Lawrence of Arabia. However, those making these claims only told half the story,

deliberately neglecting or downplaying the effect his having been raped had on his thoughts and actions.

Lawrence was captured by Ottoman Turks in Deraa in 1917 and subjected to humiliating beatings and sexual assault at the instigation of the Governor, or Bey. Rape in time of war is age-old; most people are aware of the suffering of women and girls during hostilities; however, since ancient times it has been a weapon of war used against men. The word itself is derived from the Latin *rapere* meaning to steal, seize or carry away. In the military context it was a means of stealing a man's honour, a victorious soldier emasculating a vanquished foe in the belief that by forcibly penetrating him he lost his manhood. This indignity was more often inflicted on members of the officer class in the belief that it robbed them of their authority as leaders of men, sometimes resulting in the victims' suicide. Gang rape was also considered a means of punishment in some cultures. The Ottoman Turks were infamous for inflicting it throughout the Great War on captured enemy troops, beating and gang-raping enemy officers often as a matter of course.

Prisons and garrisons often had personnel who specialized in this abuse, although there was nothing homosexual about it. The Turkish soldiers perpetrating this war crime certainly never considered themselves gay; like male rapists in prison the act has nothing to do with the sexual orientation of the attacker or victim. 'It's not sexual gratification, rather a sexual aggressor using somebody else as a means of expressing their own power and control.' (Men Who Rape: The Psychology of the Offender, by Dr Nicholas Groth).

It was a remarkable manifestation of courage, perhaps cathartic release, that Lawrence detailed what happened to him in his book Seven Pillars of Wisdom in 1926. Then as now the fear of being labelled homosexual as a result of such disclosure was a legitimate fear, society having the tendency to blame the victim of sexual assault rather than the perpetrator. Homosexuality was a taboo subject at that time; same sex rape was even more taboo. The suspicion that Lawrence was homosexual is likely to have been a natural by-product of his shocking disclosure, some readers finding a homoerotic undertone to his retelling of events. Then as now few understood the incident in its historic context, the consensus being that only homosexuals are victims of same sex rape, that a man can protect himself, and if he's raped it's because he wanted to be. If the 28-year-old Lawrence was a virgin at the time of his assault, as many biographers believe, the experience would have had a profoundly negative effect on his concept of self and sexuality. Alas, in his lifetime there were no counselling services available to men who had suffered sexual assault; they were expected to get on with their lives with a stiff upper lip.

The post-traumatic effects of same sex rape often last a lifetime; T.E. Lawrence manifested all the classic symptoms: workaholism, 'depression, anger, increased sense of vulnerability, destructive self-image, emotional distancing' (Silent Victims: Bringing Male Rape Out of the Closet by Sue Brochman, 1991). In the wake of the Great War he had difficulties with intimacy, withdrew from relationships or carried them out via mail, had problems trusting people and a defunct sex drive. Not that he ever had much interest in sex at earlier stages of his life – there is no concrete evidence of him having had an intimate relationship with anyone male or female and he seems to have willingly chosen celibacy, as many academics of his class and generation did. His family and friends attested to his sense of horror with regards to sexual subject matter in the years following the war.

Many heterosexual rape survivors question their sexual orientation, 'it's not uncommon for a victim to blame himself for the rape, believing that he in some way gave permission to the rapist.' (Adult Male Sexual Assault in the Community: A Literature Review and Group Treatment Model, Paul Isley, 1991). Recollection of involuntary physiological responses, erections or ejaculations, etc, during the event often make them question whether they deserved or wanted to be assaulted. There are certainly aspects of this post-traumatic introspection in Seven Pillars of Wisdom, which many readers have mistaken as homoerotic influences. Contrary to popular belief, Lawrence's notorious floggings aren't indicators of homosexuality; the fetish is more common with heterosexuals than homosexuals. According to noted psychologist and rape trauma therapist Dr Michael Hunter, Lawrence's behaviour was 'a recreation of the experience which marred his life, a repetition compulsion, an attempt to take control of an event which had previously been out of his control.'

His victimology isn't unique: 'People often repeat their prior traumas, literally or symbolically, both conscious and unconscious.' (Dr. Jim Hopper Ph.D. Research Associate, Boston University School of Medicine Trauma Center, Brookline, Massachusetts, USA). Psychologists also believe that Lawrence changed his name twice because he felt emasculated by his experience and wanted to escape the macho, action-man image being forced upon him by popular culture increasingly obsessed with 'Lawrence of Arabia.' By changing his name he took on another persona, left the wounded rape victim behind and became someone else for a period of time.

Over the past few decades pop biographers, historians and gay activists have made an art form of deliberately misinterpreting biographical information on notable people to sell their otherwise repetitious tomes or to push an agenda. Any figure who remained unmarried, had close same-sex friendships, or acted in a way perceived flamboyant by modern standards is automatically presumed homosexual. Evidence is not required, only innuendo; few figures escape sensational revisionism and insinuation. T.E. Lawrence was one of the first casualties of it, the psychological after-effects of having been brutally raped portrayed as sexual deviancy to sell books … In the final analysis, his sexual orientation shouldn't be an issue; if he was homosexual, it wouldn't add or subtract from his legacy, but in the interests of historical scholarship it's important to view facts in their proper context.[8]

NINETEEN

An Imaginary Person of Neutral Sex

IT WAS late summer at Chemlan, the Joyces were out, and I was sitting in a wicker chair on the balcony, the world stilled and silent in the midday heat, when it struck me forcibly again that the key to the mystery of *Seven Pillars'* dedication surely lay in the principles of Provençal poetry. My research had led me to the conclusion that Lawrence's immersion in the Middle Ages, troubadour poetry and the writings of William Morris had an underlying psychological cause far deeper than simply literary interest. When I now placed this conviction together with what I considered to be the most significant clues to the identity of S.A. – and with Robert Graves's detailed exposition of the deliberately created conundrum these clues created – it all fitted together like a jigsaw puzzle.

In the late afternoon the Joyces and I went for a drive northward along the high, winding road to the little town of Zahlé to have a meal. The open-air restaurant lay high above the distant Bekaa valley to the northeast and was full of echoes of ancient Arab culture. The tables were set on little tiered terraces shaded by small trees and islanded by irrigation channels of crystal-clear water which ran round us in their zig-zag descent of the hillside. About us Arab families were also out enjoying the balmy September air, the men in their pristine white jelabiyas puffing contentedly on their hubble-bubbles. Our thirst slaked by the ever-flowing Ksara rosé, I explained my S.A. analysis in detail to Jack and Gudrun.

Provençal love poetry was the key. Graves was always convinced – as he told me – that the dedicatee was a woman and that Lawrence, in his troubadour persona, would never have revealed her true identity but would have hidden it in the cryptic way dictated by Provençal poetic convention – by using a *senhal*, a pseudonym. Graves's explanation of S.A. is of course known but has more often than not been unjustifiably and inexplicably dismissed as not worthy of serious consideration, or has never been properly appreciated in its true context: namely Lawrence's almost obsessional passion for the Middle Ages and early French poetry, and in his abiding love of their concomitant – William Morris's quasi-medieval romances.

Graves maintained that, when put together, Lawrence's clues to the meaning of S.A., in particular those given to Basil Liddell Hart and the one Lawrence interpolated into his personal record of the writing, printing and distribution of the *Seven Pillars*, constituted an old-fashioned riddle. This would run as follows: 'S', my first, is a person; 'A', my second, is a village in Syria or property in it; and 'S.A.', my whole, is an imaginary person of neutral sex.

The solution is *Son Altesse*, or the Provençal *langue d'oc, Son Altezza* – Her or His Highness. Broken into its constituent parts, the riddle's explanation is: My first is 'Son': a person, a male offspring; my second is 'Altesse' or 'Altezza'; there is a remote village in Syria called Al-Taess forty miles south of Jerablus on the west bank of the Euphrates. Lawrence made canoe trips down the river close to this village so would certainly have known it; and Tas, or Tasa, is Arabic for a shallow drinking vessel or fingerbowl; and my whole is '*Son Altesse (Altezza)*'. This is a troubadour honorific of neutral gender, since the rules of French grammar allow it to be either female or male, and, since it is a title – Her, or His, Highness – it is, of course, not the actual name of the dedicatee but a *senhal*, an elevated idealization. In other words, it is, as Lawrence wrote in 1927, 'an imaginary person of neutral sex'; and this chimes with the two comments he made to Graves in that same year of confessional correspondence: firstly, 'S.A., the subject of the dedication, is rather an idea than a person'; and secondly, 'You have taken me too literally. S.A. still exists: but out of my reach, because I have changed.' (This, it will be recalled, was his corrective to Graves's suggestion in his first biographical draft that shortly before the capture of Damascus Lawrence had received news of a death by typhus.)

Considered cumulatively, all Lawrence's cryptic comments and hints about the dedication clearly support Graves's explanation and add to the conviction that it was what S.A. had represented, the idealization, the idea, that had died, not the muse herself. Nevertheless, it might be objected that this seems somehow too contrived and over-complicated an explanation of a dedication of a poem that appears to be essentially an earnest declaration of a deeply felt affection; and that Lawrence would, for once in this very personal instance, have considered intellectual games and literary mystification inappropriate. Yet, when I raised this point with John Mack, a professor of psychiatry as well as the author of a prize-winning biography of Lawrence, he wrote to me, 'As you know Lawrence liked to tease and set people to wondering and guessing, not necessarily deliberately but out of his own needs. I think the troubadour-love idea makes sense.'[1]

Lawrence told Graves that he had made a three-year study of Provençal poetry, and '*Son Altesse*' both embodies the convention's rule that the true identity of a dedicatee should never be revealed and simultaneously meets one of Lawrence's most deep-seated psychological needs – always to keep his feelings a well-guarded secret. In addition, and significantly, it also reflects, even if unconsciously, his life-long need to mask a real identity (Chapman) with an invented one (Lawrence).

So, is there any evidence that Lawrence had ever conceived an idealized love for a woman? It happens that there is. Mack revealed the whole story, and the girl in question – she was a girl when she first met Lawrence – was called Janet Laurie (her later married name was Hallsmith). Mack told the story in full in his biography, because of his conviction that it played a major role in Lawrence's emotional life:

> It was during the undergraduate years that Lawrence made his most important effort to establish a serious relationship with a woman. The young woman was Janet Laurie Hallsmith … The account that follows was supplied to me in interviews by Mrs Hallsmith herself. She seemed to me utterly candid within the limits of memory, and I sensed no conscious interest on her part in embellishing her story in order to claim an important association with a famous man … In 1899 Janet was sent to Oxford to boarding school and to be near the Lawrences. Two years later, her father drowned in Southampton Water and she returned home to be with her mother. She continued to visit the Lawrences in Oxford and sometimes stayed with them. She and T.E. saw each other frequently through his undergraduate years. 'I always spent Sunday afternoon at tea with him,' she said, 'and sort of watched him grow up.' Later she visited 'Ned' on occasion in the detached bungalow. Although women were not officially allowed in the undergraduate rooms, Lawrence served Janet and her sister breakfast in his room on at least one occasion.
>
> The relationship between Ned and Janet from childhood on was one of ragging and teasing. He would chide the rather tomboyish girl for not being a

boy or tease her for not being capable of doing things as well as he could. The teasing, she said, had a tender quality and she never felt hurt by it … This child-like, playful quality characterized their relationship. They never discussed their feelings about each other, especially as he seemed unable to, and she had never thought of him seriously as a suitor or mate. On the contrary, he maintained an emotional distance. Once when he was about nineteen she remarked to him, 'Ned, you never look me in the eye.' He replied, 'It gives me a painful sensation to look into your eyes.'

Janet was therefore surprised when Lawrence's interest in her took a more serious turn. She had always felt toward him as an older sister toward a clever brother, and he also inspired in her a feeling that he needed to be taken care of. Besides, he was more than two years younger and too short – he was the same height if not shorter than she was. Mrs Lawrence had wanted her to marry Bob, who was nearer her age. But Bob was "so terribly good", and he once had corrected her for using the word "pub" ("Pub is not a nice word," he had said). Janet's heart was turning to Will despite the more than three years' difference in their ages. He was the tallest and handsomest of the Lawrence boys and in her view the most "dashing".

When T.E. asked her to marry him, she was understandably taken aback. He was about twenty-one at the time, still an undergraduate, when he proposed. She had come to the Lawrences for dinner, and she and Ned had stayed at the table after the meal was over. He bolted the door so the parlour maid could not come in. 'We were joking about his brothers when he suddenly proposed.' There had been no warning, no preliminaries, such as a kiss or a revelation of feelings. Though she felt that the proposal was a serious one, in her astonishment she laughed at him. He seemed hurt, but merely said, 'Oh I see,' or 'All right,' and spoke no more about it.

Despite Mrs Lawrence's objections Janet and Will had hoped to marry, but he was killed in the war in 1915. In 1919 Janet married Guthrie Hallsmith, a war hero who later failed as an artist. Because her father was dead she asked Lawrence to give her away. At first he agreed, but just before the wedding he sent her a note saying he could not go through with it, offering as his reason that he was too short and would look silly walking down the aisle with her. But the two remained friends. He occasionally visited the Hallsmiths at their home in Newquay in Cornwall and was godfather of their first child.[2]

Lawrence did in fact attend Janet's wedding. He slipped into the church, stood at the very back, and left without a word immediately after the ceremony.[3] This account of the relationship between Lawrence and Janet has been derided by some biographers on the spurious grounds that it flies in the face of what they have determined are the known facts of Lawrence's emotional life, namely that he appeared to have little time for women and no emotional involvement with any woman who could be seriously regarded as a potential lover or partner. These commentators purposely confine the scope of their analysis to the evidence of Mack's interviews with Janet and carefully avoid taking into account another quite separate and independent talk that Mack had with Lawrence's friend, Canon Edgar Hall, which, in Mack's book, immediately follows his Laurie interviews and conclusively corroborates them.

The reason for this omission is, I suspect, that these biographers had decided that Lawrence was either homosexual or incapable of being attracted to a woman. As a result, they have been deliberately selective and unjustifiably dismissive in their treatment of the Janet Laurie story. Professor Allen is a prime culprit. He wrote: 'Some mention should be made of the story first published by John E. Mack in *A Prince of Our Disorder*. It is an account of Lawrence's alleged pre-war proposal of marriage to a childhood friend, Janet Laurie, a proposal, which was rejected. The story has not been considered credible by other Lawrence scholars.'

Along with Allen, there is one further notable sceptic, namely Jeffrey Meyers, who referred to the proposal as 'this absurd tale'. Allen, with a patronizing reluctance, admitted: 'However, even if the story does not generally convince, it does provide more evidence of the pervasiveness of the Provençal ethos, at least in its nineteenth-century form. E.F. Hall told Mack that Lawrence "worshipped [Janet] from afar". Perhaps – impelled less by heterosexual feelings than by an attitude toward life shaped by reading (and a feeling that this is what one does) – Lawrence did indeed make something like a proposal.'[4]

Did Allen seriously believe that a man as shy as Lawrence could make the very serious proposal of marriage, all because some persuasive literature has convinced him that he ought to seek out some suitable woman and ask her to marry him? This is surely ludicrous. Clearly, Lawrence's emotions were engaged, not his intellect. These two sceptical biographers are calling into question the honesty of Janet Laurie, Edgar Hall, John Mack and ultimately of Lawrence himself. More significantly, the key point that they fail to mention is that Hall's recollections are completely independent, that they vindicate Janet Laurie, and confirm the veracity of what she told Mack. One is forced to the conclusion that Allen and Meyers do not give Hall's version in full because it compromises their argument. In their youth Hall and Lawrence were close friends. Here is Hall's recollection as recounted by Mack:

I visited Lawrence's childhood friend the Reverend E.F. ('Midge') Hall and his wife on Dartmoor in Devonshire. We were talking of Lawrence's shyness when one of the Halls offered spontaneously, 'There was one girl he loved.' They seemed reluctant to reveal her identity until I told them I thought I knew, having spoken with Janet Hallsmith several months before. 'Oh, you know then,' Hall said. 'I have never mentioned it to anybody.'

And he went on to tell me that Lawrence as a youth had spoken with him of his love for Janet Laurie. Once in his undergraduate days, Hall told me, Lawrence arranged for himself, Janet and 'Midge' Hall to go boating on the Thames. But instead of taking Janet with him, he fixed it so that Midge and Janet went in a punt and he followed fifty yards behind in a canoe. Afterwards Hall asked Lawrence 'what on earth' he had done that for. Lawrence replied that he was 'observing' his friend and Janet from afar. He then added, as if to himself, 'I'm getting over the disappointment of letting the other man speak for the girl I adore. I don't know.' Hall said that he did not think Janet ever really reciprocated Lawrence's love for her. When he saw Janet Hallsmith at a later time, Hall said to her, 'You know Ned Lawrence adored you,' and she replied that she had known but could not consider him seriously as a suitor. As if to sum up his memory of the relationship of his two friends, Hall remarked, 'She was a lovely girl, a lovely girl. She was a dear. He worshipped from afar.'[5]

One hears a faint echo of the troubadours' 'La Dame Lointaine'.

Despite Janet's turning down his proposal, Lawrence behaved towards her thereafter with typical integrity, even when it became clear that she preferred his favourite brother, Will. Before going to France on active service with the Royal Flying Corps in 1915 Will had written to his brother Ned asking him to be his executor and to tell him that, if he, Will, died, he wanted Janet to have all his money. Lawrence replied from Cairo in July 1915 that he would have agreed as long as Janet was single but that it would seem that she was soon to be married.[6] Will had been in France for just a week in October 1915 when he was reported missing, presumed dead. His estate in any case amounted to very little. Will's death, when it was finally confirmed, affected Lawrence deeply. In July 1916 in a letter home he asked his mother not to pass on any of Will's papers to Janet until he had seen them; and twice, in the heat of the Arab campaign in September and November of the following year, he asked his mother for Janet's address.

Then in 1920 Lawrence seems to have heard that Janet, now married, was short of money. In an act of remarkable generosity he gave her £3000 – his share of £15,000, which had been part of an early bequest to his father from his father's sister, Lady Caroline Chapman. His father had shared this out between his surviving sons, a portion of which Will too would have received had he still been alive. This gift, an attempt perhaps to fulfil his brother's wish, is typical of Lawrence's generosity and is yet another indication not only of the affection in which he held Will but also of the fondness he retained for Janet.[7]

Lawrence and Janet remained friends and as late as 1929 he was still in touch with her. She seems to have understood Lawrence well and to have had an accurate intuition of his inner struggle, of his feeling somehow alienated from others, of what she described as 'a secret sense of unhappiness' in him.[8]

The difficulty, after much misrepresentation, of convincing the sceptical of Lawrence's true emotional orientation, and of proving that he *had* loved a woman, is that the published distortions spread over the years have insidiously become almost received wisdom and have been wrongly accepted as accurate. Janet Laurie was the first young woman in Lawrence's life. Was there another? In the summer of 1909 the twenty-one-year-old Lawrence set out for the Middle East for the first time to research crusader castles for his history degree thesis. It was to prove an arduous but exciting and instructive ordeal. He was as fit as a flea and relished it all, walking anything up to twenty-five miles a day over difficult terrain and getting to know at first hand not just the castles but also the village Arabs and their way of life, all of which was to stand him in very good stead in the looming war years. It was almost as though destiny were putting him through an apprenticeship in desert living, preparing him for a great endeavour.

A year later in December 1910 he was on his way to the Middle East again, this time to study Arabic at the American Mission School at Jebail. He must have felt a renewed exhilaration at returning to Syria. He would again have felt a surge of excitement that he had 'reached the way to the South, and all the glorious East; Greece, Carthage, Egypt, Tyre, Syria, Italy, Spain, Sicily, Crete ... they were all there, and all within reach ... of me.'[9] But now he knew that he would have the time to explore this new land and new people in greater depth and at some leisure. Later in 1911 he began his archaeological work at Carchemish, and took to life there with ease and delight. He positively revelled in it. In the later stages of these halcyon years, in December 1913, he wrote to Vyvyan Richards in England regretting that he would not be able to join him in the printing project they had planned, because he enjoyed being at Carchemish too much. He said:

> I have got to like this place very much: and the people here – five or six of them – and the whole manner of living pleases me. We have 200 men to play with, anyhow we like so long as the excavations go on, and they are splendid

fellows many of them (I had two of them – head-men – in England with me this summer) and it is great fun with them.

Then there are the digs, with dozens of wonderful things to find – it is like a great sport with tangible results at the end of things – Do you know I am keen now on an inscription or a new type of pottery? and hosts of beautiful things in the villages and towns to fill one's house with. Not to mention seal-hunting in the country round about, and the Euphrates to rest in when one is over-hot. It is a place where one eats lotos nearly every day, and you know that feeling is bad for one's desires to do something worth looking at, oneself.[10]

He worked at Carchemish under Hogarth, R. Campbell Thompson and Leonard Woolley, with a short stint in 1912 with Flinders Petrie in Egypt. In 1911 after the digs finished he went off alone in mid-July on a walking trip in a long arc northward from Carchemish, getting back to Jerablus at the end of the month. His reading at this time included 'Rabelais, Holy Grail, Rossetti, and Roland'.[11]

Lawrence was very much at ease with the Arabs and in the Arab villages, so much so that his natural shyness went almost into abeyance and he had relaxed and mutually affectionate relations with the men employed on the site, and forged friendships with Hamoudi, the excavations foreman, and Dahoum. He developed very individual ways of getting the best out of the men during the excavations of the Hittite site; he wandered far and wide through the countryside, bathed in the Euphrates, took trips along the river for both archaeological purposes and simply for adventure and pleasure, and even had a canoe with an outboard motor shipped out, which allowed him to extend the scope of his forays down the river into the Syrian hinterland. And then there were the excursions to Aleppo seventy miles south to visit people such as the Fontanas and the Altounyans, to bargain for antiquities and carpets in the suqs, and to buy supplies and staple goods for the Carchemish dig. It was indeed a golden time for him. A description of the Aleppo suqs, which Lawrence gave to Edward Leeds in a letter in the summer of 1913, reflects his delight in the life he is leading:

You should have fled down the bazaars as I did this peaceful Sunday morning buying glue and sacking and wire gauze and potatoes and embroidery and vaseline and gunpowder and Arabic manuscripts and rose sherbet and bootlaces and Damascus tiles, with a shade thermometer of 118, and an embargo upon the ice, for as much as there is an epidemic of cholera in the place. Oh the sweat in that bazaar was a salty marsh knee-deep, in which splashed perspiring camels.[12]

Some recollections of Lawrence during those days give a revealing insight into the pre-war man. Leonard Woolley wrote, 'He already spoke Arabic well and after a summer spent at Byblos (Jebail) in serious study of the language was always trying to improve his knowledge of the different dialects.'[13] And Woolley detailed Lawrence's two friendships among the Arabs at Jerablus:

> There were only two whom he regarded as friends, but of those two he was very fond. Hamoudi, our foreman, he admired intensely and was bound to him by real gratitude, for Hamoudi had saved his life at no small risk to himself. After one of his tramps (I think in the summer of 1911) Lawrence had dragged himself into Jeralbus in the throes of typhoid and Hamoudi had taken him in and nursed him. It was touch and go whether he would pull through, and just as the illness was at its worst the Turkish authorities, perhaps nervous about possible complications if an Englishman should die in their province, ordered Hamoudi to turn the dying man out; when Hamoudi expostulated he was told that if he disobeyed and Lawrence died he would be accused of having poisoned him for the sake of his money. It was a serious threat, and the village was all in favour of avoiding trouble and doing as the Turks bade; but Hamoudi stood firm, nursed Lawrence back to something like health and carried him off to Aleppo. It was in return for this that Lawrence brought Hamoudi and Dahoum to England in 1913 for a holiday in Oxford.
>
> Dahoum was his other friend. He was then a boy of about fifteen, not particularly intelligent (though Lawrence taught him to take photographs quite well) but beautifully built and remarkably handsome. Lawrence was devoted to him. The Arabs were tolerably scandalized by the friendship, especially when in 1913 Lawrence, stopping in the house after the dig was over, had Dahoum to live with him and got him to pose as model for a queer crouching figure, which he carved in the soft local limestone and set up on the edge of the house roof; to make an image was bad enough in its way, but to portray a naked figure was proof to them of evil of another sort. The scandal about Lawrence was widely spread and firmly believed. The charge was quite unfounded. Lawrence had in his make-up a very strong vein of sentiment, but he was in no sense a pervert; in fact, he had a remarkably clean mind. He was tolerant, thanks to his classical reading, and Greek homosexuality interested him, but in a detached way, and the interest was not morbid but perfectly serious; I never heard him make a smutty remark and am sure that he would have objected to one if it had been made for his benefit: but he would describe Arab abnormalities baldly and with a certain sardonic humour.
>
> He knew quite well what the Arabs said about himself and Dahoum and so far as resenting it was amused, and I think that he courted misunderstanding rather than tried to avoid it; it appealed to his sense of humour, which was broad and schoolboyish. He liked to shock. Similarly he liked practical jokes, not least those which might annoy, but his pleasure in them was so ingenuous that it was hard to take offence.[14]

It is revealing though that Lawrence hated being made to look ridiculous himself. Woolley commented, 'if you laughed at him he would at once retire into his shell and very likely withdraw altogether from your company.'[15] Woolley tells a story of Lawrence at a well in a local village where Kurdish girls were drawing water. He asked for a drink, which they gave him. They had clearly never seen anyone like Lawrence before and were so intrigued by him that, with shrieks of laughter, they pulled open his shirt to see whether his skin was white all over. He finally managed to get away almost stripped. He could not see the joke and never passed that way again, eventually telling Woolley the story but with cold indignation. Woolley commented: 'That sensitiveness to ridicule was probably due in part to his knowing that other people found it hard to take him seriously. It was hard. Physically small, with a head disproportionately large, very unobtrusive, with his quiet voice and tendency to long silences and his slow and quiet movements and a smile which if it was not entirely concerned with his own thoughts seemed to be rather deprecating and apologetic, he was not on the surface of things impressive; and however one might learn to appreciate something of what lay behind there remained a feeling of his essential immaturity. Certainly he made that impression on me, and it was not due merely to his impish humour and to a few other youthful traits, such as the fondness for "dressing up" which he had then and perhaps never got over.'[16]

One of the many anomalies of character that has fascinated people about Lawrence, and does still, is this unlikely combination of a natural, confident, charismatic power of leadership side by side with an impression (which he gave to others as well as Woolley) of immaturity – two elements of personality that one would imagine would sit uncomfortably together. But sit together they did and, it would seem, quite harmoniously much of the time.

A further verdict of immaturity and, it should be said, of irresponsibility – both perhaps part of a deep-seated nihilism – was given by Sir Hubert Young, who had been with Lawrence both in 1918 in Hejaz Operations and in 1921–22 in the Middle East Department of the Colonial Office.

Young wrote:

> Am I the only writer in this book to call him a little monkey, I wonder? And am I the only one to criticize him? If so, I shall be the only one whose account will please him wherever he is. I am afraid I always thought he was a mischievous little imp and this mischievousness was undoubtedly a flaw in his fine character. Another small failing was the vanity, which led him to pose, and tortured the

better side of his nature. He gloried in it and was ashamed of it by turns. His attitude towards publicity was that of Brer Rabbit to the briar-patch. 'Don't throw me into that briar-patch, Brer Fox,' he would protest, and all the time the briar-patch was where he longed to be. It was only when the blaze of limelight that he had himself turned on became embarrassing and even shameful to him that he made half-hearted efforts to turn it off, and by that time it was too late.[17]

Yet side by side with this assessment Young could say: 'No amount of responsibility would have been too great for T.E. I never knew him hesitate to take a decision, and I would rather have served under him than under any regular soldier I have ever met, provided that he was not himself fettered by having to answer to higher authority for what he did.'[18]

TWENTY

Candidates and Advocates

LAWRENCE'S Carchemish days were, in his own view, the happiest of his life. Throughout these four pre-war years Lawrence was on commanding form and completely in his element. He was not afraid to go, to do, to feel, even if his feelings were sometimes partially masked by his innate shyness; so this is the period when one might expect to find him having meaningful relationships, their formation made all the easier by the absence of the bourgeois restrictions imposed by his mother and by English society.

I have already mentioned his closeness to Hamoudi. Then there was his friendship with Dahoum – a friendship so often misunderstood and misrepresented. In the first years at Carchemish Dahoum had been a water-boy on the dig. It is interesting that Woolley deemed him not particularly intelligent and, until Lawrence tried to take his education in hand, he could neither read nor write. Dahoum was certainly not in the least worldly-wise yet he was quick to learn, had a good sense of humour and was often given to infectious fits of laughter. However, his horizons were inevitably limited by the customs and beliefs of his village culture and he was subject to all its parochial superstitions. Lawrence, writing home in the summer of 1911, gives an amusing account of how he and Woolley had played a trick on a local official who had pestered them for brandy. They gave him Seidlitz powder dissolved in water and pronounced some mumbo-jumbo over it. A white, smoky precipitate rose from the glass and frightened the life out of all the Arabs crowding round the Englishmen, whom they thought were practising some diabolically potent magic. Lawrence takes up the tale: 'By personal example, and the strictest orders we compelled our two water-boys to take each half a glass, and ever since they have gone about delicately, feeling their limbs, and shaking themselves, in terror lest they be changed to mares or great apes. "I drank some of that sorcery," said Dahoum on the works next day, "it is very dangerous, since by it men are turned suddenly into the forms of animals."'[1]

A brotherly friendship developed between Lawrence and Dahoum and they went on expeditions and adventures together around Carchemish and further afield, even down to Aqaba. Sometimes Hamoudi was with them, one of these occasions being a trip by canoe down the Euphrates as far as Kalaat el Nijm, some miles upriver from Dahoum's village, Allaouich. Not enough is known about Dahoum to create a rounded picture of him. He was an ordinary young Arab from an ordinary if remote village on the Euphrates. Lawrence believed his ancestry to be 'mixed Hittite and Arab' with 'possibly a strain of Armenian in him.'[2] He seems to have married at some stage during the time he knew Lawrence, because Arnold Lawrence told Jeremy Wilson that Winifred Fontana used to talk of 'Dahoum's wife', and in a letter of February 1913 to Edward Leeds Lawrence mentioned 'the engagement of my notorious "valet".'[3][4] Certainly Dahoum had a brother who married and Lawrence clearly knew Dahoum's village and family, because in 1914 the old sheikh of the village made Lawrence a present of his grandfather's prayer-carpet.[5][6] At one stage, in the winter of 1911, Lawrence had had plans to stay in Dahoum's village to learn Arabic. He writes home of him as 'the boy with whose father I may stay this winter: the boy can read & write, & so would be the best teacher of Arabic in the district'.[7] Dahoum certainly figures regularly in *The Home Letters*, and here and there in the *The Letters*. In the summer of 1911 Lawrence wrote home about him: 'The donkey boy mentioned above (Dahoum) is an interesting character: he can read a few words (the only man in the district except the liquorice-king) of Arabic, and altogether has more intelligence than the rank & file. He talks of going into Aleppo to school with the money he has made out of us. I will try & keep an eye on him, to see what happens.'[8]

Two months later he writes to Mrs Emily Rieder, a language teacher he had met at the American Mission School: 'What I wanted for the donkey boy was a history book or a geography which should be readable and yet Arab ... I have no wish to do more for the boy than give him a chance to help himself.'[9] A year later he is teaching Dahoum photography, commenting: 'I have the training of a boy – Dahoum of course – as well to see to. You have no idea how hard it is to instil elementary optics into his head in imperfect Arabic. He will put plates the wrong side out.'[10] In July 1912 he writes home: 'Dahoum is strong and I think honest'[11] and in a letter to his brother, Arnold, he says that he is continuing to learn some Arabic with Dahoum, 'who is cheaper than local labour, and who can cook and wait very well. He was six months table-boy with the Railway Engineers here.'[12] A month later Lawrence is down at the American Mission School, whose principal, Miss Holmes, was a good friend. He tells his family that he is relaxing, eating and sleeping a lot, and, when tired of reading, bathing in the sea with Dahoum, who sent his 'great salaams'.[13] By September Lawrence is back up in Jerablus and says tongue-in-cheek: 'Dahoum is very useful now, though a savage: however we are here in the feudal system, which gives the overlord great claims: so that I have no trouble with him…'[14] And: 'I don't know what Miss Holmes thought of Dahoum: she never grasped his Arabic properly, but I am more than ever struck by the beauty of it over the horrid noise that the Beyroutis make.'[15]

During January-February 1914 Lawrence and Woolley – and Dahoum – joined Captain Stewart Newcombe in Palestine to conduct what was both an archaeological expedition and a covert military survey. In Newcombe's words: 'In December, 1913, five small survey parties started to extend the Palestine surveys of Conder and Kitchener from Gaza and Beersheba southwards and to complete these maps down to Aqaba. The Palestine Exploration Fund took the opportunity to send two archaeologists to work in co-operation with the surveyors.'[16] Lawrence and Dahoum had a number of adventures in the Aqaba hinterland (which, in terms of providing first-hand knowledge of the geography and topography of the area, was to serve Lawrence well during the Arab revolt), including paddling out from Aqaba on zinc tanks to look at the ruined fortifications on a small island called Faraun. This incurred the suspicion of the Turkish authorities, and the ire of the Turkish *kaimakam*. After this the pair found themselves accompanied everywhere by a Turkish army officer and a company of soldiers. They had great fun taking the Turks on a two-day, wild goose-chase over very rough terrain along wadis and up hills, finally giving them the slip and ending up spending a bitterly cold night just below the top of Mount Hor.[17]

By March Lawrence was back at Carchemish and writing about his survey adventures to his Arabic teacher at Jebail, Miss al Akle, who at the time was in Damascus. He said that he was sorry not to have seen her in the city before he went north again and had even sent Dahoum to try to find where her school was located, adding:

> If it had not been Sunday I would have called in the morning: – but I knew that you would be beautifully dressed and singing Arabic hymns: and I was in very ancient clothes, and very dirty: and I cannot sing a single note. I wrote to you and said that I was going along the Egyptian frontier: well, with Mr. Woolley, my chief up here, we explored the Northern half (say from Gaza to Koseima – Kadesh Barnea) in about five weeks. Then we separated: I went South to Aqaba, Woolley N. towards the Dead Sea.[18]

In the summer of 1914 Lawrence mentions that Dahoum has 'a passion for high speeds' on the bicycle Lawrence had brought out to Carchemish.[19] Then there is silence about him until the war years, when Lawrence was initially based in Cairo at General Headquarters. At the beginning of January 1916 he writes home that he has been unable to get any news of Dahoum, adding: '... indeed I am afraid to send & ask. Most of the men (and boys) from that district have been sent to Constantinople, where they still are.'[20] So Lawrence was clearly not in touch with Dahoum at the start of the war and almost certainly not thereafter.

A number of writers have misconstrued this friendship with Dahoum, pronouncing it to have been so important to Lawrence that he dedicated *Seven Pillars of Wisdom* to him. However, the relationship needs careful analysis before Dahoum can be considered as a possible dedicatee. Firstly, the relationship was not homosexual. It was not even as close as that of possible literary models known to Lawrence, such as Roland and Oliver, although there might have been faint echoes of the latter, given Lawrence's preoccupations with the Middle Ages and the hero figure in medieval literature. Dahoum was in his mid-teens, Lawrence in his mid-twenties. Their friendship had all the hallmarks of that of an older with a younger brother, a teacher with a promising pupil, a mentor with a protégé. Dahoum was not Lawrence's intellectual or social peer, yet clearly Lawrence enjoyed his company – he was simply very good fun, and no threat to Lawrence's intellectual ascendancy or emotional privacy. The controlling hand was Lawrence's. He took a brotherly pride in Dahoum's eagerness and quickness to learn, while the young Arab admired Lawrence and looked up to him. They worked together on the dig and spent time together in the dig's off-season. Miss al Akle wrote: 'On one of his visits to us an Arab accompanied him, a young fellow of about eighteen years of age, named Dahoum. This young man was greatly attached to Lawrence, and from him I learnt a great deal of what the Arabs thought of Lawrence. To a question I put, Dahoum gave an answer in some such words as these: 'You ask why we love Lawrence? And who can help loving him? He is our brother, our friend and leader. He is one of us, there is nothing we do he cannot do, and he even excels us in doing it. He takes such an interest in us and cares for our welfare. We respect him and greatly admire his courage and bravery: we love him, because he loves us and we would lay down our lives for him.'[21]

It has been suggested in connection with *Seven Pillars'* dedication that Dahoum had a title, Sheikh Achmed, but there is no record of him ever being referred to by this name and no proof of it has ever been found. Dahoum was a nickname meaning 'darkness', given to him because his mother is supposed to have said that he was very dark when he was born. There might be one piece of contemporary, written evidence of him being called Sheikh Achmed, but its credibility has been doubted. It takes the form of a signature he may have used on a note he wrote to Miss al Akle, which could perhaps be read as 'Sheikh Achmed' – but if so, probably more in fun than because it was a genuine title. I have a photocopy of this note and it is certainly very hard to decipher. The late St John Armitage, a well-known Arabist and Lawrence expert, wrote: 'The claim that he signed his letter 'Shaikh Ahmad' appears to be inaccurate. He concluded, possibly to show that he had learned to write and not use a scribe, "this letter is by the hand of [i.e. written by] Shaikh Ahmad al Halabi" – [the Aleppine] – and then appended a signature, which is not clear in the reproduction but does not appear to be "Ahmad". It is certainly not "Salim", Tom Beaumont's figment of imagination which has led to the "Selim Ahmad" story.'[22]

Dahoum's candidature for dedicatee, or part-dedicatee, of *Seven Pillars* might seem to be supported by Lawrence's earlier written references to S.A., which I have already summarized as an Arab, possibly a man, who was dead. It has been thought by some that Dahoum died of typhus a few months before the capture of Damascus in October 1918. In this context the story recounted in a 1969 biography by Tom Beaumont, who had served with Lawrence in the war as a Vickers machine-gunner with the Hejaz Armoured Car Company, that Dahoum's real name was Salim Achmed is highly suspect and almost certainly a fabrication.

Beaumont died, aged 93, in 1991 and his story first appeared in *The Secret Lives of Lawrence of Arabia*. In the words of Jeremy Wilson, Beaumont, 'was also responsible for the identification of S.A. with Salim Ahmed, someone nobody else has heard of. He sold the Salim Ahmed theory to the *Sunday Times* for a large sum.'[23] Among the millions of words of Lawrence recollections there is not a single mention of the name Salim Achmed other than Beaumont's. Both John Mack and Wilson discount his tale because there is no evidence to support it. Wilson is totally dismissive of Beaumont: 'As for Salim Achmed, his creator Tom Beaumont belongs, in my view, with Richard Meinertzhagen as a tedious source of quotable (= commercial) fiction about TEL. The errors committed by Beaumont and Meinertzhagen are so crass that one can have little respect for Lawrence biographers who quote either of them. However, there are doubtless people who will keep on doing it ... A friend of mine who met Beaumont in 1985 told me that B had joked "that he would say anything anyone wanted – so long as they paid him enough!"'[24]

Wilson has also said: 'Tom Beaumont lied to make money out of his association with Lawrence ...'[25] This allegation of Beaumont's mercenariness would seem to be confirmed by a piece of cynical opportunism, which saw him alerting the press, almost certainly for payment, to Lawrence's impending departure from Bridlington in February 1935 on his discharge from the RAF. Beaumont had first written to Lawrence in 1931.

Replying to a letter of his of January 1935, Lawrence mentioned in passing that he would soon be retiring from the service and leaving Bridlington by bicycle. Within a couple of weeks the *Sunday Express* had published an article about Lawrence's retirement, which quoted chunks of his letters to Beaumont. This in turn set the whole press corps off in full cry scurrying round Bridlington looking for Lawrence and his bike. Their unwanted interest may have been no more than a mild nuisance to Lawrence but it nevertheless provoked him, uncharacteristically, into rebuking Beaumont for his inconsiderate indiscretion and offering him some timely advice in a tone of scarcely veiled irritation: 'If it's true that you got a good offer for my letters by all means take it! They are your property but the copyright (that is the right to publish) remains mine always. Sell them cheerfully but for the Lord's sake don't let the pressmen read or repeat them, it's pretty beastly to have them snooping around the place.'[26]

Beaumont's melodramatic account in *Secret Lives* claims that 'Salim Achmed' was Lawrence's 'personal assistant' during the later stages of the Revolt and went behind the Turkish lines to spy for him. In September 1918 Lawrence is supposed to have said that he was 'going to see Salim'. Beaumont then recounts that on Lawrence's return he asked him: 'Did you see Salim?' and Lawrence is supposed to have replied, 'He's finished. He's dying. He's got typhoid.' Beaumont added: 'I'm sure it was typhoid he mentioned because we all got emergency typhoid shots soon afterwards. Lawrence turned away and pulled his kuffieh over his face and I heard him say, "I loved that boy." When he turned back I could see that he had been weeping. I overheard the bodyguards talking and I caught the Arabic word for death and I saw them make gestures like Lawrence holding Salim in his arms.'[27]

On first reading, this romanticized story might not seem implausible, except that no one else has ever corroborated it and Beaumont was given to inventions and fictions. He seems, in fact, to have had a suspiciously fortuitous knack of overhearing things. For example, he said that at Lawrence's funeral Lady Astor had said to Canon Kinloch, who had officiated at the service, 'That was a bloody fine sermon, the first time I've heard you sound really sincere.'[28] However, A.W. Lawrence, who organized the funeral, emphatically denied that there was a sermon, and the printed order of service confirms his assertion; in any case, Lady Astor was a Christian Scientist and was unlikely to have heard an address by Kinloch.[29] A.W. Lawrence confirmed his distrust of Beaumont in letters to the biographer Victoria Ocampo, referring to him as 'that notorious liar'.[30]

What's more, a man like Lawrence, who, it will be recalled, is on record as saying that 'if one thinks deeply about anything one would rather die than say anything about it' would hardly talk indiscriminately, or at all, about a friend dying in so traumatic a scenario as the one in Beaumont's unlikely tale.[31] Jeremy Wilson, while believing that Dahoum was a part of the dedication, records that he most probably died in 1916, long before the final advance on Damascus, a casualty of the typhus epidemic that had followed a severe famine in northern Syria. Wilson wrote:

> Leonard Woolley, who went to the Jerablus region at the end of 1918, found that nearly half of the old Carchemish labour force had perished, and it was reported to him that almost a third of the population had died during 1916. Dahoum had remained at the site as one of the guards, and salary records for the first two years of the war show that he worked there on and off until October 1916. After this, no records survive; but postwar reports by Woolley state that, apart from Hamoudi, none of the men who had originally been appointed to watch the site had been there during the later part of the war. Carchemish is some two hundred miles north of Damascus, and it is most improbable that Lawrence heard the news directly. On the other hand, British Intelligence received a constant flow of local information from Turkish prisoners and deserters. The Arab Intelligence office at Allenby's advance headquarters had been built up by Hogarth who was interested in any news of Carchemish. If he had learned of Dahoum's death, he would have seen to it that Lawrence was told.[32]

Lawrence wrote to Farida al Akle in January 1921, 'Dahoum died some years ago, during the war, of fever.'[33] At the time of writing the most recent attempt to identify S.A. with Dahoum had been made in 2003 by an American, Sara Johnson. She cited a book, a long poem called *The Singing Caravan, A Sufi Tale*, by Sir Robert Vansittart, as providing an important clue. Vansittart, as already stated, was a collateral relation of Lawrence on the Chapman side. He and Lawrence didn't hit it off. Vansittart and his kin were rather dismissive of Lawrence's father and apparently distanced themselves from that side of the family. Nevertheless, the two men found themselves on common ground when it came to *The Singing Caravan*, and at the Peace Conference in Paris their differences were in some measure reconciled when Vansittart gave Lawrence an inscribed copy of his book, which delighted him.

The poem could have held a strong appeal for Lawrence because in some respects it mirrored his war experiences and the sense of a failed mission, as well as containing a story of lost love. The lines 'All that we had built or planned, / Toiled, bled for, crumbled at a touch, was ruined like a house of sand' would seem to be echoed in the final verse of Lawrence's dedicatory poem.[34] Johnson said, and I agree with her, that another 'compelling clue as to the identity of S.A.' is to be found in *Minorities* (Lawrence's private anthology of poetry) in the poem 'Skias Onar' (also titled '*L'Envoi*') by the Cambridge English don F.L. Lucas. This poem meant a great deal to Lawrence.

However, the main conclusions of Sara Johnson's S.A. essay are centred on Lawrence's love of Syria, particularly on an area known as the Hauran, which is described several times by Lawrence in *Seven Pillars* as the hollow land. In the section in the Oxford edition of the book headed 'On the Threshold of Syria' he talks of the Hauran as 'a huge fertile land, thickly peopled in its western half with Arab peasantry, warlike and as self-reliant and prosperous an element as any in Syria.'[35] Johnson includes a plethora of written references to this part of Syria and its likening by writers and historians down the centuries to a hollow land and makes play of the significance of William Morris's book (and poem) of the same name, *The Hollow Land*. Her argument is that Lawrence loved Morris's book and poem because they represented for him both a place and someone he loved, Syria and Dahoum. However, it should also be remembered that Deraa, the scene of Lawrence's assault and rape, is in the Hauran – hardly a place of happy memory for him.

The book *The Hollow Land* opens with words spoken by the tale's hero, Florian de Liliis: 'Do you know where it is – the Hollow Land? I have been looking for it now so long, trying to find it again – the Hollow land – for there I saw my love first.'[36] 'My love' is Margaret and towards the last third of the book Florian sees, or rather hears, her for the first time when he wakes to the beguilement of her voice as, sitting nearby, she sings the first verse of the poem, 'The Hollow Land': 'Christ keep the Hollow Land / Through the sweet spring-tide, / When the apple-blossoms bless / The lowly bent hill side.' Florian says: 'Thereat my eyes were slowly unsealed, and I saw the blessedest sight I have ever seen before or since: for I saw my Love.'[37] Can we really believe, as Sara Johnson would have us do, that whenever Lawrence read these words of Florian's about Margaret, he thought of Dahoum? Surely, he was far more likely to have recalled Janet Laurie, or perhaps another woman.

The *mise en scène* of Morris's book *The Hollow Land*, is – as so often with his romances – an ideal, lost medieval world. The story is a dreamlike fantasy played out in a half-mystical realm of mist-enshrouded lands, lordly houses, brave scions, battling knights, and wrongs inflicted and righted. It is a tale of other-worldly redemption with at its heart the love between the hero and his lady, a woman who seems at times to be almost a divinity. This love is the central theme of the book, a romance in the ideal Provençal tradition. To suggest that it mirrors a man-man love simply misrepresents *The Hollow Land*. A man's brotherly affection for a man is one thing; the love of a man for a woman is quite another.

The book ends with the lovers finding happiness and peace in a semi-paradise. Johnson includes this finale as the ending for her own thesis: 'At the end of Morris' story Florian finds his love, finds "that other face, seen in that way and no other long & long and long ago."' However, she has misread Morris, because Florian, at this specific point in the narrative, is talking about his own face. Florian has been reunited with Margaret and they walk, blissfully happy, towards what Margaret calls 'a hollow city in the Hollow Land'. They kiss and go on, coming eventually to a 'fair palace'. Florian's narration leads to the culmination of the story: 'We stopped before the gates and trembled, and clasped each other closer; for there among the marble leafage and tendrils that were round and under and over the archway that held the golden valves, were wrought two figures of a man and woman, winged and garlanded, whose raiment flashed with stars; and their faces were like faces we had seen or half seen in some dream long and long and long ago, so that we trembled with awe and delight; and I turned, and seeing Margaret, saw that her face was that face seen or half seen long and long and long ago; and in the shining of her eyes I saw that other face, seen in that way and no other long and long and long ago – my face. And then we walked together toward the golden gates, and opened them, and no man gainsaid us. And before us lay a great space of flowers.'[38]

Sara Johnson attaches importance to *The Hollow Land*, and particularly to the poem, because of a discovery she made about Lawrence's personal collection of poems, *Minorities*. It is not generally known that there are two volumes of this anthology. The second one, unpublished and privately owned, was found by chance in 1990 in a biscuit tin in the Knowles' house opposite Lawrence's cottage, Clouds Hill. It has the word *Minorities* on its spine. Incomplete, it seems to have been begun by Lawrence in or just before 1927. The final poem in both volumes of *Minorities* is 'The Hollow Land', and Johnson makes much of the fact that in the second volume the poem is placed at the very end, with forty-one blank pages between it and the preceding poem. Lawrence did this, she argues, because the poem 'The Hollow Land' had a special significance for him and in each volume he wanted it to be the high point of the anthology. This is an acceptable hypothesis but Lawrence's precise reason for the placing of the poem is open to any number of interpretations. The poem itself is hardly intellectually engaging or emotionally revealing. It is light verse, lyrical, gentle, charming. It does not evoke a person but rather a place, or places, and for Lawrence it may indeed have had nostalgic resonances – of the Hauran, perhaps, but much more likely of Carchemish itself and of his years of pre-war happiness. After all, he said, more than once, that he tended to prefer places to people. As he once told Lady Astor, his heart had 'never cared for anyone, though much for places and things'; and Leonard Woolley observed: 'He was an enthusiast for Syria; the country appealed to him more than did its inhabitants and, while he really disliked the Syrian townsman, for Syria he had a passion.'[39] [40]

The Hollow Land

Christ keep the Hollow Land
Through the sweet springtide,
When the apple-blossoms bless
The lowly bent hill side.'

Christ keep the Hollow Land
All the summer-tide;
Still we cannot understand

Where the waters glide:

Only dimly seeing them
Coldly slipping through
Many green-lipped cavern mouths
Where the hills are blue.

Another possible dedicatee whose name has often cropped up over the years is Sarah Aaronsohn, a Jewish wartime heroine and a member of the NILI spy network.

However, it is virtually certain that she and Lawrence never met. She was undoubtedly a heroine, especially to those whose ultimate hopes were for the establishment of an independent Jewish state in Palestine, and she died for her beliefs and to protect others. But would she have benefited from Arab freedom from the Turks? She was born in 1890 in Zichron Yaacov close to the Mediterranean coast south of Haifa and it was there in 1917 that she died. She had five siblings, including Aaron Aaronsohn, an agronomist of repute, who became a major liaison agent between the NILI spy ring in Palestine and British Intelligence in Cairo. The network was created by Absalom Feinberg in the spring of 1915. In the summer Alex and Rivka, Aaron and Sarah's siblings, went by American warship to Cairo to broach their plans to the British, who initially showed little interest. In August Feinberg also travelled to Cairo, where Leonard Woolley, now an intelligence officer, met him at Port Said. Woolley agreed to use Athlit, north of Zichron, for intelligence exchanges. At this time Sarah, who had married a Turkish Jew, was in Constantinople, but she returned to Zichron in November. At the end of February 1916 Woolley went by submarine to Athlit. The boat was torpedoed and he was captured. He was to spend the rest of the war interned in Turkey.

After repeated rebuffs by the British, Aaron was finally able to launch NILI in the spring of 1917. It lasted as an active spy ring until November of that year. Sarah was captured and tortured by the Turks that October, and shot herself rather than risk divulging any information to the Turks about NILI or the British. Sarah's earlier movements, which included a trip to Cairo, do not synchronize with Lawrence's and it is beyond doubt that the paths of the two never crossed. For example, during the one period (28 April to 18 June 1917) that she was accompanying Aaron in Cairo, Lawrence was in Arabia and, despite some tall tales to the contrary, never went to Athlit during the war. Leonard Woolley later confirmed in an interview with Leonard Woolf (which was later reported to Anita Engle, author of the book *The Nili Spies)* that Lawrence had never worked with NILI.[41] Engle commented, 'there is no mention in Sarah's detailed reports and letters of any contact with Lawrence by her or any member of NILI in Palestine.'[42] And nowhere in the many diaries and letters of other NILI members is there any reference to Lawrence.

The story only gained currency years later, in 1936, after a chance discussion in a hotel in California between four people, who included an author and a journalist. They saw the publicity potential of the tale and duly promoted it. The Aaronsohns in Palestine flatly denied it, but the hare was already up and running and attracting further media interest. However, since the tale had no real substance, the press eventually tired of it and it seemed to have died a death; but, astonishingly, it was resurrected and given a further lease of life by an unlikely source. Engle, confident that she had proved the story a myth, wrote an article to that effect in *The New Statesman*.[43] To her amazement, the following week a letter appeared in the journal from a Douglas Duff disputing her conclusions and claiming that Sarah Aaronsohn was indeed Lawrence's S.A. Duff, who knew the Middle East and had served with the Palestine Police, wrote: 'One morning, in the wide East Street of Bridport in Dorset, T.E. Lawrence, a few weeks before he was killed, told me that we had both dedicated a book to Sarah Aaronsohn and asked me if I had known her while she was alive. I had not, but, like him, I was her client after she was martyred ... Lawrence certainly meant the dedication for Sarah the martyr-maid of Israel. He told me so.'[44]

Engle then wrote to Duff for clarification. He replied:

> ... The meeting (with Lawrence) to which I referred took place outside Thear's Garage in the wide East Street of Bridport in Dorset. That morning I was filling my petrol tank at the garage, when a large Brough Superior motor-cycle roared up and I saw, without his seeing me, that it was Lawrence. I knew he hated recognition, and so made none, but I heard him ask the pump attendant who I was and my name given. Then Lawrence, a small man, came up and spoke to me in the strange way he had of using soldierly language, very soldierly. He asked me if I had written a recent book on Palestine, which I had dedicated to Sarah Aaronsohn. I was very flattered to think he had read my work and said so. The conversation went like this (without hoping to be verbatim):
>
> L: So you know who I am?
> Me: I do. Col. Lawrence, of course.
> L: Shaw's my name and I'm no – colonel.
> Me: I beg your pardon – I'm afraid you'll always be Lawrence in my mind. I apologize for saying so aloud.

L: Did you know Sarah Aaronsohn while she was alive?

Me: I'm very sorry that I did not. I'd have given my right arm to have done so.

L: Why?

Me: Good Lord, man, if ever there was a Joan of Arc in our days, it was Sarah!

L: Strange we two men should be here in this little town, both of us with a book dedicated to her, without either of us ever having seen her alive.

Me: Why, judging by that sonnet of yours I was sure she and you were partners in the old days.

L: We were – but without meeting.

Engle added that Duff told her that two weeks later he saw Lawrence again, who then 'made the only other reference Mr Duff heard him make to Sarah.' Lawrence is supposed to have said, 'If she had had a man for a husband, she might have been the leader of a Hebrew return with glory. It must have been hell to have been married to her when one was so unable to appreciate her.' Engle was perplexed by Duff's reported conversations with Lawrence and seems to have concluded that they might be suspect but that, if they were true, then Lawrence was indulging in 'a little wishful thinking', and that if he really had dedicated *Seven Pillars of Wisdom* to Sarah, this was also 'an afterthought'.[45]

All this puzzled me too. So I went to see Duff at his home in King Stag in Dorset. To my surprise he added to his story, saying that Lawrence had heard about Sarah's death on the heights of Makianis overlooking the Jordan valley near Tafileh in February 1918. He thought that Lawrence had recognized him at the garage because he had read Duff's book *Sword For Hire* and had also seen one of Duff's books dedicated to Sarah. He then went on to tell me that he had met Lawrence on not two occasions, as he had told Engle, but three: the first at Thear's Garage when they talked for two hours and the second at Duff's house when Lawrence just walked in and for a long while said nothing. Duff said that on that occasion he seemed very depressed and wanted to chat about old times, enquiring about one or two sheikhs he had known and mentioning Sarah, saying it was a pity she had not had a more appreciative husband, then things might have turned out differently. The third meeting, Duff claimed, was also at his house, and on that occasion his wife, Janet, had noticed that there was a button missing off Lawrence's tunic and had offered to sew it on again. Lawrence accepted and she also sewed up a pair of his pyjamas. Pyjamas? As Lawrence was leaving he seemed very grateful and is supposed to have said to Duff about his wife: 'You don't know what a lucky bastard you are.'[46]

I was now even more confused because Duff's conversation with me contradicted, in several important key respects, what he had told Engle. So I checked on his published writings held in the British Museum. I found that he had written only two books before Lawrence's death: *Sword For Hire* in 1934 and *Galilee Galloper* in 1935. The first was dedicated to his wife, the second to his wife's parents. This discovery cast a major doubt on the veracity of Duff's stories about Lawrence and Sarah. I wrote to him pointing out the anomaly and received a reply in which he said that the two books I had mentioned were the first of his to be published in the United Kingdom. He added, in order, I suspected, to explain the disparity I had found, that there was a very considerable amount of material published in the United States, the dominions and in Great Britain, in many periodicals as well as in newspapers, before any books were put out. But Duff had told both Engle and me that Lawrence had talked to him of the two of them each 'with a book' dedicated to Sarah, not an article in a periodical or newspaper; and he had told Engle that Lawrence had spoken to him only twice about Sarah. The rest of his letter betrayed a frosty impatience with what I felt were legitimate queries and ended by saying that he wished to discontinue our correspondence.

Dahoum and Sarah Aaronsohn have been the most oft-cited names associated with the *Seven Pillars* dedication, but there have inevitably been others, some outlandish, some not implausible. There has also been speculation as to whether the dedicatory poem might encompass several people or motivations in one composite person, perhaps including Dahoum as a personification of Lawrence's golden years in Syria and of the ideal of the unspoiled native, the noble savage. Another contender occasionally suggested is the Arab Revolt itself and the unique comradeship it generated for Lawrence. I was reminded powerfully of this compelling bond by what he says about it in *Seven Pillars*. He talks of the 'fellowship of the revolt' with a moving and simple lyricism: 'We were fond together, and there are here memories of the sweep of the open places, the taste of wide winds, the sunlight, and the hopes in which we worked. It felt like morning, and the freshness of the world-to-be intoxicated us.'[47]

The possibility of the Revolt itself and its tight-knit fellowship, or even of Syria (seen as a personification of Lawrence's memories of his halcyon days) playing a part in the dedicatory poem is not such a far-fetched idea and allusions to them can arguably be discerned in the stanzas. In the *Seven Pillars* manuscript in the Bodleian Library the poem differs in a few places from the version in the 1926 Subscribers' edition. Lawrence was clearly at pains in each stanza to try to ensure that the substance and sense could be read both literally and allegorically. The most noticeable textual difference is in the third verse, but the variations seem ultimately to reflect more a problem of form and rhythm than one of meaning.

To return now to Provençal poetry and to the central principles of secrecy and dissimulation demanded by the convention, it is clear that if the inspiration for Lawrence's dedication was troubadour poetry, he would have taken great care not to reveal the identity of the dedicatee, certainly not any female element of it. Hints, yes; half-truths, perhaps; but the truth? Absolutely not. The rules of Provençal love poetry not only perfectly complemented Lawrence's emotional make-up but also suited his mischievous nature. As John Mack observed, he took great delight in leading people up the garden path, even where the matter was a serious one, in which case, of course, humorous diversion and verbal sleight-of-hand would have served the essential purpose of hiding the truth.

When considering the dedicatory poem, I have often found myself thinking of Shakespeare's sonnets. While preparing to write his poem, Lawrence may have had the passing notion of doing something similar to Shakespeare, with his insoluble mystery of Mr W.H. and the dark lady. That there was not just a male 'onlie begetter' of the great Elizabethan's poems but another affection, another inspiration – a woman – could be significant in the context of Lawrence's own poem. He once wrote of Shakespeare to Robert Graves, 'There was a man who hid behind his works, with great pains and consistency. Ergo he had something to hide: some privy reason for hiding. He being a most admirable fellow, I hope he hides successfully.'[48]

The public Lawrence strictly policed his emotions but the private Lawrence was someone quite different, and his choice of poetry clearly shows this. Near the end of his time at Carchemish he made a bound volume of poems he had transcribed from *The English Review* of 1913-14. His poetic tastes were wide and this is amply reflected in his selections, but for a man regarded as having little interest in affairs of the heart it is interesting to note that of the seven poems he transcribed from the issue of April 1914 five were love poems – one, incidentally, entitled 'Shakespear [sic] and a Woman'. Dipping into the five at random you will find such stanzas as this from 'After Many Days' by H.T.W. Bousfield: 'Will you be changed? / And I? I shall be older, / Graver, maybe, appraising all your charms, / Or will the weary years have left me bolder, / Taking you into my arms?' And, from 'Lips of my Love': 'Oh, I am faint / When thy lips hang on mine / And there is ecstasy / In their mute questing, / Easting, westing.'[49]

That the undemonstrative Lawrence was drawn to such passionate poetic expressions of love for a woman may come as a revelation to some. The abiding appeal that love poems had for Lawrence (and you will also find it in *Minorities)* exposes a surprisingly romantic man, a man who outwardly betrays little feeling but who inside is brimming with emotional yearnings. In the winter of 1921–22 Lawrence had sent that draft of his dedicatory poem to Robert Graves asking him to cast his professional eye over it. In response Graves produced a very different, more metric and much-compressed version, which Lawrence gushingly praised as so much better than his original, while, typically, not incorporating a single word of it in his published poem. Lawrence also sought advice from the poet Laurence Binyon, whom he didn't know, disparaging the poem in the same self-deprecating language that he had used when contrasting his effort with Graves's re-working of it. Binyon's verdict was positive enough for Lawrence to feel justi-fied in publishing the poem in the so-called Oxford Edition.

Finally, as already stated, the dedicatory poem is deliberately ambivalent, both literal and allegorical, and this brings us full circle back to the Middle Ages. Lawrence's poem, although in modern format, reflects both troubadour poetic practice and his complex personality. It seems to be constructed to encourage the reader to indulge in all sorts of conjecture, thus ensuring that the real iden-tity of his muse would be effectively masked, safely hidden among a profusion of speculative dedicatees all competing for attention. A.W. Lawrence might, unknowingly, have been endorsing this likelihood when he wrote: 'Here I may add the suggestion that the poem which serves as dedication to the *Seven Pillars* is somewhat of a literary exercise, in memory of his youth, as well as a tribute to the person who had roused him to appreciate the potentialities of the Arab race.'[50]

His post-war friend Jock Chambers supports the theory that Lawrence wanted to create a dedicatory poem that was an enigma, open to any number of interpretations. I wrote to Jock about the poem and he replied saying that Lawrence had slaved over every word in its composition. He added that he had seen the Oxford draft of *Seven Pillars* on the table in the barrack room of B3 at RAF Farnborough, where he and Lawrence were stationed in 1922–23. To my suggestion that the dedicatee might have been a woman he said intriguingly: 'I'm not sure that TE really knew … It was written about 1923 (I think) at Clouds Hill, not at all easily, sometimes many pages each having only one line and that dead centre.' Then, significantly, he added that Lawrence, 'never mentioned any "special" woman – but he did say to me that "most men pretended to have had to do with a number of women. But I think it's just a pretence – they have only known the one."'[51]

TWENTY-ONE

The Dark Lady

So, love, I love not you but what I dream you,
My soul grows sick with clutching at a shade.
Let others seem to win the shapes that seem you:
Only our pain is never masquerade.[1]

JOCK CHAMBERS' remark to me that Lawrence had said to him that men pretended to have 'had to do' with a number of women while in fact having really known only the one, preoccupied me. Up to his departure for Carchemish the one woman in his life had without doubt been Janet Laurie. So, in those four sunlit years in Syria before the war changed him irreversibly, was there another, a woman for whom he had developed a deep affection and whom he had made a part of the S.A. dedication of *Seven Pillars of Wisdom*? To honour someone without telling them of such a profound accolade would be typical of Lawrence. He once wrote to his mother: 'Don't you ever feel that we love you without our telling you so?'[2]

So who was *Her* Highness, the 'Royal' lady of the dedication whose image and memory Lawrence would have carried with him in the desert campaign? There were certainly clues that pointed to a lost love, someone who after the war was unattainable yet still alive. Lawrence's 1927 annotation of Robert Graves's biographical draft, 'You have taken me too literally. S.A. still exists: but out of my reach, because

I have changed'³ is a significant admission, a hint dropped by Lawrence that should not be lightly dismissed as a decoy or deception. While they were at Oxford Graves had exhorted Lawrence to find a woman, specifically a woman, to help him out of his depression, and Lawrence had said that he had never been able to fall in love. However, shortly afterwards he had written to the poet to confess that he had not told him the whole truth and that there had been 'an exception', a woman who had been a part of the inspiration for his 'Arabian adventure'.

There are pointers (many of which I have already discussed), which suggest that at the heart of Lawrence lay a powerfully romantic nature, a very private world of imagination and emotion, which he protected from the curious by force of will, humour, evasion, ridicule and secrecy. He was afraid of the lack of control which might overwhelm him if he gave his feelings free rein. Spontaneous affection was not a part of his emotional vocabulary, it was something he feared. Lawrence always had to be firmly in charge of himself. A.W. Lawrence wrote of his brother: 'He had, I believe, a diffident, perhaps weak core, so controlled by his colossal will-power that its underlying presence was rarely suspected ...' and, 'His diffidence probably arose from a sense of isolation, of a barrier set by his own oddness between himself and the rest of mankind; he said, in middle-age, that it prevented any thought of marriage.'⁴

In a particularly revealing passage in *Seven Pillars* Lawrence purposely bares his inner self. In the desert at Bair on his thirtieth birthday in August 1918 he found time to take stock of both himself and his part in the campaign, and to indulge in some searching introspection:

> On this birthday in Bair, to satisfy my sense of sincerity, I began to dissect my own beliefs and motives, groping about in my pitchy darkness, full of the wailing of the underworld. My self-distrusting shyness held a mask, often a mask of indifference or flippancy, before my face, and puzzled me. My thoughts clawed at this apparent peace, wondering what was underneath, knowing that it was only a mask because, despite my trying never to dwell on what interested me, there were moments too strong for control when my will burst out and frightened me.
>
> I was very conscious of the bundle of powers and entities within me: it was their character which hid itself. There was my craving for being liked: – so strong and nervous was it that never could I open myself to another, to make him my friend. The terror of failure in an effort so important had frightened me from trying; and besides there was the standard, for intimacy seemed shameful unless the other could make the perfect reply, in the same language, after the same method, for the same reasons.

There was a craving for being known and famous, and a horror of being known to like being known. My contempt of my passion for distinction had made me refuse every offered honour. I cherished my independence almost as a Beduin did, but found I could realise it best by making another remark upon it, in my hearing. My impotence of vision showed me my shape best in painted pictures, and only the oblique overheard remarks of others taught me my created impression. So an eagerness to overhear and oversee myself was my assault upon my own inviolate citadel.

The lower creation I avoided, as an insult to our intellectual nature. If they forced themselves on me I hated them. To put my hand on a living thing was degradation to me: and it made me tremble if they touched me or took too quick an interest in me. This was an atomic repulsion, the power which guarded the intact course of a floating snowflake: but the opposite would have been my choice, if my head had not been tyrannous. I had a longing for women and animals, and lamented myself most when I saw a soldier hugging a girl in silent ecstasy, or a man fondling a dog: because my wish was to be as superficial and my gaoler held me back.

He hated the fact that his being was incarcerated in flesh:

To recognise our possession of bodies was degradation enough, let alone to enlarge upon their needs and attributes. These others were outwardly so like me that I would feel shame for myself, seeing them wallow in what I judged shame: since the physical could be only a glorification of man's cross. Indeed the truth was always that I did not like myself.[5]

A person's private choice of poetry may, when decoded, provide a revealing insight into the hidden persona. I am in accord with Henry Thoreau, who said: 'Poetry is a piece of very private history, which unostentatiously lets us into the secret of a man's life' – the devotee's as well as the poet's. *Minorities* is one such key and it opens a door to the inner Lawrence. The poems in *Minorities* were written by Lawrence into 'a little Morrell-bound note-book', which he gave to Charlotte Shaw in 1927, explaining that its title dictated the choice of poems: 'One necessary qualification was that they should be in a minor key: another that they should sing a little bit.'[6] The following year he again mentioned the book to Charlotte: 'You know that tiny anthology of poems I sent you? It travelled with me for years, and there is not a poem in it I have not read 50 times.'[7] Lawrence confessed that he couldn't write poetry but he believed nonetheless that it was 'the crown and head, the only essential branch of letters.'[8] It was sometimes specific parts and phrases of a poem that he sought to provide the verbal magic he enjoyed most, 'moments' that triggered a flight into space of his entire consciousness 'upon these vibrations of perfect sound.'⁹ If Lawrence chose the poems in *Minorities* for their content not their form, or, as he put it, for their matter not their manner, it would be a mistake always to detect autobiographical allusions in them. That is not to say, however, that some of them didn't have an especially personal meaning for him or encapsulate something deeply felt in his life. In my view, *Minorities*, read discerningly, provides revealing insights into the hidden Lawrence.

His choice for inclusion in his anthology reflects a person with strong emotions and a love of the romantic, someone who was drawn to nostalgia, nostalgia for irrecoverable things, times, relationships, experiences, with the accent on wistfulness and regret – a love undeclared or lost, a challenge not met or failed, hopes unfulfilled or dashed, the futility of life, and the inevitability of death. Sometimes there is an optimistic entry, or some light-hearted verse, but the dominant note, in keeping with the book's title, is in a minor key redolent of what Lawrence seemed to feel was a sense of sadness at the heart of things.

At least twenty of the 112 entries are love poems, and, as you might expect, the poet with the greatest representation is William Morris, with ten poems, followed by James Thomson with seven; Flecker, Edward Thomas, Swinburne, Sassoon, Shelley, Blake and Hardy, with four apiece; and Dowson, John Davidson, Ralph Hodgson, A.E. Housman and Alice Meynell with three each. This list in itself gives an idea of Lawrence's very lyrical, almost elegiac taste and reflects an imagination nurtured not only by Provençal poetry but also in some measure by that of the nineties and the Edwardian decade.

In 1923 he wrote to Graves about *Minorities*, 'you'll be astonished at my sweet tooth, if ever you see that discreditable collection.'¹⁰ Among the love poems are a number that certainly encourage the belief that there is a correlation with Lawrence's own life, which seem to hold a mirror up to some emotional experience of his own. Firstly, an excerpt from the third verse of 'The Lover,' by John Crowe Ransom:

> ... O love, do you know the secret now
> Of one who would not tell nor touch?
> Must I confess before the pack
> Of babblers, idiots, and such?¹¹

And from 'Spell-bound' by Morris:

O golden love that waitest me,

The days pass on, pass on a-pace,
Sometimes I have a little rest
In fairest dreams, when on thy face
My lips lie, or thy hands are prest

About my forehead, and thy lips
Draw near and nearer to mine own;
But when the vision from me slips,
In colourless dawn I lie and moan,

O dearest, scarcely seen by me —[12]

Two others seem to suggest something deeply felt in Lawrence's life: 'Bride Song' by Christina Rossetti with the opening lines:

Too late for love, too late for joy,
    Too late, too late!
You loiter'd on the road too long,
    You trifled at the gate:
The enchanted dove upon her branch
    Died without a mate;
The enchanted princess in her tower
    Slept, died, behind the grate;
Her heart was starving all this while
    You made it wait...[13]

And the resonance of George Herbert's lines:

Love bade me welcome; yet my soul drew back,
    Guilty of dust and sin.[14]

There is one particular love poem in *Minorities*, however, that clearly had a very special significance for Lawrence. This is F.L. Lucas's 'Skias Onar', which I mentioned earlier. It was first published in *The New Statesman* in 1924.

The poem's theme, unfolded with an aching poignancy, is essentially of the impossibility of translating ideal love into a living reality, of the fervent longing that lies at the heart of love and is never satisfied, never fulfilled, and of the tragic impossibility of true union, of becoming one with another person. The poem is suffused with the troubadour ethos. Lawrence waxed lyrical about Lucas's poems and their effect on him as soon as he came across them. Shortly after reading 'Skias Onar' he was commenting on it in a postscript to a letter to E.M. Forster: 'Who is F.L. Lucas, by whom have been two excellent poems lately in the *New Statesman* ... Really excellent, I mean: a sure, rounded, polished, fluent, fluting voice. Really, really, good.'[15] Five years later, in 1929, when the Hogarth Press published *Time and Memory*, a collection of Lucas's poems, Lawrence wrote to David Garnett describing their effect on him as, 'so low-toned and they creep in and over my spirit like lianas ... I think I've been through the book about 20 times, and can't place it in myself. I like them awfully. It's like hearing myself speak perfectly, on every other page. He just says what I've felt inarticulately.'[16]

Earlier, in 1927, at RAF Miranshah, he had again talked about 'Skias Onar' with great animation and feeling, this time with his friend Harry Banbury, whom he had first met in 1924. Banbury wrote: 'He read it over to me. The last line, "Only our pain is never masquerade," was spoken with such force and intensity as to make me realize that there was an expression written by another which he felt fitted with his own feeling, and in uttering it he expressed his own self.'[17] Jeremy Wilson wrote that Lawrence was 'deeply affected' by the poem, especially by the last verse.[18] Wilson told me that there existed a privately owned proof of the dedicatory poem to S.A., onto which Lawrence had written this last verse, which reads:

So, love, I love not you but what I dream you,
    My soul grows sick with clutching at a shade.
Let others seem to win the shapes that seem you:
    Only our pain is never masquerade.[19]

The first four stanzas of 'Skias Onar' are:

One thing I craved, one thing you would not grant me –
    (Oh, nothing you *could* give me, you denied) –
Your love's for others. Yet they shall not supplant me:
    Others – they, too, shall pass unsatisfied.

I craved your love. And what you could, you gave me,
    Your body's beauty; yet I sought the soul.
Not loving me, dear child, you could not save me:
    Yet all your love could not have made me whole.

For thus men's hearts have ached since man's beginning;
    Beauty can blast, Love cannot wholly bless.
We stretch vain hands—pure hands alike and sinning;
    But Beauty cannot give, nor Love possess.

As, in old tales, when wraiths of lovers perished
    Glimmered once more on eyes that wept them dead,
Still from the living arms that vainly cherished,
    A smoke, a dream, the subtle phantom fled …[20]

The poem's fifth and last verse, which so affected Lawrence, encapsulates an anguished longing for a love whose true existence is only in the heart and mind of the poet, a love whose human recipient is ultimately a 'subtle phantom', a haunting personification of a mystical enchantment. This suggests strongly that Lawrence, with his most individual emotional pathology, had a very similar, highly refined response to love and that he identified completely with Lucas's experience and interpretation of it. Such ideal love (the key to troubadour love) is a powerful driving force. The imagined is a far more potent agent of inspiration than the real.

By now I had no doubt that a female element of S.A. did exist, an ideal love for a real woman that had been transfigured onto an almost otherworldly plane, and that this love was one of the principle motivations in Lawrence's relentless efforts to gift the Arabs freedom. My years of wondering and wandering down the byways of Lawrence's secret emotional life were, I sensed, reaching their *dénouement*. I had scoured all the known written material relating to the dedication of *Seven Pillars* and to Lawrence's deepest feelings (rarely revealed though they were). I was convinced I had finally found the answer, or part of the answer. Robert Graves's support and corroborations were to prove central to opening the door to discovery. I had written to him laying out my conclusions about the dedication.

He had been very interested and had invited me to stay with him in Majorca, where he lived. During that two-week visit in the mountains we had long discussions about his friendship with Lawrence and about the dedication to *Seven Pillars*. We were of like mind about it. Each day under the unchanging blue of the Mediterranean sky we would stroll from his house along the winding road high above the sea into the postcard-pretty hilltop village of Deya. Cutting a colourful dash in his baggy, khaki shorts, Mexican top and wide-brimmed straw hat, Graves told me more about his conversations at Oxford with Lawrence, who, he said, had been extremely knowledgeable about Provençal poetry. He added that he felt that Lawrence had very occasionally seemed to come close to revealing further clues to the dedication. Later John Mack told me that he thought Graves's and my conviction that the dedication was tied into Provençal poetry and troubadour love rang true, given Lawrence's secretive emotional nature.

Graves and I were now sure that there were three key pieces of evidence relating to the dedication: firstly, Lawrence's admission to him that there *had* been 'an exception', a woman who had inspired him; secondly, the coded information hidden in the two books that Lawrence had curiously forced on his attention when the two men were at Oxford; and thirdly, Lawrence's written comment to the poet in 1927 that 'S.A. still exists: but out of my reach, because I have changed.' The books were the ones to which I have already referred: Hewlett's medieval romance, *Richard Yea-and-Nay*, and the short stories by Morley Roberts. Why had Lawrence thrust these books on Graves? Not because he was deliberately using him to throw the curious off the scent with a false trail, as some have, in my view, erroneously concluded, but because Graves was a muse-poet and Lawrence knew that he would draw the right inferences from the books where others might not. He had clearly felt an urge to tell Graves the truth but, typically, in a veiled form.

Lawrence wrote home from Carchemish in 1912, 'not many books will be read 6 times by me, unless they have a little more than prose in them.'[21] He read the romantic *Richard Yea-and-Nay* at least nine times and dubbed it 'a masterpiece' and 'an outstanding book.'[22] [23] It is a love story about Richard Coeur de Lion and Jehane de Saint-Pol, and is set in France and, more significantly, in Syria at the time of the Crusades. The historical content of the book was clearly well-researched; even verses of Provençal poetry in the troubadours' original tongue of Old Occitan are included. Lawrence obviously delighted in the colourful depictions of the Middle Ages, of mounted knights and shining armour, heraldic insignia, castles under siege, and heroism in the heat of battle. But anyone who thinks that he liked the book solely for its historical, martial or literary content should think again.

The book – like *The Well at the World's End*, and *The Hollow Land* – is above all a love story full of evocative and lyrical description. An example of this is the opening paragraph of chapter fourteen, 'How the Leopard was Loosed', which describes Richard's heart-ache as he remembers the long-ago days in France when his love for Jehane was magically new. The author described his book as 'this chronicle of Anjou and a Noble Lady'[24] – the beautiful, spirited Jehane, Jehane of the Fair Girdle, Bel Vezer in her *senhal* persona. Much space is devoted to describing her loveliness, sweet personality and intelligence, her high-born qualities, her bravery, the love that she and Richard have for each other and the obstacles that rise up to prevent its happy resolution. There is a rich supporting cast too, including Bertrand de Born, Richard's friend, who engages in troubadour *tenzons* (impromptu versifications) with him, each vying to sing a better poem than the other's; and the villain of the piece, the Marquess of Montferrat, who schemes for Richard's death. It is the perfect *mise-en-scène* of Lawrence's beloved medieval world, and Graves and I felt sure that the haunting love story at its heart mirrored something deeply felt in Lawrence's life.

In the context of the dedication of *Seven Pillars*, the important part of the story comes towards the last third of the book. In order to save Richard from Montferrat, Jehane sacrifices her chances of a future with Richard by going on a dangerous journey by donkey high into the Lebanese mountains to the stronghold of the Old Man of Musse, to beg his help. This sinister yet strangely wise Lord despatches two of his assassins to kill Montferrat while in return Jehane agrees to remain forever with the Old Man as a ransom. Richard and she will never be together again. Years later they are poignantly but only momentarily reunited, but afterwards she returns to the mountains of the Lebanon.

I was convinced, as was Graves, that the two books Lawrence had suddenly given him – this story of Richard Coeur de Lion and Jehane, of a man who returns to his homeland leaving his love behind in the mountains of the Lebanon; and the short story of the sea captain who is haunted by the memory of his wrecked ship – were Lawrence's way of telling Graves that during the war there had been a woman who meant a great deal to him, a woman who had perhaps been behind enemy lines, but with whom, because he had irrevocably changed, he felt he couldn't resume any serious engagement after his return to England on the cessation of hostilities in Syria.

Over the years I had pieced together all this half-coded information and now, after long deliberation and heart-searching, I suddenly knew. The identity of the woman who was the female aspect of S.A. had been staring me in the face. She *was* an Arab, she lived in Syria, and she *had* known Lawrence very well. I sought and found her, and wrote to her over several months. Her first written contact with me was via a schoolmaster who was close to her. He was writing on her behalf because she had recently fallen, fractured her thigh and was recovering in hospital. He ended by saying what a wonderful person she was. Eventually she invited me to come to see her. On a glorious morning of sunshine the Joyces drove me up into the foothills of Mount Lebanon. I asked them to drop me near the village where she lived. Then I walked with mounting excitement and trepidation along the winding lane that snaked upward into the mountains, its white, powdery surface muffling the sounds of my footfall and adding to the extraordinary quiet and serenity of the great hills all around me. She had described her house to me and, as I came round a corner towards the village, there it was, with its segment of garden above the little lane and its great cedar of Lebanon standing sentinel over it. Now aged eighty-four, she stood waiting for me, just outside her garden door, walking-stick in hand, smiling quizzically.

I was at once struck by her quiet poise, her gentleness and her dignity. I knew she was a Christian Arab, a Quaker by conversion – a simple, altruistic, no-frills expression of faith for which Lawrence might well have had considerable empathy. But more significantly, I knew she had been a fervent believer in Arab Nationalism, a movement in which, of course, Lawrence too had had an abiding interest. I had thought that she would be unaware of the importance the visit held for me. I was soon disabused of this illusion. I sensed that she knew why I had come. I also sensed from the start that this was something she would be reluctant to talk about. Yet she somehow managed to convey this to me without saying a word and with that customary Arab courtesy and kindness I had come to appreciate so much and which was at once both charming and disarming.

Later I came to realize that what on the surface appeared to be a childlike unworldliness in her masked a strong, shrewd woman with a probing sense of humour. This humility disguised as innocence has misled some, who never met her and knew little about her, into believing her to be guileless and without intellectual depth. This I soon found to be false. If you evaded or indulged in half-truth, or tried to impress with grandiose argument wrapped in a self-important gravitas, she would glance sideways at you with a knowing smile and, to your initial embarrassment, your pretence would be instantly punctured.

I stayed with her for a week. Her little house had a cool, spacious hall with a high ceiling and an attractively tiled floor with rooms leading off. When you sit and talk with someone day after day without the pressures of time or the limitations of a formal interview, simply enjoying each other's company, you hear and learn things you would not if you had come with an appointment and a prepared agenda. Over the long, sunny days, as we drank tea and ate home-made sweetmeats, sitting out in the garden, it dawned on me that the received view of her that she was simply a sweet, ingenuous person who had taught Lawrence Arabic and fallen under the spell of his personality and his encyclopaedic knowledge, was quite off the mark. No, Farida al Akle – or Farida Akle as she sometimes signed herself to me – was a special person, quite delightful, with an inner strength and dignity that touched and impressed everyone who met her. Reserve and simplicity should not be mistaken for timidity and shallowness.

After I returned to England we maintained our correspondence and she became a wonderful friend, always loving, always concerned for my welfare, yet never intrusive. By now she was aware that I believed her to be a part of Lawrence's *Seven Pillars* dedication. As our letters became more friendly and trusting, we talked more and more about it; but when I put my reasons to her, she became concerned that it might not be true, because, as she said to me: 'He never told me.' She had always shunned any kind of publicity. Yet, despite her concern, she couldn't suppress her sense of humour and frequently signed herself 'F.A. not S.A.'. However, the intensity of my youthful desire to identify her with the dedication began to alarm her. She wrote to A.W. Lawrence asking him to cast his eye over my book when it appeared to ensure that she wouldn't be publicly identified in print with the *Seven Pillars* dedication. He wrote to me reiterating Farida's concern, quoting her as saying she had been 'sick' about it and had been caused 'great anxiety and worry'. He added that he was sure such an identification was wrong, 'disregarding the evidence that the person in question died not later than 1918'; and he wrote again saying that his view of Farida agreed with that expressed in a letter to the *Sunday Times*, which had quoted the Arabist and travel writer Freya Stark. This letter had been written in response to a series of hastily compiled but reasonably well-researched articles in the *Sunday Times* in 1968. These were based on a variety of new information and 'revelations', which had come into the possession of the newspaper and had resulted in the writers being given access to the then embargoed Lawrence archives in the Bodleian Library, Oxford.

A.W. Lawrence wrote dismissively to me that, 'the facts of the matter … had been adequately stated in the letter by Miss Freya Stark', adding that it agreed with his knowledge of Miss Akle as well as with the tone of the correspondence between her and his brother.[25] Freya Stark's quoted comment about Farida reads: 'There is a nice woman here named Faridi who taught T.E. Lawrence Arabic down at Jubail when he was wandering among the old Syrian forts on his first coming East. I believe she is one of the few women he ever writes to – not beautiful, but with a good intelligent rough face and manner – and very kind to me.'[26]

Farida's anxiety had been aggravated by the imminent publication of the heavily promoted biography, *The Secret Lives of Lawrence of Arabia*. Like Lawrence she was a very private person, much disturbed by the thought of any publicity or sensation that might envelop her when the biography was released. She told me later, very apologetically, that my beliefs had panicked her into recruiting A.W. Lawrence to help prevent any *published* linking of her with S.A. If at the time I had appreciated the depth of her anxiety, I would have withdrawn from the field rather than upset her.

She had already heard that in their treatment of the S.A. conundrum in their articles the *Sunday Times* writers had devoted space to dismissing Graves's and my views by quoting her denial. They later reiterated this in their book, which had been developed from the articles, quoting Farida: 'However, she herself has written to at least two people emphatically denying that she is S.A. "I am not S.A. and this is the truth. T.E. never fell in love with any woman. He could not … T.E. wished that S.A. would be a mystery that is difficult to solve."'[27] This apparent denial and A.W. Lawrence's letter to me constitute what might be termed 'the case' against Farida being a dedicatee.

Let me present the case for it. Firstly, citing Freya Stark's description of Farida seemingly to imply that Lawrence might not have found her attractive seems unconvincing to me. You do not have to be beautiful to attract. What's more, Freya Stark was writing in 1928 when Farida was forty-six and had inevitably lost the bloom of early youth. However, in a photograph taken seven years earlier she has both an arresting beauty and a nobility of expression – high cheekbones, jet-black hair, dark eyes, a direct gaze, smooth, creamy skin, and finely sculptured lips. I knew at least two people who had known her and who agreed with that assessment. And I have in my possession a much earlier, youthful photograph of her, in which she exudes a sweetness of nature and a delightful charm, in a school grouping sitting in the centre cross-legged on the ground with one child in her lap and another nestling against her side. This is the young Farida that Lawrence would have known.

So, what *did* Lawrence feel about her during his pre-war years in Syria? Firstly, a disproportionate deference has sometimes been accorded A.W. Lawrence in matters concerning his brother. Lawrence was unlikely to have talked to anyone about any feelings he had for her, let alone to his youngest brother, who was only nine years old when Lawrence met her and still in his teens during the war and just after. Besides, as has been shown, Lawrence very rarely, if ever, exposed his emotions and wouldn't have done to a brother who, he said, never got enthusiastic 'except in denunciation' and whom he considered to have 'so little patience, so little breadth of judgement'.[28] And, as I have mentioned, Leonard Woolley endorsed this, commenting that Lawrence 'was frightfully reserved about himself' and 'if he showed signs of sentiment, as very occasionally he did, he would at once turn them to ridicule. I do not remember his ever admitting to any affection for anybody, though I knew perfectly well that in the case of certain people the affection was there and was deeply felt.'[29]

Lawrence first met Farida in early August 1909, when she was twenty-seven and he twenty-one, on his trek through Syria to study Crusader castles. He called in at the American Missionary School where Miss Holmes and her staff gave him a cordial welcome and generous hospitality. He stayed a few days before walking on northward along the coast to Batroun and Tripoli on the second stage of his tour. Farida described his arrival at the school: 'One hot day in the summer of 1909 a weary traveller stood knocking at the door … The maid who opened the door, seeing the dusty, tired-looking traveller with the bundle tied on his back, thought him one of the German tramps that were going about the town at that time.'[30]

Lawrence returned to England but was back at the school in the harsh Syrian winter of 1910 to study Arabic before joining Hogarth in mid-February in Beirut to travel up through the snow-blanketed hinterland to Carchemish to start his archaeological work. In an article, solicited for publication after Lawrence's death, Farida outlined his two-month stay in picturesque Jebail:

> He arrived on Christmas Eve, and was received very enthusiastically by those who knew him from his first short visit. From that day Lawrence made the school at Jebail his second home. He had not been long with us before we all realized that amongst us was a unique personality, a man with high ideals and aims, with keen intellect, and great ability – he possessed such a wide knowledge on so many subjects that the staff rightly named him the Encyclopaedia. He was of a very shy, quiet nature and loved to dress very simply, giving little attention to outward appearance. The material things of life had no attraction for him, and money he only valued for its convenience. He had a wonderful charm about him; and his kindheartedness easily won him a way into the hearts of those with whom he came in contact. Even the little schoolchildren were drawn to him as by a magnet, and would come up to him with confidence carrying their broken dolls and toys, which he would spend hours mending, and perfect work he made of it. Lawrence's stay meant a great deal to us; he entered into the very life of the school. His advice was often sought and he always proved to be a wise adviser and a man of sound judgment.[31]

To paint a true picture of a relationship as elusive as that between Lawrence and Farida requires sensitive analysis and treatment and a need to read between the lines without misinterpretation or misrepresentation. I travelled again to Syria and visited Farida a second time. Our friendship deepened and she seemed now to see me as a kind of protégé. This I found very moving and I constantly reminded myself that she had to be treated in return with the utmost honesty and integrity. I had to ensure that what I finally wrote about her would be what I was convinced was true, factually supported wherever possible, and not simply what I *wanted* to be true. It was a difficult and complex charge. Whenever we talked of her long-ago days with Lawrence she seemed to enter a private world of both rich and painful memories, of intense nostalgia for what had been, and what might have been. She gave the marked impression of being torn between two warring and irreconcilable urges – to acknowledge that there had indeed been a signifi-cant relationship between herself and Lawrence and at the same time to prevent it from being exposed to the world.

So was there something special between them? Lawrence stayed for almost two months at Jebail, from Christmas 1910 until towards the end of February 1911. Living in the same house, meeting each other every day over many weeks in the seclusion and intimacy of the school afforded the perfect opportunity for the socially shy Lawrence to get to know the young Farida. Most importantly, it was a relationship that was free to develop both naturally and in unusual privacy. For Lawrence, and for Farida, the school at Jebail provided a unique environment for the creation of an enduring bond, an environment he had never known before and would never know again. A lot has been made of Lawrence's claimed prefer-ence for male company, especially after the war, but the fact that he spent nearly two months at Jebail almost exclusively in the company of women – and Farida's in particular – seems to have been oddly overlooked. At what other time in his life was Lawrence given such an opportunity?

During his time in Syria Lawrence was to make many visits to the school, and Farida was often in his thoughts. In a home letter from Jebail of 22 January 1911 he mentions that he is making a careful survey of the castle and reading Arabic with 'Miss Fareedah', 'who is wonderful'.[32] In April he wrote from Jerablus that he hoped to visit the school when the digs finished at the end of June and later he talked of perhaps wintering in Jebail.[33][34] In early July, as already mentioned, he tells Mrs Rieder that he is going to ask Farida for a few simple books to help Dahoum to learn to read.[35] Three months later he is telling Mrs Rieder that Farida 'is going to have a letter: "The strange, marvellous and most wonderful adventures of an ancient book: written in the tongue of the Saracens, and purporting a discourse of a hermit in the Holy Land."'[36] In a home letter of 2 January 1912, written in abbreviated form, he notes: 'Miss Fareedah away,' and three weeks later, writing again to Mrs Rieder, he sends Farida his 'salaams'.[37][38] His concern for her well-being is evident when, three days after that, he is telling his family that Miss Holmes 'has been a little too hard lately on Miss Fareedah, who has nearly broken down.'[39]

However, the most significant letter is undoubtedly the one Lawrence wrote, yet again to Mrs Rieder, on 20 May 1912. He tells her that he has had an Arabic postcard from Fareedah and then says:

> I want to know also about Miss Fareedah: she joined you, I see, at Damascus: I had hoped to come down this summer to Jebail, and to have seen her, but an unknown male has given us £5000 and the B.M. has added £2000 and the whole 7 is to be spent here: so there are lots and lots more digs to come – and immediately a second season in September. For some reason Mr Hogarth is very anxious to make me learn Arabic; and so I am going to stay here July & August alone. I hope to go home at Xmas, and to carry Miss Fareedah away with me for six-weeks in England. There will be more digs in Feb. but all through Jan. Miss Holmes will be bereft (inshallah!).[40]

In this personal context the words 'carry away' are undeniably romantic, especially when applied to a young, single woman, and even more so when applied by Lawrence. Is there anywhere else on record another example of Lawrence using such romantic language about a young woman, other than perhaps about Janet Laurie? Lawrence's hopes of bringing Farida with him to England were ultimately dashed because his limited funds wouldn't run to it.[41]

However, it's possible that the startling, and no doubt disturbing prospect of her son bringing a young Arab woman home with him had been met with disapproval by his mother. It is significant to note that his plans to take Farida with him to England were laid well before he was to bring his Arab friends from the Carchemish dig, Sheikh Hamoudi and Dahoum, to Oxford for a month in mid-July 1913 – and that seems to have been more on impulse than planned. He made no mention of bringing the two Carchemish men home until as late as June 1913 in a letter to Hogarth – 'I expect to get back about mid-July, and may bring the Hoja and Dahum with me: which will shock you.'[42] His taking the two to England was in part a thank-you for their having looked after him so caringly when he was seriously ill with dysentery in 1911. Hamoudi had, as mentioned, bravely kept Lawrence in his own house and nursed him back to health.

When Lawrence was at the Jebail School, his room was next to Farida's. Teaching and learning Arabic was not the only occupation that brought them constantly together. Farida had a deep interest in Arab history and they talked often about the Arabs one day gaining their freedom from the Turks. She described this to me: 'T.E. and I had a good deal in common. We were both deeply interested in books on the Arab world and the Arabs of the desert, and archaeology. These were the main subjects of our talks and interest. Besides I was at the same time helping him with his Arabic. This gave me a closer touch with him and helped me to know him and understand him better.'

On Saturday mornings the two of them would sometimes go down to a cliff near the sea and look for prehistoric artefacts; they would slide down the sand dunes, he with his arm around her. She said, 'He visited all the convents near Jebail and got acquainted with the monks, and once he bought two large volumes which he spent no end of time cleaning and mending, and afterwards he left them as a present to the School.' She told me one day, 'He loved flowers, he loved everything that is beautiful – for he was lovely himself.' And there were too the little giveaway signs of affection so rare with Lawrence. She told me: 'I had found the girls' school in an untidy state and had set about cleaning up the floor on my hands and knees. Ned thought I was being overworked but said nothing, he simply held my arm to help me up the steps on my return to the other building. He didn't really like touching people so I knew how much this really meant.'

On another occasion there was a communal meal in the main dining-room but the smell of kerosene from one of the heaters was so strong that Farida felt nauseous and rose and took her plate and went and ate in the hall. Without a word Lawrence got up and joined her so that she should not feel alone.

But most revealing of all perhaps is that on St Valentine's Day 1911 Lawrence gave her a present of a miniature travelling valise, a little trunk, as an earnest of his wish to take her to England. She said:

> His gift to me was this small travelling case. You see, he and I used to talk so much about my going to England with him and that is why he thought of the valise. Where he got it from I have no idea. He attached a card to the handle and on it wrote the word 'steamer' and the names of all the towns I would stop at and other travelling information. I gave him a small book, a 'manuscript'. I made it from a matchbox lined over with old, rotten leather. It looked as if it

was brought from some digs in Byblus. He was thrilled with it and took it with him to England.

He told her that her Valentine's present to him had been the best of all presents. On another occasion he gave her a gift of a needle-box.

She knew Dahoum quite well because Lawrence brought him to see her several times. On one occasion at a signal from Lawrence the two started gabbling away in the Aleppine dialect of Arabic and she couldn't understand a single word, which provoked much merriment all round. Another time the pair arrived to visit her in the middle of the night when Farida was then staying in the hills opposite Broumana, her family's village. They slept on the roof and in the morning when she reproached them for not having knocked and come in, Lawrence said, 'Well, we couldn't wake you at an hour like that, could we?' She told me that 'Ned' jealously guarded his privacy, his freedom. He could not stand people who raised their voices and, when they did, he would put his hands over his ears. She had never met anyone so sensitive to others. He seemed to sense if something was wrong almost before it occurred and seemed to know what one was thinking most of the time. In those early days, she said, he wore his hair long and lank and it often fell over his eyes. She would tease him by saying, 'Would you like me to get a hair-clip and pin it up for you?' He would just smile. She noticed too that he seemed especially concerned about her welfare and was always watching to ensure that she was happy in her work and in her life generally.

As we sat in the sunshine under the cedar in her little garden, our gentle chats about Lawrence and his time with her at Jebail seemed so relaxed, so easy, joyous as well as nostalgic. They were punctuated by comfortable silences when the sound of distant voices or the faraway drone of a car somewhere in the hills would drift across the valleys to us. She would smile wistfully to herself as she recalled all these memories of a long-ago idyll.

Suddenly she said: 'You know Richard, I am different from the rest, the only dark one in the family, with dark hair and dark eyes. When I was young I was very thin and looked quite tall … Yes, that is what I looked like when T.E. was with us. I think he rather liked slight figures. The long dress was the fashion then.' Then she added, almost sotto voce, 'Perhaps I knew Ned differently from others. He was my student, young and rare. He was blooming like a flower, but he was crushed.' For a moment she was silent. Then she said quietly, 'He was altogether in the spirit. The flesh did not count much, it was simply a case for that great soul.' She was silent again, and then said, 'I am comforted to know that Ned did not live to an old age;

he used to tell me that up to 45 is a good age for a man to live, not more.'

Some years before this she had written about Lawrence to a close friend: 'From the first I knew what he was, I knew that boy would never think of getting married. How did I know it? I cannot tell you. He would not know what to do with a wife and children.' (With regard to Farida's comment that she was 'very thin and looked quite tall,' it is interesting to note that Janet Laurie too was tall and 'exceedingly slim'.)[43]

Our talks continued, and gradually, emotionally, and with some difficulty, Farida revealed the depth of her relationship with Lawrence and how he had seemed to open up to her. She said that he once said to her: 'Help does not come to us from outside but from within.' Years later he was to tell his Clouds Hill neighbour, Dick Knowles, something very similar: 'It's my experience that the actual work or position or reward one has, doesn't have much effect on the inner being, which is the important thing for us to cultivate.'[44] Farida told me that she and Lawrence seemed indeed to have an intuitive understanding of each other's moods, feelings and thoughts.

Mrs Rieder seems to have become an unofficial go-between and covert orchestrator of the relationship. She and Miss Holmes sensed the closeness of the two and would observe them, fascinated. Farida told me that Mrs Rieder used to say to her 'Oh, Ned would do anything for you.' Typically in character, Lawrence initially tried to keep his hopes of taking her to England secret from her; Farida said to me: 'For some reason or another he never used to let me know what he did and what he said concerning me. He had deep respect to my feelings. Would you believe it if I tell you that in the beginning he never said a word to me about my going with him to England, but he wrote to Mrs Rieder about it. I can tell you many incidents of that sort: telling others but not to me. He was so shy with me …' She continued: 'He was so reserved, so thoughtful, so sensitive to the feeling of others that he would avoid saying anything that he thought others might not like.' But she added: 'He was at the same time a little imp full of humour, full of boyish mischievousness; just the sort you would love.'

One morning, sitting in the garden, she said to me, 'I have been reading again some of his letters that were written fifty years ago. They were fresh and sweet and I could hear Ned's voice talking to me through them.' On another occasion she confided to me with a warm smile, 'In spite of the fact that he used to receive letters by the hundreds, the greater part of which he didn't even look at, he never missed answering any of my letters.'

It should also be emphasized that Farida just as much as Dahoum would have benefited from Arab freedom and that she and her family suffered great hardship and hunger during the war. At one point early in the revolt Lawrence actually seems to have been contemplating some limited expansion of the Arab campaign into Lebanon itself.[45] Farida's family village was Broumana but during the war she taught at the American School for Girls in Beirut. She told me how she had to walk for four hours up into the mountains to get home. Her mother would meet her halfway with a jug of water. The Turks would not allow anyone to take supplies up to the mountain villages but she and her sister devised a deception to smuggle food to Broumana. The bridge over the river controlling the routes into the hills was manned by Turkish soldiers to ensure nothing got through. She received word from her mother that the need for food had become desperate. She and her sister went down to Beirut and bought some wheat from the market. They had to return over the bridge with the river in spate. A young girl, who had been sent down by Farida's mother, was hiding among the reeds. Farida's sister carried the bag of wheat on her head while Farida approached the guards and diverted their attention. Her sister waded through the river and gave the wheat to the girl and waded back again. She had been up to her waist in water and became ill after having to walk soaking wet all the way back to Beirut.

Farida reminded me that a third of the Lebanon had been close to starvation and that many died. She herself had had first-hand experience of the terrible plight of the people. She said: 'I was living away from Broumana at the time. One morning where I was, there was a knock at the door. I opened it and saw a young man standing there. He said, "Please, could you let me have a shovel." I asked him why he wanted it. He replied, "My brother has just died outside my house and I want to cover him with sand."' Towards the end of the war conditions became so bad that she and her family believed that they too would die of starvation. She told me that she thought Lawrence would somehow manage to come to her during the war, and she heard stories of what she later learned was the assault on him at Deraa. She also heard that there was a price on his head. But she wasn't to see him again until 1926 (I thought of Richard Coeur de Lion returning to his homeland while Jehane remained in the mountains of the Lebanon).

As a result of our many conversations, I was all the more convinced that Farida was a part of the S.A. dedication. Later we continued to write to each other and I felt that she seemed close to revealing something that she had kept to herself all through the years. Then a letter came and I found myself reading:

Now the important side of my letter is to tell you briefly what T.E. is to me. It is extremely hard to write and even to speak upon this subject. I do it to rest your mind and to continue your search for the real S.A. I hope you will find her. In 1909 I had the great opportunity of meeting T.E. and to get to know him personally. This was one of the greatest events of my life if not the greatest ... A deep friendship grew between us: it was a friendship that was founded on spiritual values. It was a spiritual unity of a soul with a soul. I can't express it in any other way. Lawrence lived in his spirit not in his body. He was marvellous. Such experience was most elevating most uplifting to me. You asked me if I loved him. Oh dear! Who couldn't have loved him!! Love never fails, it is eternal, it never dies but it suffers in proportion to the love one has. Now Richard I have brought you into the inner sanctuary of my life. Some day you may experience this spiritual unity that surpasses all understanding. I need not ask you that it is a secret to be kept.

I sat for some time, stunned by what I had read. Even though she had talked of my continuing to look for S.A. I knew now that my quest was complete. I knew that she had revealed to me an hitherto unknown truth about a gentle, almost ethereal relationship between herself and Lawrence, which had been intensely private. For them love was of the heart and soul, not of the body. It was the exquisite harmony of finely-attuned kindred spirits, a rare but perfect match. It reminded me of what Lawrence had described in *Seven Pillars*, in the self-regarding reflections of his thirtieth birthday, as the only kind of intimacy he could ever accept, an intimacy that called forth from each 'the perfect reply, in the same language, after the same method, for the same reasons.'

I understood too that, because she had such integrity and was innately humble, Farida would never have considered or presented her feelings for Lawrence – or his for her – as a love affair. The epithet seemed trite when applied to them. She would never even have made a claim privately (until now), and certainly not publicly, to have been loved by Lawrence, let alone to have been a part of the S.A. dedication – quite simply because, as she had said to me, he never told her she was, and also because a genuine humility would have prevented her from doing so.

But she *did* write to me: 'I can't say I won't agree with you, Richard, all I want you to understand is that T.E. never told me about S.A. so I can't claim to be S.A. and I can't proclaim it to the world. I am happy and content just as I am. If you are determined to mention me in your book, you will have to be very clever in the method you use ... This is a serious and sacred subject to me.'

Now, all these years later, I sensed that Lawrence's legendary status inclined her to feel, with that self-effacement so characteristic of her, that time had somehow distanced him from her, that he now walked on a grander stage, that he belonged to the world, that her relationship with him, sacred though it was to her, might not be of notable significance in the greater scheme of things. She once said to me, 'I am glad I knew him long before the world had touched him; he was great then to me.' However, I was sure by now that the relationship *was* significant and that it would provide a profound, revealing and much-needed new insight into Lawrence. Farida later wrote to me that now that I knew the truth about her relationship with Lawrence she hoped I wouldn't betray her confidence. She said: 'It was sacred to me. It is deeply hidden in my heart; I have no wish or desire to expose it to the light and to the world. It is my comfort to keep it to myself.' I was now convinced and for the first time the matter to me was virtually beyond dispute. To reveal what she had revealed to me had, I subsequently discovered, cost her much heartache. Almost immediately she followed up her confessional letter to me with another, which only reinforced my conviction and in which she said with a touching concern, 'I wonder what you thought of my letter if you really got it? I haven't written the like of it to anyone before. I wanted you to know the truth.'

I wrote to Robert Graves in confidence and included a transcription of Farida's confession to me about her relationship with Lawrence. He replied, 'I am now convinced by the letter – but shall not of course divulge the secret – that Farida was S.A. "The Vigil" is a confirmation,' adding, 'I like the way she opened to you: it was a terrific compliment; and it must have done her a lot of good herself to have someone honest to confide in.' 'The Vigil', by John Pettie, is a painting in the Tate Gallery in London of a knight kneeling at an altar in ritual self-dedication; Farida had obtained a postcard of it on her visit to London in 1926. She sent it to me with the inscription: 'May you strive to enter into the Knighthood of the heroes of old who gallantly stood for justice, for peace and righteousness.'

However, when the *Sunday Times* book appeared with all its 'revelations', including the S.A. / Salim Achmed story – which wasn't exposed as almost certainly bogus until much later – both Graves and I, inevitably, had doubts about our understanding of S.A., doubts raised by the ambiguities and contradictions thrown up by the *Sunday Times*' explanation of the dedication, which, at least initially, seemed persuasive. Yet Graves still stood firmly by the troubadour interpretation (as did I) and certainly had no time for Dahoum's candidacy. As he wrote to me, 'Achmed was a red herring, of course; though T.E. had a David and Jonathan thing with him at one time.'

I also wrote to John Mack about Farida and the dedication. As I have already mentioned, he replied: 'My own thought about S.A. is that the object of the dedication is a composite of people, qualities and fantasies and that Miss Fareedah probably played a part in it. As you know Lawrence liked to tease and set people to wondering and guessing, not necessarily deliberately but out of his own needs. I think the troubadour-love idea makes sense.'[46] And Mack is by no means the only one to believe that Farida was, or was a part of, S.A. Among others, a Professor Denis Jerome, a history lecturer at Damascus University, also believed that the dedication of *Seven Pillars of Wisdom* was to her. He said, 'She was a charismatic, modern-thinking bluestocking. She could have inspired him in the way that the Dark Lady inspired Shakespeare.'[47]

In the context of the troubadour ideal it is interesting to note that in 1920, when Lawrence would have been turning his thoughts to the dedication and to the content and form of his poem, he received a letter from Farida in which she said, 'I never told you that my great desire was (when young) to be an Arab princess. I mean to say to have been born among them as an Arab princess.'[48] *Son Altesse* and Her Highness immediately spring to mind. A similar concept had perhaps sprung to John Mack's mind too when he wrote: 'For Lawrence present life was measured always against an ideal of the imagination, particularly a medieval ideal, and his most important actions, especially during the war years, may be seen as efforts to impose upon grimmer circumstances, to which he had also to adapt, his utopian imaginings. Lawrence recognized that this idealistic question was to some extent a family problem shared with his brothers. In a letter to his family, written soon after arriving at Carchemish, he referred to himself as 'an artist of sorts and a wanderer after sensations' and he reassured his parents that 'one of us must surely get something of the unattainable we are all feeling after'.[49] Fareedah el Akle, with whom he found so much in common, seems to have possessed a feminine counterpart to Lawrence's hero fantasies.'[50] Mack then quotes Farida's remarks to Lawrence about her youthful wish to be a princess.

Lawrence and Farida corresponded intermittently after the war, sometimes in humorous vein. When she wrote, uncertain whether he wanted to write, he replied, 'Of course I'll write to you: why did you ever think I wouldn't? It was only bad manners for the man to begin the correspondence with the lady.' Towards the end of the letter he says, 'I hope you will be able to come to England some day, as we always talked about.' Farida wrote back in mischievous riposte to his tongue-in-cheek opening, 'So you expect the lady to start the correspondence!

And what if she happens to be an oriental being, whose customs and ways are just the reverse of yours???'[51]

Separated by many years and miles and having lived divergent lives in distant countries, Farida and Lawrence were to meet for the last time in the unsympathetic surroundings of a London café during her visit to France in 1926 as the Syrian Delegate to the International Women's Congress in Paris. She wrote that he had ridden for four hours on his motorcycle to see her. It is a bitter irony that this very last meeting was spoiled for her by the presence of, of all people, Mrs Rieder, which prevented Farida from being alone with Lawrence for long. Writing about this last meeting, she said that during their talk Lawrence had explained, in detail, about the Chapmans and his father's inability to marry his mother: 'He gave me the whole story of the family. He knew of it when he was still a little child, a mere boy. When I bade him goodbye he said to me, "This family ought to die out, we are all eccentric." There was sadness in his voice when he said these words. Ned possessed a very delicate and sensitive conscience.' She added that she had somehow always known that he would never marry, partly because of the irregularities of his family history. Here yet again, whenever his illegitimacy and his forbidden Irish heritage intruded on his thoughts, Lawrence was seized by an urge to self-denigration – even in Farida's company. His abiding dismay at the consequences of his father's extramarital romance, his painful awareness of his grand but tabooed ancestry – the unapproachable, unbending Chapmans – and his ineradicable conviction that he was an illegitimate upstart, 'an Irish nobody', lurked as always behind his words.

Farida wrote to me again soon after. It was as though talking to me about that last poignant meeting with Lawrence had stirred long-dormant memories. She asked: 'When and where did Ned write to Robert Graves saying, "You have taken me too literally. S.A. still exists but out of my reach because I have changed?" From India? The word "changed" struck me. It was just a week or so before he went to India that he came down to London to see me and I was at the same time preparing myself to return home. I said to him then, "Ned, you have so changed I wouldn't have known you." He was silent.'

Of course, this admission by Lawrence – that S.A. was not dead but out of reach because he had changed – had indeed been penned from India, yet again in 1927, on that draft of Robert Graves's biography of him. Lawrence had written it less than a year after Farida's own comment to him about his having 'so changed'. The coincidence is tantalizing. She enlarged further upon their final meeting in another letter:

I first saw him with RAF uniform on and he just looked like a knight of old. However, the Ned I knew in his early twenties was deeply marked by the ravages and severity of his war experience; as he had once remarked to me 'Farideh, my war experience was horrible!' Also the burden of his moral disappointment was heavily weighing on his soul and had forced him to seek the humble corners of oblivion. That wonderful refreshing and lovely smile on Ned's face was no more.

When she wrote to me of Mrs Rieder's presence preventing her from having much time alone with Lawrence, I could sense that she had been on the verge of tears. Her handwriting became shaky and I could almost hear her faltering voice saying the words she had written: 'If you have an opportunity like that which I had, don't miss it – like I did.'

At home in the Lebanon once more she had written to Lawrence about their meeting and of her disappointment. She told him how sad she had been not to have had more time alone with him, and he had replied, 'If I had known, we could have gone off for ten minutes quietly together.' Farida told me that in that fateful year of 1927, when Lawrence went to India, she felt that it might have been a burden to him to continue to write to her. And so, at the cost of much personal anguish, she just stopped. She said: 'I knew he would understand – and he did.' That unforgettable, unspoken goodbye must have seemed like an epitaph for her lost youth, a haunting reminder of the transience of all the bright mornings of the heart.

One of the most elusive, delicate and lovely relationships of Lawrence's life had come to its unremarked end. Farida continued her life of teaching in the Lebanon, but her memories of those far-off days at the school in Jebail, when two young people found in each other a very private but very real joy, remained always vividly alive, full of a nostalgia and a happiness too deep to express. This will sound melodramatic but, having been Farida's friend and the recipient of what I came to realize were some of her innermost secrets, I know it was all exactly as she told me.

The warm glow of our own friendship remained undimmed but time plays tricks with the continuity of things and somehow our letters grew fewer and fewer until, finally, there was an empty silence, a silence for which I have never been able to forgive myself. Farida died in 1976 at the age of ninety-four. I did go back to Broumana, one last time, years later. As always, the Lebanese summer was hot and the land cowered motionless under cloudless skies. The little road and the little house were still there but the house was now lived in by people I didn't know.

Yet it seemed to be quite empty, quite lifeless without her. I stood and watched the door to the garden, thinking that she would suddenly be standing there, smiling sweetly at me, walking-stick in hand. And did I see, just for a moment, three young people sitting in the sun on the wall by the roadside, laughing and talking and joking together, their youthfulness and eager delight in each other's company lighting up everything around them? But Farida and Lawrence and Dahoum were, of course, not there. How could they be? And yet, somehow, I felt they were. I turned then and walked quietly away, the pressing demands of today and the half-laid plans of tomorrow seeming suddenly meaningless beside the memories of yesterday that filled my heart and mind.

Appendix 1

THE CHAPMAN COAT OF ARMS

Some chance information I received about the Chapman family escutcheon led to a puzzling discovery which in turn revealed what may be one of the most extraordinary, and hitherto unknown, family connections of Lawrence's life, and of which it is very likely he himself may have had no knowledge at all. In a side-wall of a handsome and sizeable rectory in the English county of Wiltshire there is a window containing a stained glass panel of the Chapman escutcheon. The current owner of the house was keen to find out the full story behind this coat of arms. Some research suggested an extraordinary possibility, which at first seemed hard to believe, that T.E. Lawrence and General Allenby, the moving forces behind the success of the Arab Revolt, were distantly related by marriage.

This substrand of Lawrencian genealogy starts with the Wiltshire rectory. Built of the lovely local hamstone, Donhead House lies in the idyllic hamlet of Donhead St Andrew, which is hidden away in a hollow of the gentle hills around the town of Shaftesbury. It transpires that the Rector of Donhead in 1875 was one Horace Edward Chapman, an old Etonian and a graduate of Downing College, Cambridge. The Rector was clearly a wealthy man – the seventh son by two marriages of David Barclay Chapman, a successful banker – because by 1901, he supported at Donhead, in addition to his family, eight live-in servants. In the 1870s he became embroiled in the High Church Oxford Movement and only escaped serious censure by the Church of England because his bishop happened, to his good fortune, also to be a High Churchman.

Chapman ceased to be the Donhead incumbent in 1891, later converted to Roman Catholicism, but remained master of Donhead House. Later, when he became ill, his representatives retained the gift of the living. He eventually went to live in Hastings and died in 1907. He was an interesting man, being a top class chess player among other accomplishments. He had two daughters, the one of immediate interest being the eldest, Adelaide Mabel Chapman. On December 30th, 1896 in the Parish Church of Donhead St Andrew she married Edmund Henry Hynman Allenby, then aged thirty-five and a Captain in the sixth Dragoons, and later, of course, famous as Field Marshal Sir Edmund Allenby, First Viscount Allenby of Megiddo. One of the witnesses at his wedding was a Florence Chapman. It seems the names Mabel and Florence were favourite Chapman christian names, in England as well as Ireland.

The reader may say at this point that this story has some peripheral interest but that Chapman is a reasonably common name and why should the Donhead Chapmans have any connection with the Chapmans of Westmeath? Quite so. Yet they probably do, even if perhaps distantly. The fact that the Chapman escutcheon had been incorporated in a window at Donhead House certainly strongly suggests that Horace Chapman was related to the baronets of Killua, or thought that he was.

And there is an even more perplexing corollary to this. Into the story now comes another Chapman relation, a Desmond Chapman-Huston, a writer and a member of an Irish, County Leitrim family, whose mother was a County Monaghan Chapman and claimed Lawrence's father, Thomas Chapman, as her kinsman.[1]

If a touch snobbish, Chapman-Huston cuts a rather noble, romantic, adventurous, outspoken yet oddly lonely figure. From his autobiography it would appear that his Anglo-Irish family were impoverished gentry, but he certainly mixed in 'high life' in both Ireland and England, was mentioned in despatches in the First World War, worked in the theatre, dabbled in politics, and became a writer and a biographer of the aristocracy and Royalty. In or around 1910 he went to live at Donhead House. Horace Chapman had died and it was now the seat of the baronet Sir James Pender, who was, or became, a friend of Chapman-Huston's. Why the peripatetic writer came to live there in the first place is a puzzle (or just possibly an amazing coincidence), unless he had had a family connection, however tenuous, with Horace Chapman which had brought him to live there with the Penders as a kind of genteel lodger.

Chapman-Huston subsequently developed an ambition to write about his claimed famous kinsman, Lawrence of Arabia. There existed a copy of *The Golden Reign* by Clare Sydney Smith, into which had been loosely inserted a letter from Clare to the painter Augustus John. Clare's command of English appeared to be not too good. To write a book she would undoubtedly have needed some help. In the National Archives there is a letter dated June 16, 1939 from Major Desmond Chapman-Huston to the Officer in charge of Records at the Air Ministry, seeking the exact dates of Lawrence's RAF postings. The letter begins: 'I am engaged in editing a Memoir of the late Colonel T.E. Lawrence by Mrs Sydney Smith, wife of Air Commodore Sydney W. Smith, O.B.E., which is to be published this autumn.'[2]

Chapman-Huston may even have completed a biography of T.E. Lawrence himself. Called *Ned: An Intimate Study of Lawrence of Ireland and Arabia*, it was to have been published by John Murray Ltd. The mystery deepens because Chapman-Huston died in 1952 with his book apparently still in its proof stages. It was last heard of in the possession of the man to whom Chapman-Huston had willed his papers. This man has never been identified and John Murray, some years ago, claimed not to have any manuscript in their possession. However, Chapman-Huston did commission a portrait of Lawrence by the Austrian painter Herbert Gurschner which was to have served as a frontispiece to his book. Probably painted largely from photographs, full of symbolic imagery and suggesting elusive secrets, it is a self-consciously posed, quasi-religious likeness. Near the end of his life Chapman-Huston presented this portrait to the National Gallery of Ireland.[3]

Appendix 2

FARIDA AL AKLE

Farida al Akle was born in 1882 into a Christian Arab Greek Orthodox family which originally came from Bikfaya in the Lebanon. One of her uncles was Bishop of Antioch. They were well-known and well respected in Beirut where the family had settled. Her father, Ibrahim al Akle, and one of his four brothers, were world-renowned goldsmiths known for their intricate filigree designs, and employed a forty-strong workforce. The highly detailed work ultimately resulted in eye-strain and the family moved up to Broumana in the hills where they bought a silk factory. In 1888 the crop failed and Farida's parents were forced to sell land and silverware. Her father kept his factory and some land. He once said to her: 'I shan't leave you much but I will leave you a good name.'

While attending the Girls' High School of the Society of Friends in Beirut she became a Quaker. She trained as a schoolteacher and taught at Friends' and American Mission schools in both Lebanon and Syria, among them the American Mission School in Jebail, where in 1909 she met T.E. Lawrence, whom she tutored in Arabic.

During the First World War she taught initially in the Bill Medain quarter in Damascus and later at the American Girls' School in Bourge in Beirut. She became Principal of the Junior Department of Broumana High School in 1922, represented Syrian Protestant Women at a Regional Conference in 1924 and was the Syrian delegate to the International Women's Congress in Paris in 1926, when she came to England and met Lawrence for the last time. She was also a delegate to the International Missionary Conference in Jerusalem in 1928. Her teaching career included service at Ras il Matin at Broumana; the Jebail Mission School (1907–13); in Damascus (1913–14); in Beirut (1914–21); and again in Broumana from 1922.

To mark her retirement from teaching in 1942 (she had broken records for the longevity of her career) a special testament was presented to her from the Syrian Committee of the Friends' Service Council which paid fulsome and glowing tribute to her, both as a teacher and a person. It said in part:

> Her deep love for, and understanding of, children, her sympathy in their difficulties and her wise advice and practical helpfulness have made an indelible impression on many lives; and her leadership has been an inspiration to the teachers who have worked with her…Her influence has not been confined to the Broumana work. She is known and loved in many other places.

Farida never married, and for the rest of her life she lived in her own house in Broumana. She died in 1976 at the age of 94.

Appendix 3

CHAPMAN OF KILLUA

RYCHARD CHAPMAN (of Husbands Bosworth, Leicestershire, England)

WILLIAM

JOHN (dsp.c.1600. Received land grants in Kerry, Ireland, 1589, through cousin Sir Walter Raleigh)

BENJAMIN (granted Killua estate, Clonmellon, County Westmeath, Ireland by Cromwell, 1667; m. secondly Elizabeth Robinson of Wexford with issue; m. firstly Anne Parkinson of Ardee), by whom:

WILLIAM (b. 1668. d. 1734) — Thomas (to America) — Katherine (b. 1672. d. 1728.
(m. Ismay Nugent of Clonlost)   (has issue) m. William Copeland, 1695)

BENJAMIN (m. Anne Tighe of Mitchellstown)
(High Sherrif of Meath, Westmeath; d. 1779), by whom:

SIR BENJAMIN ———— **SIR THOMAS** (m. 1808 Margaret Fetherstonhaugh of Bracklyn Castle) — William
(m. Anne Lowther of Staffordstown 1776.   (2nd Bt. b. 1756; kt. 1780. d. 1837), by whom:
Cr. Baronet 1782.
MP.Dr.of Laws.dsp.1810)

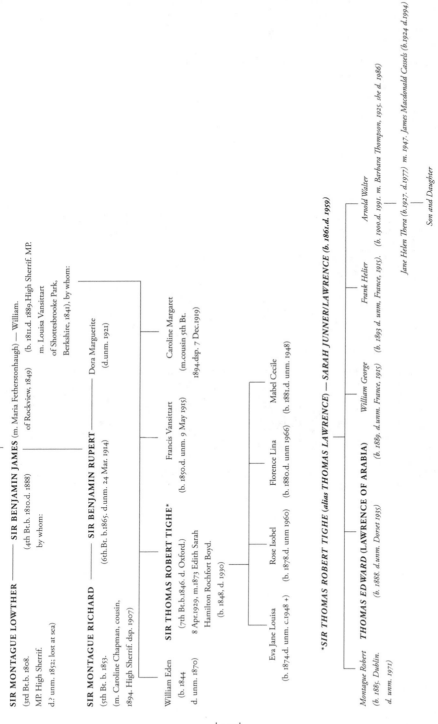

SIR MONTAGUE LOWTHER ——— **SIR BENJAMIN JAMES** (m. Maria Fetherstonhaugh) — William.
(3rd Bt.b. 1808.   (4th Bt.b. 1810.d. 1888)   of Rockview, 1849)   (b. 1811.d. 1889.High Sherrif. MP.
MP: High Sherrif.   by whom: m. Louisa Vansittart
d.? unm. 1852: lost at sea)   of Shottesbrooke Park,
                                                                                        Berkshire, 1841), by whom:

SIR MONTAGUE RICHARD ——— **SIR BENJAMIN RUPERT** ——— Dora Marguerite
(5th Bt. b. 1853.   (6th.Bt. b.1865, d.unm. 24 Mar. 1914)   (d.unm. 1921)
(m. Caroline Chapman, cousin,
1894. High Sherrif. dsp. 1907)

William Eden   **SIR THOMAS ROBERT TIGHE***   Francis Vansittart   Caroline Margaret
(b. 1844   (7th Bt.b.1846. d. Oxford.)   (b.1850.d. unm. 9 May 1915)   (m.cousin 5th Bt.
d. unm. 1870)   8 Apr.1929, m.1873 Edith Sarah   1894.dsp. 7 Dec.1919)
                  Hamilton Rochfort Boyd.
                  (b. 1848. d. 1930)

Eva Jane Louisa   Rose Isobel   Florence Lina   Mabel Cecile
(b. 1874.d. unm. c.1948 +) (b. 1878.d. unm 1960) (b. 1880.d. unm 1966) (b. 1881.d. unm. 1948)

***SIR THOMAS ROBERT TIGHE (alias THOMAS LAWRENCE) — SARAH JUNNER/LAWRENCE (b. 1861.d. 1959)**

Montague Robert   ***THOMAS EDWARD (LAWRENCE OF ARABIA)***   *William George*   *Frank Helier*   *Arnold Walter*
(b. 1885. Dublin.   *(b. 1888. d.unm. Dorset 1935)*   *(b. 1889. d.unm. France, 1915)*   *(b. 1893 d. unm, France, 1915).* *(b. 1900.d. unm. Barbara Thompson, 1925. she d. 1986)*
d. unm. 1971)

                                                                                        Jane Helen Thera (b.1927. d.1977) m. 1947. James Macdonald Cassels (b.1924 d.1994).

                                                                                        Son and Daughter

| 255 |

Appendix 4

LAWRENCE – JUNNER

LAWRENCE

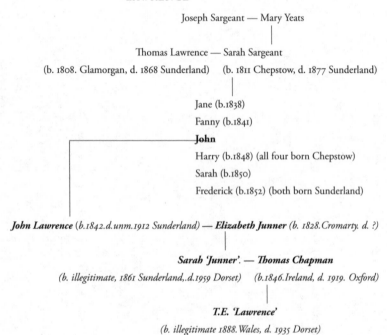

Joseph Sargeant — Mary Yeats

Thomas Lawrence — Sarah Sargeant
(b. 1808. Glamorgan, d. 1868 Sunderland)   (b. 1811 Chepstow, d. 1877 Sunderland)

Jane (b.1838)
Fanny (b.1841)
John
Harry (b.1848) (all four born Chepstow)
Sarah (b.1850)
Frederick (b.1852) (both born Sunderland)

John Lawrence (*b.1842.d.unm.1912 Sunderland*) — ***Elizabeth Junner*** (*b. 1828.Cromarty. d. ?*)

Sarah 'Junner'. — ***Thomas Chapman***
(*b. illegitimate, 1861 Sunderland,.d.1959 Dorset*)   (*b.1846.Ireland, d. 1919. Oxford*)

T.E. 'Lawrence'
(*b. illegitimate 1888. Wales, d. 1935 Dorset*)

JUNNER

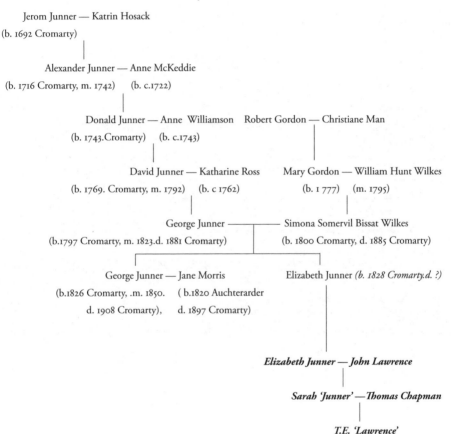

Jerom Junner — Katrin Hosack
(b. 1692 Cromarty)

Alexander Junner — Anne McKeddie
(b. 1716 Cromarty, m. 1742)   (b. c.1722)

Donald Junner — Anne Williamson   Robert Gordon — Christiane Man
(b. 1743.Cromarty)   (b. c.1743)

David Junner — Katharine Ross   Mary Gordon — William Hunt Wilkes
(b. 1769. Cromarty, m. 1792)   (b. c 1762)   (b. 1 777)   (m. 1795)

George Junner ———— Simona Somervil Bissat Wilkes
(b.1797 Cromarty, m. 1823.d. 1881 Cromarty)   (b. 1800 Cromarty, d. 1885 Cromarty)

George Junner — Jane Morris   Elizabeth Junner *(b. 1828 Cromarty.d. ?)*
(b.1826 Cromarty, .m. 1850.   (b.1820 Auchterarder
d. 1908 Cromarty),   d. 1897 Cromarty)

Elizabeth Junner — John Lawrence

Sarah 'Junner' — Thomas Chapman

T.E. 'Lawrence'

MS OF DEDICATORY POEM TO *SEVEN PILLARS OF WISDOM*

To S. A.

I loved you, so I drew these tides of men into my hands, and wrote my will across the sky in stars
To gain you the seven-pillared house [Freedom] [worthy] of freedom], that your eyes might be shining for me
When I came.

Death was my servant on the road, till we were near and saw you waiting;
When you smiled, and in sorrowful envy he outran me, and took you apart
Into his quietness.

So our love's earning was your cast-off body, to be held one moment
Before earth's soft hands would explore all your face, and the blind worms transmute
Your failing substance.

Men prayed me to set our work, the inviolate house, in memory of you;
But for fit monument I shattered it unfinished, and now the little things
Creep out, and patch themselves hovels in the marred shadow
Of your gift.

Appendix 6

MAP OF THE MIDDLE EAST IN 1915

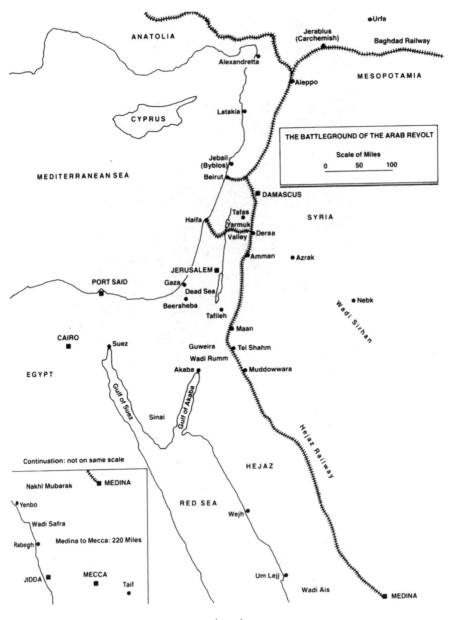

Appendix 7

LAWRENCE AND CHAPMAN AT REST

Clouds Hill, TEL's cottage at Moreton, Dorset.
(National Trust, England)

The recumbent effigy of T.E. Lawrence at St Martin's
Church, Wareham, Dorset; it was carved in Purbeck
stone by Eric Kennington between 1935 and 1939.

The grave of Thomas Chapman, TEL's father,
Wolvercote Cemetery, north Oxford.

Notes

ABBREVIATIONS

AB Jeremy Wilson, *Lawrence of Arabia: The Authorised Biography of T.E. Lawrence* (William Heinemann Ltd: London 1989).

BHF A.W. Lawrence (ed.), *T.E. Lawrence By His Friends* (Jonathan Cape: London 1937).

BL The British Library, Euston Road, London.

BLAM British Library Additional Manuscript.

BOL Bodleian Library, Oxford.

DG David Garnett (ed.), *The Letters of T.E. Lawrence of Arabia* (Jonathan Cape: London 1938).

HL M.R. Lawrence (ed.), *The Home Letters of T.E. Lawrence and his Brothers* (Basil Blackwell: Oxford 1954).

HR Harry Ransom Humanities Research Center, University of Texas, Austin, Texas, USA. T.E. Lawrence Collection,

IWM Imperial War Museum, Lambeth Road, London.

IWM-ST Imperial War Museum, Research material for The Sunday Times book, *The Secret Lives of Lawrence of Arabia*. Phillip Knightley & Colin Simpson (Nelson: London 1969).

JM John E. Mack, *A Prince of our Disorder: The Life of T.E. Lawrence* (Weidenfeld and Nicolson: London 1976).

JTELS Journal of the T.E. Lawrence Society.

MB Malcolm Brown (ed.), *The Letters of T.E. Lawrence* (J.M. Dent & Sons: London 1988).

NA The National Archives, Kew, London.

SPW T.E. Lawrence, *Seven Pillars of Wisdom* (Jonathan Cape: London 1935).

SPWO T.E.Lawrence, *Seven Pillars of Wisdom: The Complete 1922 'Oxford' Text* (J. and N. Wilson: Fordingbridge, Hampshire 2004. Single vol.).

S-S 1922–26 J. and N. Wilson (eds), *T.E. Lawrence: Correspondence with Bernard and Charlotte Shaw, 1922–1926 Vol. 1* (Castle Hill Press 2000).

S-S 1927 *Vol. 2* (2003).

S-S 1928 *Vol. 3* (2008).

S-S 1929–35 *Vol. 4* (2009).

THBRG & THBLH Robert Graves & Liddell Hart, *T.E. Lawrence: Letters to his Biographers* (Cassell: London 1963).

TEL T.E. Lawrence.

I. A MEETING

1. Sir Ronald Wingate, *Wingate of the Sudan* (John Murray: London 1955), pp. 177–8.
2. Sir Ronald Storrs, *Orientations* (Ivor Nicholson & Watson: London 1937), p. 179.
3. Clayton-Wingate Papers (C-W), Durham University, Box 407/4. Letter of 22.XI.16.
4. *Ibid.* Box 470/4, 12.11.16.
5. THBLH, p. 97.
6. BLAM 45983A. Pocket Diary, 1917. May 8.
7. Admiral of the Fleet, The Earl of Cork and Orrery, *My Naval Life: 1886–1941* (Hutchinson: London 1943), pp. 103–4.
8. George Antonius, *The Arab Awakening* (Hamish Hamilton: London 1938), p. 322.
9. SPW, p. 323.
10. S-S, 1927, p. 130.
11. S-S, 1929–35, p. 238.
12. C-W, Box 145/6, Arab Affairs, July 1917, Part 1.
13. Jean Beraud Villars, *T.E. Lawrence* (Sidgwick and Jackson: London 1958), p. 151.
14. *Ibid.*
15. Polly A. Mohs, *Military Intelligence and the Arab Revolt* (Routledge: Abingdon, Oxon 2008), p. 218.
16. *Ibid.* p. 133.
17. William Rothenstein (ed.), *Twenty-Four Portraits* (Allen & Unwin: London 1920), [D. G. Hogarth on TEL]. No pagination, but folio 87.
18. The Earl of Cork and Orrery, *op. cit.* p. 100.
19. IWM, Typescript K59492, p. 122. Pierce Joyce in a BBC talk, July 1941.
20. BLAM 45915. Message-pad notes, folio 48, verso.
21. *The Arab Bulletin.* (Cairo. 1917). (Archive Editions: Cambridge 1986). Vol.2, p. 347.
22. BLAM 45983A. Pocket Diary, 1917. May 11-13, 15.
23. *Ibid.* June 5.
24. BLAM 45915. 55 verso.
25. *Ibid.*
26. THBRG, p. 16.
27. C-W, Box 146/1. (& cf. Note 3).
28. *Ibid.*
29. Hogarth Papers. Middle East Centre for Arab Studies, St Antony's College, Oxford. 30 September 1917.
30. BLAM 45983A. Pocket Diary, 1917. June 6–9, 11, 13.
31. NA, FO. 882/7. FO 29. Sir R.F. Wingate to TEL, 14.7.1917.
32. Royal Archives, Windsor Castle. RA GV Q2521/103 (Part) 31.7.1917.
33. Hogarth Papers. Letters home from D.G Hogarth 1917-18, 20(ii), 28(ii), 29(ii), 30(ii). (& cf. Note 29).
34. Chalmers Roberts, *World Today* Vol. 49, No. 5, July 1927, p. 442.
35. Polly A. Mohs, op.cit. p. 154.

36. THBLH, p. 153.
37. JM, p. 442.
38. BHF, p. 398.
39. *Ibid.* p. 426.
40. Storrs, *op. cit.* pp. 39–40.
41. BHF, p. 158.
42. *Ibid.* p. 248.
43. *Ibid.* p. 453.
44. John Buchan, *Memory Hold the Door* (Hodder & Stoughton: London 1940), p. 218.
45. Priscilla Napier, *Late Beginner* (Michael Joseph: London 1966) p. 150.
46. BHF, p. 150.
47. TV documentary, *Lawrence and Arabia*. Omnibus, BBC 2, 18 April 1986.
48. DG, pp. 813–14. To Eric Kennington, 6.VIII.34.

2. IRISH INITIATIONS

1. DG, p. 85.
2. S-S, 1929–35, p. 130. Letter of 26.3.31.
3. Buchan, *op. cit.*, p. 214.
4. BHF, p. 425.
5. Storrs, *op. cit.*, p. 518.

4. A TERRITORIAL ROOT IN THE PROPER PLACE

1. S-S, 1927, pp. 41–2.
2. S-S, 1922–26, p. 30. Letter of 4.1.23.
3. TV documentary, *Lawrence and Arabia*. (cf. Ch 1. Note 47).
4. THBLH, p. 79.
5. BHF, p. 272.
6. DG, p. 301.
7. BHF, p. 215.
8. BLAM, 45903. T.E. Lawrence to Charlotte Shaw, 28.ix.25 and S-S, 1922–6, p. 150.
9. DG, p. 655.
10. MB, p. 333.
11. *Ibid.* p. 326.
12. Wyndham Lewis, *Blasting and Bombardiering* (Calder & Boyars: London 1967), p. 240.
13. Letter to the author from Elizabeth Newcombe.
14. DG, p. 533.
15. JM, p. 5 and p. 472.
16. NA. State Papers, Ireland. (SP 63/146/41). Sir Henry Wallop to Sir Francis Walsingham, October 16, 1584.
17. NA. State Papers, Ireland (SP 63/146/41). Sir William Herbert to Lord Burghley, September, 1589.

5. A HUGE GRANT OF COUNTY MEATH

1. MB, pp. 333–4. TEL to John Buchan.
2. National Library of Ireland. 'Catalogue of Valuable Antique and Modern Furniture, Silver Plate, Old Sheffield Plate, Library and 200 Oil Paintings to be sold at Killua Castle, Westmeath, by direction of General R.S.Fetherstonhaugh, 2 June 1920'.
3. MB, p. 301.
4. AB, p. 667.
5. HR. Letter from Flora Armitage to Basil Liddell Hart, 25.1.54.
6. BLAM, 45903, Folio 76.
7. TV documentary, *Lawrence and Arabia*. (& cf. Ch 1. Note 47).
8. BLAM, 45904. Folio 5. Letter from TEL to Charlotte Shaw, 21.5.28.
9. A.W. Lawrence (ed.), *Letters to T.E. Lawrence* (Jonathan Cape: London 1962), p. 185, and Royal Archives, Windsor Castle. George V. (RA GEOV 27350). Letter from Lawrence to Lord Stamfordham, January 26th, 1928.
10. JTELS, Vol VI, No. 1, Autumn 1996. Harold Orlans, 'The Ways of Transgressors are Hard', p. 20.
11. HR. Folder 1, Box 10. Celandine Kennington, 'Re Chapmans of Killua', p. 2.
12. JM, p. 474, note 77 and p. 525, note 68.

6. ANCESTRAL VOICES

1. Knight of Glin, David J.Griffin, Nicholas K.Robinson, *Vanishing Country Houses of Ireland* (Irish Architectural Archive & The Irish Georgian Society: Dublin 1988) pp. 12–13.
2. DG, p. 37. Thomas Chapman in conversation with Oxford don Ernest Barker.
3. cf. note 1.
4. Edmund F. Dease, *A Complete History of the Westmeath Hunt* (Brown & Nolan: Dublin 1896), p. 85– passim.
5. Samuel Lewis, *A Topographical Dictionary of Ireland* (S. Lewis & Co.: London 1837). See under Clonmellon.
6. National Library of Ireland. Manuscript department. Ms. 2726.
7. *Westmeath Guardian*. Friday, 25 January 1907, p. 3.
8. *The Irish Times*, 10 September 1944.
9. BOL, Lawrence Papers. Transcript of letter from TEL to Florence Hardy, 21.i.24; and AB, p. 743.
10. AB, p. 743. TEL to his mother, 18.v.24.

7. FASHIONABLE MARRIAGE

1. National Library of Ireland. Reynell Papers. Ainsworth 412. Unmarked. Black book of press cuttings, 14 April 1868, p. 39.
2. *Westmeath Examiner*. Saturday, 11 December 1886, p. 2.
3. *Ibid.* Saturday, 21 May 1887, p 3.

4. Barbara Casey. Conversation with author.
5. *Ibid.*
6. BLAM 45903. TEL to Charlotte Shaw. 14.iv.27.
7. *A Complete History of the Westmeath Hunt.* (cf. Ch. 6. Note 4 above), p. 85– passim.
8. cf. Note 1.
9. BL. *Daily Express*, Dublin Edition, 26 July 1873, p. 3.
10. cf. Note 1.
11. *Ibid.*
12. Barbara Casey. Conversation with author.
13. *Ibid.*
14. Phillip Knightley & Colin Simpson, *The Secret Lives of Lawrence of Arabia* (Nelson: London 1969), pp. 7-8.
15. BOL. Lawrence papers, Ref. MS. Res. c. 569.
16. HR. cf. Ch.5. Note 11. Celandine Kennington, 'Re: Chapmans of Killua', p. 2.
17. *Ibid.* p. 7.

8. THE ABANDONED SISTERS

1. Barbara Casey. Conversation with author.
2. Lily Montgomery. Conversation with author.
3. cf. Ch.5. Note 11. Celandine Kennington, 'Re: Chapmans of Killua'.
4. MB, p. 333.
5. HR. Letter from Bob Lawrence to Basil Liddell Hart, 28.ii.55. (& cf.Ch 5. Note 5).
6. *Ibid.* letter from Eric Kennington to Liddell Hart, 29.4.54.
7. *Ibid.* letter from Bob Lawrence to Liddell Hart, February 1955.

9. A DOUBLE LIFE

1. JTELS, Vol. VI No. 2, Spring 1997, p. 37.
2. HL, p. 265.
3. *Ibid.* p. 435.
4. *Ibid.*
5. *Ibid.* p. 450.
6. *Ibid.* p. 269.
7. *Ibid.* p. 256.
8. JM, pp. 12–3.
9. HL, p. 481.
10. *Ibid.* p. 483.
11. BOL. Lawrence Papers, Ref. MS Reserve. C.569, and JTELS, Vol. VI No. 1, Autumn 1996, pp. 20–1.
12. MB, p. 192.
13. TEL to Robert Graves. 28.6.1927. (omitted from THBRG p. 48). Houghton Library, Harvard, USA.

14. MB. p. 333.
15. THBLH. p. 78.
16. Christies New York Catalogue, Thursday, February 26, 2004. The Spiro Family Collection. Part III. p. 64. Item 61.
17. *Ibid.*
18. Malcolm Brown. *T.E.Lawrence*. (British Library History Series: London 2003), p. 108.
19. A.W Lawrence. *Biographical Notes*. (Two typed pages). May 12, 1985. BOL. Lawrence Papers.
20. IWM-ST. Box No.I. p. 2. Comment by A.W Lawrence on draft of biography: *The Secret Lives of Lawrence of Arabia.*

10. A STANDING CIVIL WAR

1. Barbara Casey. Conversation with author.
2. Robert Graves, *Lawrence and the Arabs* (Jonathan Cape: London 1927), p. 13.
3. IWM-ST, Celandine Kennington to Lady Hardinge. 30 July 1954.
4. JTELS, Vol. VI No. 2, Spring 1997. Malcolm Brown, 'Behind the Genteel Façade', p. 45.
5. Malcolm Brown. Conversation with author.
6. JM, p. 13 and p. 474, note 69.
7. BLAM, 45903 Folio 27. and S-S 1927, p. 61. TEL to Charlotte Shaw. 14.4.27.
8. JTELS. Vol.VI. No.I. p. 24. TEL to D.G.Hogarth. & BOL. Lawrence Papers.
9. BLAM, 45904 Folio 27. TEL to Charlotte Shaw. 28.8.28.
10. AB, p. 943.
11. THBLH, p. 78.
12. *Ibid.*
13. AB, p. 984, note 28. A.W. Lawrence to Jeremy Wilson.
14. Louisa Young, *A Great Task of Happiness* (Macmillan: London 1995), pp. 254–5.
15. Flora Armitage, *The Desert and the Stars* (Faber & Faber: London 1956), p. 19.
16. S-S 1927, pp. 59–61.
17. Lord Robert Gilbert Vansittart, *The Mist Procession* (Hutchinson: London 1958), p. 166.
18. S-S 1922-26, p. 178.
19. JM, p. 8.
20. BOL. Exhibition booklet (1988), 'T.E. Lawrence: The Legend and the Man', p. 9.
21. BOL. Lawrence Papers. Two typed pages by A.W. Lawrence headed 'Biographical Notes'. May 12th, 1985.
22. Harold Orlans, *T.E. Lawrence: Biography of a Broken Hero* (McFarlane & Company: Jefferson, North Carolina, USA 2002), p. 138; and Jeremy Wilson, telstudies@lists. netlink. co.uk 1997 (nb. website was being reconstructed 2012).
23. J.M.Wilson (ed.), *T. E. Lawrence: Letters to E.T. Leeds* (The Whittington Press: Andoversford 1988), p. 114.
24. JM. p. 27.

25. DG. p. 61.
26. JM. p. 29.
27. BHF. p. 11.
28. JM. p. 11.
29. JTELS. Vol. VI No. 2, Spring 1997, p. 35. A.W. Lawrence in conversation with Malcolm Brown.
30. JTELS. Vol. VI No. 1, Autumn 1996. Harold Orlans, 'The Ways of Transgressors are Hard'.

11. A CHILD OF SIN

1. Barbara Casey. Conversation with author.
2. BLAM, 45904. 17.v.28.
3. MB, p. 333
4. Sunderland Public Library. National Population Census, 1861. R.G. No. 3784, pp. 47–8.
5. MB, p. 333.
6. *Ibid.* p. 345.
7. S-S 1922–26, p. 175.
8. Barbara Jones, Information Services Manager, Lloyd's Register, London. Email.
9. JM, p. 9.
10. Elizabeth Newcombe. Letter to the author.
11. JTELS, Vol X No. 1, Autumn 2000, p. 9. Gillian Stevenson & Martin Riley, 'A Dash of Scandinavian'.
12. *Ibid.* p. 8.
13. AB, p. 743. Letter to his mother of 18.v.24.

12. MY NATIVE LAND

1. IWM. T.E.Lawrence Exhibition, 2005–6, Item 14. Deed Poll.
2. BLAM, 45903 Folio 184. TEL to Charlotte Shaw. November 10th, 1927.
3. *Ibid.* Folio 182. TEL to Charlotte Shaw. 1.xi.27. (actual date of letter was 1 December).
4. *The Contemporary Review*, December 1974, p. 314.
5. H.S.Ede (foreword & running commentary by), *Shaw-Ede. T.E.Lawrence's Letters to H.S.Ede 1927–1935.* (Golden Cockerel Press: London 1942), p. 12. Letter of.1.xii.27.
6. MB, p. 318.
7. *Ibid.* p. 316.
8. BLAM, 45904 Folio 220. TEL to Charlotte Shaw. 16.ix.34.
9. HR. Letter from Irene Magan to Celandine Kennington.
10. AB, pp. 789-90 & p. 1139, note 42; & BOL, Lawrence Papers. Letter (photocopy) to R.T.R.P. Butler.
11. BOL. Lawrence Papers, Ms.b55. Letter from TEL to Colonel Pierce Joyce. March 19th, 1929.

12. AB, p. 789. TEL to Edward Eliot, 16.6.27.
13. AB, p. 1139.
14. MB, p. 336. TEL to John Buchan. 1927.
15. *Ibid.* p. 330. TEL to Dr A.E .Cowley, 19.v.27.
16. *Ibid.* p. 283. TEL to E.M Forster. 17.vi.25.
17. *Ibid.* p. 465. TEL to Charlotte Shaw. 16.ix.32. & BLAM 45904. Folio 180.
18. DG, p. 649.
19. *Ibid.* p. 744.
20. *Ibid.* p. 447.
21. JM, p. 446.
22. BHF, pp. 461-2.
23. DG, p. 722.
24. Wyndham Lewis, *Blasting and Bombardiering*. (Calder & Boyars: London 1967). p. 240.
25. Harold Orlans, *Biography of a Broken Hero*, p. 127. (cf. Ch.10. Note 22).
26. *Irish Times*, 10 December 1985. An Irishman's Diary (Eileen O'Brien). (From an article by W.Thomas in *The Irish Historical Review*).
27. *Ibid.*
28. The Times Bookshop, Wigmore Street, London, Autumn 1961. Sale catalogue no. 2, Rare Books, p. 19. Colonel Pierce Joyce's copy of *Seven Pillars of Wisdom*, with letter from TEL (facsimile) inserted.
29. THBRG, pp. 186–7.
30. MB, p. 345.
31. S-S 1922–26, p. 29.
32. Paul Tunbridge, *With Lawrence in The Royal Air Force* (Buckland Publications Ltd: Sevenoaks 2000), pp. 38–9.
33. Dominic Winter Book Auctions. (The Old School, Maxwell Street, Swindon, Wiltshire), Wednesday, 2 March 2005. Catalogue, p. 37. Letter from TEL to Colonel Dyas, c. 1923. (Facsimile).
34. BHF, p. 316.

13. CRAZED WITH THE SPELL OF FAR ARABIA
1. From first verse of 'Arabia' by Walter de la Mare.

14. THE LAST AND LINGERING TROUBADOUR
1. S-S 1927. p. 138.
2. THBRG, p. 81.
3. THBLH. p. 84.
4. From poem 'Lepanto' by G.K Chesterton.
5. *T.E. Lawrence: Letters to E.T. Leeds.* (The Whittington Press. Andoversford, 1988), p.x.
6. HL, p. 441.
7. *Ibid.* p. 443.

8. *Ibid.* p. 560.

9. DG, p. 294.

10. BOL. Lawrence Papers, transcript. (Original in Kilgour Collection, Houghton Library, Harvard University, USA) & cf. *T.E. Lawrence, Towards 'An English Fourth'* (Castle Hill Press: Fordingbridge 2009). Introduction, pp. xiii, xiv and 45.

11. list2 – telstudies.org 28.01.09. (nb.website was being reconstructed in 2012).

12. Letter from Elizabeth Newcombe to the author. 22.09.68.

13. BOL. Lawrence Papers, and MB, pp. 168-9.

14. DG, p. 431.

15. MB, p. 253.

16. THBRG, pp. 8–9.

17. *Ibid.* pp. 15–17.

18. A.W. Lawrence (ed.), *Oriental Assembly by T.E. Lawrence* (Williams & Norgate: London 1939), p. 26.

19. THBRG, pp. 15–18.

20. SPWO, p. 812.

21. THBRG, p. 55.

22. HR. *Texas Quarterly*, Autumn 1962, Vol. V Number 3, p. 48 (Facsimile).

23. THBLH, p. 64.

24. *Ibid.* p. 68.

25. *Ibid.* p. 143.

26. *The Saturday Review,* New York. USA. 15 June 1963. pp. 16–17.

27. For expanded version of the *Saturday Review* article see Robert Graves, *Poetic Craft and Principle* (Cassell: London 1965), pp. 185–95.

28. Robert Graves, *Between Moon and Moon* (Moyer Bell Ltd.: New York 1990), pp. 132–3.

29. Jonathan Black. The Graphic Art of Eric Kennington (exhibition booklet). (College Art Collections: University College London 2001), p. 31.

15. I'D RATHER MORRIS THAN THE WORLD

1. THBRG, p. 74.

2. Dan H. Laurence & Daniel J Leary (eds) *Flyleaves*. George Bernard Shaw. (H. Thomas Taylor: Austin, Texas, 1977). p. 40.

3. THBRG, p. 74.

4. DG, p. 512.

5. HL, p. 184.

6. BHF, pp. 395, 397.

7. E.Bishop, *The Debt We Owe. The Royal Air Force Benevolent Fund 1919–1969.* (Longmans: London 1969).

8. T.E. Lawrence. *Secret Despatches from Arabia.* (Golden Cockerel Press: London 1939), p. 126. (First published as *Twenty-Seven Articles*, August 20th, 1917 edition of The Arab Bulletin, Cairo.)

9. William Rothenstein (ed.), *Twenty-Four Portraits* (cf. Ch 1. Note 17).
10. HL, p. 110.
11. A. W. Lawrence (ed.), *Oriental Assembly*, p. 143.
12. BHF, pp. 83–4.
13. MB, p. 481.
14. BLAM, 45904 Folio 12. TEL to Charlotte Shaw, 30.6.28.
15. Augustus John, *Chiaroscuro* (Jonathan Cape: London 1952), p. 208.
16. Clare Sydney Smith, *The Golden Reign.* (Cassell: London 1940), p. 6.
17. Internet: Lawrence List 018. (website under reconstruction 2012).
18. MB, p. 502.
19. Clare Sydney Smith, *The Golden Reign* (Fleece Press: Upper Denby 2004), pp. 20-21.
20. BHF, pp. 311–2.
21. *Ibid.* p. 271.
22. BLAM, 45903 Folio 76.
23. THBRG, pp. 186–7.
24. MB p. 481.
25. JM, p. 41.
26. BHF, p. 52.
27. *Ibid.* pp. 52–3.
28. THBRG, p. 48.
29. THBLH, p. 50.
30. BHF, pp. 383–4.
31. HL, p. 64.
32. *Ibid.* p. 66.
33. Jesus College Magazine. IV. (1935). pp. 343–5. Article on TEL.
34. J.N.L. Baker, *Jesus College, Oxford 1571-1971* (Oxonian Press: Oxford 1971), p. 108.
35. BHF, p. 83.
36. DG, p. 85.
37. S-S 1927. pp. 46–7.
38. S-S 1929-35. pp. 46–7.
39. S-S 1927. p. 90.
40. *Ibid.* p. 125.
41. *Ibid.* p. 123.
42. BHF, p. 500.
43. DG, pp. 639–40.
44. DG, p. 244.

16. THE WELL AT THE WORLD'S END

1. A.G. Ferrers Howell, *Dante and the Troubadours* (University Press: London 1921), p. 197.

2. *Ibid.* p. 64.

3. J.F Rowbotham, *The Troubadours and Courts of Love.* (Swan Sonnenschein & Co: London 1895), p. 12.

4. A.J Denomy, *Fin Amors: The Pure Love of the Troubadours, its Amorality and Possible Source.* (Medieval Studies, Vol.VII. 1945), p. 175.

5. J.F Rowbotham, *op. cit.* p. 189.

6. William Morris, *The Well at the World's End: Vol 2.* (Pan/Ballantine Books: London 1971), pp. 82-83.

7. SPWO, p. 6.

8. M.D. Allen, *The Medievalism of Lawrence of Arabia* (Pennsylvania State University Press: University Park, Pennsylvania 1991), pp. 53–7 – passim.

9. HL, p. 304.

10. DG, p. 511.

11. BHF, p. 92.

12. Jeffrey Meyers, *The Wounded Spirit*, (Martin Brian & O'Keeffe: London 1973), p. 124.

13. MB, p. 236. TEL to Lionel Curtis. 14.v.23.

14. Meyers, *op. cit.* p. 123.

15. AB, p. 703.

16. AB, pp. 703–4 and 1128.

17. Phillip Knightley & Colin Simpson, *The Secret Lives of Lawrence of Arabia* (Panther Books: London 1971), p. 43.

18. BHF, p. 385.

19. IWM-ST, Box No2. 69/48/2. White file marked 'masochist'.

20. BHF, p. 119.

21. BOL, Lawrence Papers, Ms.d49. Letter from TEL to E.H.R. Altounyan, 28 December 1933.

22. E.H.R. Altounyan, *Ornament of Honour* (Cambridge University Press: Cambridge 1937), p. 55.

17. BODY AND SOUL

1. MB, p. 389.

2. *Ibid.* p. 408.

3. *Ibid.*

4. BLAM, 45903 Folio 22.

5. *Ibid.* Folio 68.

6. MB, p. 236.

7. *Ibid.* p. 233.

8. Hector Bolitho, *The Angry Neighbours* (Arthur Barker Ltd.: London 1957), p. 139.

9. Virginia Quarterly Review (USA). Vol.21. No 4. Autumn, 1945. 'T.E. Lawrence:

Some Trivial Memories', by Margot Hill. pp. 589 and 596.

10. Colonel R Meinertzhagen, *Middle East Diary* (The Crescent Press: London 1959), p. 39.
11. BHF, p. 114.
12. Thomas Jones, *A Diary with Letters, 1931-1950* (Oxford University Press: Oxford 1954), p. 149.
13. HL, p. 147.
14. BHF. pp. 542–3.
15. Clare Sydney Smith, *The Golden Reign* (Cassell), p. 164.
16. MB, p. 360.
17. *Ibid.* p. 429.
18. IWM-ST. Box ref. Misc 196 (2904).*Recollections of Life in the Tank Corps 1916-18 and of T.E. Lawrence 1923-25.* by A.H.R Reiffer. Typescript of letter of April, 1970 (23-41/3).
19. S-S 1927, p. 76.
20. BOL, Lawrence Papers, and MB, p. xxviii.
21. BHF, pp. 591–2.
22. S-S 1927, p. 61.

18. THE CITADEL OF MY INTEGRITY

1. MB, p. 165–6. T.E. Lawrence to Deputy Chief Polical Offices, Cairo (Colonel W.F. Stirling). June 28, 1919
2. T.E. Lawrence, *Seven Pillars of Wisdom.* (Folio Society: London 2000), pp. 373–75.
3. SPWO, pp. 501–2.
4. S-S 1922-26, pp. 70-71.
5. Storrs, *op. cit.* p. 446.
6. Meinertzhagen, *Middle East Diary*, pp. 32–3.
7. From two unpublished letters from Theodora Duncan to Helen Cash (10.6.66 & 30.11.66). Author's transcripts.
8. John Godl, 'The Disputed Sexuality of T.E. Lawrence', www.firstworldwar.com/features/telawrence.

19. AN IMAGINARY PERSON OF NEUTRAL SEX

1. John Mack. Letter to the author, 13 September 1968.
2. JM, pp. 64–5.
3. Emma Smith, *The Great Western Beach* (Bloomsbury: London 2008), p. 243.
4. M.D. Allen, *op.cit.* p. 56.
5. JM, pp. 65–6.
6. AB, pp. 226–7 & 1017, and BOL, Lawrence Papers.
7. AB, pp. 637–8.
8. JM, p. 21.

9. HL, p. 66.
10. DG, p. 161.
11. A.W. Lawrence (ed.), *Oriental Assembly*, p. 51.
12. *T.E. Lawrence: Letters to E.T. Leeds.* op.cit. p. 47. (cf. Ch. 10. Note 23).
13. BHF, p. 88.
14. *Ibid.* p. 88–9.
15. *Ibid.* p. 90.
16. *Ibid.* pp. 90–1.
17. *Ibid.* p. 125.
18. *Ibid.* p. 127.

20. CANDIDATES AND ADVOCATES

1. HL, pp. 169–70.
2. *Ibid.* p. 221.
3. www.telstudies.org/analysis/asher017.htm (nb. website was being reconstructed in 2012).
4. *T.E.Lawrence. Letters to E.T. Leeds*, op cit. p. 61.
5. HL, p. 293.
6. *Ibid.* p. 292.
7. *Ibid.* p. 176.
8. *Ibid.* p. 173.
9. DG, p. 119.
10. HL, p. 213.
11. *Ibid.* p. 222.
12. *Ibid.* p. 226.
13. *Ibid.* p. 227.
14. *Ibid.* p. 229.
15. *Ibid.* p. 232.
16. BHF, p. 105.
17. DG, p. 166.
18. *Ibid.* p. 168.
19. HL, p. 299.
20. *Ibid.* p. 311.
21. BHF. p. 80.
22. T.E. Lawrence List Archive. (Internet).
23. T.E. Lawrence List. July 1, 1998.
24. T.E. Lawrence List Archive. (nb. T.E. Lawrence List websites were being reconstructed in 2012).
25. *Ibid.*
26. AB, p. 926 and BOL, Lawrence Papers.
27. Knightley & Simpson, op.cit., pp. 190–1.

28. *Ibid.* p. 313.
29. Jeremy Wilson. Telephone conversation with author.
30. Harvard University, USA, Houghton Library. Victoria Ocampo. Letters.
31. HL, p. 304.
32. AB, p. 544.
33. *Ibid.* pp. 544 & 1100 and BOL, Lawrence Papers.
34. JTELS, Vol. XII No. 2, Spring 2003. Discoveries Part II. Sara Johnson. p. 52.
35. SPWO, p. 360.
36. William Morris, *The Hollow Land* (Thomas B. Mosher: Portland 1900), p. 11.
37. *Ibid.* p. 63.
38. *Ibid.* pp. 96–7.
39. MB, p. 481.
40. BHF, p. 93.
41. Anita Engle, *The Nili Spies* (Hogarth Press: London 1959), p. 230.
42. *Ibid.* pp. 232–3.
43. *The New Statesman*, 22 December 1956.
44. *Ibid.* 5 January 1957.
45. Engle, *op. cit.* pp. 235–7.
46. Douglas Duff. Interview with author at King Stag, Dorset, 12 November 1967.
47. SPWO. p 6.
48. MB. p. 284.
49. BHF, p. 486.
50. *Ibid.* p. 592.
51. Jock Chambers. Letter to author. 7 December 1967.

21. THE DARK LADY

1. From the poem 'Skias Onar' by F.L. Lucas.
2. HL, p. 304. TEL to his mother, spring 1915.
3. THBRG, p. 17.
4. BHF, p. 590.
5. SPWO, pp. 679–80, 684–85.
6. S-S 1927, p. 187.
7. BLAM, 45904. Folio 3. 8.v.28.
8. DG, p. 370.
9. Jeremy Wilson (ed.), *Minorities.* (Jonathan Cape: London 1971), p. 20.
10. THBRG, p. 22.
11. Wilson, *op. cit.* p. 193.
12. *Ibid.* p. 81.
13. *Ibid.* p. 119.
14. *Ibid.* p. 113.
15. DG, p. 467.

16. Wilson, *op. cit.* p. 262.
17. BHF, p. 544.
18. Wilson, *op. cit.* p. 31.
19. Jeremy Wilson. Telephone conversation with author.
20. Wilson, *op. cit.* p. 220.
21. HL, p. 206.
22. *Ibid.* p. 193.
23. BLAM, 45904. Folio 9. 15.6.28.
24. www.Abebooks.co.uk. 2006.
25. Letter from A.W. Lawrence to author. 6 July 1968.
26. Freya Stark, *Letters from Syria* (John Murray: London 1942), p. 39. Letter of January 7, 1928.
27. Knightley & Simpson *op. cit.* p. 187.
28. S-S 1927, p. 76.
29. BHF, p. 92.
30. *Ibid.* p. 76.
31. *Ibid.* pp. 77–8.
32. HL, p. 129.
33. *Ibid.* p. 148.
34. *Ibid.* p. 174.
35. DG, p. 115.
36. *Ibid.* p. 123.
37. HL, p. 182.
38. DG, p. 135.
39. HL, p. 188.
40. DG, p. 138.
41. AB, pp. 114 & 996. Letter from TEL to Mrs André Rieder. 7.1.1913. and BOL, Lawrence Papers. Transcript.
42. DG, p. 155.
43. Emma Smith, op.cit. p. 247.
44. BOL, Lawrence Papers, Ms.d56. TEL to Dick Knowles, July 14, 1927.
45. DG, p. 230–1 and AB, p. 1075.
46. John Mack. Letter to author. 13 September 1968.
47. *The Sunday Times*, 5 July 1998. News Section. p. 13.
48. BOL, Lawrence Papers, Ms.d60, and JM, p. 100. Fareedah al Akle to TEL. 30 March 1920.
49. HL, pp. 147–8.
50. JM, p. 100.
51. MB p. 173.

APPENDIX 1: THE CHAPMAN COAT OF ARMS

1. Desmond Chapman-Huston, *The Lamp of Memory; Autobiographical Digressions* (Skeffington and Son Ltd: London 1949), pp. 27, 36–7, 59–62.

2. NA. (AIR 1/2697). Letter of June 16, 1939 from Major Desmond Chapman-Huston to the Officer in charge of Records at the Air Ministry.

3. Charles Grosvenor, *An Iconography: The Portraits of T.E. Lawrence* (The Otterden Press: Pasadena 1988) pp. 96–8.

Bibliography

ARCHIVES

All Souls College, Oxford. Letters, memorabilia.

Ashmolean Museum, Oxford. Archives.

Bodleian Library, Oxford. T.E. Lawrence Papers (including Ms. *Seven Pillars of Wisdom*).

British Library, Euston Road, London. T.E. Lawrence Papers, (manuscripts, diaries, message-pad notes, letters, photographs, books).

Dorchester Museum, Dorset. Lawrence Collection (letters).

Harry Ransom Humanities Research Center, University of Texas, Austin, Texas, USA. T.E. Lawrence Collection.

Houghton Library, Harvard University, USA. Kilgour Collection.

Huntington Library, San Marino, California, USA.

Imperial War Museum, Lambeth Road, London.
> Research documents for Sunday Times book, *The Secret Lives of Lawrence of Arabia*.
> T.W. Beaumont Papers.
> G. Dawnay Papers.
> F.G. Peake Papers.
> W.F. Stirling Papers.

Jesus College, Oxford. Library.
> 'Examiners' Copy' of TEL's Crusader Castles thesis (Ms. J/160/7).
> Some TEL letters.

Liddell Hart Centre for Military Archives, King's College London.
> Sir E.H.H. Allenby Papers.
> P.C. Joyce Papers.

Middle East Centre, St Antony's College, Oxford.
> D.G Hogarth Papers.
> T.E. Lawrence Papers.
> S.F. Newcombe Papers.
> Sir H.W. Young Papers.

The National Archives, Kew, London.
> FO 371. Political: correspondence.
> FO 686. Jiddah Agency Papers.
> FO 882. Arab Bureau Papers.
> SPI 63. Elizabeth.vols. xxvii, xxviii.
> WO 33. War Office reports and papers.

WO. 95. War diaries.

WO 106. Directorate of Military Operations & Military Intelligence – papers.
The National Library of Ireland.

Manuscript department: Ms. 965. Books of Survey and Distribution for Counties Westmeath and Longford, known as 'the Down Survey of the Cromwellian Plantation of Ireland' (lists recipients and lands granted in 1666–8). Family collections & manuscripts.

Palestine Exploration Fund, Manchester Square, London. Archives.

Pembroke College, Cambridge. Sir R. Storrs Papers.

Royal Archives, Round Tower, Windsor Castle, Windsor, Berkshire.Letters.

Sudan Archive, Durham University Library. Papers of Sir G.F. Clayton and Sir F.R. Wingate.

BOOKS

Aldington, Richard, *Lawrence of Arabia* (Collins: London 1955).

Allen, M.D., *The Medievalism of Lawrence of Arabia* (Pennsylvania State University Press: University Park 1991).

Altounyan, E.H.R., *Ornament of Honour* (Cambridge University Press: Cambridge 1937).

Altounyan, Taqui, *In Aleppo Once* (John Murray: London 1969).

Anderson, Scott, *Lawrence In Arabia* (Doubleday: New York 2013).

Antonius, George, *The Arab Awakening* (Hamish Hamilton: London 1938).

Armitage, Flora, *The Desert and the Stars* (Faber & Faber: London 1956).

Asher, Michael, *Lawrence: The Uncrowned King of Arabia* (Viking: London 1998).

Baker, J.N.L., *Jesus College Oxford 1571–1971* (Oxonian Press Ltd.: Oxford 1971).

Barr, James, *Setting the Desert on Fire* (Bloomsbury: London 2006).

Bishop, E., *The Debt We Owe. The Royal Air Force Benevolent Fund 1919–1969* (Longmans: London 1969).

Black, Jonathan, *The Graphic Art of Eric Kennington* (exhibition commentary & catalogue) (College Art Collections: University College London 2001).

Bodleian Library exhibition booklet, *T.E. Lawrence: The Legend and the Man* (Bodleian Library: Oxford 1988).

Bolitho, Hector, *The Angry Neighbours* (Arthur Barker Ltd.: London 1957).

Boussard, Léon, *Le Secret du Colonel Lawrence* (Éditions A.M.: Paris 1946).

Boyle, Andrew, *Trenchard* (Collins: London 1962).

Brémond, E., *Le Hedjaz dans la Guerre Mondiale* (Payot: Paris 1931).

Brown, Malcolm, *Lawrence of Arabia: The Life, The Legend* (Thames and Hudson: London 2005).

Brown, Malcolm (ed.), *T. E. Lawrence: In War and Peace* (Greenhill Books: London 2005).

Brown, Malcolm (ed.), *The Letters of T.E. Lawrence* (J.M. Dent & Sons: London 1988).

Brown, Malcolm. T.E.Lawrence (The British Library Publishing Division: London 2003).

Buchan, John, *Memory Hold the Door* (Hodder & Stoughton: London 1942).

Cadell, James, *The Young Lawrence of Arabia* (Max Parrish: London 1960).

Canny, Nicholas. *Making Ireland British 1580-1650* (Oxford University Press, Oxford 2001).

Chapman-Huston, Desmond, *The Lamp of Memory* (Skeffington and Son Ltd: London 1947).

Clayton, Sir Gilbert F., *An Arabian Diary* (University of California Press: Berkeley 1969).

Cork and Orrery, Earl of, Admiral of the Fleet, *My Naval Life 1886–1941* (Hutchinson: London 1943).

Dease, Edmund F., *A Complete History of the Westmeath Hunt* (Brown & Nolan: Dublin 1896).

Devas, N., *Two Flamboyant Fathers* (Collins: London 1966).

Dixon, Alec, *Tinned Soldier* (Cape: London 1941).

Dockter, Warren, *Churchill and the Islamic World* (I.B. Tauris: London 2015).

Dominic Winter Book Auctions. March 2nd, 2005. Catalogue. (Printed Books & Maps. Dominic Winter, The Old School, Maxwell Street, Swindon, Wiltshire).

Dooley, Terence. *The Decline of the Big House in Ireland.* (Wolfhound Press. Dublin.2001).

Ede, H.S. (foreword & running commentary by), *Shaw-Ede. T.E. Lawrence's Letters to H.S. Ede 1927-1935.* (Golden Cockerel Press: London 1942).

Engle, Anita. *The Nili Spies.* Hogarth Press. London. 1959.

Faulkner, Peter (ed.), *William Morris, Selected Poems* (Carcanet Press: Manchester 1992).

Ferrers Howell, A.G., *Dante and the Troubadours* (University Press: London 1921).

Florence, Ronald, *Lawrence and Aaronsohn* (Viking Penguin: New York 2007).

Forster, E.M., *Two Cheers for Democracy* (Edward Arnold: London 1951).

Garnett, David (ed.), *The Letters of T.E. Lawrence* (Jonathan Cape: London 1938).

Gaunt, Simon, and Kay, Sarah, *The Troubadours* (Cambridge University Press: Cambridge 1999).

Grainger, John D, *The Battle for Syria 1918–1920* (The Boydell Press: Woodbridge 2013).

Graves, Robert, *Between Moon and Moon* (Moyer Bell Ltd: London & New York 1990).

Graves, Robert, *Lawrence and the Arabs* (Jonathan Cape: London 1927).

Graves, Robert, *Poetic Craft and Principle* (Cassell: London 1965).

Graves, Robert, and Liddell Hart, B.H., *T.E. Lawrence to his biographers, Robert Graves & Liddell Hart* [letters, notes, commentaries] (Cassell: London 1963).

Grosvenor, Charles, *An Iconography: The Portraits of T.E. Lawrence* (The Otterden Press: Pasadena 1988).

Gullett, H.S., *The Australian Imperial Force in Sinai and Palestine* (Angus and Robertson: Sydney 1923).

Hewlett, Maurice, *The Life and Death of Richard Yea-and-Nay* (Macmillan: London 1900).

Hynes, James Patrick, *Lawrence of Arabia's Secret Air Force* (Pen and Sword Aviation: Barnsley 2010).

James, Lawrence, *The Golden Warrior* (Weidenfeld and Nicolson: London 1990).

John, Augustus, *Chiaroscuro* (Jonathan Cape: London 1952).

Johnson-Allen, John, *T.E. Lawrence and the Red Sea Patrol* (Pen and Sword Military: Barnsley 2015).

Jones, Thomas, *A Diary with Letters, 1931–1950* (Oxford University Press: Oxford 1954).

Kirkbride, Sir Alec, *A Crackle of Thorns* (John Murray: London 1956).

Knight, Ronald, *T.E.Lawrence: A Brief Chronology* (T.E.Lawrence Society: Oxford 1990 & 2014).

Knightley, Phillip & Simpson, Colin, *The Secret Lives of Lawrence of Arabia* (Thomas Nelson: London 1969).

Knight of Glin, Griffin, David J., Robinson, Nicholas K. *Vanishing Country Houses of Ireland* (Irish Architectural Archive & The Irish Georgian Society: Dublin 1988)

Knowles, Patrick, *"An Handful With Quietness"* (Privately published by E.V.G. Hunt: Weymouth 1992).

Knowles, Richard, *Precious Caskets* (The Fleece Press: Denby Dale, Wakefield 2003).

Korda, Michael, *Hero: The Life and Legend of Lawrence of Arabia* (HarperCollins: New York 2010).

Laurence, Dan H. & Leary, Daniel J (eds) *Flyleaves*. George Bernard Shaw. (H. Thomas Taylor: Austin, Texas, 1977).

Lawrence, A.W. (ed.), *Letters to T.E. Lawrence* (Jonathan Cape: London 1962).

Lawrence, A.W. (ed.), *Oriental Assembly* (Williams and Norgate: London 1939).

Lawrence, A.W. (ed.), *T. E. Lawrence by his Friends* (Jonathan Cape. London.1937).

Lawrence, M.R. (ed.), *The Home Letters of T. E. Lawrence and his Brothers* (Basil Blackwell: Oxford 1954).

Lawrence, T.E., *Crusader Castles*. Intruduction & Notes by Denys Pringle (Clarendon Press: Oxford 1988)

Lawrence, T.E., *Military Report on the Sinai Peninsula* (Castle Hill Press: Fordingbridge 2008).

Lawrence, T.E., *Revolt in the Desert* (Jonathan Cape: London 1927).

Lawrence, T.E., *Secret Despatches from Arabia* (Golden Cockerel Press: London 1939).

Lawrence, T.E., *Seven Pillars of Wisdom: The Complete 1922 Text*. Two vols. (Castle Hill Press: Fordingbridge 1997).

Lawrence, T.E., *Seven Pillars of Wisdom* (Jonathan Cape: London 1935).

Lawrence, T.E., *The Diary kept by T.E. Lawrence while travelling in Arabia during 1911* (Garnet Publishing: Reading 1993)

Lawrence, T.E., *The Mint* (Jonathan Cape: London 1955).

Lawrence, T.E. (T.E. Shaw), trans. *The Odyssey of Homer* (Oxford University Press: Oxford 1935).

Lewis, Samuel, *A Topographical Dictionary of Ireland* (S. Lewis & Co: London 1837).

Lewis, Wyndham, *Blasting and Bombardiering* (Calder & Boyars: London 1967).

Liddell Hart, B.H., *'T.E. Lawrence' in Arabia and After* (Jonathan Cape: London 1934).

Lockman, J.N., *Scattered Tracks on the Lawrence Trail* (Falcon Books: Whitmore Lake 1996).

Mack, John E., *A Prince of our Disorder: The Life of T.E. Lawrence* (Weidenfeld and Nicolson: London 1976).

Marriott, Paul J., *The Young Lawrence of Arabia 1888-1910* (Privately published by author: 1977).

Marriott, Paul and Argent, Yvonne, *The Last Days of T.E. Lawrence* (The Alpha Press: Brighton 1996).

Meinertzhagen, Colonel R., *Army Diary 1899 - 1926* (Oliver and Boyd Ltd: Edinburgh 1960).

Meinertzhagen, Colonel R., *Middle East Diary* (The Cresset Press: London 1959).

Meyers, Jeffrey, *The Wounded Spirit* (Martin, Brian & O'Keeffe: London 1973).

Mohs, Polly A., *Military Intelligence and the Arab Revolt* (Routledge: Abingdon, Oxon 2008).

Monroe, Elizabeth, *Britain's Moment in the Middle East: 1914-1956* (Chatto and Windus: London 1963).

Montgomery Hyde, H., *Solitary in the Ranks* (Constable: London 1977).

Morris, William, *Golden Wings and Other Stories* (Newcastle Publishing Co.: Van Nuys, California 1976).

Morris, William, *The Early Romances of William Morris* (J.M. Dent and Sons: London 1907).

Morris, William, *The Hollow Land* (Thomas B. Mosher: Portland 1900).

Morris, William, *The Well at the World's End* (Pan/Ballantine Books: London 1971).

Mousa, S., *T.E. Lawrence: An Arab View* (Oxford University Press: Oxford 1966).

Napier, Priscilla, *Late Beginner* (Michael Joseph: London 1966).

Nicolson, Harold, *Peacemaking 1919* (Constable: London 1933).

Norman, Andrew, *T.E.Lawrence Tormented Hero* (Fonthill Media Limited: 2014).

Nykl, A.R., *Hispano-Arabic Poetry and its Relations with the Old Provençal Troubadours* (J.H. Furst Company: Baltimore 1946).

O'Brien, Philip M., *T.E. Lawrence: A Bibliography* (Oak Knoll Press: Delaware 2000).

Ocampo, Victoria, *338171 T.E. (Lawrence of Arabia)* (Victor Gollancz Ltd: London 1963).

Orlans, Harold, *T.E. Lawrence: Biography of a Broken Hero* (McFarlane & Company: Jefferson, North Carolina, 2002).

Preston, R.M.P., *The Desert Mounted Corps* (Constable: London 1921).

Reynolds, J.S., *Canon Christopher of St Aldate's* (Abingdon Abbey Press: Oxford 1967).

Richards, Vyvyan, *Portrait of T.E. Lawrence* (Jonathan Cape: London 1936).

Rogan, Eugene, *The Fall of the Ottomans* (Allen Lane/Penguin Random House UK: 2015).

Rolls, S.C., *Steel Chariots in the Desert* (Jonathan Cape: London 1937).

Rothenstein, William (ed.), *Twenty-Four Portraits* (Allen & Unwin: London 1920)

Rowbotham, J.F, *The Troubadours and Courts of Love.* (Swan Sonnenschein & Co: London 1895)

Sanders, Liman von, *Fünf Jahre Turkei* (August Scherl: Berlin 1919).

Sattin, Anthony, *Young Lawrence* (John Murray: London 2014)

Seward, Desmond, *Wings over the Desert* (Haynes Publishing: Sparkford, Yeovil 2009).

Sims, Wing Commander R.G., *The Sayings and Doings of T.E. Lawrence* (The Fleece Press: Denby Dale,Wakefield 1994).

Sims, Wing Commander R.G., *Cats and Landladies' Husbands: T. E. Lawrence in Bridlington.* (Some recollections)(The Fleece Press: Denby Dale, Wakefield 1995).

Smith, Emma, *The Great Western Beach* (Bloomsbury: London 2008).

Stark, Freya, *Letters from Syria* (John Murray: London 1942)

Stirling, W.F., *Safety Last* (Hollis and Carter: London 1953).

Storrs, Sir Ronald, *Orientations* (Ivor Nicholson & Watson: London 1937).

Sydney Smith, Clare, *The Golden Reign* (Cassell: London 1940).

Sydney Smith, Clare, *The Golden Reign* (Fleece Press: Upper Denby 2004).

Tauber, Eliezer, *The Arab Movements in World War I* (Frank Cass and Co. Ltd: Abingdon 1993).

The Arab Bulletin 1916-1919. Four vols.(Cambridge University Press, Archive Editions: Cambridge 1986).

Thomas, Lowell, *With Lawrence in Arabia* (Hutchinson: London 1925).

Thompson, V.M., *Not a Suitable Hobby for an Airman* (Orchard Books: Long Hangborough 1986).

Tunbridge, Paul, *With Lawrence in the Royal Air Force* (Buckland Publications Ltd: Sevenoaks 2000).

Vansittart, Lord Robert, *The Mist Procession* (Hutchinson: London 1958).

Vansittart, Lord Robert, *The Singing Caravan: A Sufi Tale* (Gregynog Press: Newtown, Montgomeryshire 1932).

Villars, Jean Beraud, *T. E. Lawrence* (Sidgwick and Jackson: London 1958).

Weintraub, Stanley, *Private Shaw & Public Shaw* (George Braziller: New York 1963).

Weintraub, Stanley and Rodelle, *The Literary Impulse* (Louisiana State Univerity Press: Baton Rouge 1975).

Williamson, Henry, *Genius of Friendship* (Faber and Faber: London 1941).

Wilson, Jeremy. (ed.), *T. E. Lawrence: Letters to E.T. Leeds* (The Whittington Press: Andoversford 1988).

Wilson, Jeremy (ed.), *Minorities* (Jonathan Cape: London 1971).

Wilson, Jeremy, *T.E. Lawrence* (Exhibition catalogue) (National Portrait Gallery Publications: London 1988).

Wilson, Jeremy, *Lawrence of Arabia: The Authorised Biography of T.E. Lawrence* (William Heinemann Ltd: London 1989).

Wilson, J & N. (eds), *T.E. Lawrence. Towards 'An English Fourth'* (Castle Hill Press: Fordingbridge 2009).

Wilson, J. & N. (eds), *T.E. Lawrence, Correspondence with Bernard and Charlotte Shaw.* 1922–1926. (Castle Hill Press: Fordingbridge 2000). (Vol 1); 1927. (Vol. 2). 2003; 1928. (Vol. 3). 2008; 1929-35. (Vol. 4). 2009.

Wilson, Peter. (ed.) *T.E. Lawrence: Correspondence with Henry Williamson* (Castle Hill Press: Fordingbridge 2000).

Wingate, Sir Ronald, *Wingate of the Sudan* (John Murray: London 1955).

Winstone, H.V.F. (ed.), *The Diaries of Parker Pasha* (Quartet Books: London 1983).

Winstone, H.V.F., *The Illicit Adventure* (Jonathan Cape: London 1982).

Winterton, Earl, *Fifty Tumultuous Years* (Hutchinson: London 1955).

Woodward, E.L., *Short Journey* (Faber and Faber: London 1943).

Woolley, Leonard, *As I Seem to Remember* (Allen and Unwin: London 1962).

Woolley, Leonard, *Dead Towns and Living Men* (Oxford University Press: Oxford 1929).

Woolley, Leonard, and Lawrence, T.E., *The Wilderness of Zin* (Stacey International: London 2003).

Yardley, Michael, *Backing into the Limelight* (Harrap: London 1985).

Young, Louisa, *A Great Task of Happiness* (Macmillan: London 1995).

Young, Sir Hubert, *The Independent Arab* (John Murray: London 1933).

Zeine, Z.N., *The Struggle for Arab Independence* (Khayats: Beirut 1960).

JOURNALS, NEWSPAPERS, RADIO, TELEVISION

BBC 2 (television). Omnibus. April 18, 1986. Documentary: Lawrence and Arabia.

Daily Express, Dublin Edition. July 26th, 1873.

Encounter. October, 1970. (Anglo-Irish, by James Morris).

Jesus College Magazine. IV. (1935).

Journal of the T.E. Lawrence Society. 1991 to present day (P.O.Box 728, Oxford OX2 9Z).

Joyce, Pierce. BBC radio talk. July 14th, 1941. Typescript. Imperial War Museum.

Medieval Studies. Vol.VII. 1945. Denomy, A.J. Fin Amors: The Pure Love of the Troubadours, its Amorality and Possible Source.

Quarterly Statement of the Palestine Exploration Fund. Journal.1935. Newcombe, S.F. Personal Reminiscences.

Roberts, Chalmers. World Today. Vol. 49. No5. July.1927.

Royal Society of Antiquaries of Ireland. 54. 1924.

Texas Quarterly. Autumn 1962, Vol.V, Number 3. T.E. Lawrence Collection, Harry Ransom Humanities Research Center, University of Texas, Austin, Texas, USA.

The Contemporary Review.Vol XLI. Jan–Jun, 1882.

The Contemporary Review. December, 1974.

The Irish Times. September 10th, 1944.

The Irish Weekly Times. March 1st, 1941.

The New Statesman. December, 22, 1956.

The Saturday Review. New York. June 15th, 1963.

The Sunday Times. July 5, 1998. News Section.

Virginia Quarterly Review (USA). Vol.21. No 4. Autumn, 1945.

Westmeath Examiner: 11 December 1886, 1 January, 21 May 1887, 22 April 1990.

Westmeath Guardian: 31 July 1873, 25 January 1907.

Acknowledgments

First and foremost I must thank my publisher Antony Farrell of The Lilliput Press, for having had the courage to take on a book which does not follow the conventional biographical format and which is more a personal quest than a chronological coverage of a life. He has given the book his usual perfectionist treatment and, aware also of the uniqueness of its illustrations, has accorded them prominent exposure.

Those who have given me help along the way are legion and I cannot name them all. I owe the greatest debt of gratitude to two people – Patrick Wynne-Jones and Malcolm Brown. Patrick's advice and support have been unstinting from the very inception of the book many years ago. When I felt that I had reached an impasse, or became demoralised by the seeming magnitude of the task I had set myself, it was he who assured me that the story I had to tell was one well worth the telling and that I had the ability to tell it. He has come to know the book as thoroughly as I do and over the last five years has patiently acted as unpaid textual and historical adviser. And then Malcolm Brown. One of the world's foremost Lawrence scholars and chroniclers, he has given me both enthusiastic encouragement and crucial advice on structure, content and form, and then generously crowned the considerable time and effort he had devoted to this by writing the Foreword to the book. His championing of it in its infancy gave my motivation a renewed impetus when otherwise it might have faltered.

Of my editors at Lilliput I must firstly thank Sean Farrell, whose enthusiasm for and commitment to the book was wholehearted from the moment it landed on his desk. He did an extremely thorough edit which played a major part in shaping the finished product, while his keen application to a difficult task was a real morale-booster. I also owe gratitude to the late Charlie Naper, who was given the brief of assessing the book for publication, whose thumbs-up gave it the green light, and who applied himself assiduously to the initial stages of the in-house editing process. Also I must thank Djinn von Noorden, Lilliput's senior editor, who honed, refined, and, where necessary, productively re-shaped the text into what I now feel is a final, well-balanced, well-polished form. And finally, not forgetting Suzy Freeman for her energetic and creative promotion and marketing.

The scope of the book necessitated research in many archives and I thank their staff for the guidance they gave me through labyrinths of documentation. Among these institutions and people I would mention in particular the manuscript department of the National Library of Ireland in Dublin; the Sudan Archive in Durham University Library; the Middle East Centre at St Antony's College, Oxford; and, in London, the British Library, the National Archives in Kew, the Newspaper Library in Colindale, and the Imperial

War Museum. In the USA Richard Workman, Research Librarian at the Harry Ransom Humanities Research Center at the University of Texas in Austin, for furnishing me with some key documents. And, of course, I am most grateful to Mr Michael Carey of the Seven Pillars of Wisdom Trust for use of quotations from Lawrence's writings and letters.

On a more personal level I would like to acknowledge the invaluable help given me by the following people: Sally Critchlow, a friend and a professional literary editor, who went through the book and alerted me to textual errors which had escaped notice; Eugene Sheridan in County Westmeath in Ireland for several photographs and whose detailed knowledge of the Chapman family he kindly shared with me; Peter Metcalfe, one of Britain's foremost Lawrence collectors, who knows more about him than most of his biographers and who was the source of a constant flow of material which strengthened the book's narrative and arguments; and Susan Williams in the USA, a Lawrence expert herself, who has never failed to lift my spirits by insisting that the book is an important contribution to Lawrence scholarship. I would also like to thank the world's leading Lawrence authority, Jeremy Wilson, who would often, when I had drawn a blank in some controversial area, put me on the right track or supplied important information.

I also owe a debt of gratitude to the many who assisted me with research, or who kindly provided accommodation – or both. In Ireland: the late Niall Fallon (a close friend, a pillar of support always, and a fount of information on Anglo-Irish families and the history of Westmeath) and his widow, Patricia, for putting me up on innumerable occasions at the family home in Hill of Down; Audrey Naper at Dublin University, whose family connections opened the doors to many of the Big Houses of Westmeath and who visited them with me; Nick Kindersley and his late wife, Susie, at Newcastle House in County Longford, who were key to the discovery of rare and unknown Chapman family photographs. In Westmeath: John Bellingham of Glencara, a kind and generous host and a fellow aficionado of the Middle East, who smoothed the path to many a useful informant in the County; the Ogle family of Dysart, for photographs and anecdotes; and the late and delightful Barbara Casey (née Fetherstonhaugh) of Rockview for her colourful memories of Lawrence's Irish family and her infectious sense of humour. I must also mention my friends Christopher and Jane Dick from County Kildare, who took some evocative photographs for me of Lawrence's family home, Killua Castle, and related places. Then, in England: the Bowen-Wright family who put me up in Sunderland, where I made significant discoveries about Lawrence's mother's antecedents; George and Iris Williams in Cornwall for photographs and for sharing their unrivalled knowledge of Lawrence's time in Plymouth; and Rhona Martindale for patient and painstaking transcription of many letters. Finally, in the Middle East, my friends Jack and Gudrun Joyce, who gave me generous hospitality in both the Lebanon and Damascus and whose considerable knowledge of the region, its peoples and its life was crucial during one of the most important stages of my research.

Index

14–17; doubts about revolt 14–15; dreamworld 161–2; dress 13, 97; dual personality 44–5; eccentricity 36, 107–8; emotional reticence 180–1; fabrications 103; family support 142–3; fear of families 105, 191; film depiction 3–4, 20; flagellation complex 118; funeral, grave 4, 146, 216; generosity 182; Great War 5–6; handwriting 155; Hogarth's death 123; homosexuality alleged 162, 168, 181, 182, 189, 190, 197, 198, 207, 213; illegitimacy 32, 47, 48, 57–9, 86, 89, 93–4, 97–8, 127, 129, 143; *Illustrated Travelogue* 45; impotence 154–5, 195; India 123–4; immaturity 208; inheritance 95; insight into women 166; interests 21; Killua hopes 69–70; kindness 21–2; Late Late Show appearance 666; loner 21, 107; Laurie, Janet 201–5, 226, 240, 243; love of France 14; Magan's opinion 84; mask ix, 97; marriage options 188–9, 202; masochism 168, 196–7; medals 106; medieval interests 169–72; Morris influence 162, 178–9, 199; mother's influence 100–2, 104–5, 167; mother's origins 96, 116; motivates tribal chiefs 13–4; motorbike crash 4; Oxford studies 154, 168; Paris Peace Conference 19; parents visit Ireland 93; physical contact 188; portraits 20, 252; pre-Raphaelite 157, 158, 172, 177, 183; practical jokes 187, 207, 210–11; professed poverty 102–3; promotes Arab autonomy 19–20; Provençal/troubadour poetry 144, 154, 156, 170, 171, 174–7, 179–10, 181, 233; public persona 44–6; RAF service 46; rape victim 118, 146, 154, 166, 168–9, 186, 189, 192–8; repetition compulsion 196; resemblance to Rose 81; romantic 225, 227; Ross, Aircraftman xi, xii, 124; Royal Artillery 58, 87, 107; S.A.132–6, 147–55; 'Scotch' grandmother 121; self-

denigration 248; self-inquisitor 5, 227–8; self-revulsion 186; sense of failure 26, 127; sensitivity 208, 242; sexuality 150, 154–5, 162–7, 181–4, 185–91, 192–98; Shakespeare 224; 'Shortarse' 182; shyness 163; sisters 39, 40, 70, 77, 81, 82, 83, 84, 86–8, 99, 150; size 163; Smith, Clare Sydney 164–56; surnames 103, 122–3, 125–6, 129, 198; technician 21; 'Uncrowned King of Arabia' 22; vanity 209; Victoria Cross 16; visits Killua 125; water-like 23; Wilson's opinion 8; women's company 163–4, 187, 239

Lawrence, Thomas 48, 116–18
Lawrence, Thomas and Sarah (Sunderland) 115, 116–17
Lawrence, Will: birth certificate 89; character 144; estate 96; father in Ireland 94; death 96, 108, 204; intellect 143; letters to parents 145; Oxford studies 144; preferred by Janet Laurie 202, 204; religiosity 100; unknown grave 146
Lean, David xiii, 3–4, 20, 31
Leeds, E.T. 106, 142, 162, 206, 211
Leith, Scotland 118
Leitrim 252
Letters of T.E. Lawrence 146
Lewis, Wyndham 127
Lifeboat Institution 82
Light of the World 157
Lissoy, Co. Westmeath 71
Liverpool 118
Lloyd's Register 116, 118
Lord of the Rings, The 159
Loughcrew House, Co. Meath 34
Louis VII 176
Lucas, F.L. 185, 217, 230–2
Lutterworth, Leicestershire 50

Mack, John 22, 101, 107, 121, 169, 181, 195, 201, 203, 215, 224, 233, 247
Madden, Sarah 112